Nature's Experts

Nature's Experts

SCIENCE, POLITICS, AND THE ENVIRONMENT

STEPHEN BOCKING

Rutgers University Press
New Brunswick, New Jersey, and London

Second paperback printing, 2006

Library of Congress Cataloging-in-Publication Data

Bocking, Stephen, 1959–
    Nature's experts : science, politics, and the environment / Stephen Bocking.
        p. cm.
Includes bibliographical references and index.
    ISBN 0–8135–3397–X (hardcover : alk. paper) — ISBN 0–8135–3398–8
(pbk. : alk. paper)
    1. Environmental policy. 2. Environmental sciences. I. Title.
    GE170.B65 2004
    333.7—dc22

2004003815

A British Cataloging-in-Publication record for this book is available from the British Library

Manufactured in the United States of America

For Mom and Dad

CONTENTS

PREFACE

Most people see it as self-evident that scientific knowledge is relevant to environmental affairs. Scientists study the global climate system, identifying signs of a warming world. A forestry agency uses science when deciding how much timber can be cut each year. Environmental organizations marshal data to demonstrate that a pollutant is toxic and must be controlled. Biotechnology firms manipulate the DNA of crops in hopes of creating new markets for seeds and pesticides. Environmental politics may be replete with conflicting interests and attitudes, but all parties appear to agree, at least, that science is essential.

And yet, never has the relation of science to environmental politics been as actively debated as it is today. Observers cite countless issues that lack resolution—from global climate change to neighborhood contaminants—even after decades of research. Scientists provide multiple views of problems, unable to agree on what advice to offer. Science is widely viewed as too closely tied to powerful interests, especially in industry and government. According to some critics, the act itself of defining environmental problems as scientific hinders consideration of their political and economic dimensions—especially inequalities of power and wealth.

This book is about science in environmental politics: how it contributes to resolving environmental problems; and how, frequently enough, its contribution is ineffective or heedless of people's concerns. Many scholars have examined science and politics in recent years, and I draw on this work. However, this book also makes a distinctive contribution to the discussion. In the first chapter, I begin by taking a walk in New York City, demonstrating how issues of science and politics are all around us. I then examine various aspects of environmental affairs: the role of science as a source of authority, the connections between science and environmental values, and the contribution of science to natural resources management, international environmental issues, and decisions about risks. Most studies of science in environmental politics focus on just one aspect—say, international issues, or risk. I argue, in contrast, that there are elements common to all, and that our understanding of each can be enhanced by considering all of them together. These elements can also be understood in terms of two characteristics that are necessary for science to contribute to resolving rather than exacerbating environmental controversies. First, science must be effective in the sense of actually influencing attitudes and actions. This depends, in turn, on its credibility and relevance. Second, science must be democratic: contributing to a transparent, accountable environmental politics, in which people have access to the information they need to present, and discuss, their views of the world.

My own interest in environmental science and politics began in the study of the recent history of ecology. In an earlier book I examined the connections between ecology and environmental politics as they had evolved between the 1940s and the 1990s in the United States, Great Britain, and Canada. Since then I have continued to pursue the study of science and politics and to teach in this area at Trent University. I would therefore like to thank the students of my course, "Environmental Science and Politics," who over the years have had first crack at many of the ideas presented in this book. With each class split almost evenly each year between the humanities and the sciences, the students also convinced me that this could be a productive area for interdisciplinary work. I have tried here to express that interdisciplinary ideal, drawing on the work of scholars in many fields who have worthwhile things to say about science and politics.

I would also like to thank my colleagues and friends, at Trent University and elsewhere, who shared ideas about science and politics, and gave much support during an interesting time. Taarini Chopra served well as my research assistant, and Trent University provided helpful funding. Helen Hsu, formerly of Rutgers University Press, offered early encouragement, and for the last two years Audra Wolfe has been a wise, supportive, and patient editor at the Press. Two anonymous reviewers provided very useful comments. My thanks as well to my father, Richard, from whom I have learned much regarding the politics of genetic engineering, and to my mother, Winnifred, for unceasing interest and encouragement. To Barb Znamirowski, wonderful colleague and companion, my love and gratitude. Best thanks of all to my kids: Paul and Emma.

PART I

Introduction

CHAPTER 1

Encountering Science and Politics

❧

Environmental matters are widely seen as matters of science. The U.S. Environmental Protection Agency, the European Environment Agency, Environment Canada, and other such agencies invest in scientific research, obtain advice from scientific committees, and assure interest groups that their decisions are based on science; regulations they administer usually define the environment in terms—parts per billion, cases of cancer per million—requiring measurement and interpretation by scientists. Environmentalists, although sometimes ambivalent about the effects of science and technology, in practice draw heavily on scientific expertise: national environmental organizations recruit professional scientific talent, while community groups solicit volunteer scientists from the local university. Businesspeople insist just as firmly on the importance of basing environmental policies on "sound science." So do the media: scientists are ubiquitous in television coverage of environmental controversies, newspapers report on the environment in their "science" sections, and *National Geographic* marked the 2002 Johannesburg environmental conference by asking scientists—not economists, poets, or politicians—to explain the state of the world.[1]

All these institutions call upon scientists to interpret environmental problems that range from the global to the individual. Climate negotiations are framed by scientific results provided by the Intergovernmental Panel on Climate Change. Responses to contaminants—from routine releases by industrial facilities, to the dust and smoke over lower Manhattan after September 11, 2001—are guided by scientific understanding of these hazards. Scientists evaluate the environmental impacts of dams, highways, and other developments, and scientific assessments are used in deciding how many fish may be caught or where trees may be cut. Individuals draw on scientific advice in considering the hazards of running on hot smoggy days or whether to spray herbicide on their lawns. More than perhaps any other political issue, the environment is defined in terms of the search for, and argument over, the "facts" about nature. In defining these facts, science is primary: as Barry Barnes and David Edge note, "Science is near to being *the* source of cognitive authority: anyone who would be widely believed and trusted as an interpreter of nature needs a license from the scientific community."[2]

Science often even determines what becomes an environmental issue in the first place. Several of the most serious environmental problems, such as the transport of toxic contaminants over long distances, depletion of the stratospheric ozone layer, and climate change, were only recognized as problems once scientists had described them. Indeed, the view that an issue only exists once science has described it is pervasive in environmental politics. For instance, I am writing this on a hot September day, the air tinted an unhealthy orange. The Ontario provincial government has just announced it will upgrade its air quality monitoring network. It already measures ground-level ozone, which, as a product of hot days and chemical reactions in the atmosphere, is usually a problem only in summer. Soon the network will also measure fine particulates, which may be present throughout the year. As a result, the television reporter explained, poor air quality days may now occur at any time of the year. In effect, "poor air quality" has become a state that only exists once it can be measured scientifically. Such is the authority of science in environmental affairs.

Science and Controversy

Science is widely viewed as a source of reliable knowledge about the natural environment and the impacts of human activities. But it is much more than that. Scientists and scientific knowledge play several roles in environmental politics, shaping not only regulatory decisions and other environmental protection initiatives, but also the processes by which decisions are made and initiatives are taken, as well as the debates and controversies that surround these processes. The science itself is often a focus of debate. In countless environmental controversies, opposing parties assemble scientific evidence, expressing their conflicting interests or values in terms of scientific knowledge. Citizens are increasingly unwilling to accept uncritically the judgments of experts, and this has become one of the primary political dynamics of environmental decision-making. Often this resistance reflects awareness of the close ties between scientists and powerful economic and political interests—as evidenced, for example, in current controversies regarding agricultural biotechnology. In a society in which environmental affairs can be the scene of intense disputes over divergent worldviews and conflicting interests, the portrayals of the environment provided by scientists are themselves often fiercely contested. Thus, while science is widely considered essential to environmental affairs, its role is fraught with tensions and contradictions.

A Walk in the City

One way to begin exploring these matters is by examining some specific environmental issues. Some months ago, I encountered several such issues during a single day. Early one Saturday, after a workshop at the Marine Biological Laboratory at Wood's Hole, Massachusetts, I traveled down to New York to see my son, who was on his first visit to the city. The day began in Brooklyn, where he was staying in a house in the Williamsburg neighborhood. It's an intriguing place: older homes, diverse shopping streets, industries past their prime. It is also, though, within the "lead belt" of New York: lead still contaminates many of its streets and homes, more so than in most other areas of the city, and indeed most of the country.

Lead was once an inescapable, and inescapably toxic, aspect of American life. Since the 1970s, however, it has been removed from its chief sources: gasoline, paint, and the solder used in cans. This is an environmental success story, tallied in the drop in mean blood lead levels of American children: from 13 micrograms/deciliter (μg/dL) in 1970, to 3 μg/dL today. This progress has often been attributed to the influence of science: as research demonstrated the dangers of lead (scientists have even determined how many IQ points children can expect to lose at each level of exposure) governments responded by progressively tightening regulations, lowering the level of lead considered to be dangerous. In New York this level dropped from 60 μg/dL in 1970 to 40 in 1975, to 30 in 1981, to 25 in 1986, and to 10 μg/dL in 1992.[3]

But the story about science and lead has been far from straightforward. After all, it has been known at least since 1923 that lead can damage the brain. However, instead of effective action, there were decades of disputes over the evidence of harm and over what should be done. These were played out in a variety of arenas: scientific journals and meetings, negotiations for regulations proposed by the Environmental Protection Agency, the writing of advisories for physicians by the Centers for Disease Control and Prevention, lawsuits against polluters. The debates often turned not just on how to respond to the evidence, but on the reliability of the evidence itself. Different specialists provided contrasting interpretations, sometimes, it appeared, less because of scientific differences than because of their ties to economic interests. Scientists associated with industry tended to downplay concerns, attributing most cases of exposure to natural sources. Scientists also differed on how to respond to new information: some urged immediate action, while others argued for stronger evidence before acting.[4]

Today, however, there is a fixed standard: lead poisoning is defined as a blood level at or above 10 μg/dL. When a child exceeds this level, as happens most often in neighborhoods like Williamsburg and Bedford/Stuyvesant where the houses are old and often poorly maintained and many families are struggling economically, the system swings into action. The child's environment is examined and remedial measures are taken. These may include advice to the family, orders to the landlord, and even, if necessary, moving a family into emergency housing until the source (most likely, lead paint) has been cleaned up.

This standard is a product of scientific evidence. It also reflects one of the constraints of bureaucracy: the need for a stable basis for regulatory decisions. The problem, however, is that what we know about lead is still changing rapidly. Over the last twenty years more knowledge of its impacts at low levels has accumulated, and there is now much evidence of effects even at levels below 10 μg/dL, including impaired intelligence and behavioral changes. Some argue now that there is a need to reassess policies in the light of these results. According to Richard Canfield of Cornell University, "nontrivial damage is occurring below the C.D.C. level of concern. Both the C.D.C. and the World Health Organization need to reassess their policies in light of this research."[5]

But other factors are also at work, making it difficult to say conclusively that specific cases of impairment are attributable to lead: the overall health of the child and mother, nutrition, home environment, and other factors may also play roles. And while it is agreed that lead-based paint applied before it was banned in 1978 is the single greatest source, other factors may also be important, albeit to an uncertain degree. Brooklyn accommodates newcomers from many countries, and exposure is tied to places of origin where lead is more widespread in the environment and in consumer products—even a deodorant from the Dominican Republic was found to have very high levels of lead. In 2002, 35 percent of the most serious lead cases in New York could not be traced to paint at all. Many sources of lead also persist in the outdoor environment—sidewalks, soil, even lead paint on the elevated subway stations of the J line that travels through Williamsburg—but the significance of these sources is not entirely understood, since most research has focused on indoor sources.[6]

Debate continues about lead in Brooklyn and elsewhere in the urban environment: eighty years after the first notice of its dangers, there is still uncertainty about its sources, its effects, and what should be done. A matter of environmental justice is also now inescapable: lead now disproportionately affects poorer families. The issue may have been put on the public agenda by science, but the questions have shifted beyond what can be resolved by scientists alone.

We take the J train to Manhattan, then transfer and head uptown to Central Park. Our destination is The Reservoir, to run the track around it (that is, my son will run; I'll just find a bench and read). Originally part of the city's water system, the reservoir received water flowing south from the Croton River. Of course it no longer has that function, just as the Croton River is no longer the chief source of the city's water. The Catskill Mountains now fulfill that role, meeting about 90 percent of demand. Rain and snow, captured in lakes and reservoirs, is sent to the city through deep and long tunnels: about 15,000 gallons per second. The water is very pure, requiring chlorination, but not costly filtration. In the late 1980s, however, the city faced a new requirement, in the form of the Environmental Protection Agency's Surface Water Treatment Rule of 1989. The rule requires either filtration of water supplies, or a watershed control program that can minimize potential for contamination by *Giardia* cysts and viruses. The alternatives for New York were clear: to meet these regulations by building a new filtration plant, at a cost of between $6 and $8 billion, and extra operating costs of $300 million each year, or to put in place a watershed plan for the Catskills, at a cost of only perhaps $1 billion. As a result, in 1997 New York signed an agreement to buy land and take other steps to protect the Catskills environment, and therefore its own water supply.[7]

This choice, and the watershed program itself, were effective examples of using science to guide decisions regarding this valuable resource. Knowledge of pollutants such as pathogens, nutrients and sediments, and their sources, effects, and means of control guided design of the plan. The influence of this knowledge was evident in both its overall priorities and its specific actions, including protection of land near lakes and streams and advice to farmers on environmentally sound land use practices. Most fundamentally, the program demonstrated awareness of the links between protecting an ecosystem and ensuring its capacity to provide amenities such as clean water. As ecologists have often argued, intact ecosystems can provide a host of services, from steady supplies of water to a moderate climate, that could otherwise be provided only at great expense.[8] Protecting nature, in other words, makes good economic sense, as demonstrated by ecological science.

But a closer look shows how the role of science in decisions about New York's water is anything but straightforward. Managing a watershed is a complex undertaking, with countless factors influencing the quality of the water that pours out of it. As a result, scientific claims regarding the connection between protecting land and safeguarding the water cannot but be highly uncertain. And in fact, the driving force behind this program was not ecological science, but something much more certain: the new EPA regulation. The city was assured it could meet its obligations by investing in watershed protection. Whether this would actually result in a meaningful improvement in water quality was, essentially, beside the point. Scientists had not, at any rate, identified imminent threats to the water supply, at least of an ecological nature—indeed, the population of the watershed had not increased since the Civil War. And not just its justification lacked scientific foundation; so did major aspects of the program itself. Much of the investment by the city was not for ecological protection, but for compensating rural landowners and investing in economic development in the watershed. This was to mollify watershed residents, traditionally resentful toward New York, who feared the program would result in tighter controls on their activities, with all the benefits going only to their giant neighbor. It is even unclear how much of the watershed the city will actually protect.[9] Thus, a program seemingly framed in terms of scientific knowledge is in fact an amalgam of science and legal, economic, and political maneuvers.

Thirsty, we head downtown to Greenwich Village for a drink. This neighborhood has its own recent history of experts and politics. When Jane Jacobs lived here in the 1950s, she was a careful student of the life of the city. And

when proposals were made to raze blocks of the neighborhood, first for housing and then for a cross-Manhattan expressway, she and many others fought back,
defeating both projects. What was striking in this controversy—one of the key
episodes in the history of the twentieth-century American city—is how it was
framed in terms of expertise, especially arguments about who best understood
cities and what they needed. Jacobs argued for the street-level expertise of those
who actually lived in the city and cherished its chaotic nature. She excoriated
professional planners, who viewed the city from above and misunderstood everything they saw. In *The Death and Life of Great American Cities* she explained
that the "pseudoscience of city planning and its companion, the art of city design,
have not yet broken with the specious comfort of wishes, familiar superstitions,
oversimplifications, and symbols, and have not yet embarked upon the adven-
ture of probing the real world."[10] Her antagonist, Robert Moses, New York's
Master Builder, valued above all else efficiency and rapid movement; for him,
opposition could only stem from ignorance. "The current fiction is that . . . any
busy housewife who gets her expertise from television, radio and telephone is
endowed to plan in detail a huge metropolitan arterial complex good for a century. In the absence of decisions by experts, no work, no arts, parks, no nothing
will move."[11] This conflict between the expert quest for efficiency and mobil-
ity and the contrasting interest in complexity and contingency has been a persistent theme in environmental controversies involving science.

We head south a few more blocks, ending our walk in Battery Park City.
On September 11, 2001, dense smoke and inches-thick deposits of fine powder
briefly made this environment one of the most toxic in the world. The atmosphere contained asbestos, PCBs, and a huge variety of combustion byproducts,
which made respirators mandatory. A fleet of vacuum trucks swept in, and the
Environmental Protection Agency set up an extensive monitoring system, sampling air and drinking water. A week after the tragedy the agency announced
that air quality was acceptable and that local water quality had not been affected.

But many remained concerned about hazards, especially asbestos, and the
long-term health effects for those closest to the site—firefighters and other res-
cue workers—as well as thousands of workers and residents. Smoke from lin-
gering fires, scratchy throats, the "World Trade Center cough"—all suggested
there were things to worry about. Experts, however, reassured the public that
bad smells and symptoms were not proof of damage. As one medical expert explained, "The visceral human reaction to this is, this smell is not natural, so there
must be something wrong, something toxic," but no reliable conclusion about
toxicity could be drawn simply from smell.[12]

This contrast between public concern and official reassurance had several
consequences in the months after 9/11. There was distrust, born of a sense that
not all that was known was being said or that authorities charged with protecting the public did not themselves know enough to do so. For those living nearby,
the uncertainty was particularly unsettling. They received too little advice: should
they refinish their floors to remove the hazard, or would that simply raise more

dust? Was special equipment needed, or just a damp towel? That no firm answers were available was itself unsettling. As one resident noted: "It's such a uniquely American thing to think that science can provide an objective truth, but no one has an answer to these kinds of questions."[13] In the absence of firm advice, residents relied on their own instincts: some cleaned up and went on with life in the city, a few decided their future lay in the suburbs.

And in fact, it became clear in the months after the event that the first reassurances were too confident. There were huge uncertainties, and ignorance, about the health consequences. Partly this was a matter of bureaucracy: no one agency had overall responsibility for ensuring that all environments were tested, and apartments and other indoor spaces simply fell through the cracks. But especially, there was just too much that was new: there was nothing against which scientists could compare this unprecedented mix of combustibles and fragments, and so very little could be said with certainty. The EPA had made decisions about what needed to be measured, relating to sizes and types of particles and their likely distribution. These decisions were based on limited information and subsequently affected what knowledge would, and would not, be gathered.

With limited knowledge, those making decisions had to choose, as is often the case, which evidence and which "message" to emphasize. As the EPA's Inspector General reported in August 2003, the agency, advised by the Council on Environmental Quality (and through the Council, by the White House), chose to be reassuring, to downplay the hazards. This too is a pattern often encountered in environmental controversies. The consequences were also familiar: distrust and cynicism toward officialdom. People may also not have taken all the precautions that a franker presentation of the uncertainties might have encouraged; nor were opportunities pursued for scientists to be guided by people living in the area (the real experts on this environment), so as to ensure that all relevant locations would be examined for hazardous substances.

We can reflect briefly on the lessons about science and politics apparent within just a few square miles of one city. In every issue encountered, scientific knowledge plays a role in framing the questions at stake. However, continually evolving scientific information, and pervasive uncertainties, mean that science cannot merely provide the "facts." Experts are often required to make decisions regarding what to test, and how to advise the public; these decisions then provide many opportunities for other factors—economic values, political priorities—to influence scientific judgments. The relations between experts and the public are also unexpectedly complex, with people sometimes distrusting advice or rejecting expert prescriptions, particularly when those prescriptions embody assumptions or values that are not widely shared. Such outcomes demonstrate how applying science to environmental challenges cannot be a matter just for experts. It is necessary, rather, if science is to be applied effectively, and if people are to feel that their concerns have been addressed, to find some way of conducting research as a joint activity, shared between experts and people. Environmental challenges today—persistent hazards such as lead, or novel ones such as office towers reduced to dust, protecting a watershed, or planning a vital city—are too important to be left to the experts.

Outline of Chapters

These challenges—the elusiveness of reliable knowledge, the difficulty in determining how much knowledge is necessary for informed decisions, the challenge of drawing on this knowledge in ways that do not impede and can even reinforce democracy—are central to understanding the place of science in environmental politics. The ultimate challenge, as Sheila Jasanoff has expressed it, is at the heart of environmental politics: how is knowledge to be connected to actions that advance our visions of natural and social well-being?[14] Each of the chapters in this book provides a perspective on this challenge.

I begin by examining why we listen to scientists in the first place. The authority of science has many sources, including its success in providing both theoretical and practical knowledge about the world, and a reputation for methods of inquiry that assure a disinterested but critical perspective on reality. But just as important are the diverse efforts by government agencies, environmental organizations, business, and the media to reinforce this authority. The authority of science, in other words, is not simply self-evident; it is a phenomenon embedded within environmental politics, constructed and asserted whenever participants in environmental politics require it to support their positions. Countless controversies have demonstrated that knowledge of a phenomenon, and control over how this knowledge is communicated, affords a powerful means to assert control over the phenomenon itself. As Gary Lease notes, "A contest over what is allowed to represent reality . . . is a struggle over that reality itself."[15]

But this authority is also being challenged. Scientific uncertainty, the negotiated character of scientific knowledge, and its frequent irrelevance to the actual environments in which people live have all served to undermine the status of science as reliable and relevant. The challenge has been especially felt during controversies, when science often exhibits close ties to political and economic interests. Awareness of these ties—especially as manifested in the increasing role of industry in financing research—has eroded the boundary between science and politics, and hence the status of scientists as objective experts. Claims that scientific knowledge should be understood less as an objective representation of reality than as a social construction, the product of the specific contexts—political, economic, and cultural—within which science is done, have undermined its authority. The ultimate outcome is that the traditional assumptions governing the relation of science to environmental politics—that science is objective, reliable knowledge, remote from political or economic interests—are no longer valid. It is necessary, therefore, to develop a new understanding of this relation.

In the middle section of the book I explore what this new relation might look like, in terms of four broad realms of environmental politics. I begin by examining the relation between science and environmental attitudes and values. Many argue that science, and in particular the discipline of ecology, can serve not just to describe nature, but to suggest appropriate environmental values, and even as a guide to conduct within our environment. Others, however, argue that this approach to the relation between science and values is an effort to imbue particular ethical preferences with the authority of science; ultimately, it represents the ambition to redefine environmental decisions as scientific rather than political matters.

In subsequent chapters I sharpen my focus, to consider how science is applied within three realms of environmental politics, each possessing its own nexus of institutions, interests, and forms of knowledge. The first of these is natural resources management. Professional resource management has been viewed since its early days as a scientific matter. However, the limits of science have become increasingly evident: in pervasive uncertainties regarding the state of resources and the impacts of harvesting, and in the failure of science to prevent depletion of resources around the world. Science has also been implicated in recent crises involving unsustainable resource use, as well as in a broader critique of resource management: that it imposes a view of nature defined in terms of efficiency and uniformity, unresponsive to evolving public attitudes and values, and irrelevant to the complexity and unpredictability of nature. But there are also many efforts underway to redefine how science contributes to resource management, by taking into consideration the need to adapt to changing conditions, to consider entire ecosystems rather than just the resources of immediate interest, to respond more effectively to public values, and to permit communities to play more effective roles in resource management.

No environmental issues are more closely identified with science than those that affect the global environment. We rely on the scientific community to identify and explain the significance of problems such as depletion of the stratospheric ozone layer and global climate change because the events and behaviors that impact them occur on scales of space and time remote from our daily experience. But with these problems the challenges of forging effective links between science and policy are especially evident. After years of extensive research, effective action on climate change remains elusive, amid concerns about its economic implications and different views regarding responsibility for the problem and its solution. These obstacles to effective action make it necessary to examine closely global climate science, to identify its political dimensions and implications, and to consider whether its emphasis on predicting the future global climate is enabling the science to be as politically effective as it might be.

Society is still in the early stages of addressing the global climate issue— if, indeed, it will deal with it at all. In contrast, there is an extensive record of regulatory action relating to the more familiar hazards of industrial society, such as contaminants in drinking water or in the air. Several novel hazards are also now demanding attention, such as genetically engineered food crops. These hazards, viewed in terms of risk, have become the major focus of regulatory agencies such as the Environmental Protection Agency, and they are now used as a justification for heavy investment in scientific research. The hope was that this science would provide an objective, widely accepted rationale for regulation, avoiding political controversy. In fact, risk science itself has often become a focus of contention. This has occurred both because the science used in risk assessment has embedded in it many political assumptions and implications, and because people have their own concepts and understanding of risks, encompassing broader political and cultural dimensions not readily captured by scientific analysis. Controversies have arisen over such questions as who should be able to make decisions regarding risks; these questions are sharpened by widespread distrust of regulatory authorities and governments generally. One outcome has been greater interest in approaches to risk that are more explicitly framed in terms of the political dimensions of environmental hazards.

These four areas of environmental affairs—values, natural resources management, global environmental problems, and risk—raise many questions regarding science. An essential one is: what are the characteristics of effective environmental science—that is, science that has some impact, either on our view of the world or on our actions? Answering this question requires first that we move beyond the simplistic dichotomy, often invoked, of "good" and "bad" science. This dichotomy obscures the diversity of factors and priorities that determine effectiveness. Scientists certify through peer review that research results are reliable, but then they complain that they are nevertheless ignored by policymakers. Policymakers object that such research is not relevant to real-world problems, fails to consider political or economic constraints, or provides only uncertain conclusions. Citizens complain that scientific information is not translated into terms comprehensible to lay people without advanced training, or is not relevant to issues or hazards as they understand them. Environmental research receives many, often mutually inconsistent criticisms. The challenge, addressed in chapter 7, is to find our way through these, to identify how science can be both credible scientifically and effective politically.

A second essential question is inherent in the place of science within democratic societies. It has been argued persuasively that environmental policy should be democratic, for both pragmatic and idealistic reasons. These arguments have been extended to science, given that it is an essential element of the environmental policy process. But the counter-argument is often made that science, to be credible, cannot also be democratic: truth is found through discovery, not voting, and not everyone's views are of equal value. Letting scientific decisions be made democratically, some say, leads to absurdities such as school boards requiring "creation science" to be taught alongside evolution. This argument has been extended to policy issues that draw substantially on science: that such issues are simply too complex for those lacking specialized knowledge, and opening them to democratic decision-making will relegate scientific information to the periphery, with the likely outcome of complex problems being ignored or addressed inadequately. This tension between democracy and expertise is a familiar one—evident in John Dewey's account of the emergence during the twentieth century of both individual citizens as a political force and large corporate and government organizations guided by experts.[16] The tension is, if anything, intensifying: while experts and large organizations encounter ever more distrust and demands for citizen participation, many pressing environmental problems, such as climate change and depletion of the ozone layer, are invisible to ordinary citizens, occurring as they do at scales beyond the experience of any individual.

Complicating this tension is the fact that scientists are not the only people able to make convincing claims of special insights into nature. Many groups claim distinctive experience and knowledge of the environment: those who experience nature through work—fishers, farmers, loggers, or wilderness tourism operators; those with daily experience in a particular environment, such as residents of a community next to an industrial facility; those who experience nature through recreation; and indigenous peoples, who assert a special relationship with nature. The origins of the environmental movement itself can be attributed as convincingly to the experience of ordinary citizens as to the knowledge of experts.

Neither is the meaning of democracy self-evident. Officially, everyone is for it, and some form of citizen participation is a near universal requirement for environmental policymaking to be considered legitimate. At the same time, systems of democracy are in flux. There is no agreement about preferred forms of democracy: respect for traditional representative democracy is in decline, and new forms of democracy are emerging. Democracy is under stress, with citizens detaching themselves from political institutions and from civic life in general while political leaders seek themselves to bypass the process.[17]

The central problem is the reconciliation of democratic values with the technical nature of environmental issues. In recent decades this challenge has only sharpened: environmental problems have become ever more technically complex, while people have become more distrustful of expert authority. Can the people—often lacking formal scientific training—be relied on to make the "right" decisions with respect to environmental problems that often have considerable and complex scientific content? Conversely, can scientists and other elites make decisions about environmental matters that take account of public concerns and values? Many have responded with a "no" to either or both questions. Environmentalists and some environmental scholars argue that the environment cannot survive democracy—left to the popular will, it will be degraded and depleted, as individuals act in uncoordinated pursuit of their self-interest. Environmental protection, therefore, requires limits on democracy, with a larger role for elites, including scientists, in governing humanity's relationship with its environment. On the other hand, many critics of science have argued that scientific expertise is incapable of ensuring environmental protection, either in the broader public interest or in terms of the interest of other species. According to this view, science is unable to provide the reliable knowledge needed to guide environmental protection, or it is tied too closely to powerful interests.

It might be suggested that a choice must be made between technocracy, in which rational decisions are made by technical experts at the cost of neglecting certain public values, particularly those that cannot be expressed in scientific terms; and democracy, emphasizing responsiveness to public concerns and public participation in decisions, but at the expense of not fully considering the scientific details of environmental problems.[18] This tension between technocratic expertise and democratic values is a familiar one, and many writers have made important contributions toward its resolution. Countless citizens engaged in environmental controversies have made their own efforts at this reconciliation, asserting their democratic right to participate while drawing on available expertise. I will draw on these ideas and experience, especially as they relate to the four areas of environmental affairs addressed in this book. Scholars of environmental science and politics have traditionally considered each of these areas in isolation. Indeed, only in the last few years have there been tentative efforts to cross the boundaries between them—as in, for example, work done within the International Human Dimensions Programme on Global Environmental Change on linking actions at the local and global levels.[19] My objective is to demonstrate that while each has distinctive elements, they also share common challenges regarding the effective and democratic use of science in environmental politics.

A Note on "Science"

Studies of contemporary science and public affairs commonly refer to "science" and the "scientific community." So will I, as a matter of convenience. I will also refer to the "environmental sciences" as those areas of science relevant to environmental affairs. But it is necessary to remain aware of the heterogeneity of environmental science and the need to apply a broad definition of science itself. In this book, "science" encompasses scientific knowledge about the world; the application of this knowledge in pursuit of practical goals; and the institutions of scientific research and its application to these goals, within government, universities, and the private and nonprofit sectors.

The subject matter of environmental science is similarly diverse. Let me give an example. When I studied the history of the relation between ecology and environmental politics, I noted the diversity of methods, theoretical principles, and practical applications that developed within the single branch of ecology devoted to the study of ecosystems. Great Britain's Nature Conservancy, the Hubbard Brook Ecosystem Study in New Hampshire, the Oak Ridge National Laboratory in Tennessee, and the University of Toronto each developed a distinctive approach to the study of ecosystems and the application of knowledge to practical problems.[20] And this was within only a single branch of ecology: there are several other branches of the discipline, devoted to the study of organisms, populations, or communities, and drawing on diverse theoretical and practical perspectives. In turn, ecology is only one discipline within a diverse environmental science community that ranges from toxicology to fisheries biology to atmospheric chemistry. The proliferation of environmental concerns and agencies over the last fifty years has seen the emergence of environmental science as a large and diverse body of activities: complex, pluralistic, and multidisciplinary. New realms of scientific inquiry have formed, encompassing new institutions—government agencies, universities, industry and citizens' groups—and new forms of expertise and their application. As public concerns and policy priorities have shifted, so too has the center of gravity of this scientific activity. When concerns about protecting natural areas are prominent, there is greater demand for ecologists. When attention is focused on the human health implications of environmental risks, toxicologists and epidemiologists are sought after. Controversies regarding global warming bring atmospheric chemists and computer modelers to the fore.

Scientific debate over environmental issues has also shifted: from relatively closed, small groups of experts to larger groups, from a wider variety of institutions. Environmental science is, in short, a diverse and diffuse collection of institutions and areas of knowledge, the boundaries of which are always open to negotiation. This has implications for both the effectiveness of science and its openness to democratic values. The complexity of the scientific community has disadvantages: the range of specializations and institutions can hinder communication and construction of a common understanding of the environment. But it also has advantages, particularly in terms of reinforcing the capacity of the environmental sciences to fulfill their diverse roles in society. Ultimately, this diversity is essential to the capacity of science to both provide accurate portrayals of nature and enhance democratic features of environmental policy.

CHAPTER 2

The Uncertain Authority
of Science

When we want to know more about the state of the earth, or of a city, we start by asking scientists. It is their views, on topics ranging from the ecology of clean water to the health consequences of lead, that we accept most readily as reliable and useful. This is interesting, because scientists are certainly not the only source of knowledge about the environment. Activists and policymakers engage daily in environmental affairs, while other experts—political scientists, sociologists, and environmental historians, among others—devote careers to understanding how and why we consume, protect, and argue over our environment. And every one of us has a lifetime's experience of using, enjoying, or thinking about this environment. And scientists do not always provide clear answers: their advice is often uncertain, addresses some problems but neglects others, serves powerful interests while denying public preferences.

Nevertheless, the image of science as rational and relevant—truth speaking to power—remains persuasive. It has been the basis for a social contract persisting since the 1940s: that science, given sufficient funding, will generate both reliable knowledge and social and economic benefits. In America this view reached its height in the 1960s, when scientific expertise underpinned "rational" approaches to waging war, planning cities, eliminating poverty, and reaching the moon. Although now eroded, that view remains influential. This notion that scientists can provide truthful, objective, trustworthy knowledge about nature I refer to as the authority of science. When it has this authority science plays essential roles in environmental politics; without it, its status can simply evaporate.

As significant as the authority of science are the frequent challenges it encounters. While scientific knowledge retains tremendous influence, there is widespread reluctance to take this knowledge at face value. Those who use this knowledge are often interrogated: Is the scientist competent, properly trained, able to ask appropriate, relevant questions? Are there any uncertainties? Did political or economic interests influence this information? Was the information used legitimately, or was it used to justify decisions made for other reasons? This dual character of science—as authoritative knowledge, and as knowledge whose authority has been widely challenged—is central to understanding its place in environmental politics.

Why Do We Listen to Science?

Most obviously, we listen to science because it works. Science has provided both technological innovations and solutions to practical problems. This view had special resonance during the twentieth century, and perhaps most powerfully after the Second World War, when it was seen as having helped assure victory through ingenious inventions like radar, penicillin, DDT, and the atomic bomb. In the postwar era, these technologies gave powerful testimony to scientists' claims of special insight, according them unprecedented prestige and authority and, especially in the United States, generous funding for research—from which was expected, in return, a steady flow of technological innovations. That this flow continued, with moon landings, modern medicine, computers, biotechnology, and many other novelties, confirmed for most that science indeed describes the world as it really is. In environmental affairs, the postwar authority of science was epitomized by confidence that the same strategies that had won the war could be applied to defeating "enemies" in nature, such as insects or fire.[1]

Scientists have gained authority not only through technology but by accumulating impressive empirical and theoretical knowledge: the predictions of plate tectonics, making sense of the shapes of continents; the success of evolutionary theory in providing a unified explanation of fossils, embryology, biogeography, and other apparently unrelated phenomena; knowledge of the structure of DNA, making sense of heredity; and the accuracy and precision of predictions in quantum electrodynamics, to note a few examples. Together, new technologies and new forms of explanation testified convincingly for a commonsense realism: that there exists a real world, independent of ourselves and our values, and that science, while fallible, can provide true and useful accounts of this reality.[2]

But scientific authority has never been simply a byproduct of knowledge. Rather, the conduct of research has been shaped by scientists' views of how they can best establish their status as providers of reliable, rigorous knowledge. One aspect of scientists' tendency toward self-validation is that knowledge has tended to be considered most persuasive when presented as universal: true everywhere, independent of local interests and circumstances. As a result, in studies of the environment, as in other areas of science, universal knowledge has tended to be the object of pursuit. In the early nineteenth century Alexander Humboldt and others formulated general theories of desiccation to make more convincing their conclusions regarding the relation between deforestation and climate change. In the early twentieth century industrial hygienists reinterpreted the unique combinations of noise, dust, and danger found in individual factories in terms of the effects of standardized substances or conditions; this knowledge, grounded in general principles, was considered superior to the experience-based knowledge of employers and workers. Today, ecologists study flows of matter and energy, developing principles of ecosystem functioning that are independent of particular species or habitats. And as Bruno Latour describes, scientists in the Amazon reinterpret the relation between soil and vegetation in terms of standardized characteristics, reducing local peculiarities to categories that make sense anywhere.[3]

Related to this view of the virtues of universal knowledge has been the notion that science is most authoritative when it speaks with unanimity. Assessments of global environmental issues, for example, tend to be considered reliable when they are based on a consensus among experts. One consequence has been that such assessments limit themselves to scientific matters, avoiding contentious political issues; within science, they focus on the hard physical and chemical sciences, eschewing the complex ecological phenomena about which consensus can be more elusive. This "design for consensus" and for authority may thus be pursued even at the expense of practical relevance.[4]

Knowledge has also usually been considered most authoritative when presented in the form of numbers.[5] The demand for quantitative knowledge has shaped environmental research: driving the creation of new categories of understanding, such as yield and risk, that can be expressed mathematically; reducing debate over alternative courses of action to the calculation of costs and benefits; assigning a privileged role in policy to forms of expertise better able to provide quantitative results; encouraging efforts to attach numbers even to supposedly intangible environmental attributes such as beauty.

Another consequence of the status accorded to generalized, quantitative knowledge has been the tendency of scientists, especially in newer fields, to seek links with disciplines already widely viewed as authoritative. For example, between the 1950s and the 1970s the U.S. Atomic Energy Commission provided ample support for ecological research. However, ecologists, conscious of their lower status within atomic laboratories dominated by the physical sciences (some viewed them as "butterfly collectors") sought to enhance their authority by adopting research methods and equipment used by physicists, such as radionuclides and computer models. In a different arena, industrial hygienists studying lead poisoning and other occupational diseases pursued a similar strategy, emphasizing principles of internal medicine when explaining the link between environment and health, thereby applying forms of explanation considered legitimate by chemists and physiologists.[6]

Scientists have asserted authority not just on the basis of the universal, quantitative aspects of scientific knowledge, but also by invoking the process by which this knowledge is created, and the nature of the scientific community itself. Since the Enlightenment, the scientific community has been widely viewed, at least ideally, as a collective of free individuals pursuing neither private gain nor political ideology, but simply the truth: an image of freedom and cooperation that is both unique and a model for society. Robert Merton codified the "scientific ethos" said to govern this community:

> *Universalism*: evidence is open to all; there are no privileged observers;
>
> *Communism*: knowledge is collectively arrived at and is owned by all;
>
> *Disinterestedness*: nature is approached without prior wishes that it be one way or another;
>
> *Organized skepticism*: nothing is immune from doubt.[7]

Thus, knowledge developed by one scientist is not private property, but is freely publicized, to be verified by other researchers. Any scientist will discard knowledge, no matter how cherished, that is contradicted by experience. Truth is achieved efficiently and honestly, unsullied by ideology, dogma, or private interest. This image of science, and its pervasiveness in the postwar era, must be placed in context, including the defense of science during the cold war as part of a free society.[8] Science as objective knowledge was considered a hallmark of Western thought, in opposition to the notion of science as shaped by political or economic influences, as Soviet historians had begun to argue in the 1930s. More generally, aspects of scientific practice and forms of argument have been transferred to the political sphere, not least by demonstrating that conflicts can be resolved peacefully and that it is possible to explain the world in terms of concrete causes and effects—both demonstrations underpinning contemporary political authority and accountability.[9] Portrayals of science as the objective pursuit of truth have thus played important political roles in the postwar world.

Many scientists today would agree that, apart from fraud or ideological contamination, these norms do in fact describe how the scientific community works; indeed, their authority depends on how well they convince others of this. Accordingly, in fields from conservation biology to climate change research, scientists will portray themselves, whatever their personal convictions, as objective researchers, engaged in disinterested, skeptical inquiry. But this image of science has also become highly contentious in recent decades.

Drawing the Boundary between Science and Politics

Authoritative scientific knowledge—convincing and useful, expressed in universal, quantitative terms, created through disinterested, objective inquiry—can be persuasive because it is everything that politics is not. On the other hand, if science comes to be viewed as merely the expression of political preferences, then its methods, results, and interpretations will all be open to question. Accordingly, as Thomas Gieryn explains, scientists and those who use science insist on the distinction between science and politics, engaging in "boundary work": the reconstruction of scientific results for public use in ways that demonstrate that these results, and how they were obtained, are distinct from (although often relevant to) politics.[10] Scientists may engage in boundary work themselves; often, however, the key role, particularly in complex matters such as global ozone depletion or climate change negotiations, is taken by knowledge brokers, who mediate between the scientific and political communities, asserting the reliability and authority of scientific results while translating them into language that is accessible and meaningful to nonscientists.[11]

While scientific knowledge is presented as universal, produced through unvarying norms of disinterested objectivity, the strategies of boundary work (like politics itself) are preeminently local, shaped by whatever circumstances— institutions, audiences, issues—prevail in a particular situation. As a result, the boundaries between science and politics are usually ambiguous and flexible, shifting in relation to changing circumstances. For example, while scientists today construct firm boundaries between their work and social attitudes, nineteenth-century European colonial scientists accompanied their calls for ecological reform with demands for social reform, such as better treatment of indigenous peoples. Similarly, while contemporary scientists tend to distinguish their view of nature from that provided by indigenous knowledge, colonial scientists often drew on indigenous knowledge, recognizing the value of insights gained from long experience of living off the land.[12]

The extent to which the authority of science depends on boundary work can be especially evident during times of crisis, when the shortcomings of science put its authority at risk. At such times boundary work is pursued intensely. One instance occurred after the collapse of northern cod populations off Newfoundland in the early 1990s. The loss of this resource—for centuries a mainstay of the Newfoundland economy—caused much economic hardship. Prior to its collapse, the fisheries had been managed on the basis of extensive research, and scientists were closely involved in debates over how many fish it was safe to catch. Their participation continued right up to the actual collapse. Nevertheless, some fisheries scientists argued that a major reason for the collapse was interference in science by economic and political factors. In particular, government scientists alleged they were prevented from expressing their concerns openly. The solution, they argued, would be an independent institution for fisheries science, insulated from political and managerial pressures.[13] Thus, the apparent failure of science to contribute to effective fisheries management became, for scientists, an opportunity to stress the importance of boundaries between science and politics, and to emphasize thereby that it was not science, but politics, that had been at fault.

A crucial question about the boundary between science and politics is its location: where, in the continuum between hard data and messy questions of responsibility, does science end and politics begin? For several reasons, the pervasive tendency in environmental politics has been to draw the line to favor science: to define problems so that they require scientific solutions, thereby converting political controversies into technical puzzles. This drawing of boundaries is itself intensely political, dependent on local contexts in which knowledge is closely wrapped up with interests and ideologies.

The Contexts of Scientific Authority

For several decades a chief arena for the exercise of the authority of environmental science has been administrative agencies: the U.S. Forest Service, the Environmental Protection Agency, Environment Canada, and many others. The formation of these agencies can be traced to emerging problems of resource supply, and new risks to health and the environment, that compelled redefinition of the environment as a collective responsibility subject to regulatory authority. A characteristic feature of this redefinition has been the transformation of scientific knowledge into distinct arenas of professional practice, imparting authority both to expertise and to the agency employing it, adhering to the model of behavior described by Max Weber, in which bureaucracies assert power through specialized expertise and control of information, justified by their claim to be the only means by which the complexities of modern society can be managed.[14] This was the path followed by experts within national agencies during the early twentieth century, including foresters at the Forest Service, agricultural researchers at the Department of Agriculture, and economists at the Department of Commerce. Each agency developed a corps of scientific expertise and thereby bolstered its capacity to assert authority over an area of national economic life. After World War II, and especially after the 1960s, many more agencies took shape, each justifying the expansion of government regulatory authority on the basis of scientific authority.

The result, in areas ranging from economic development, to planning, to education, has been an ever-expanding application of administrative rationalism: seeking, with the guidance of technical expertise, rational and efficient solutions to the problems of society, translating the authority of science into political power.[15] As Weber argued, the greatest value of technical expertise to a bureaucracy is in reinforcing its authority. By this view, the public interest is to be determined not democratically, but through expert analysis, with this interest then pursued by disinterested, objective experts, who protect the public from the errors they might make if they had direct responsibility. An unbridgeable gap is maintained between the public and "expert cultures": technical experts present their knowledge as neutral fact, insulated from public accountability by a wall of bureaucracy.[16] The legitimacy of administrators implementing policy, exercising discretion in applying legislative directions that provide only general guidance, relies on their authority as experts, and they rely on science to buttress their arguments when obliged to defend them, in court or elsewhere. As Ted Greenwood notes, "decision-makers . . . have strong incentives to claim that their actions and arguments are grounded in knowledge, not interest or values, and can often thereby muster support . . . the pretense of knowledge yields power."[17] Framed in terms of science, administrative decisions are thereby warranted to reflect reality rather than merely political preferences. Agencies also rely on expertise as a means of resolving the tension between common law's insistence on individualized proof of causal injury and the frequent impossibility of establishing this proof in cases of environmental harm.[18] In the absence of definitive proof of harm the imposition of environmental regulations must instead be grounded in confidence in expertise.

A series of symbiotic relationships therefore emerged between scientists and administrative agencies: as an area of concern—agricultural productivity, forest management, the workplace environment, clean water—became defined as a collective concern and a government responsibility, the relevant administrative agency became a new locus of expertise and specialized professional practices. In return for imbuing administrative decisions with authority, scientists enjoy not only the opportunity to develop and apply their professional expertise, but also an increase in their own authority thanks to the parallel between general scientific knowledge and the administrative preference for standardized operating principles and regulations.[19] This authority is exercised at whatever level experts work—by a forester managing a stand of trees, or through decisions at forest service headquarters—because of the experts' capacity to shape basic categories of thought and language and thereby to influence people's perceptions of what exists, how it should be understood, how it can be controlled.[20] And this exercise of expertise justifies not just particular decisions, but the practice of administrative rationalism itself: issues are defined as strictly technical, discouraging attention to their political dimensions and focusing debate not on the ends (about which it is assumed that all agree) but on the efficiency and effectiveness of the means. Defining a decision as scientific shifts responsibility for its consequences from the political system to science, and so can discourage potential opponents.

This symbiosis of expert and administrative authority, and the attendant redefinition of political issues as technical, are reinforced by the constellation of expertise that accumulates within and around administrative agencies. Scientists within universities, industry, and government share assumptions regarding knowledge and its role in the political process, as well as certain values and policy goals. These experts (often collectively referred to as policy networks or communities) also tend to enjoy privileged access to the political system, where they shape both policies and their implementation, framing definitions of what is and is not feasible, guiding the flow of information to senior bureaucrats and elected officials, shaping support for certain policies and denying support to others.

Asserting the Authority of Science

Since the 1960s the ideology of administrative rationalism has become a favorite target for environmentalists. That agricultural scientists and the chemical industry could make all the decisions regarding pesticides; that industry and resource agencies would alone determine how forests were to be exploited; that nuclear energy, with all its implications, was the exclusive province of the Atomic Energy Commission: these and other closed worlds of expertise and associated interests came to be viewed as significant reasons for failures to consider public concerns, including the interests of other species.[21] As a result, a central theme of environmental politics over the last four decades has been the effort to change where decisions are made: not within these closed worlds, but in the public view. But the striking aspect of the resulting transformation of many arenas of decision-making—from the closed world of administrative rationalism to the glare of controversy—has been that the status of science as authoritative knowledge has endured. This is striking, but not surprising: when we examine environmental controversies, we can see how the interests of all parties involved demand that the authority of science be maintained.

Certainly, environmentalists tend to see science as an essential resource, enhancing the persuasiveness of their accounts of environmental problems. As Sheila Jasanoff notes, "science is environmentalism's favorite battleground."[22] Environmentalists have often drawn on scientists' authority, relying on their capacity to recognize the risks of toxic chemicals, climate change, ozone layer depletion, and other hazards. Many environmental groups, including some traditionally associated with confrontational tactics, such as Greenpeace, now act as conduits between scientists and the media, seeking to ensure that the latest information on environmental problems is widely available. This reflects the increasing tendency of some environmental organizations to take on tasks that governments are unwilling or unable to do, including gathering and disseminating information and even commissioning research. Even those few radical environmentalists who have presented visions of a chaotic world facing ecological breakdown have tended to argue that such a future would require the prescriptions of authoritative experts armed with knowledge and computers.[23]

Those in industry—environmentalists' frequent adversaries—are perhaps even more enthusiastic promoters of scientific authority, appealing consistently to "sound science" as the only reliable basis for decisions. This focus on science is often reinforced by the news media, yet another receptive audience for authoritative expertise. More generally, businesspeople, like environmentalists, see science as firm ground from which to argue—confirmation that their views are based on reason, not emotion or interests. Often enough, this invocation of "sound science" is, as Elisa Ong and Stanton Glantz conclude, the product of "sophisticated public relations campaigns controlled by industry executives and lawyers to manipulate the scientific standards of proof for the corporate interests of their clients."[24] Defining a problem in scientific terms implies that action—including regulation of industry activities—must wait until scientific standards of proof have been satisfied. Science-based arguments are attractive for other reasons as well. Industry often has the most scientific resources, particularly in research-intensive fields such as biotechnology. In a debate framed in terms of science they can control what information is available, outgunning any opponents. (At the same time, they also tend [as do some environmental organizations] to emphasize an emotional message: biotechnology firms stress the importance of good nutrition for children, timber companies display expanses of green forests—while obscuring the scientific details of the technology.[25]) A further advantage to industry of defining environmental problems as scientific is that debate on more fundamental matters is forestalled: changes in consumption practices or in the structure of society, or critical analysis of the economic activities that contribute to environmental problems in the first place, are rendered irrelevant. Finally, the political commitments involved in appealing to "sound science" have often been evident. In the early 1980s, for example, Anne Gorsuch of the Environmental Protection Agency used an appeal to better science to mask the Reagan administration's political agenda of deregulation.[26]

The authority of science, therefore, can be traced not just to the intrinsic nature of scientific knowledge, but to the interests—scientists, administrative agencies, environmentalists, business—that authority serves. This can be viewed idealistically: authoritative expertise promises agreement on the nature of environmental challenges, giving impetus to solving them. Viewed more cynically, advocates on all sides of a controversy can evade responsibility for their value choices, hiding instead behind the protective veil of science. Certainly, this second view can help explain a persistent feature of environmental controversies: the agreement between adversaries regarding the authority and value of expertise. One consequence of this agreement is that debate tends to shift readily from whatever political, economic, or moral values or interests may be at stake to focus instead on scientific issues.[27]

Industry may encourage environmental research on strictly pragmatic grounds, as when certain environmental problems are also business risks. The insurance industry's early interest in studies of climate change is one example of this. And in these controversies environmentalists and industry find the news media a receptive audience for authoritative scientific knowledge. Journalists prefer to present themselves as objective, and they will draw on the authority of science to reinforce this perception. The authority of science is also often reinforced through the choice of stories to be covered. Writers and editors prefer stories with a clear message, and so will cover issues in which the hazards or culprits are more obvious and the relevant scientific information more clear-cut and conclusive, rather than fuzzy and uncertain. There are exceptions, however: the media, seeking to appear balanced, will sometimes emphasize uncertainties— a tendency most evident in its portrayal of a scientific community divided over climate change, underestimating the actual consensus among scientists.

Scientific authority, then, has many sources. Scientists assert their authority by invoking the universal and quantitative character of scientific knowledge and the disinterested objectivity of the scientific community. Administrative agencies, their credibility tied to professional expertise, continually emphasize the relevance and reliability of the scientific knowledge they cite. Participants in controversies—environmentalists, businesspeople, the media—seek, for their own purposes, to reinforce the status of science as a source of reliable knowledge. The result is a paradox: the authority of science, justified in terms of a capacity to generate facts true in every context, is continually recreated out of local materials, its particular form the product of specific circumstances, in the research community, environmental bureaucracies, or public controversies.

Not only do the purposes of asserting scientific authority vary—encompassing justification of both stringent environmental protection and weaker regulations, depending on the interests at stake—but so do the discourses, or ways of understanding and valuing the world, that underpin expertise. For example, the late 1960s were often described as the "age of ecology," testifying to this discipline's newly acquired authority and to recognition of the complexity and fragility of nature. This discourse of ecology can be compared to the at least equally influential discourse of economic rationalism. While an ecological discourse privileges expertise that explains, say, how a wetland functions and why it should be protected, economic rationalism favors experts who can explain how to drain the swamp and convert it to useful purposes. According to this discourse, nature is not complex and fragile, but simply matter awaiting conversion to something that humans can use, under the guidance of expertise devoted to control and transformation. Within this discourse economic expertise is especially favored, while expertise that emphasizes complexity and uncertainty, including ecology, is distrusted.[28]

Challenging Scientific Authority

When the light of the first atomic bomb reached him, Robert Oppenheimer thought of the words from the Bhagavad-Gita, "I am become death, the destroyer of worlds." His colleague, Kenneth Bainbridge, uttered a phrase less memorable, but more relevant to the suddenly altered role of physicists: "Now we are all sons of bitches."[29] Bainbridge realized that the capacity to destroy had shattered the myth that scientists could remain detached from the uses to which their knowledge is put, and from politics generally. The episode epitomizes a major feature of environmental politics over the last four decades: doubt regarding the status of science as objective, neutral knowledge, and a blurring of the boundaries between science and politics. The consequences for the authority of science have been immense.

For two decades after World War II science was broadly viewed as politically neutral, generally progressive, and best able to flourish when left to develop autonomously.[30] (There were exceptions—in particular, the Frankfurt School of critical theorists were led by the experience of the war to question whether scientific progress necessarily results in human progress: it had not prevented Nazism and the Holocaust, nor the use of atomic weapons.[31]) By the late 1960s, however, a reluctance to defer to experts had become more widely evident, especially in America. Cases of misconduct—misrepresentation or fabrication of results—were one factor, although such behavior was usually perceived as isolated violations of scientists' own code of conduct and therefore did not impugn their collective competence and objectivity.[32] More significant challenges to expertise came through practical experience, with the initiatives of the "best and the brightest," from planning war to planning cities, generating unexpected and sometimes disastrous consequences, not least because of a failure to understand how complex systems, whether societies or cities, actually work. It became evident that technical ability does not imply competence in matters of political and social judgment.[33] Accompanying this was a decline in respect for experts as disinterested authorities. Instead, they often came to be seen as just another interest group, more concerned with their own influence and status than with the general progress of society, and too often allied with dominant political, economic, and institutional interests. Rachel Carson's *Silent Spring* is a classic text of this reassessment of expertise. Carson was influential not just because of her knowledge of DDT, but because she placed this knowledge within a general critique of chemical expertise: its narrow focus on instrumental goals, such as controlling pests; its dismissal of ecological and human health concerns; and its close ties to agricultural and chemical interests.

Ever since, challenges to expertise have been a central feature of environmental politics. Some challenges relate to the nature of environmental science itself, including doubts regarding its capacity to provide adequate and reliable knowledge, questions concerning the role of judgment and negotiation in science, and critiques of how science relates to other forms of knowledge. Debates throughout the 1980s and 1990s regarding the objectivity of scientific knowledge, the implications of relativistic perspectives, the deconstruction of the concepts of nature and of science, and critiques of expert knowledge as oppressive to communities that live near particular industries, resources, or habitats have all been part of an active controversy concerning the authority of environmental scientists to determine who should be permitted access to and control over nature.

For a range of complex issues—from the ecological impacts of climate change to the long-term health consequences of toxic chemicals—scientists are often unable to provide conclusive advice. This may reflect incomplete theoretical understanding, or insufficient research, or merely the great complexity of natural and human systems. As a report by the Heinz Center for Science, Economics, and the Environment noted, knowledge of many aspects of the American environment remains inadequate as a basis for decisions.[34] The National Research Council agrees, noting that "[a]ssessments that provide useful, credible scientific information to decision makers in a timely and politically acceptable manner remain the exception rather than the rule."[35] Frequent experience of how inconclusive scientific information can be has undermined its authoritative image.

Particular problems for the authority of science have been posed by awareness of pervasive uncertainty (incomplete knowledge about a phenomenon) and ignorance (lack of awareness of even the existence of a phenomenon). In an uncertain world, a single answer is rarely possible; in a world in which there are large areas of ignorance, there may be no answer at all, particularly in policy-relevant areas that push scientific inquiry to the outer edge of accepted facts.[36] The complexity of ecosystems, the unpredictable consequences of human activities, and the fragmentary nature of scientific inquiry, in which disciplines and institutions probe certain aspects of nature more deeply than others, together generate deep gaps in knowledge. At the same time, scientists are being called upon to answer ever more complex questions, about, say, the cumulative impacts of several industries on a river or other ecosystem, or the regional consequences of climate change. Such questions, regarding problems that have long-term but uncertain implications and that extend across regional or global scales, with causes and effects often widely separated in time and space, may often be unanswerable.[37] Ignorance and uncertainty can be constructed in other ways as well: opponents of an initiative justified on the basis of scientific evidence (such as action on climate change) will often focus attack not on the initiative itself, but on the science underpinning it. The examination of scientific evidence in adversarial situations, such as a courtroom, also highlights its uncertainties. Bringing to bear several scientific disciplines or approaches on a problem can also magnify uncertainties, simply by demonstrating that science provides many partial, sometimes contradictory perspectives rather than a single "truth".[38]

Whatever its causes, the failure to provide definitive answers encourages doubts regarding the authority of science, since it contradicts the notion that only a single truthful scientific description of the world can exist. Environmentalists find that science cannot provide the support (in the form of specific information) that they expect of it; regulatory agencies find that science provides only fragmentary grounds on which to base their decisions; parties to controversies find that scientific evidence does not resolve, but only exacerbates divisions.

There is an increasing realization as well that many significant problems in environmental politics do not lend themselves, even in principle, to scientific solution. There are many reasons for this: these problems have political, economic, or moral dimensions regarding which science is silent; scientists provide not one answer, but a range of answers to questions asked of them, because of the complexity of these questions or because of gaps in scientific understanding; and finally, science itself is often shaped by political or economic interests, including those that contribute to the problems in the first place. These matters are considered in more depth in later chapters.

Another reason for questioning the authority of scientific knowledge is awareness of how this knowledge is actually created. Scientists rarely simply gather data and then move unambiguously toward a conclusion. This is rare indeed in environmental science, where the questions—about the long-term effects of contaminants, or the status of fish populations, for example—are often at the outer edge of scientific understanding. Making sense of a complex world—

determining which observations are relevant, what they mean, how they connect to what we already know—usually takes a great deal of judgment. And convincing other scientists, creating a consensus on new knowledge, can require plenty of negotiation. These negotiations are shaped by many factors, including scientists' training, ambitions, and disciplinary perspectives. Scientists will often disagree about what data are relevant, or what they mean, especially if specialists from different disciplines are working on the same problem. For example, study of a contaminant may bring together a toxicologist, an epidemiologist, and an environmental chemist, each with his or her distinctive methods and standards of evidence. Scientists may also be prone to particular biases and tacit assumptions. Those who engage in forecasting, for example, tend to assume that the future will be like the immediate past. Scientists also tend to give greater weight to evidence from fields with which they are more familiar.[39]

These aspects of how scientific knowledge is created are unavoidable, but they are also often viewed as problematic. It is often assumed (both within and outside the scientific community) that if scientists disagree there must be some kind of polluting influence at work: one side may be incompetent or fraudulent, or one (or both) sides may have fallen prey to ideology or the influence of economic or political interests. The fact that scientists negotiate is often taken to imply that not simply empirical data, but more idiosyncratic factors, such as the relative power of scientists or their negotiating skills, may determine what becomes knowledge.

And finally, challenges to the authority of science sometimes stem from how scientific knowledge relates to other ways of understanding our complex world. Science is celebrated for its success in generating universal knowledge. This has encouraged scientists to reorganize the diverse heterogeneity of nature into uniform, standardized formats, amenable to precise control and analysis—in effect, extending the laboratory ideal into the world.[40] But as numerous scholars have noted, there is often a sharp contrast between scientific knowledge and the knowledge held by those who live in a particular place. This knowledge is often far more appropriate to local conditions, because it can take into account the subtle but crucial variations that scientists seeking general knowledge may not be able to appreciate. Michael Thompson's study of flooding and erosion in the Himalayas and Brian Wynne's study of scientists, sheep farmers, and radioactive contamination in England's Lake District both demonstrated how general knowledge relates poorly to local conditions and forms of expertise, and how scientists had difficulty accepting this local expertise as "scientific" and therefore reliable.[41] In addition, tacit prescriptive commitments embedded in scientific knowledge, especially relating to controlling and transforming nature, may fit poorly with local attitudes that emphasize adaptation and coexistence.[42] Studies of alternative forms of knowledge, particularly indigenous knowledge, have undermined the authority of science by rendering visible the assumptions embedded within scientific practice. By demonstrating that knowledge can be obtained by means antithetical to those employed by scientists—qualitative rather than quantitative observation, eschewing experimentation, with information communicated through stories and oral traditions, often bound to social and cultural values and beliefs—indigenous knowledge demonstrates that science is not the only way to understand the world. Ultimately, science is seen as irrelevant to, or even a deliberate misunderstanding of, the places in which people live.[43]

These features of contemporary science—its inadequacy in the face of complex environmental problems, its negotiated character, and its relationship with other forms of knowledge—have all been the basis for challenges to its authority. But what has often given such challenges special force are certain aspects of contemporary environmental politics. These include public and legal controversies over the environment, in which a harsh light is often directed on the ambiguities and uncertainties of scientific knowledge; the involvement of economic interests, especially industry, in funding scientific research, leading to questions regarding the objectivity of science; and the status of science in relation to structures of power in society, generating a widespread view that science serves not as disinterested knowledge, but to reinforce these structures. Each of these aspects has generated critical examination of science, undermining its status as reliable, objective knowledge.

Science in Controversies

Environmental controversies have proliferated since the 1960s, as citizens and activist groups have asserted their concerns and the restricted communities that once dominated environmental and natural resource management have opened up. Across countless issues, from regulating industrial emissions to determining forest cutting plans, many (but by no means all) decisions once made quietly by industry and government are now open to a broader range of participants.

Science has become a major part of these controversies, provoking concerns and structuring and informing debate. Indeed, these controversies often stem from divergent scientific views regarding the existence, significance, and responsibility for environmental problems. Is the climate really changing? How important are the health effects of electromagnetic radiation? From which power plants does acid rain falling on Vermont or Ontario originate? As experience has shown, such questions can also generate years of debate. Scientific information alone rarely compels closure, especially when the stakes are high; in fact, uncertainties often only continue to accumulate.

Within the scientific community, an inability to provide precise, decisive answers is not usually considered problematic; rather, it is seen as a necessary condition, stemming from the fact that science is an unfinished enterprise (witness the clichéd conclusion of a scientific paper: "more research is needed"). Scientists are relatively trusting of their colleagues' results: tolerant of the informal craft skills intrinsic to field and laboratory practice, the informed interpretations necessary to make sense of uncertain results, the frequent lack of agreement on interpretations. These are viewed as inevitable: tentative results illustrate the elusiveness of definitive proof as scientists negotiate their way toward eventual consensus on new knowledge.[44]

However, in public controversies these tacit features of scientific practice provide many openings through which to challenge scientific authority. Controversies, particularly in the courtroom, cast a harsh, unflattering light on scientific knowledge. Uncertainty is viewed as inadequacy, interpretation as mere opinion, lack of consensus as evidence that science cannot yet justify any action. The spectacle of different experts interpreting the same thing differently contradicts assumptions about their objectivity. Scientific information itself often becomes the focus of controversy, as participants line up with opposing scientific assessments and deconstruct the science of their opponents, critiquing methods and assumptions, disputing uncertainties, and using those uncertainties to discredit others' results. Those who do not accept a decision can always find experts to back up their objections. Non-scientists, once happy to defer to experts, are increasingly willing to critique them. Beginning in the 1970s courts often examined not just agency decisions, but the scientific arguments underpinning them. In numerous cases, they set aside decisions because they found these arguments inadequate.[45] Opponents of regulation highlight the absence of definitive proof regarding many hazards and dispute regulatory decisions through close examination and critique of their scientific basis. In effect, litigation has become an alternative channel for debating science, and in courtrooms the ethos of skeptical mistrust toward all testimony has inevitably been directed toward science. The result is often harrowing for scientists subjected to cross-examination, as the assumptions and interpretations underlying their evidence are pulled apart.[46] Brian Wynne notes how scientists providing legal testimony find themselves in

> an alien system which does not share science's own informal social norms, presumptions and institutional factors restricting to a socially pragmatic level the questioning of agreed knowledge. This is also true of scientists in any external context; but legal settings not only do not share those presumptions, they also possess an ethos that runs totally counter to them. Legal processes enshrine scepticism and mistrust: cross-examination has a duty to question as fully as possible the adversary's case in front of the judge or jury.[47]

Crucially, science in legal contexts demonstrated the possibility that more than one interpretation—more than one set of "facts"—is possible. As Ted Greenwood argues, "the institutions and procedures of American administrative government, designed as they are to place high dependence on judicial and quasijudicial proceedings and intended to encourage decision-making based as far as possible on science and engineering knowledge, in fact exacerbate political controversy by focusing attention on conflicting interpretations of deficient knowledge."[48]

Members of the public also engage in critiquing science. For example, in the late 1980s the environmental impact assessment process for a large pulp mill in northern Alberta provided a forum for local residents to challenge directly the quality of expert testimony provided by the scientists hired to review the mill's impacts. As one resident stated:

> [The Environmental Impact Assessment] goes on to say that "there is a large uncertainty in the emission rate estimates for the cooling pond." And that "the rates are educated guesses." I am a household engineer, and in my educated opinion . . . and I am an educated person . . . this is bullshit science. Where do you get off making enigmatic predictions that will affect my lungs and those of my family?[49]

Evidently, scientists' participation in controversies often undermines their authority as objective experts. The problem is founded in a contradiction: expert judgments are usually presented as neutral and objective, but they are then used to justify positions and decisions that are inherently political. As Dorothy Nelkin explains:

> [t]he authority of scientific expertise has rested on assumptions about scientific rationality. The interpretations and predictions of scientists are judged to be rational and immune to political manipulation because they are based on data gathered through objective procedures. But scientific expertise is enlisted by all sides of disputes as a means to either defend or challenge the legitimacy of policy decisions. The willingness of scientists to lend their expertise to various factions in widely publicized disputes contributes to the political challenge, but it also is problematic. For, ironically, as scientists debate the various sides of politicized issues, their involvement undermines assumptions about the objectivity of science, and these are precisely the assumptions that have given experts their power as the neutral arbiters of truth.[50]

In practice, the perception that experts can disagree—inevitably disagree, when they become involved in controversies—highlights how doing science always involves some judgment, and how these judgments can be shaped by values, as well as by professional, economic, and political factors. The realization that experts are not infallible, and do not have access to some unique, objective methods or perspectives, has resulted in an opening up of science beyond the scientific community. The details of science itself, once seen as the province of scientists, become themselves controversial: what to study, how studies should be designed, how results should be assessed. One of the most basic of the details brought to light in controversies concerns levels of proof. Scientists favoring high standards of evidence will argue that there is no proof that a given pollutant is harmful and that dissenting scientists are tainted by nonscientific, emotional tendencies; other scientists will argue that those demanding high levels of proof also have unscientific commitments, such as ties to industry or a skepticism regarding regulations generally.

Science can even intensify controversies, providing evidence for all sides of the debate, fueling the dispute instead of resolving it. Fractured along lines of discord, such as that between environmental and corporate interests, scientific knowledge reinforces political differences.[51] Environmental activists criticize corporate science as favoring narrow economic objectives over the public good, while their opponents decry as "junk" research that identifies new environmental hazards. This notion of "junk science" is frequently invoked by the private sector: while not precisely defined, it generally refers to science that can justify environmental or health regulations or is consistent with the precautionary principle; thus, it is often invoked to discredit environmental claims and statements of alarm or caution generally.[52] It is often contrasted with "sound science"—another rhetorical phenomenon that reflects the public relations priorities of industry more than an effort to enhance scientific quality. By such means are debates polarized, with each side finding in the other's representation of nature further rationale for disagreeing.

One irony of all this is that the authority of science is eroded by efforts to reinforce it. Consider what is happening when industry officials invoke the need for "sound science" when arguing for more studies before action, while environmentalists appeal to scientists for credible statements of just how bad problems already are. Both parties are insisting that science provides authoritative support for their positions. But in doing so they undermine this authority—not just by putting the phenomenon of scientific disagreement on public display, but by implying that science owes its authority, at least in part, to the claims made by those who invoke it in controversies. In effect, the authority of science is itself revealed as a political entity. This renders it as open to challenge as any other claims made by participants in a controversy.

The authority of science becoming itself a political matter is one manifestation of how the border between science and politics has been blurred. Another has been the emergence of a "fifth branch" of science advisors: hybrid communities that combine scientists, government officials, and actors from other sectors, including business and environmental groups.[53] These hybrid communities are scattered across the entire area of environmental affairs: from risk assessment to resource management to climate science. A common feature, however, is that they make it necessary to find new ways of thinking about how science relates to policy, beyond the simple linear model of knowledge originating in the scientific community and then being applied in society. Scientists may be as wrapped up as policymakers in the regulatory process, churning up science and politics, evaluating their results in the light of political, social, and moral values.[54] At the same time, nonscientists are involved in setting scientific priorities, evaluating the relevance of scientific results, and making judgments that combine scientific and nonscientific considerations. The products of such a community may look like science, but they are much more: as William Leiss notes, the "'number' selected for an environmental standard only appears to be derived directly from the pure disinterested inquiries of the laboratory; in fact, it usually represents a rough compromise among vested interests, balancing science, politics, and economy on the knife-edge of potential catastrophe."[55] With scientists and nonscientists trading roles, the boundary between science and politics is eroded, weakening the image and authority of science as a realm distinct from the world of interests and values.

Many scientists are unhappy with all this, and especially with how scientific disputes have become public, tarnishing (in their view) the image of science as a source of rational knowledge. This is also problematic for science-based regulatory agencies, because it challenges the scientistic assumptions that often prevail in these agencies, impugning their authority and hence their effectiveness. Environmentalists are also troubled by this, because it means that science is often unable to provide straightforward support for their arguments.

These challenges to the authority of science also have consequences for the controversies themselves. Scientific evidence is rarely able to compel closure. No matter how well-researched an issue might be, there are always more unknowns and more unexamined possibilities; science tends to raise more questions than it can answer, expanding the realm of ignorance more rapidly than the realm of what is known. Even results widely considered to be the product of "good science" will rarely provide the "right answer" that will immediately resolve policy disputes. Expert information is not enough protection against skepticism, and so disputes over science tend to be intractable, especially when they are bound up with the consequences for regulation.[56]

Industry and the Authority of Science

The relations between industry and researchers powerfully shape the politics of environmental science. Industry supports a great deal of research, for a variety of purposes: to guide the harvesting of natural resources, to develop new products, to meet regulatory requirements, and so on. This has several implications for the authority of science. Industry has an interest in maintaining the authority of the expertise for which it pays; at the same time, the ties between industry and science have served as another avenue by which the authority of science as objective knowledge has been challenged.

These challenges have taken several forms. Industry support for research inevitably raises the question of what benefits it derives from this investment. Funding usually comes with strings attached. Choice of projects is affected by this support, with a stronger focus on applied, "practical" subjects. This is of special concern with respect to the environment, since so many issues relate only indirectly, or not at all, to industry priorities. Industry will also often dominate research on a particular issue or hazard, limiting opportunities for other interests to develop their own scientific perspectives. In a controversy there may be only a few, if any, independently financed studies that can be arrayed against a mass of corporate-backed research.

The authority of industry science has also been challenged on the basis of the confidentiality of research results—a practice considered inimical to the pursuit of objective knowledge. Industry often dictates the terms under which research is conducted, and scientists routinely agree to keep both methods and results secret for a period of time, or to withhold the data on which conclusions are based. Inevitably, these confidentiality arrangements inhibit the exchange of information, with commercial interest overriding the public's interest in sharing knowledge.[57] Researchers are often contractually obliged not to disclose even dangers to public health.[58] When data are not publicly available, there is no independent check on the results or interpretation of industry-sponsored research.

Research results themselves can be affected by industry support. Given the negotiated character of research results, it is generally possible to manipulate them to obtain the desired outcomes. Outright cheating may be rare, but there are more subtle ways of ensuring that research provides appropriate results: by not testing high enough doses of a suspected toxic substance, for example, or by not exposing research subjects for a long enough period. Studies of publications in biomedical journals have found that researchers funded by, or with other ties to, industry tend to report more positive results relating to company products than do independent researchers.[59] A similar conclusion has been derived from studies of industry-sponsored research in chemicals.[60] According to the authors of one of these studies, ties to industry also affect the direction of research: scientists linked to industry were more than twice as likely to take commercial considerations into account when choosing research topics as were those without such funding.[61] A similar pattern has been evident in climate research funded by energy companies, generally downplaying concerns about climate change.[62]

Of course, these are only the most recent episodes in a long history of industry experts allowing their evaluation of risks to be shaped by economic interests. The classic example is the tobacco industry, whose persistent efforts to obfuscate were epitomized by a notorious 1969 internal document explaining that "doubt is our product."[63] Another case was asbestos: industry scientists concealed what they knew and suspected, while governments wishing to protect this industry turned a blind eye to health concerns.[64] Industry has often used science to defend itself against public concerns, paying for studies designed to minimize damaging findings, hiring scientists to support industry perspectives, attacking opposing scientists. Corporations, including high-profile firms such as Monsanto and Dupont, and their consulting firms have manipulated studies required by regulatory agencies, on topics such as the movement of pesticides and the residues on food products.[65]

This accumulating evidence of how science has served political and economic interests, often in ways counter to the public good, has generated much greater wariness regarding the ties between researchers and economic interests. Some leading journals—particularly in the biomedical field—require authors to disclose financial ties with industry. Advisory boards have chosen to exclude from review committees scientists with financial interests.[66]

One of the consequences of this wariness, and of the erosion of the authority of industry science generally, is that industry now provides much of its support for environmental research indirectly, through institutions perceived as independent. Over the last two decades these institutions have proliferated: large formaldehyde producers organized the Formaldehyde Institute; pesticide manufacturers formed the American Crop Protection Association; and the Center for Indoor Air Research acts on behalf of the tobacco industry.[67] In each case, industries pool their research resources while presenting a united front. The relations between these institutions and industry are not always clear, but their justification is: presented as independent, their research results carry much more authority than do those generated by the industry itself.

But while scientists and corporations have sought to obscure the relation between industry and science by "laundering" funds through these institutes, many such arrangements appear to leave unchanged both corporate expectations and scientists' understandings of these expectations.[68] In practice, these institutes tend to downplay risks associated with the products of the industry from which they receive their funding, or to present scientific perspectives that are otherwise favorable to corporate interests.

Industry support for "independent" research has been most evident, and most controversial, within universities. Widely considered to be independent, beholden to no interest but the pursuit of knowledge, university scientists carry greater authority than any other form of expertise. A direct result is that industries have greatly increased their funding of university researchers. In the United States, corporate contributions to universities increased from $850 million in 1985 to $4.25 billion less than a decade later. Universities have welcomed this trend, perceiving several benefits, including contracts, donations, and access to industry research facilities. Governments have as well, seeing opportunities to lessen universities' dependence on funding, as well as for faster commercialization of innovations in biotechnology and other fields. Governments have also encouraged corporate giving to universities through a law allowing universities to patent the results of federally funded research and through tax breaks for corporations investing in academic research.[69] Shared funding arrangements between government and industry leverage the latter's influence over university research. In Canada, for example, the Natural Sciences and Engineering Research Council (NSERC)—the chief national science funding agency—has several programs to encourage closer ties between universities and industry. Its "Industrial Research Chair Program," NSERC tells industry, "sets up a distinguished researcher and research team in an area of importance to you"; shared-cost research granting programs encourage university researchers to pursue topics relevant to industry; and "Industrial Postgraduate Scholarships" support students who are then required to spend at least 20 percent of their time working at company facilities.[70] Academic scientists themselves often have financial interests in their research; one study found that one third of articles by University of Massachusetts scientists had one or more authors who stood to make money from results they were reporting, either as patent holders or through some other relationship to industry.[71]

But industry-university ties have also aroused substantial controversy. Besides the specific issues just noted, there is the more general concern that universities rushing to respond to market forces and funding opportunities will place less emphasis on independent critical thought, whether in their research or in their students, for example by favoring in hiring decisions faculty that are more likely to work on topics consistent with industry interests. Industry also tends to exercise substantial influence over the direction and even the results of university research, supporting researchers with a track record of studies that reflect industry's point of view.[72] Opposition to such arrangements reflects, in part, unease regarding the privatization of public universities, the influence of economic interests on institutions that are meant to pursue the public interest, not profit. More generally, there is concern that these arrangements would diminish the ability of universities to provide objective information about contentious topics.[73] For example, it may be more difficult for universities to investigate concerns about genetically modified organisms as corporations become more dominant in funding research in this area. This has certainly been a theme in controversy surrounding an agreement between the University of California at Berkeley and Novartis, a biotechnology company (since replaced by its successor firm, Syngenta). The company is providing about $5 million each year for plant research and is also providing access to databases. In return it has received seats on university and department research committees and the first right to negotiate licenses for a portion of the discoveries made by the Department of Plant and Microbial Biology, including the results of research funded by governments as well as by itself. It has restricted academics' freedom to discuss the arrangement. Critics view the Novartis-Berkeley deal as undermining trust in Berkeley's capacity to provide an impartial view of genetic engineering.

Similar questions can be raised regarding the relationship announced in November 2002 between Stanford University and several corporations, led by ExxonMobil. These corporations will give the university $225 million over ten years for research on energy technologies that can also reduce greenhouse gas emissions.[74] As Stanford itself acknowledges, these companies will be able to influence the research agenda of the Global Climate & Energy Project by encouraging development of commercial technology: "[o]ne of the critical roles for the sponsors is to bring their understanding of the global marketplace to help guide the Project into productive and promising areas likely to lead to solutions that can have wide application and significant impact." Funding of the project is only assured to 2005, with further funding dependent on "successful progress" as evaluated by the sponsors.[75] While research on cleaner energy technology is obviously important, it might be asked whether this support will affect the capacity of Stanford scholars to pursue technologies less amenable to commercialization or to examine policy options that are counter to the interests of the energy industry. Arnold Relman, former editor of the *New England Journal of Medicine*, summed up his view of the impact of close industry ties on the credibility of university research: "The academic institutions of this country are allowing themselves to be the paid agents of the pharmaceutical industry. I think it's disgraceful."[76] Relman was speaking about biomedical research, but analogous concerns can apply to other forms of academic research, including those relating to the environment.

The impact of industry-funded research on the environmental policy agenda has also generated considerable discussion. Especially in areas where industry is the dominant source of funding, this sort of relationship is seen as shifting the agenda toward private (and away from public) interests. In many cases regulation depends on information supplied by industry. Although this research may be mandated by government, when performed by industry it becomes proprietary and closed to public scrutiny. Actors with productive interests, such as forestry or energy companies, typically have an institutional and economic advantage over those representing non-economic interests. In effect, science is often on the side of the polluters, because they pay for the tools and techniques required to assess the problem as well as the expertise that applies them. As Melody Hessing and Michael Howlett note, industry "has supplied much of the baseline data, up-to-date technical information concerning abatement technology, and cost-benefit analyses concerning production, pollution, and abatement, from which regulatory standards have been set."[77] This can reinforce problems of regulatory capture, when close identification with industry hinders regulators' ability to protect the public interest. Environmentalists especially worry about regulators' uncritical acceptance of industry data.

A more subtle influence of industry on environmental regulation is expressed through the assumption implicit in the regulations themselves: that they must be based on data, not moral values or political preferences. For example, Monsanto has argued that its products, such as genetically engineered crops, should be judged strictly in terms of evidence based on science. Monsanto has an interest in making this argument: it has a great deal of experience with a science-based regulatory system, and entry of other considerations into the process would raise the cost of getting products approved. In effect, for Monsanto the most efficient way of creating a market for a product is to ensure that the regulatory process is strictly science-based.[78]

More generally, critics see a predominant role for industry in science as a dangerous linking of science with power: those who already have substantial economic and political influence are able to buy scientific clout as well, and they can then use this clout to convince others of their view of the world. Industry (often in partnership with government) can legitimate its decisions, reassure citizens that risks are minimal or under control, and provide ideological support for current practices or conditions. This takes place, however, at the cost of the authority of science as objective knowledge.

Scientific and Political Authority

Relations between industry and science are one aspect of the larger issue of the relationship between science and political authority. According to the tacit postwar "contract" between science and society, scientists receive financial and institutional support; less tangible, but equally important, is recognition of their role as an objective, neutral, and universal authority, with other forms of knowledge marginalized and disenfranchised. In return, they use their knowledge to express their allegiance to society's elites, supporting their interests, viewing the world through their eyes, and legitimating their authority over the rest of society.[79] They legitimate the values of the stronger actors in society—the private sector, states, or international organizations—and provide the technology by which to assert mastery over nature and people. By defining science as universal and abstract, scientists obscure the contexts in which knowledge is created, evaluated, and applied. This universal knowledge is then appropriated by elites, who present this view of reality as the only one possible.[80] Following Gramsci's notion of cultural hegemony, these elites persuade subordinate groups to accept their view of reality, and its accompanying political and ideological preferences, as natural and normal.

This relation between science and dominant interests has several consequences. One is that certain assumptions about society, the world, and the possibility of controlling and predicting events and developments in the world become embedded in the ideas and practices of science. How scientists define problems speaks as much to political imperatives as to the nature of the problems themselves. Scientific models reproduce implicit assumptions about cultural and political conditions and social identities, particularly by assuming that these remain static or change only marginally; thus, existing institutions and structures are taken as "natural."[81] Tacit assumptions about users and audiences, and about the interaction between experts and the public, are also embedded in scientific knowledge; these may then serve as unnegotiated social prescriptions.[82] Thus, the culture of science embodies a range of assumptions: that the natural purpose of knowledge is control and prediction; that standardization of environmental measurements and concepts is natural, even though this also imposes standardization on society; that uncertainties in scientific knowledge can be contained within the private scientific sphere, because they would otherwise be misunderstood by the public; and that local lay knowledge is worthless.[83]

One of the chief practical implications of these relations between science and power is that problems are often defined as technical rather than political. According to Samuel Hays, "One of the most pervasive political impulses of the world of expertise is to drive the context of decision-making underground, beyond the purview of the general public, by imbedding it in enormous and complicated detail that makes it all but impossible to grab hold of."[84] When societal problems are defined as technical, the view of science as objective and free of particular political values rules out political change as an option, thereby disallowing alternative political visions. Alternative ideas about the relations between humans and other species, or about economic systems, or democracy, are excluded. In effect, science supports a conservative view of society, rejecting all but minor adjustments in the social order.[85]

By justifying the existing order as the only possibility, science perpetuates injustices. There are many examples of this. In colonial India, forest authorities drew on science to justify separating indigenous forest users from their resources. In California, science legitimated the exclusion of certain ethnic groups from coastal and river fisheries. The reshaping of rivers of the American west through engineering was accompanied by a concentration of authority within managerial agencies and the exclusion of smaller water users from decision-making.[86] The environmental justice movement has been spurred by governments and industrial interests invoking expertise when they dismiss concerns about unequal exposure to environmental hazards; the resulting climate of suspicion has extended to science, encouraging interest in alternative ways of understanding hazards. Professional expertise has justified excluding the public from decisions regarding resource use—and as a result, this expertise has become a target of the environmental movement's arguments for open, democratic forms of decision-making. This is the backdrop, then, of debates concerning science and its relation to political authority: as this relation and its practical consequences have been recognized, they have also been critiqued.

One illustration of this dynamic between science and political authority can be derived from changing views of administrative agencies. Carson's *Silent Spring* was an eloquent example of how a more general critique of the authority of science emerged from environmentalism. While Carson drew on scientific evidence of the ecological impacts of pesticides, she also raised questions regarding the authority of certain forms of expertise, and related interest groups, and their right to make decisions that have implications for the general public. Since the 1960s, these concerns have been broadened to administrative agencies generally. Resource management has been criticized as too narrowly defined, excluding both ecological realities and public concerns. Institutions that emphasized efficiency of wood production, like the Forest Service in the United States and the Forestry Commission in Britain, came under intense scrutiny. For many the problem was the centralization of authority within specialized professions, and the close ties between professions, interest groups (especially corporations), and government agencies that share a consensus concerning their objectives and how to achieve them and tend to exclude groups outside these arrangements, known in the United States as "iron triangles."[87] In particular, critics noted, simplistic and standardized scientific representations of issues seemed to coexist with centralized, standardized administrative practices. The nuclear industry attracted special attention, not only because of its environmental implications, but because it served as the paradigm of secretive decision-making, buttressed by the notion that expertise could solve any problems. Critiques of industry and agencies extended to questioning the notion that there exists a single public interest to be identified and promoted by these agencies. Indeed, since the 1960s this notion has broken down and has been replaced by the assumption that surrounding almost any topic there are likely to be a constellation of competing interests.

Other, increasingly influential discourses have also, by expressing skepticism toward administrative rationalism and the expertise it employs, helped to reduce the authority of science. In particular, increasing interest in economic rationalism, including market-based approaches to environmental regulation such as carbon taxes and emissions trading, have constituted a challenge to the authority of science, because, in its terms, only certain kinds of expertise are seen as relevant or useful. This discourse also expresses a distrust of government practices that rely on expertise, as seen, for example, in dismissal of "command and control" regulation.

Significant challenges to the authority of science have also emerged through critiques of international development practice. Since the 1940s the concept of development, as pursued by bilateral aid agencies and by international institutions such as the World Bank, has been based on the transfer of expertise—in farming, dam-building, or high technology—to developing nations. This, in turn, has been based on the notion that there is universal knowledge, relevant to any context, that simply needs to be imported to assure progress. This progress occurs, in part, by displacing local knowledge, which is often seen as a hindrance to modern development. Interpretations contrary to the dominant scientific perspective are rejected as naïve, inadequate, and unscientific.[88] However, this view has received heavy criticism over the last three decades, in part because of the damage done by development projects: from inappropriate agricultural technology to the mania for dam-building in India and elsewhere. Awareness of the ideological, economic, and political priorities embedded in development expertise, including the transformation of former colonies into modern industrialized nations, and the imposition of control over territories and peoples, has also shaped this critique.[89] The Green Revolution, once lauded as a successful application of science to meet the food needs of a growing world population, is now widely condemned for neglecting the social factors of food production—a neglect that was only possible because it was assumed that technical expertise could be divorced from the social and political contexts of its application.[90] Scientific agriculture, far from being a neutral input, sets in motion a cycle of dependency: scientists' efforts to optimize outputs through standardized mass production involve negation of farmers' knowledge. New seed types, fertilizers, and pesticides require farmers to reorganize farming routines, deny their knowledge of diversity and complexity, and abandon their methods of learning and adapting to changing conditions. In effect, their knowledge is organized right out of the process, and they are reduced to following the standardized practices prescribed by scientists.[91]

Critiques of such transformations make two general points. The first is to stress that knowledge is tied to power. Awareness of the relations between power and knowledge have encouraged some protest movements to work outside of established social and political arenas, focusing more on the questions being asked than on the answers.[92] As Michel Foucault suggested, "[New social movements] are an opposition to the effects of power which are linked with knowledge, competence, and qualification: struggles against the privileges of knowledge. But they are also an opposition against secrecy, deformation and mystifying representations imposed on people. . . . What is questioned is the way in which knowledge circulates and functions, its relations to power."[93]

The second critique is rejection of the concept of universal knowledge. Instead, it is argued that knowledge is always tied to the context in which it is created and applied. In other words, all knowledge is local. Scientific knowledge is the product of the intermingling of facts and values, interests and political priorities, and different actors will arrive at different constructions of scientific reality. This corresponds to the challenge posed by postmodernism: rejecting the privileged status of scientists as the sole source of reliable knowledge, emphasizing instead the value of knowledge, tied to local contexts, that is held by less powerful groups.[94] Postmodernism challenges the modernist belief that there is or can be a single perspective or language that can be used to describe and define complex social and political realities, and that a single, final, accurate description of the world is possible. Ulrich Beck's critique of modernity has also been influential. According to his concept of "reflexive modernization," a critical perspective has now, particularly as a result of environmental degradation and other unexpected consequences of modern industry, been turned onto science itself, which has led to a questioning of the assumptions on which science is founded.[95] Beck's critique is also reflected in cross-cultural comparisons of knowledge, undertaken by anthropologists and other scholars. In the past, such comparisons tended to view Western science as the benchmark for evaluating other forms of science. Western science would be seen as rational, value-free, and context-independent; in contrast, traditional knowledge would be seen as more closely tied to values and the local context and to immediate pragmatic concerns.[96]

Some of the most incisive questioning of the authority of science in environmental politics has been derived not from critiques by Beck, Foucault and others, but, as I have described, from experience in actual controversies. Paradoxically, many of the sources of the authority of science have also provided the basis for challenging it. Industry asserts the reliability of "sound science," but the economic ties between scientists and industry lead to a questioning of this authority. Science is relied on in legal proceedings, but its credibility also comes under sustained attack there. Science is seen as essential to administrative rationalism, but as that approach has been challenged, so has the science that underpins it.

That the authority of science is not simply an intrinsic property of descriptions of nature but a political entity—created by scientists and by those who use science—has had several implications. Some scientists find the notion disturbing; they see it as an opening of science to political distortion, undermining the rational foundation for decisions—part of a "flight from science and reason."[97] Other scientists, however, have accepted, even welcomed, an understanding of how their ideas and methods are affected by the environments in which they work, and how the status of science as value-free, objective knowledge is historically and culturally situated. Certainly, the notion does raise difficult problems for scientists, including whether they can be involved in the regulatory process without risking their neutral status, and whether their contributing at all to policymaking erodes democratic decision-making.

The view of science as not neutral but embedded within its political and economic contexts, and as having and pursuing its own agendas, has been widely (if tacitly) accepted: science is considered useful, certainly, but it is not to be applied uncritically. For example, it is widely understood that even in the absence of regulatory capture agency officials may have other political objectives (such as a preferred outcome of the regulatory process itself), and that they are able to exploit scientific uncertainties to construct conclusions consistent with these objectives. Environmental Protection Agency officials acknowledge that an expert's position can generally be predicted in advance: with the "neutral" expert exposed as a convenient fiction, their goal has become to balance diverse points of view so as to appear impartial.[98]

But these critiques, and a decline in public deference to expertise generally, have not meant that science has become less important. The regulatory system still has an enormous appetite for scientific expertise, as do debates and initiatives generally in environmental affairs. However, expert claims are now more than ever before subject to questioning, and on the basis of not just the reliability of the claims themselves, but of the process by which the claims are developed: the process must be scientifically credible, but also transparent to observers and open to participation. Confidence in administration discretion and professional independence has been replaced by public scrutiny, strict timetables, stringent standards, and an insistence that all claims be testable.[99]

For environmental organizations, a practical challenge has been to work out how to rely on science for evidence to support their claims while remaining aware of the ties between science and the interests these organizations critique. They, like citizens generally, do not just receive official information passively; they actively respond to it, interpreting it within its context, incorporating the perceived trustworthiness of the institution that is providing the science, reconsidering the boundary between science and other forms of knowledge, taking responsibility for aspects of knowledge that were once seen as falling within the domain of science, and fitting all this together with their own understanding of the world and their own agendas. This active response implies that the more citizens know, the less willing they are to defer to experts.[100] There is widespread skepticism over the veracity of scientific information, grounded in awareness that it is provided by agencies, industries, and other interest groups that have a vested interest in the outcomes of policy debates. In particular, the striking correspondence between available scientific information and the interests of those providing the information has often been noted. For example, information on biotechnology provided by the Canadian department of agriculture has elicited considerable skepticism because it promotes the products of genetic engineering to the exclusion of alternative agricultural technologies. In documents such as "Biotechnology: Science for Better Living," this Canadian government agency emphasizes the supposed benefits of biotechnology while minimizing or ignoring possible risks.[101] As the department itself has noted, the goal of its communication strategy is not to communicate information, but to leave readers with a positive feeling about biotechnology.

What implications can we draw from the erosion of the authority of science? To some, this erosion implies that science has no constructive value in politics, or at least no more value than any other perspective: everything, scientific knowledge included, is relative. David Collingridge and Colin Reeve express this view neatly: they argue that "scientific expertise can *never* be of use to policy," because scientific knowledge will always either be accepted too uncritically, because it is consistent with an already existing elite policy consensus; or encounter an overly critical environment, in which adversaries are sharply divided and scientific claims are subjected to heightened scrutiny, resulting in endless technical debate.[102] Certainly, awareness of the nature of science today—uncertain and contested, tied to powerful interests, with limited public access to information, and too little participation in decisions involving science—might convince one of the difficulty of finding feasible ways forward. In this context, predispositions to accept or to distrust science may more often reflect other ideas about society: those disposed to a rational worldview and to existing social hierarchies will see science as useful knowledge, while those with more humanistic leanings and egalitarian inclinations will be more reluctant to view science as a reliable and sufficient basis for policy.[103]

But we need to know about nature if we are to make appropriate decisions. This, of course, is why there has been so much interest in recent years in working through the relation between science and politics. One of the chief conclusions of this work has been that it can be most productive to acknowledge explicitly the political nature of knowledge. According to Sheila Jasanoff, when scientists and policymakers insist on a clean demarcation between the science and policy components of their tasks, policymaking becomes more difficult; when the boundary is intentionally blurred, achieving agreement on actions becomes easier. Others argue that a constructivist perspective on science can actually improve its position in society, reminding us that science, for all its rationality, is a very human activity.[104] Thus, while the value-bound character of science cannot be denied, this does not mean that scientific knowledge cannot be used in policy. Rather, it can only be evaluated by considering all aspects of how it is produced and used, not merely holding it up as an artifact to be compared against nature's pattern.[105]

PART II

Science and Politics in Environmental Affairs

CHAPTER 3

Science and Environmental Values

☙

*A*s we were driving across America in the summer of 2002, my kids and I stopped at a rest area on Interstate 90 in Wisconsin. There we found a plaque celebrating "The Nation's Hardest-Working River":

> From its source at Lac Vieux Desert to the Mississippi River at Prairie du Chien, the Wisconsin River descends 1,071 feet in 430 miles. Twenty-six power dams utilize 640 feet of the fall of the river to produce an annual average of one billion kilowatt hours of electrical energy. The Wisconsin Valley Improvement Company, created after passage of state enabling legislation in 1907, operates a system of 21 reservoir dams in the upper valley designed to store water during high flow periods for use in the downstream power dams during periods of low flow. The reservoir system, in addition to enhancing power production, diminishes flood damage and enriches the recreational potential of the valley. The system of private development and management under state regulation, made possible by the 1907 legislation, is unique and has enabled the Wisconsin River to earn the title "The Nation's Hardest-Working River."

That the river, now "improved" into a series of tightly regulated reservoirs, can be celebrated as "hard-working" says a great deal about the attitudes toward nature that have informed this transformation.

Environmental politics is about such transformations and the choices they imply: to dam a river or allow it to flow unimpeded; to harvest a forest or protect it. These choices, in turn, reflect certain attitudes about values—for instance, that the value of the Wisconsin River can be measured by its transformation and by the "work" it can do for humans; or that the value of a forest is set by its timber production and not by the habitat it provides for other species.

Science is implicated in many of these choices. Most obviously, it provides the means with which to act on choices to exploit or to protect nature. Some scientific fields—such as geology, chemistry, and biotechnology—provide the tools for exploiting resources. Others, such as conservation biology, facilitate environmental protection, for example by identifying the habitat required by endangered species. This view of science—as knowledge that enables us to act on our choices but is independent of those choices—is widely held, not least because it reinforces the image of science as politically neutral. Science as a realm of facts, distinct from values—echoing David Hume's distinction between what is and what ought to be—remains a touchstone of how many scientists see themselves and how science is viewed by others. Avoiding the naturalistic fallacy (that because something exists, it must be good) is viewed as elementary to sound reasoning. At the same time, it is widely acknowledged that the boundary between facts and values is not watertight: arguments about what we ought to do are necessarily informed by knowledge of what is. The argument that we ought to protect endangered species can be informed by the knowledge that certain species are at risk of extinction, without this knowledge itself justifying their protection.

But many writers, including some scientists, prefer to go further, viewing this boundary between facts and values as a stepping stone: suggesting that science can provide instruction as to appropriate conduct toward other species, inspiring ethical preferences and moral imperatives. Some argue that historically science has inspired exploitation and domination, providing not just the means, but the justification for converting the earth into a collection of commodities. Others, however, have proposed that science, especially ecology, can inspire a more respectful environmental ethic, teaching us not only how, but why the earth should be protected.

But such a view of science—implementing, even inspiring value choices while providing objective knowledge—is itself problematic. Science is bound up in these choices: it constrains our awareness of which choices are available, and it warrants that certain choices reflect not simply political or economic preferences, but the actual state of the world, and are therefore viable and realistic. Thus science not only responds to environmental priorities, but helps to create them. It strengthens the hand of those who wield it. Study of one species will focus attention on the value of that species; in contrast, study of entire ecosystems will tend to favor ecosystem values. Information regarding endangered species can strengthen support for conservation; information regarding timber productivity can strengthen support for logging. Use of cost-benefit analysis gives greater weight to the views of economists. These relations between science, choices, and values reflect how science is not simply an independent source of knowledge, but is embedded within the political and economic institutions that shape our relationship with the environment. Science is therefore implicated in our environmental values, and, indeed, in how our ideas about nature—about what is fit for exploitation, and what is worth protecting—have changed over time.

Science and Domination

Some environmentalists and historians attribute environmental problems to the values of modern society, especially the view that nature exists to be dominated and exploited by humans. According to Carolyn Merchant, close ties developed between this exploitative perspective and modern science as it emerged during the Scientific Revolution of the 1600s. Galileo, Newton, Descartes, and other scientists depicted nature in terms of physical principles, explaining phenomena in strictly materialistic, mechanistic terms. This depiction served as both instrument and rationale for manipulating nature: a dead and passive world displaced an earlier view of the earth as an organic, living entity that commanded a more restrained, respectful attitude.[1] Feminist scholars have also argued that the status of science as objective knowledge, independent of its context, is tied to the assumption that the world is an object to be dominated and controlled. It does so by justifying the belief that one can manipulate the world without being affected by one's actions, and so can despoil nature without fear of consequences.[2]

Other aspects of the modern scientific perspective are said to reinforce this mechanistic orientation. Experimentation—the preferred method of scientists—requires control and manipulation, serving thereby as a practical expression of mastery over nature. Specialized knowledge legitimates the division of nature into separate units, to be studied in isolation and exploited for profit. Proof of scientific progress is to be measured by the practical efficacy of knowledge, especially improved human well-being, perpetuating the ultimate objective of Western science: the mastery of nature in the service of humanity. In several respects, therefore, mastery over nature became central to the modern scientific enterprise—encapsulated in Francis Bacon's statement of science: "the Knowledge of causes, and secret motions of things, and the enlarging of the bounds of Human Empire, to the effecting of all things possible."[3] These ideas emerged alongside a reinterpretation of the relation between God, nature, and humanity: all creation was now said to require superintendence and thorough transformation.

By 1800 science could provide a considerable commentary on humanity's relationship with the natural world. Enlightenment ideals, especially confidence in progress through rational effort, reinforced the view of science as the instrument by which the world could be manipulated for human benefit. Linnaeus's *The Oeconomy of Nature* (1749) exemplified this "imperialist" view and the grounding of the authority of its descriptions of a rational, mechanistic nature in an attitude of detached objectivity.[4] From such ideals were drawn attitudes regarding nature across many realms: the suppression of fire and shifting cultivation in favor of settled agriculture; the drive to replace forest folklore with a rational, scientific forestry, beginning perhaps with the French Forest Ordinance of 1669; the design of English country gardens, infused with an ethos of precise regulation of nature; the expansion of European settlement across the North American continent, led by scientific expeditions taking inventory of resources;

and, more generally, a growing sense of command over a wider territory, as a result of discovery, colonization, and the formation of empires. Such attitudes complemented the instrumental view of nature engendered by the industrial revolution and by capitalism: a storehouse of resources, implying no obligations beyond meeting human needs, permitting a focus on means—the efficient use of technology to master nature—while ignoring the problem of ends.

Mastery of nature through science has therefore been a persistent theme throughout the modern era. But mastery has not always meant unrestrained exploitation. It has also implied careful tending, husbandry, and improvement of nature, reinforced by biblical imperatives of stewardship, expressed through forest and agricultural management. By the 1870s Germany had created a model of science-based forestry, effectively reiterating the historic importance of trees to German culture and national identity, but in the lexicon of nineteenth-century professional science: university chairs, research programs, and an extensive specialist literature. This model of professional management was subsequently disseminated to India and elsewhere, including the United States, where Gifford Pinchot applied lessons from Europe to the formation of the U.S. Forest Service. By 1900 expertise had come to be seen as essential to the control of nature. In the North American conservation movement, resource management was defined by businesspeople, politicians, and scientists as a technical matter: science, backed by government, could ensure efficient use of resources for the general welfare.[5] The rise of professional resource management also marked a divergence in social roles for scientists, between those acting as activists outside industry and government, often providing wide-ranging critiques of resource use, and managers, who viewed social activism as unprofessional and who focused on efficiency of production. As noted in chapter 2, with the formation of public and private organizations expertise became closely associated with bureaucratic authority, with resource professionals basing much of their authority on an ideal of rational objectivity.

Ties between bureaucratic and scientific authority often formed on terrain defined by the interests of powerful state and private actors. For instance, Donald Worster describes how science and the domination of nature and humanity were combined in irrigation systems of the American west. Just as winding natural waterways were replaced by straight, sterile lines of concrete irrigation canals, so too was lost the promise of freedom, as represented by local control over water resources. Both were displaced by engineered water management systems, designed and managed by technical experts and in the service of government agencies and industrial agriculture. Worster concluded that "the brigade of hydraulic engineers . . . had more to do with making the modern West than all the fur trappers and cowboys and sheepherders there ever were": imposing a comprehensive, rational system of irrigation, ensuring (through scientific expertise) efficient control of both natural and human communities.[6]

The drive to dominate nature through science was similarly evident after

World War II, with the embrace of industrialization by the developing world and by international and national aid agencies. The dream of modern development transforming traditional societies captured the imagination of Third World leaders and the World Bank alike, encouraging investment in power stations, ports, highways, and other infrastructure. In India, Africa, and Latin America large dams became a symbol of the mastery of nature through science and technology, just as they had in the United States and in the Soviet Union. In the last two decades of the twentieth century dams, and the hardship, waste, and destruction that so often accompany them, have inspired a powerful reaction, with critics like Vandana Shiva arguing that they demonstrate how science and economic growth together can destroy the diversity and sanctity of life.[7] The displacement of indigenous knowledge by modern science has accentuated these concerns.

The domination of nature is often noted as intrinsic to modern industrial agriculture. Diverse ecosystems are replaced by artificial monocultures, divorced from the natural environment and engineered for maximum productivity, demanding intensive control through pesticides and other technologies. And most recently, the notion of a domineering, mechanistic science has been invoked in critiques of genetic engineering, with the view of plants and livestock as simply bundles of genes to be manipulated considered the ultimate expression of a reductionist perspective. As such, genetic engineering is said to display an ideology of control and manipulation.[8]

Inevitably in unequal societies, as new ways of manipulating nature are created, they become available as instruments for the exercise of power, and so become an instrument not for furthering the general welfare but for upholding the interests of the powerful. According to William Leiss, "If the idea of the *domination* of nature has any meaning at all, it is that by such means—that is, through the possession of superior technological capabilities—some men attempt to dominate and control other men. The notion of a common domination of the human race over external nature is nonsensical."[9] Viewed in these terms the question involving domination is that of identifying the oppressors and the oppressed. According to Merchant, Shiva, and other feminist writers, science has been historically an instrument for the domination of nature and women. Others have portrayed science as being in the service of powerful interests—irrigation agencies, wealthy farmers, governments, the World Bank, biotechnology firms—with nature and much of human society—smaller farmers, peasants, indigenous peoples—subject to their will.

Alternatives to Domination

However prevalent this relation between science and domination, it has also often been argued that the study of nature is consistent with alternative perspectives: a critique of industrialization, and a view that humans are only one among many species and that our objective should be not domination, but peaceful harmony, expressed through lives of simplicity and humility. These contrasting visions serve to remind us that nature, interpreted by countless individuals in many contexts, has rarely spoken with a single voice.

Gilbert White provided a classic statement of what Donald Worster described as an "arcadian" view, in *The Natural History of Selborne* (1788). Nature was seen as a system in regulated harmony that could not be overly disturbed without changing, and perhaps destroying, the balance and equilibrium of the whole. White, and subsequent authors within the Romantic tradition, such as Henry David Thoreau, grounded this perspective in sympathetic, holistic observation, by naturalists who saw themselves as part of, not separate from, nature; who rejected the view of science as the sole source of authoritative knowledge; and who sought to generate not general theory, applicable in all contexts, but knowledge of a specific place.[10]

Natural theology—the intellectual tradition in which God was understood through his works in nature—had ambiguous implications for the relationship between humans and nature. It might be interpreted as supporting an environmental ethic: if all species perform some function in God's plan, then this implies, as Linnaeus suggested, a value to every species. Alternatively, natural theology suggested that nature, having been created by a wise and beneficent Creator, would tend toward stability and balance. Humans would be therefore free to manipulate it to serve their needs. Science could assist by surveying and classifying nature and identifying useful resources.

In the eighteenth and nineteenth centuries other aspects of science had similarly ambiguous environmental implications. The field sciences were integral to European imperial expansion, as botanists, naturalists, and other scientists traveled the globe, identifying natural resources or research opportunities. But by the early nineteenth century some scientists had also begun to express concerns regarding the consequences of this expansion. On the island of Mauritius, Pierre Poivre, like a few scientists elsewhere, developed a sophisticated environmental perspective on colonial practices, eventually convincing authorities to enact laws controlling deforestation. This tended to occur first on tropical islands, whose small size and status as symbols of paradise enhanced scientists' persuasiveness. Alexander von Humboldt also contributed, by demonstrating that forest loss, and resulting climate change, was of continental significance, buttressing the "desiccationist" theory linking forest cover to climate (and ultimately to the economic security of the colonies). Through the influence of such scientists, forest conservation became in India, and eventually in southern Africa and elsewhere, an accepted task of colonial governments, effectively extending the role of the state.[11]

Critiques of the impacts of imperial expansion were mirrored by concerns regarding the impacts of industry and urban expansion. In the nineteenth century governments of industrial nations transformed themselves, assuming a wider range of responsibilities. Economies were demanding more resources, cities were growing, and environmental dangers to health were multiplying. In response, aspects of the environment with immediate economic or health implications began to be perceived as public responsibilities. It became accepted that government should address public concerns, even to the extent of regulating or restricting private activities. For example, stagnant water, a source of malaria and other diseases, could be "conquered" through drainage or by installing fountains, as in France and elsewhere.[12] By the end of the century urban water supplies in several industrial nations were being provided by municipal governments, reflecting the new importance of government as mediator of the relationship between society and the environment.

As governments expanded their roles, so did science. In Britain chemists aggressively asserted their authority as objective experts on water purity, even when their advice was of uncertain reliability. These efforts showcased the developing role of expertise, as reflected in new professional groups, such as the associations of sanitary engineers and public health physicians that formed in America. These groups would argue heatedly over their rival prescriptions for protection of public health. By the turn of the century ideas of reform also encouraged perceptions of a close relation between the urban environment, human behavior, and social order.[13] In a variety of ways, therefore, science was implicated not only in industrialization and domination over nature, but in a reaction against the damaging impacts of these processes, particularly as expressed through the burgeoning role of the state in regulating private activity.

These ambiguities—both support for, and critique of, domination of nature—were also evident in evolutionary thinking. While Darwin's theory tended to imply not harmony but struggle, and while the notion of "survival of the fittest" was often used to justify dominion over nature (as well as inequalities within human society), it also suggested a kinship between humanity and other species, while the record of species extinction over evolutionary time implied the fragility of life's diversity. (As I note below, conservation biologists today, like E. O. Wilson, make a similar argument.) By the end of the nineteenth century, as a result of work by Darwin, George Romanes, and other students of animal behavior, and as popularized through "realistic" animal stories like those by Ernest Thompson Seton, animals were portrayed as feeling, thinking, and suffering beings, encouraging more humane treatment.[14]

The advent of Darwinism, and these portrayals of animal character, extended into the twentieth century a longstanding debate on human-animal relations, largely framed in terms of the ethics of vivisection and the adequacy of mechanistic explanations of animal physiology and behavior. From René Descartes's argument for the irrelevance of human ethics to insensible, unthinking animals, to John Locke's contrasting assertion of a moral duty to avoid cruelty to animals, to John Ray's description of animals as God's creatures, requiring benevolent stewardship, ethical attitudes toward animals eventually became the focus of organized campaigning. In Britain, agitation by the Society for the Prevention of Cruelty to Animals (formed in 1826 and made the Royal Society in 1840) culminated in the 1876 Cruelty to Animals Act, which focused on vivisection. Debates concerning this act drew the participation of much of Britain's scientific elite.[15]

To many nineteenth-century observers science was certainly not inconsistent with nature conservation. Most famously, George Perkins Marsh, in *Man and Nature* (1864), reinforced concerns about species extinctions and forest clearing, drawing on international evidence of human impacts, including arguments by European colonial scientists, particularly in India. Marsh's portrayal of a harmonious world torn apart by greed and ignorance was widely influential, particularly in the United States.[16] During the nineteenth century scientists sought in several instances ways of linking their professional identity with particular environmental values. For example, by the 1890s scientists in California had developed a distinctive professional role, emphasizing field study and environmental advocacy. Many scientists became activists, particularly as cofounders or participants in the Sierra Club (led by John Muir).[17] Similarly, in Russia conservationist attitudes had begun to be expressed by the 1850s, particularly by zoologists and agronomists at Moscow University and the Moscow Agricultural Society. By 1900 Russian scientists had developed several arguments for conservation, including the need for areas to be set aside for study.[18]

By the Second World War science had begun to underpin a critique of the global impacts of industrial and military activity. In 1948 two books offered Malthusian and to some extent ecological perspectives on a growing human population in a finite world: William Vogt's *Road to Survival*, and Fairfield Osborn's *Our Plundered Planet*. In the 1950s public concern about radiation—the first global environmental hazard—emerged in debates about the health effects of nuclear fallout. Studies indicating the accumulation of radioactivity in the Arctic, and of strontium 90 in cow's milk (and eventually in teeth and bones), added to these concerns. New institutions, some instigated by scientists (such as the International Union for the Conservation of Nature and Natural Resources, formed in 1948), also indicated the emergence of an international perspective on environmental issues.[19]

But this emerging international environmental perspective had its own ambiguities, evident when we consider portraits from space of the earth. Many have argued that this view—an icon of the environmental era—inspired a global environmental ethic. But as Sheila Jasanoff has noted, not only were there many antecedents to this image of a global environment, but it took another twenty years, and publication of the Brundtland Commission's report, *Our Common Future* (1987), for environmental problems to be more widely defined as global. This global image, mediated by American technology, also rendered invisible those problems, such as dirty air and contaminated drinking water, that are not apparent from space but nevertheless affect billions.[20] People themselves, and the political and economic inequities that some believe to be at the root of environmental problems, are rendered imperceptible by this image. According to Wolfgang Sachs, in generating a conception of the earth as a physical system, such an image projects a "transnational space where the existence of nations, the aspirations of communities or other human realities fade into irrelevance when compared to the overwhelming presence of the natural earth."[21]

The Gaia hypothesis is perhaps the most widely known attempt to provide a scientific basis for a global environmental ethic. It too, however, is highly ambiguous. In the mid–1970s James Lovelock suggested that organisms have the homeostatic capability of maintaining optimal conditions for life on Earth.[22] The idea, and especially its message of interdependency, attracted wide interest. But while Lovelock drew on his scientific understanding of the global ecosystem in developing his hypothesis, many scientists have resisted its seemingly mystical implications (is the earth a living organism, sharing a name with a Greek goddess?) or have been reluctant to embrace the challenge it poses to the fragmented perspectives of conventional scientific disciplines and to explanations of ecological phenomena strictly in terms of individuals. Does the hypothesis represent some kind of coming together of science and environmental values? If so, does it imply a need to protect the earth's homeostatic capability, or does it suggest that the earth is able to adjust to whatever stresses humans impose on it? Or is it perhaps a strictly scientific approach to understanding the earth as a single integrated system, without any value implications? That such questions can still arouse debate three decades after its introduction illustrates how the hypothesis lacks definitive ethical implications..[23]

From these diverse instances we can sense the ambiguities in the relation between science and environmental values: supporting and critiquing the domination of nature, justifying both exploitation and protection. New knowledge has unpredictable consequences, particularly for human interests or other values. Environmental values have imposed a variety of demands on science, for knowledge about air and water quality, patterns of land use, health, or cleaner technologies. Beyond generating new research agendas, the influence of environmentalism is also evident in how knowledge of the natural world has come to be structured in terms of public concerns. Environmental and conservation concerns have encouraged formation of a range of new disciplines, from forestry and wildlife management to toxicology and environmental chemistry. The structure of these disciplines—their core ideas and the boundaries between them and political priorities—represent the outcome of negotiation between public concerns and scientific perspectives. For some scientists these outcomes have been very positive, particularly in terms of greater research funding. But while some scientists have welcomed public prominence and social relevance, others have retreated into their labs because of perceived risks to scientific credibility and autonomy. These complexities are especially evident in ecology, the discipline most often associated with environmental values.

Values and Ecology

In the 1960s Barry Commoner gained attention as an environmental prophet through his "Four Laws of Ecology": everything is connected to everything else, everything must go somewhere, nature knows best, and there is no such thing as a free lunch.[24] Simple, easily understood, with great rhetorical power, they were widely viewed as basic principles of conduct distilled from scientific knowledge of ecology. Commoner is just one of many environmentalists who have argued that ecology can be the basis for environmental values.

Undoubtedly, ecology can assist in implementing environmental values. Ecologists can determine, for instance, how large an area of old-growth forest must be to ensure a viable, self-sustaining ecosystem. Protection of endangered species requires considerable ecological information, about food, habitat requirements, and human impacts. Even in the absence of agreement as to why an area should be protected, science can provide signposts toward agreement on how it can be protected. On the other hand, debates over what kind of nature we want to preserve or recreate, within national parks or elsewhere—to allow fire, for example—are more complex. Science can inform these debates, for example by providing information about the history of fire in particular ecosystems, but it may provide little guidance as to what nature is to be protected.[25] It can extend our realm of moral concern: by demonstrating that a "swamp" is a thriving wetland, or that a barren desert harbors unique species, ecology expands the list of what we may choose to care about. But this does not imply that ecology mandates a particular choice: while scientists can demonstrate that an ecosystem is diverse, or that pesticides or habitat loss may have an impact on certain species, this does not necessarily account for why we might wish to be concerned about the ecosystem or these species in the first place. Instead, science can most readily underpin rationales for protection that are expressed in terms of human needs: for resources, for ecosystem services such as clean water, or (as has often been the motivation for ecologists) for protected research areas.

But many, like Commoner, have argued that ecology may not just help implement, but actually inspire environmental values. In the 1960s the environmental movement pushed this view of ecology to center stage. Ecology was portrayed as subversive of dominant intellectual traditions: the modern, rational worldview, mastery over the world, the separation of science from values.[26] In magazines such as *The Ecologist*, and in countless statements by activists, ecology was presented as a prescriptive science, warning that humanity had acted contrary to the laws of nature, and presenting instead an alternative ethic.[27] According to one writer, "[e]cology was the science which could interpret the fragments of evidence that told us something was wrong with the world—dead birds, oil in the sea, poisoned crops, the population explosion. . . . What it meant was—everything links up. . . . Here was a new morality, and a strategy for human survival rolled into one."

The use of ecology to underpin environmental values is especially evident in the work of two individuals: Aldo Leopold and Rachel Carson. Both have been celebrated for their efforts to incorporate an ecological understanding into our relationship with nature. Carson gained immediate attention when her *Silent Spring* was published in 1962, while Leopold, who died in 1948, was rediscovered in the 1960s when his *Sand County Almanac* (1949) became an environmental classic.

A forester and wildlife manager, Leopold published an early textbook of wildlife management, *Game Management* (1933), in which he presented implications of new ideas in animal ecology, including the essential role of predators in regulating prey populations. He also drew on ecology in formulating his "land ethic," presented in *A Sand County Almanac*. It became an influential statement of environmental values, in part, according to J. Baird Callicott, because Leopold framed his argument in terms of science. According to Leopold, Charles Elton and other ecologists had demonstrated how ecological communities function as assemblages of interacting species, consuming and being consumed by each other.[28] These communities, not individuals or species, would therefore be the appropriate unit for a conservation ethic. This merging of values and science was exemplified in Leopold's best-known statement: "A thing is right when it tends to preserve the integrity, stability, and beauty of the biotic community. It is wrong when it tends otherwise."[29] The merging could only occur on the terrain of ecology, a discipline viewed by Leopold and by his subsequent disciples as an alternative to specialized scientific studies that, in the pursuit of rationality, drain meaning and beauty from nature.[30]

Rachel Carson was the most eloquent and influential advocate of a link between environmental values and ecology. The link was central to her popular books about the oceans, to *Silent Spring*, and, indeed, to her own passions for both nature and science. By the 1950s she had become increasingly concerned about the consequences of modern science, including the new synthetic pesticides, such as DDT, and this became a chief theme of *Silent Spring*: how science and technology, carelessly applied, were enabling the "unthinking bludgeoning of the landscape," destroying nature and threatening life, including humans.[31]

With this theme in mind, we can read *Silent Spring* in several ways. It is an assemblage of scientific information on the environmental impacts of pesticides, and it presents some alternatives to these chemicals. It is also an attempt to elicit an emotional reaction to this information—an objective perhaps most evident in the "fable" with which Carson begins her book, in which a peaceful American countryside is invaded by a mysterious and dangerous substance. But *Silent Spring* is also a work of political advocacy, presenting arguments about both the kinds of knowledge that should be used in making decisions about pesticides, and who should make these decisions. These decisions, she argued, should be based on an ecological view of nature. There is a natural order, a web of life, that through "checks and balances" is able to maintain ecological stability; and that web must be allowed to function.[32] The great danger is that these decisions are made by scientists and industries that are considered to be uniquely knowledgeable, but that in fact perpetuate an arrogant ignorance of ecology. As she famously concluded, "[i]t is our alarming misfortune that so primitive a science has armed itself with the most modern and terrible weapons, and that in turning them against the insects it has also turned them against the earth."[33]

Such arrogance, she also insisted, demonstrated the need for democratic guidance of science: citizens themselves have much to say and must not be silenced
by the authority of expertise. Progress, Carson argued, depends not on scientists or officials, but on "the people who first spoke out against the reckless and
irresponsible poisoning of the world that man shares with all other creatures,
and who are even now fighting the thousands of small battles that in the end
will bring victory for sanity and common sense in our accommodation to the
world that surrounds us."[34]

By the late 1960s numerous ecologists, including Commoner, Eugene
Odum, Paul Ehrlich, and Frank Fraser Darling were pursuing their own efforts
to derive political implications from ecological ideas, from the cycling of nutrients to the relation between the diversity of species and the stability of ecosystems. Eugene Odum was one of the most prominent ecologists to stress the
stability of nature, particularly in his account of how ecosystems change over
time: through a process of orderly and predictable development, culminating in
a largely unchanging state of maturity.[35] This view of ecosystems was a foundation of much ecological research in the 1960s, including the development of
computer simulation models. It was also widely invoked in the popular literature of the environmental movement: the stability and balance of ecosystems
were portrayed as an appropriate model for humanity. Odum and other ecologists welcomed the link between their science and environmentalism, although
their advocacy often had only loose ties to their research—Ehrlich, for example,
spoke out on human population growth, among other topics, while focusing in
his research on the evolution and ecology of butterflies. But other ecologists
viewed more coolly the novel prominence of their discipline; one complained
of "the word 'ecology' . . . being dragged back and forth . . . like a smelly red
herring."[36]

By the 1960s ecological science was having an impact on environmental
politics. Wetlands and deserts, once seen as worthless, were now perceived as
interesting and worth protecting, while habitats, such as forests, once valued only
in economic terms were also appreciated as diverse ecosystems. The Marine
Mammal Protection Act of 1972 and the Endangered Species Act of 1973 reflected the view derived from ecology that not just some, but all species, together with their ecosystems, should be protected. These values also led to new
arenas for application of ecological expertise. The professionalization of park
management during the 1960s and 1970s, and its reorientation toward ecological priorities generated a larger role for ecological knowledge in national parks.[37]
In studies of water pollution, the focus on chemical characteristics most relevant
to human uses, such as bacterial content, was broadened to encompass ecological parameters that measure the overall health of aquatic ecosystems. These applications of ecology reinforced the already widespread sense that ecology could
provide the basis for environmental values.

Many ecologists have continued to pursue roles as environmentalists, drawing on their authority as scientists to "speak on behalf of nature."[38] Indeed, since

the late 1990s ecologists have redoubled their efforts to take on this role.[39] And unlike the 1960s, when prominent ecologists like Odum and Ehrlich acted as individuals, they are putting more institutional weight behind their message, particularly through the Ecological Society of America. Conservation biologists have been most active in this area: they have defined their discipline in terms of both scientific questions and environmental concerns, seeking to reshape how humans understand living nature, assembling diverse concerns regarding endangered species, deforestation (particularly in tropical forests), and wilderness preservation into a single global environmental crisis of biodiversity.[40] Often evident in this has been an underlying assumption that science can provide the basis for unanimity on environmental values. Michael Soulé, for example, argues that the current diversity of views of nature can be explained, in part, as the result of ignorance of science—more knowledge, it is implied, will lead to more agreement.[41]

For two decades Edward O. Wilson has been the most prominent exponent of an environmental ethic grounded in biological science. He has often argued, most recently in his 2002 book *The Future of Life*, that such an ethic, which he described as "the only guide by which humanity and the rest of life can be safely conducted through the bottleneck into which our species has foolishly blundered," can be inspired by knowledge: of our place in nature and of our evolutionary kinship with all other species.[42] This knowledge, according to Wilson, can awaken instincts we already possess, encoded within us through evolution, that will compel us to assume responsibility as stewards of life: "[i]t is not so difficult to love nonhuman life, if gifted with knowledge about it. The capacity, even the proneness to do so, may well be one of the human instincts. The phenomenon has been called biophilia, defined as the innate tendency to focus upon life and lifelike forms, and in some instances to affiliate with them emotionally."[43] Thus, the foundation of biophilia is our evolutionary kinship with other species, and this constitutes a universal, biological basis for human attitudes toward nature, limiting variations imposed by local differences in culture and society. Stephen Kellert, with Wilson, has expanded the biophilia hypothesis into a classification of diverse attitudes toward nature.[44] The overarching practical implication, Wilson concludes, is the preservation of diversity: "We should judge every scrap of biodiversity as priceless while we learn to use it and come to understand what it means to humanity. . . . An enduring environmental ethic will aim to preserve not only the health and freedom of our species, but access to the world in which the human spirit was born."[45]

Wilson's ideas are compelling, not least because they are expressed so elegantly. They have also provoked much debate. The assertion of an essentially genetic basis to environmental attitudes echoes Wilson's earlier arguments regarding sociobiology: that human social behavior can be explained in biological terms. The claim of close ties between an environmental ethic and science also renders the ethic vulnerable to criticism as elitist—it implies that only those with sufficient education (and perhaps, only those possessing the social advantages that ensure access to such education) can fully appreciate the biophilic ethic—and, indeed, nature itself.

Ecology has also been drawn on by non-ecologists to support particular environmental values. One of the most prominent such efforts is deep ecology. Essentially, this view asserts that nature has intrinsic value, independent of whatever instrumental uses we have for it. The argument has often been linked to science. Carolyn Merchant has identified ties between deep ecology and challenges to mechanistic theories of nature, such as David Bohm's physics of process, Ilya Prigogine's thermodynamics, and chaos theory: these are, she argues, deep ecology's "scientific roots."[46] However, the complexities and ambiguities of deep ecology and science are best considered in terms of deep ecologists' accounts of the relation between their view and ecology. As presented by Arne Naess, George Sessions, and other writers, this relation has at least three dimensions. First, in historical terms, they trace the origins of deep ecology to the 1960s and to the influence of ecologists such as Leopold and Carson, as well as to the prominence generally of scientific ecology at that time. By warning of an environmental crisis, scientific ecology is said to have demonstrated the need for deep ecology. In general, deep ecologists view scientific ecology in realist terms, as providing authoritative, unproblematic descriptions of nature. Thus, environmental problems are seen at least in part as problems of education; as Sessions argues, "the magnitude and severity of the global ecological crisis must be fully appreciated."[47] The second dimension of the relation between deep ecology and scientific ecology is more philosophical, and more indirect: that scientific ecology "inspired" deep ecology, not through any specific conclusions, but through its general orientation toward systems and the interdependence of species. By demonstrating the complexity and diversity of nature and the status of humans as only one species among many, ecology is said to be able to encourage a sense of humility that is consistent with deep ecology's ecocentric perspective. And finally, there is a prescriptive relation between scientific ecology and deep ecology: ecologists can guide the application of deep ecology, by demonstrating the need for preserving wilderness and advising on appropriate size and shape of protected areas. Conservation biology is thus the practical arm of deep ecology.

However, deep ecologists have also resisted identifying too closely with scientific ecology. While taking at face value scientists' warnings of ecological crisis, they draw an explicit contrast between their perspective and scientific, or "shallow" ecology, which fails to ask deeper questions about the relations between society and nature. Deep ecologists often express distrust of conventional scientific expertise and its ties to industry and government. They stress that knowledge of nature can be best obtained not through research or by reading scientific reports, but by direct experience, generating, as Muir and Thoreau did, an intuitive understanding deeper than any insights generated by science.[48] Critics of deep ecology also note that the link between ecological science and an ecocentric perspective is a tenuous one—science can as easily justify an alternative perspective in which humans remain the center of concern but are recog-

end

— maybe we
need both
somewhere in
between

Science and Environmental Values 61

nized as dependent on healthy ecosystems.[49] And finally, deep ecologists rarely mention the current work of active ecologists, preferring to invoke general "insights," such as the relation between diversity and stability of an ecosystem, that many ecologists are skeptical of. This is the ambiguity of deep ecology: trading on the authority of science and its accounts of environmental crisis, deep ecologists nevertheless also argue that their ultimate purpose and justification transcend it.

?

Besides deep ecology, many other perspectives on humanity and nature invoke the "lessons" of science. Often these perspectives embody a contradiction: advocating a critical perspective on modern science while accepting modern ecological science as an ethical guide.[50] For example, bioregionalism, in calling for a sense of identity with, and knowledge of, one's own region, relies on ecological knowledge for guidance in fitting political and economic structures within ecosystem boundaries. At the same time, these relations are ambiguous: some describe bioregionalism as a "science," while others see it as an environmental ethic or cultural sensibility. Some bioregionalists are wary of science, seeing it as antithetical to local knowledge and sensibilities; according to Michael Vincent McGinnis, to understand a bioregion one should "take to the wind, feel the breath of air, witness the diversity of the city or village you inhabit"—evidently do anything but go to the science textbooks.[51] Social ecology, of which Murray Bookchin is the most prominent exponent, draws on scientific knowledge to support its claims that nature is cooperative, not hierarchical, and can therefore serve as a model for a more egalitarian society.[52] Together, deep ecology, social ecology, and bioregionalism exemplify how, outside the scientific community, ecology has often been viewed as not merely a specialized discipline, but a holistic, integrative perspective. For some, "ecology" is not science at all, but an ethical perspective or political movement. Thus, while drawing on ecology, especially as a source of scientific authority, these perspectives often have only a tenuous link with ecology as it is actually done by ecologists.

Several philosophers have argued that ecology can provide the basis for environmental values. According to J. Baird Callicott, knowledge of ecology leads directly to protective environmental values:

> Deforestation of the most tropics, unrestrained burning of fossil fuels, exponential human population growth *is* deleterious to the health and integrity of the biosphere. Therefore, we *ought* to preserve tropical forests, reduce our consumption of fossil fuels, and stabilize and eventually reduce the human population. Connecting the latter *is* with the latter *ought* is the value we place on the health and integrity of the biosphere, the most encompassing community of which we are members. . . . If such a value is not as universally espoused as family-scale values or ethnic-scale values, that is because such concepts as biotic community, ecosystem, and biosphere are newly formed scientific ideas, while such

concepts as family and tribe are primitive. The remedy is universal ecological education.[53]

Similarly, Holmes Rolston has argued that the sciences are central to our appreciation of nature: they tell us what nature really is and how it got that way, making
our experience of nature richer.[54]

Some historians as well have argued that ecology has played a central role
in formulating and justifying environmental values. Donald Worster develops
the most extensive argument for a historical relation between ecology and environmental ethics: he argues for an "arcadian" tradition in ecology that began
with Gilbert White and that describes nature in terms of harmony and balance.
In contrast, the "imperial" tradition in ecology focused on exploitation of resources. Carolyn Merchant described ecology as an alternative to both the domination of nature and the dominant sciences: "Ecology has been a subversive science
in its criticism of the consequences of uncontrolled growth associated with capitalism, technology, and progress—concepts that over the last two hundred years
have been treated with reverence in Western culture."[55] Other historians, including John Opie, Roderick Nash, and Thomas Dunlop, have portrayed ecology as
forming the scientific foundation of environmentalism and as a central reason
for the emergence of environmentalism as a mass movement in the 1960s.[56]

There have been many other efforts to relate science to environmental values. Scholars of environmental politics often see ecology as a source of the "lessons of nature." According to Sylvia Noble Tesh, environmentalism itself
apparently originated in the 1960s, through the efforts of a select group of writers—Carson, Leopold, et al.—that advocated a perspective grounded in the
"Laws of Ecology."[57] William Leiss argued in 1979 that "ecology establishes
guidelines within which a society that hopes to achieve a sustainable relationship with the biosphere must circumscribe its activities. In this sense, ecology
has been termed the 'critical science.'"[58] Similarly, Donald Elliott notes that
while nature teaches the connectedness of all activities, most environmental law
regulates pollutants separately, thereby "violat[ing] the basic principles of ecology." Ecology, Elliott argues, can serve as a model for not just the content, but
the process of environmental protection: "[l]ike nature, we can feel our way by
trying a diversity of techniques on a small scale and adapting as we learn which
are most successful."[59] Green political thought is underpinned at several points
by ecological science: its concern with ecological crisis, respect for ecological
integrity, acknowledgment of ecological interdependence, and acceptance of ecological limits to growth.[60] According to John Barry, "part of the novelty of the
green political perspective lies in it being the first political outlook so informed
by and grounded in modern science." He also notes, however, that knowledge
cannot function as the sole guide to political thought.[61]

These arguments for a relation between ecology and environmental values—in accounts by political scientists and historians of a role for ecology in

fostering environmentalism; in philosophers' efforts to develop an environmental ethic grounded in ecology; and in the advocacy by deep ecologists, bioregionalists, and others—all share a view that scientific ecology provides objective, accurate descriptions of the world, particularly by identifying a tendency toward balance or stability.[62] These descriptions underpin a critique of the dominant assumptions of Western culture and an alternative vision that celebrates the intrinsic value of nature. The descriptions, and their implications in terms of environmental values, are then disseminated to the wider public by scientists or by gifted communicators such as Rachel Carson. Changes in values compel, or are hoped to compel, a new politics.

Two observations can be made regarding these claims that ecology underpins environmental values and political change. The first is that it provides an avenue by which debates over the nature of scientific knowledge—the "science wars"—enter environmental discussions. According to some scholars, claims that science is not just an objective portrayal of nature, but the product of interests and values, undermine its authority, and in doing so give license to those who would exploit nature: if nature is simply an artifact created out of our own thoughts and values, how, it is suggested, can it be worth protecting? As Michael Soulé and Gary Lease argue, "certain contemporary forms of intellectual and social relativism can be just as destructive to nature as bulldozers and chain saws."[63] Unfortunately, this debate has sometimes tended toward caricature. For example, Soulé describes the deconstructivist alternative to objectivism as stipulating that "it is impossible to know nature at all" and that there is no basis on which to determine that any account of nature is more valid than any other account.[64] That efforts to place science within its social context provoke such a reaction underlines how claims of environmental values can be viewed as so closely linked to, even dependent on, scientific claims.

A second observation is that these claims imply that the roles of scientists in environmental politics can be defined in terms of their personal values. Thus, the arcadian impulses of Gilbert White, the romantic outlook of Thoreau, the utilitarian perspective of Gifford Pinchot, and the ecological sensibilities of Rachel Carson shape the contributions of each of these individuals to environmental affairs. At the same time, as ecologists draw on ecological concepts of stability, balance, competition, and cooperation to derive lessons concerning human conduct, these concepts shape ecologists' role in environmental politics. Whether nature is seen as orderly, deterministic, and balanced or as chaotic, unpredictable, and unstable also influences the ability of scientists to assert their expertise. Scientists have been more influential when they have had a clear message, and this has been more readily available when nature appears intelligible.[65] However, as I argue throughout this book, explanations of scientists' contributions to environmental politics will be inadequate if they are based only on their personal values and attitudes toward nature.

History and Ecology

Ecology, then, has often been invoked as a basis for environmental values. However, a closer look at the history of this discipline provides much ground for challenging such efforts. The history of ecology demonstrates the complexity of the relation between ecology and environmental values. Originating within a variety of institutional contexts, and the product of diverse professional ambitions and opportunities, ecology had coalesced as a distinct discipline by 1894. Although this was also the time, in North America, of the progressive conservation movement, ecology lacked the ties with industry or government characteristic of professional resource management. Nor did it have any necessary link with environmentalism: far from being a unified, holistic perspective, ecology was an amalgam of fragmentary perspectives. The various subdisciplines of ecology, such as plant ecology, animal ecology, and limnology, would retain distinct identities far into the twentieth century.

Ecologists had similarly diverse perspectives on environmental questions. While some advocated protection of natural areas in order to preserve research sites, others contributed advice on managing and controlling nature, especially in the service of agriculture. In the United States it developed in both "pure" university contexts (such as the University of Chicago) and more practically oriented land-grant colleges. Thus, after 1880 Stephen Forbes at the University of Illinois linked ecology and the work of the Illinois Natural History Survey and the State Entomologist, so that ecology could be applied to the problem of insect pests troubling farmers. At the University of Nebraska, Charles Bessey and his student Frederick Clements promoted a school of plant ecology that had significant ties with agricultural research and the challenges facing prairie farmers.[66] Other ecologists attracted private patronage, allowing them to avoid the focus on immediate problems characteristic of agricultural research stations. Such work sometimes had environmental implications. For example, Daniel Trembly MacDougal encouraged Americans to appreciate the desert environment, portraying it not as harsh and unforgiving, but as a place where life could flourish if adapted to those conditions.[67]

By the 1920s ecology was traveling a variety of pathways. In Britain concern about pollution and its impacts on salmon and other species, together with belief in the need for scientific knowledge as a basis for government action, encouraged study of freshwater pollution. A Water Pollution Research Board was established in 1927, followed two years later by the research station of the Freshwater Biological Association at Windermere.[68] British ecologists, led by Arthur Tansley and Charles Elton, pursued research, including its practical implications for imperial resource management.

In the 1920s Soviet ecologists had considerable influence, advocating protected areas for ecological study and the application of ecology to regional planning and rehabilitation of degraded land. By the early 1930s their message had been obliterated by Stalinists intent on creating a new society on the basis of a conquered, broken nature. Nevertheless, while it existed, Soviet conservation demonstrated the complexity of factors influencing environmental politics: inter-agency conflict, and the desire of agencies to protect their own interests; contrasting ideas concerning the value of basic science and the value of undisturbed nature; the role of expertise in determining human-nature relationships; and the efforts of a scientific community to respond to changing political conditions.[69]

In America, the Bureau of Biological Survey, while fostering research on wildlife, also sought to control, and even eliminate, predators. Eventually, ecologists, led by Leopold and Elton, among others, began to build a scientific basis for wildlife management. Their efforts also laid the groundwork for changing American attitudes toward wildlife, by showing how nature is organized: predator and prey relations, trophic levels, niches, and food chains. Their influence was evident in how nature writers wrote less about individual animals, and more about the "web of life." This broader view of nature increasingly encompassed predators, who came to be seen less as evil pests than as a natural part of this web.

Leopold is today the most well-known, but in the 1930s other ecologists also presented their discipline as able to provide a synthetic critique of human society. Perhaps the most prominent were Clements and Paul Sears.[70] This synthetic perspective was, in part, rooted in their experience of the prairie Dust Bowl and their conviction that destructive land use practices could be reformed on the basis of the equilibrium in natural communities, as described by ecologists. Clements's views on ecological succession and climax implied that undisturbed nature was the best guide for land use.[71] Nevertheless, such arguments did not lead to sustained government interest in ecology, and farmers resisted ecologists' prescriptions. Clements's message also had less resonance for ecologists in countries where virtually the entire landscape displayed the marks of human activity. Tansley, like other British ecologists, argued that ecological theory should incorporate human agency, not treat it as an invasive impact on otherwise natural communities. He and his colleagues also advocated creation of a network of nature reserves, and an institution—the Nature Conservancy—to manage them and support ecological research, thereby linking closely their professional ambitions and their desire to protect ecological communities.[72]

Plant ecologists were not alone in considering the implications of their discipline for society. Animal ecologists at the University of Chicago under Warder Clyde Allee argued that human society could learn from the cooperation found in nature.[73] In South Africa, ecologists followed a different path. During the 1930s Jan Smuts—general, politician, botanist—pursued his vision of a united South Africa. He drew up a comprehensive political and scientific program of ecological research, based on a philosophy of holism. It also helped justify, for Smuts, a policy of racial segregation and political oppression. In his view, races deserved respect, and rights, according to the level to which they had evolved. They also had to remain within their allotted positions, kept there by force when necessary. Other South African ecologists explored the implications of Smuts's vision of holistic ecology. According to J. W. Bews, races had

achieved different levels of development: while some were still affected by local climate and ecology, others had evolved to be more independent of their environment. The races must, therefore, live separately, each according to their level
of development and appropriate relation to the environment. Racial segregation
was thus for Bews a legitimate response to the diverse ecologies of races, ensuring ecological and social harmony.[74]

More recently, many ecologists have resisted incorporating humans within
their discipline, remaining skeptical toward the incipient discipline of "human
ecology" and resisting those who, like Sears, defined ecology as a synthetic,
critical perspective on society.[75] The notion of ecology as a "subversive science"
presented by Paul Shepard in 1969 did not take root within the discipline. Instead, efforts to synthesize ecology with critiques of society have largely developed outside the natural sciences. Ecologists have often resisted a link between
ecology and environmental values, in part because of concerns that such a link
would weaken the scientific status and objectivity of ecology. They have also
tended to draw away from the study of sites affected by human activity, stressing instead the need to preserve undisturbed areas for ecological study; in this
view, only "pristine" areas can provide reliable knowledge.

Apparent links between ecology and environmental values have sometimes
concealed other, more complex factors shaping the discipline. For example, while
competing strategies of pest control in 1960s America could be described as reflecting contrasting attitudes of domination over nature or coexistence, these strategies were also shaped by political and institutional factors, including antagonism
between federal and state agricultural research establishments and efforts to obtain environmentalists' support in the competition for research funds.[76] Ecologists have also benefited from ties with institutions often considered antagonistic
to environmental values. In the United States, for example, ecosystem ecology
emerged in large part through a close relationship with the Atomic Energy Commission. AEC laboratories at Oak Ridge and elsewhere became major centers
for ecological research, and ecology was seen as contributing, in a variety of
ways, to the AEC's nuclear mission, even as the AEC was being vilified by environmentalists.[77]

Thus, contrary to assumptions of a direct relation between ecology and
environmental values, the story is more ambiguous: ecologists' pursuit of environmental goals most often reflects specific intellectual, institutional, and political circumstances—a mosaic of responses to diverse local conditions. Just
as ecologists pursue a vast range of research topics, from the evolutionary strategies of individual species to the movement of nutrients in ecosystems, so too
have they drawn diverse links between their science and environmental concerns.

Certainly, just as educated, middle-class individuals in Western societies
tend to view themselves as environmentalists, so too do most ecologists. Indeed,
ecologists have particular reasons to possess environmental values: they spend
much of their working life in nature (some, like E. O. Wilson, even chose the
profession for this reason[78]), and their research sites may have been threatened

by human activities. But predispositions to enjoy nature and to wish it to remain unspoiled, the product of personal experience and preferences, do not imply a necessary link between ecology and environmental values. When we seek, for example, to account for Aldo Leopold's ecological values, should we focus on his scientific training, or on the decades he spent working out-of-doors—an experience likely to instill protective environmental values in anyone, scientist or not? Leopold may have used ecological concepts, such as those provided by Elton, to imbue his ecological values with scientific authority, but this is distinct from them serving as inspiration for these values.

The trail between environmental values and ecology is further muddied by its impact on other forms of knowledge, particularly that of indigenous people. As Ramachandra Guha and others argue, ecologists—presuming to speak authoritatively for nature—can supplant the voices of marginalized communities, whose knowledge of their local environment is derived from daily experience, not scientific training.[79] The conflict has been especially apparent in the history of wildlife protection in the developing world, where nature reserves have often displaced communities or separated them from the resources on which they depend.

While some ecologists today are active environmentalists, some also question efforts to derive environmental values from ecology, and not just because of concerns that such efforts impugn their objectivity as scientists. Using nature—where disturbance is the norm, and 99 percent of all species that ever existed are now extinct—as an ethical guide is always problematic. It has become especially so in recent years. Since the 1970s ecologists have questioned accounts of stability and order in nature. Instead, the world now appears erratic, unpredictable, surprising; and the emphasis is on change and disturbance caused by fire, wind, pests, and other disruptions in nature, as well as on the heterogeneity and instability of ecosystems.[80] Such a view, Worster argues, reflects back onto nature the disorder and turbulence characteristic of modern industrial capitalism, which has rendered nonsensical any notion, or even possibility, of stability in human affairs.[81] But it can also be traced to ecologists' observations of nature, as mediated by their methods and theories. As I note in chapter 4, expectations that a harvested resource, such as a fish population, will tend toward stability can be so far off that they endanger the resource. Forests protected from fire become ever more susceptible to catastrophic blazes. Several ecologists, such as C. S. Holling, have described the complex patterns of stability and instability of animal populations.[82] Ecologists have shown how a landscape may exhibit any of several possible states, depending on chance combinations of fire, soil, water, seeds, and so on. At any given time there may be stability for certain species within an ecosystem but not for others, and there is no one time at which every species can achieve an optimal balance.[83]

Chaos theory has become central to much of our understanding of nature, challenging assumptions of mechanistic predictability. The basic idea is straightforward: small differences in initial conditions can result in large, apparently random changes. For ecology, a chief implication is that change and disturbance are an inevitable part of nature. Robert May, one of the first ecologists to apply chaos theory, found that mathematical models could not adequately describe changes in animal populations, such as outbreaks of gypsy moths in eastern forests or the cycles of lynxes in sub-Arctic Canada. According to Daniel Botkin, a prominent exponent of the role of chaos in ecology,

> Until the past few years, the predominant theories in ecology either presumed or had as a necessary consequence a very strict concept of a highly structured, ordered, and regulated, steady-state ecological system. Scientists know now that this view is wrong at local and regional levels . . . that is, at the levels of population and ecosystems. Change now appears to be intrinsic and natural at many scales of time and space in the biosphere. Wherever we seek to find constancy . . . we discover change. . . . We see a landscape that is always in flux, changing over many scales of time and space, changing with individual births and deaths, local disruptions and recoveries, larger scale responses to climate from one glacial age to another, and to the slower alterations of soils, and yet larger variations between glacial ages.[84]

These insights into ecology, undermining notions of stability and elevating change, disturbance (such as fire), and chaotic behavior into inevitable components of ecosystem processes, complicate attempts by ecologists to specify which features of plant and animal communities are "natural" and are to be protected. With no consensus on the optimal state of an ecosystem, ecology can provide no clear norms for when a community is natural or healthy.[85] This perspective on ecology, itself rooted in particular approaches to ecological research (Botkin's book, *Discordant Harmonies*, is not just an exposition on chaos, but an argument for computer modeling, his preferred research method), challenges some of the ethical implications that have been drawn from ecology.

In particular, the dynamic perspective poses a challenge to Leopold's land ethic and its invocation of ecological stability. In response, Callicott has suggested modifying the land ethic. While acknowledging that disturbance may be a normal part of nature, Callicott argues that what is new are the larger and longer scales on which humans disturb. The land ethic could be revised accordingly: disturbances of a certain size are consistent with ecological stability and integrity; beyond that, they would be prohibited.[86] Of course, this poses a new challenge: many natural disturbances, such as hurricanes, are huge, while humans can do significant damage to ecosystems on much smaller scales. Inevitably, the advantage of clarity that once justified basing an environmental ethic on science would be lost.

On the other hand, Worster argues that even with ecologists' embrace of change and disturbance, there are lessons to be drawn from nature. These combine instruction on what we should value, including interdependencies in nature, with the diversity of forms of change and how to draw on the wealth of models of successful problem-solving in natural and human communities. Such lessons, Worster stresses, are imbued with the authority of science: they "stand up well because they are based not merely on private fantasies but on knowledge."[87] However, it is worth noting that the knowledge Worster invokes can be more readily viewed as familiar truisms of natural history rather than as conclusions from contemporary ecological research. Again, therefore, in seeking ethical lessons from ecology, it has become necessary to draw back from the ideas that actually engage practicing ecologists.

The paradox becomes obvious: while ecology is widely invoked as a basis for environmental values, ecologists themselves doubt whether it can serve in this role. This suggests that such efforts rely on an unfamiliarity with the science of ecology. Commoner's four laws, for example, are a highly simplified and distorted view of ecological theory. While ecology is said to suggest that "everything is connected to everything else," in fact ecologists have found that while some species are important, other species can be eliminated without large effects on their community. In contrast to assumptions that ecology provides a holistic view of nature, in practice ecologists focus on energy or nutrient flows, or on predation and competition, applying perspectives that can be highly reductionistic. The diversity/stability hypothesis is still often invoked, long after it has been significantly revised by ecologists. What is especially striking, then, in the ecology invoked by non-ecologists, is that while it trades on the authority of science, it does not correspond to ecology as practiced by scientists.

The difficulty in drawing clear lessons from ecology is reflected in arguments used by those who seek to justify exploitative attitudes towards nature, such as the Wise Use Movement: if change is normal, then there is no basis for arguing that clearcutting, grazing, or other activities are destructive; in fact, such activities may mimic forms of change that are seen as "natural." For example, in 2001 the Ontario Ministry of Natural Resources created a furor by developing guidelines for forest cutting that, it suggested, would emulate fires and thereby "create a more natural landscape pattern."[88] In response, environmentalists noted that cutting, unlike fire, has a variety of damaging ecological impacts. The episode demonstrated how both sides in a controversy could draw on ecology to support contradictory conclusions.

Beyond these ambiguities, the argument that ecology, and science generally, can have a central role in inspiring environmental values has several problematic implications. First, the notion of an elite defined by its expertise instructing the wider public is a highly simplistic view of the origins of environmental values. As historians like Samuel Hays argue, these values have tended to spread less through dissemination from authority figures than through people's own experiences, their changing economic and social conditions, and their desire to improve their quality of life. For example, Americans have been more likely to value wilderness as a result of their visits to national parks, made possible through longer vacations, more disposable income, and better transportation options, than because they read John Muir. More generally, Hays argues for the need to distinguish between the world of environmental ideology (primarily academics and related intellectuals) and the world of environmental practice (larger and more diverse, rarely referring directly to the works of the intellectuals, preoccupied instead with ideas directly applicable to practical circumstances), with neither world much aware of the ideas of the other.[89] Corroborating this account, Willett Kempton and his colleagues have described how people have their own complex views—"cultural models"—regarding environmental values, which rarely refer to deep ecology or other ideologies, and which intellectuals writing on environmental values themselves rarely mention.[90] Sociologists have provided other insights into the origins of environmental values, such as post-materialism—the view that progress cannot just be defined in terms of ever-increasing consumption.

The diversity of contemporary environmental values is itself an argument against the view that they are derived from ecology. From wilderness preservation, to concerns about global scarcities, to the impacts of industrial facilities on marginalized communities, such diversity cannot be merely the result of the influence of a few scientists or other intellectual leaders. Environmental concerns are part of a larger transformation of ideas about the nature of power in society, the role of government, skepticism toward expert authority—all factors left out of a focus on ecological ideas. Given this, it may be more accurate to argue that science does not inspire environmental values, but serves to activate and provide guidance in applying preexisting values, particularly by raising awareness of certain issues that potentially affect everyone, thereby encouraging expression of collective, community-oriented values over values associated strictly with private gain: that is, the concerns of citizens, not consumers, as Mark Sagoff makes the distinction.[91] On this basis, we can give more attention to other ways of justifying our actions, perhaps in terms of human values or on other grounds. While scientific knowledge can suggest how we might achieve certain goals, defining the goals themselves requires us to draw on other sources of insight.

The political goals and preferences embedded in the view of ecology as the foundation for environmental values are also problematic. As John Dryzek explains, those who emphasize the need for new environmental values are seeking different kinds of subjectivity, different ways individuals can experience the world. There is little concern with institutions, or politics, beyond the individual: "green romantics want people to be different; and when they are, then everything else is expected to fall into place."[92] However, this leaves unexamined the many complex ways in which scientific ideas actually wield influence in society. Instead, it seeks to imbue a particular ethical preference with special authority, implying that that preference should supersede all others: it is nonnegotiable, because it is founded in objective reality. Bob Pepperman Taylor notes that the "attractiveness for environmental ethics of building on science rather than moral and political traditions grows out of the seduction of scientific certainty, a certainty that would put an end to the very need for democratic politics."[93] Ultimately, efforts to derive a scientific basis for environmental ethics exhibit the same reasoning as does the use of science in many areas of public policy: by attaching the authority of science to one's position, one makes it appear less arbitrary because it is grounded in something beyond individual preferences. Such a view is often seen in scientists' pronouncements about environmental values: there is more than a hint of the idea that it is necessary to move beyond "politics"; to instead derive ethical ideas from first principles based on science. This is problematic for two reasons. First, scientific knowledge is always subject to revision, rendering futile efforts to use it as a stable basis for environmental values. And second, such a perspective depends on the view that science is itself situated outside of politics. But as I outlined in chapter 2, science does not exist in some objective, apolitical space. Observations of nature, including those made by scientists, are mediated by ethical values, as well as by other aspects of prior experience and ideas about the world. These observations cannot then serve as the foundation for values because they do not exist independent of those values; rather, they are given meaning by our preexisting knowledge and beliefs, including whatever values we have already attached to nature.[94] Efforts to formulate a system of environmental values on a foundation of science—particularly when these efforts proceed in isolation, only presented to the world once fully constructed—are thus likely to be seen as illegitimate, because those asked to assent to these values had no part in formulating them, and because the authoritative role of science in this formulation may not itself be explicitly justified, but only assumed.

When theorists invoke ecological science in support of particular environmental values they are also making a claim regarding how, and by whom, environmental values can be best determined: that this is a task requiring experts, who are able to understand the scientific basis for these values. The public, in contrast, cannot be relied upon to determine appropriate environmental values. Ultimately, therefore, in invoking science to support environmental values, these theorists are expressing a distrust of democracy. This distrust is itself rooted in a belief that people who lack special knowledge of environmental science or philosophy—that is, most people—lack environmental values. This perspective, however, is contrary to what we find when we examine public attitudes: not a commitment to destroying nature for economic benefit, but an appreciation for unspoiled nature, and widespread concern regarding the impacts of humans upon the environment. Environmental protection efforts have not been imposed on an indifferent populace by experts holding the appropriate environmental values, but are a response to widely held values. Efforts to derive environmental values from science therefore miss the point, because they obstruct access to discussion about them by the very people—that is, the public—who have historically led in defining them.

The effort to use science to shift discussion of environmental values beyond politics also invalidates the possibility of dissent. As Richard Rorty argues, the only democratic guide to conduct are the choices that people make themselves: there is no possibility of normative evaluation independent of the democratic process, such as would be derived from science.[95] Since there is no reason to suppose that environmental values are independent of other human values (humans can, after all, feel concern for species other than their own), these values can be examined and discussed within a democratic process.

How might science and environmental values be discussed constructively? Rather than developing a scientific foundation for ethical values, one possibility is to focus instead on providing the scientific advice needed to implement environmental values that are already widely held. As we've seen, ecology, in particular, informs some widely invoked environmental principles, such as Leopold's land ethic. A challenge, however, is in moving from these principles to concrete advice, to be applied in specific situations, that can withstand challenge not only within scientific arenas but in the legal and political contexts that are so erosive of scientific authority. According to Kristin Shrader-Frechette, this can't be done: general principles are inadequate in these contexts. What is needed, she suggests, are scientific approaches that can generate testable predictions, useful explanations, and clear, practical applications. Such ideas, she argues, can be best derived from an understanding of species within particular situations.[96]

But general scientific ideas can have a role to play: not as an apolitical basis for environmental values, but by contributing to debate about environmental values and how to implement them. One such idea may be that of ecosystem integrity. In the Great Lakes region a community of scientists, policymakers, and others have been seeking to develop such a concept and to apply it to this complex ecosystem. The concept has both normative and empirical aspects. The objective of the 1978 Great Lakes Water Quality Agreement, for example, was "to restore and maintain the chemical, physical, and biological integrity of the waters of the Great Lakes Basin Ecosystem." In normative terms, this commitment acknowledged that the Great Lakes ecosystem has intrinsic value, and that human society is obliged to live in harmony with it.[97]

Scientifically, the elaboration of the concept of ecosystem integrity has occurred, at least in part, because of the inadequacy of more narrowly conceived perspectives. Study and management of separate components of the environment—fish populations or water chemistry, for example—provided no basis for either understanding or ameliorating the multiple stresses imposed on Great Lakes ecological communities: pollution, loss of habitat, over-fishing, and the intrusion of exotic species such as the zebra mussel.[98] Ecologists have developed both theoretical and empirical perspectives on ecosystem integrity. One such perspective views ecosystems as complex systems that develop and maintain some internal organization and identity and that possess both homeostatic and self-organizational capability. An ecosystem is said to exhibit integrity if, when subjected to disturbance, it has an organizing, self-correcting capability to recover toward a state that is normal for that system.[99] Efforts to specify indicators of ecosystem integrity have focused on those that integrate the impact of the diverse stresses imposed by humans and that are meaningful to those who must participate in efforts to restore or maintain ecosystem integrity.[100]

In recent years the International Joint Commission has applied these perspectives on ecosystem integrity to the Great Lakes, within a broader view of the nature of the ecosystem concept. According to this view, no one definition of an ecosystem is the scientific "truth," appropriate for all purposes. Rather, the concept must accommodate a variety of definitions, constructed at different scales and levels of organization of ecosystems, so that the concept will be relevant to all the purposes for which these definitions may be created.[101]

The use of terms such as "ecosystem health" or "integrity" to define the objectives of ecosystem management is, in effect, an effort to define objectives that will have both scientific and social meaning—in effect, to translate raw ecological knowledge about the abundance and number of species, or their habitats, or the flows of nutrients and energy, into terms that nonscientists can understand and appreciate. But it is more than simply an effort to communicate scientific information: "ecological integrity" or "ecosystem health" also imply a particular course of action. While invoked as a means of placing management on a scientific footing, they imply an integration of science with certain values, such as concern for the well-being of future generations. It also follows that such terms cannot be defined simply through scientific research. Instead, their definition requires discussion within society, to identify what values particular communities attach to their surrounding environments.

Such a formulation is of necessity ambiguous. According to Shrader-Frechette, the integrity concept is vague, understandable only in terms of general, qualitative judgments, and therefore useless.[102] But another view is possible if we consider integrity within its political context. Protecting and restoring a complex ecosystem such as the Great Lakes demands not only new science, but new politics: a new relationship between expertise and citizens; more open, collaborative decision-making; cooperative ways of managing a region that is shared and used in many ways. Management must, in essence, be democratized: all citizens, not just experts and officials, should be able to participate in discussions about resource values, policies, and alternative futures.[103] Such discussions can be difficult when, as in the Great Lakes region, different interests have different, sometimes conflicting priorities. However, ambiguous as it is, the concept of integrity provides a basis for discussion of environmental goals among all these interests. Just as an ambiguous concept can serve usefully as a basis for discussion within a divided scientific community,[104] so too, within the environmental community, can a concept such as integrity. Within such a context ecologists may, therefore, act not as privileged purveyors of an environmental ethic, nor as experts within adversarial processes, but as contributors to a societal consensus on a preferred environment. Such a consensus can then bolster local environmental stewardship. The concept of ecosystem integrity, then, while reflecting a diminished confidence in the capacity of senior governments to impose solutions to environmental problems, instead imposes a greater responsibility on individuals and local institutions.

The concept of ecosystem integrity illustrates how science can relate to

environmental values in ways other than as an objective guide. Several philosophers have argued persuasively for such an alternative role. Their motivation is
pragmatic: if, they ask, discussions of values are focused on the long-term project
of developing a replacement for the assumptions of modernism, perhaps by drawing on ecology, what should be done in the meantime? They suggest instead an
experimental approach that recognizes the complexity of current problems, uncertainties in our knowledge, the likelihood of error, and the existence of a broad
range of public environmental values. Social learning can best be achieved not
through a quest for ethical perfection, or through insistence on insulating values from politics, but through collective inquiry, creative conflict mediation, and
public deliberation over values and policy goals. As Bryan Norton suggests, some
areas of intellectual discourse should not be tied tightly to scientific ideas. In
particular, discussion of possible worldviews is less suited to drawing on scientific ideas (and the accompanying assumption that there is a single "right" answer) than are the more pragmatic discussions of what can actually be done in
response to environmental challenges today.[105] In short, agreement on reasons
for action is less important than agreement on the action itself.[106]

The advantages of a more pragmatic approach to environmental values over
efforts to seek a single, scientifically grounded value can be illustrated in terms
of a hypothetical campaign to protect an area that is both a potential source of
valuable timber and a significant habitat for many species. One approach might
be to develop a rigorous, ecologically grounded argument for the intrinsic value
of the area as wilderness, and to then seek to convince the public, government,
and industry of this value. But this would take a long time, and the area would
likely be logged first. Another approach would be to respond to the diversity of
values that people might already have regarding this area: some may see possibilities for backpacking and canoeing; others may be appalled by the sight of
ugly clear-cuts; some may enjoy knowing that at least a few areas will survive
untouched for their grandchildren; some may even have read and been convinced
by the deep ecology literature. The point is that there are many reasons why
people may favor wilderness protection, and a campaign to protect an area will
be more effective if it taps into all those reasons, rather than seeking to impose
a single, ecologically justified reason. We are motivated to appreciate nature for
many reasons, rooted in history and culture, beyond its value as a repository of
useful resources.[107] To justify respect for the intrinsic value of nature merely in
terms of science impoverishes discussion. Certainly the grizzly bears won't care
whether protection was justified scientifically.

This approach highlights the challenge of science in relation to environmental values: not to use it as an infallible guide to these values, but to ensure
that political institutions are able to provide for the free expression and examination of values, particularly those that stem from people's own experience, while
drawing appropriately on science to inform them. This challenge has often been
encountered in addressing contentious issues in natural resources management,
as I discussed in chapter 4.

CHAPTER 4

Science and Natural Resources Management

$\sim$

The Ocean Sciences Center occupies a spectacular site on a rocky promontory overlooking the Atlantic Ocean, north of St. John's, Newfoundland. Inside, oceanographers and fisheries scientists work on making sense of the North Atlantic, charting a course to the sustainable use of its resources. But when I visited in 1997 I could not avoid another, more disconcerting impression. Five years before, in 1992, the cod fishery had collapsed, and thousands of Newfoundlanders had lost their jobs on fishing boats and in processing plants. The center's exhibits discussed this collapse and reviewed several possible explanations for what had happened. But there was no tidy conclusion, no definitive account—simply an expression of the uncertainty of science. The uncertainty persisted at the time of my visit. By late 2002, after ten years of severely restricted fishing, stocks had still not recovered; the number of mature cod was only one per cent of what it had been in the early 1980s. Scientists had to acknowledge that "even after a decade of research they do not know what has prevented the cod stocks from recovering."[1] The story of the cod fishery—discovery, exploitation, depletion, and uncertainty about the reasons for the collapse—could be told for many fisheries, and indeed, for many resources around the world.

For two centuries science has been considered essential to exploiting natural resources. Since the origins of resource management in Europe, its elaboration in empires and colonies, and its application to resources in North America and elsewhere, decisions regarding forests, fisheries, wildlife and other resources have been considered the domain of technical professionals. Today, agencies such as the United States Forest Service, the Canadian Department of Fisheries and Oceans, a multitude of provincial and state agencies, and transnational bodies such as the International Council for the Exploration of the Sea (ICES), as well as many resource companies, employ thousands of professionals who use science to guide the efficient and sustainable use of resources.

But the world's resources are in crisis. Most of the world's fish stocks are being fished at or beyond their capacity: as Daniel Pauly, a fisheries scientist at the University of British Columbia, put it, the impact of fisheries on marine life has been "equivalent to that of a large meteor strike on terrestrial life."[2] On land, forests are being depleted and degraded, igniting controversies in North America, Southeast Asia, Latin America, and elsewhere. Regardless of the specific re-source, exploitation has tended to follow a consistent pattern: new stocks are discovered and are then exploited intensively, often to the point of collapse, be-fore regulatory agencies can respond effectively. This pattern, and the boom-and-bust economics that tends to accompany it, helped instigate the creation of resource management agencies in North America, but it remains after a century of experience with these agencies a persistent feature of how we use resources.[3]

Resource crises stem not only from overexploitation, but from conflict be-tween resource users. Many such conflicts relate to forests, as for instance be-tween industry and environmentalists, or between harvesters responding to the global timber trade and those meeting local needs for forest products. Some of the most complex conflicts relate to the world's fisheries: between industrial and subsistence fishers, commercial and sport fishers, or between fisheries and the use of water for other purposes: power generation, irrigation, or waste disposal. For example, Pacific coast salmon exhibit some of the most challenging prob-lems in resource management, the result of a diversity of resource users and interests, as well as competing ideas regarding the roles of governments, the pri-vate sector, individuals, and other actors in resource management.[4]

Such crises transcend science. They are the product of larger forces: humanity's demand for resources, the appetite of the market, corporate power, or political paralysis. Resource conflicts may stem from opposing values or in-terests, and so will resist resolution through research. Crises and conflicts have occurred even in the face of warnings from scientists; indeed, scientists have often attributed such crises to a failure to follow their advice.[5]

But resource science has also been implicated in these crises.[6] Often, fish-eries and forests have been depleted even while being managed scientifically. When it collapsed in 1992 the Newfoundland cod fishery was being managed by a well-funded and respected fisheries research agency. Today, the ICES notes that "despite a large and technically complex input to fisheries management, most stocks in the ICES area (the northeast Atlantic and Baltic Sea) are overex-ploited and in some cases depleted."[7] And in spite of a century of scientific management of forests across North America, conflicts over the use of forests, and concerns regarding their depletion, continue. Science, clearly, is no pana-cea for resource conservation problems.

Why is this? One explanation may be ineffectiveness: the inability of sci-entists to overcome entrenched political and economic interests. Short-term prof-its generated by rapid exploitation may be so tempting that scientific warnings will be ignored. Scientific advice may be subjected to political interference, as Canadian fisheries scientists argued occurred with the cod fishery.[8] It can be especially difficult for scientists to encourage conservation when, given a complex environment, they are unable to provide clear, unambiguous advice. Such complexities have also meant that scientific advice can be and has been used to support competing positions, generating confusion and paralysis. This was illustrated by the degradation of the Great Lakes fishery over the last century, in the face of confusion over which impact on these lakes—overfishing, pollution, or incursion of exotic species—was a more significant factor in its decline.[9]

But much remains unsaid if we invoke merely "ineffectiveness" in explaining crises and conflicts in science-based resource management. Many view science as not merely permitting, but justifying exploitation. The Canadian writer Farley Mowat spoke for many critics when, in discussing the forest industry, he condemned "the Byzantine computer models, double-speak, and selected scientific data used by the industry to conceal its crime."[10] In 1996 a British report argued that scientists had to accept some blame for depleted fish stocks, as their advice had been used to justify overfishing.[11] Such claims echo a more general critique of science as the rational justification for the exploitation of nature. Scientific management is widely viewed as seeking only efficiency— ever larger fishing boats or mechanized tree-cutting systems—at the expense of ecosystems and local economies. In addition, the definition of resource management as a technical problem, amenable to solution through science, is also said to hinder consideration of broader concerns, such as overconsumption and unequal access to resources, that many consider to be at the root of resource crises. Far then from being neutral, science has been viewed as an instrument of dominant interests: with support from industry and government, science helps ensure that other interests and values, including a preference for preservation over exploitation, as well as other sources of knowledge, are excluded from resource decisions.

Two crises, then, are evident in resource science and management. The first is a crisis of sustainability: the degradation of resource stocks around the world. The second is a crisis of effectiveness and legitimacy: the widespread perception of an inability to respond effectively to the diverse and often conflicting values and interests associated with natural resources. These twin crises have intensified debate over the role of science in a changing, uncertain world. Can science encourage sustainable use of resources? Can it help resolve, rather than exacerbate, resource conflicts? Such questions are being asked ever more frequently, encouraging many resource institutions to reconsider how they use science.

One immediate conclusion has been that more effective resource management will not come simply through more, or better, science. Instead, it is necessary to reconsider both the roles and the practice of resource science. Ultimately, the objective must be to provide accurate, timely knowledge of resources and ecosystems, while incorporating new knowledge into management practices.

Resource science must also find ways to be more responsive to the concerns, priorities, and knowledge of diverse interests. It must find ways of learning from experience: both failure and success. Many experiments in alternative approaches to resource management are under way, aimed at addressing these requirements. Before discussing these alternatives, however, it is appropriate to examine conventional approaches to using science in resource management.

Conventional Resource Management Science

Typically, science in resource management has addressed two kinds of questions. The first relates to the condition of the resource. How many fish are in the ocean, of what species, age, and size? How many trees are in the forest, and how rapidly are they growing? The second kind relates to the impact of human activities, especially harvesting. How many fish can be caught without endangering the stock? How often can a forest be harvested? How can forest growth be enhanced?

The role of science implied by such questions can be better understood if we examine the practice of, for instance, North American forest management. Beginning with an intact forest, management typically involves a sequence of steps: harvesting; replanting (by artificial and/or natural restocking); management of regrowth through weeding, pest control, and fire protection; and eventually, harvesting of the second-growth forest. Scientific expertise contributes at every step: aerial and ground surveys to estimate potential yield; artificial regeneration, using improved specimens of selected species, to enhance productivity; design of cutting practices, guided by (among other considerations) knowledge of the terrain and other features of the forest environment; and estimation of the optimal date of second harvest, using models of tree and stand growth.

These elements of forest management practice share an underlying objective: the replacement of a complex, diverse forest with a simpler one, consisting of one or a few species of trees all of the same age.[12] The objective is maximum efficiency of production, through a forest of trees of similar age, harvested just at the point at which their biological productivity begins to decline. With such a forest, it is also possible to estimate precisely, using inventory data and standardized yield tables, the quantity of timber and the rate of growth. In contrast, forests composed of numerous species, with individual trees of varying age and productivity, produce timber at a slower rate, and so are considered less efficient; estimates of available timber will also be less precise. An even-aged forest of one species can also be harvested more quickly and efficiently by modern machinery. In essence, therefore, the goal is to reconstitute in nature the standardized efficiency of a factory, producing commodities harvested to meet the demands of world markets. These elements, in turn, reflect deeper commitments and assumptions regarding nature and the role of expertise.

Views of Nature

Resource science is often said to be engaged in a "quest for certainty"—an ambition expressed in the form of precise, accurate predictions of the future state of the resource. Management decisions are based on the assumption that such predictions are accurate. For example, the planning of forestry "cutting cycles"—designed to ensure that the amount cut each year is balanced by new growth—is based on the assumption that trees grow at a predictable rate and will be available for harvest at a predictable future date (a cycle may range from 40 to 100 years, depending on species and growing conditions). Similarly, fisheries stock assessment and management relies on accurate predictions regarding how many fish will be produced each year by those left uncaught. Such predictions, in turn, depend on several assumptions about nature: that it can be understood in terms of mechanistic, predictable laws; that it will behave deterministically; that the future will be like the present and the recent past; that nature tends towards stability and is little affected by small changes, and thus is unlikely to generate surprises.[13]

Another assumption about nature relates to the usual focus of management on species of immediate economic interest. It is assumed that certain components of nature (including species) can be understood in isolation and manipulated without affecting other aspects of nature. For example, growth curves of individual species form the basis of sustained yield forestry. Using these curves, foresters can harvest trees when their growth is at its maximum rate. Other aspects of the environment—non-economic plant species, or wildlife—can be ignored. Similarly, fisheries scientists may assume that a fishery can be understood and predicted on the basis of knowledge of the birth, growth, and mortality rates of an individual species, with less attention paid to other components of the ecosystem. Thus, stock/recruitment models focus on single-species fish populations, downplaying the importance of habitat or other ecological factors, while maximum sustained yield models assume that the maximum yield of one species can be removed from the system without changing the system itself.[14]

These assumptions illustrate an argument to which I will return below: that judgments regarding value and purpose are inevitably embedded in resource management science. They may be merely implied, as in science that pursues efficient timber production under the rubric of the public interest; or they may be expressed openly. This normative dimension must be recognized and opened to examination and discussion through processes that allow communities to deliberate concerning how they use or protect natural resources and what is their preferred relation to nature generally.

Role of Expertise

The concept of the "tragedy of the commons" has often been invoked to justify conventional resource management. As popularized by Garrett Hardin in 1968, it is said to apply to any resource to which many people have access. If the resource is depleted or damaged through overuse—the forest is cut down, the fish are caught—all users will lose. They therefore have a collective interest in restraining their use. The tragedy is that no individual has any incentive to think in collective terms: if only one person cuts fewer trees, or catches fewer fish, the resource will still be depleted, and that person will have simply lost her share.[15] This is where resource management agencies come in: they impose this collective interest, forcing users, through the regulatory authority of government, to restrain their use.

These agencies are viewed as providing an objective perspective on sustainable resource management, remote from self-interested users. Within them, the role of scientists, particularly those employed by government agencies, is to provide an objective, rational view of resources that reflects neither the interests of resource users nor political preferences, but simply the facts of nature. Using these facts, grounded in testable theories and impartial data, management can avoid being swayed by local interests and political conditions. As I will note, this tenet, like the concept of the tragedy of the commons, has been sharply criticized, but it remains an important element of the public image of resource professionals. Reinforcing this image, agencies such as the Bureau of Land Management and the Forest Service commonly portray themselves as the middle ground between opposing interests in resource conflicts, especially industry and environmental groups. Criticism from both sides reinforces their image of neutral objectivity. Similarly, in the aftermath of the northern cod crisis, Canadian fisheries scientists were quick to implicate political interference with science; the solution, they argued, would be an independent institution able to provide unbiased, objective scientific advice.[16]

Critiques of Resource Science

Conventional resource management has been the subject of many critiques. Some have focused on its immediate environmental impacts or its economic and social consequences; others have addressed its fundamental assumptions. For example, the tragedy of the commons, far from being inevitable, relies on assumptions regarding the motivations of individuals, the rules governing use of resources, and the nature of the resource itself; all these assumptions can be challenged.[17] The notion that management institutions provide an objective perspective, independent of economic interests, has also been challenged.

Many of these critiques have also been directed at resource science. Two aspects have been especially questioned: the assumption that nature can be understood and its future predicted; and the political implications of its status as objective knowledge.

Resource Science and Uncertainty
Nature is always changing, often faster than we can understand, as a result of both natural processes and our own activities. Our knowledge must al-

ways therefore be incomplete, uncertain, and riddled with areas of ignorance. According to Ray Hilborn, a Canadian fisheries scientist, "[u]ncertainties snap at the resource manager like a pack of wild dogs."[18] There is much that scientists do not know: as Doug Hay (another fisheries scientist) commented regarding Pacific fish stocks: "If you're asking me what's going on . . . the answer is, I don't know, and I don't think anybody does."[19]

Uncertainties about fish are understandable: they move rapidly and cannot be seen or counted directly. More surprising, perhaps, is our uncertain knowledge of trees. As industry critics have pointed out, forest inventories provide, at best, an imprecise measure of the resource. Aerial photos—the most common inventory technique—tend to miss local variations and details. Even direct field measurements are often in error, overestimating growth rates and stand volumes. According to Ken Drushka, inventories are "more often than not . . . outdated, speculative, or just plain wrong."[20] And as Elizabeth May, an environmentalist, concludes: "Overall, Canada doesn't have much better science to figure out how much wood is available than to figure out how many fish were in the waters off Newfoundland."[21] The long temporal dimension of forestry magnifies the challenge: to set sustainable cutting levels, foresters must predict the state of a forest a century from now, on land that may never before have supported artificially planted trees, in an era of unprecedented climate change. In such a context, one must talk not just of uncertainty, but of ignorance, with even the relevant questions, let alone the answers, obscured.

There are many sources of uncertainty and ignorance in resource management.[22] Several relate to the gathering of knowledge about resources:

- *Research Limitations.* There are usually limits to the effort that can be devoted to assessing the state of a resource. This may reflect limited funds (particularly for long-term monitoring—a perennially neglected area of research) or a belief that some resources (such as fish in smaller lakes) are not valuable enough to be monitored continually. The consequence will be insufficient information for effective management.
- *Observation Uncertainty.* Measurement and sampling error can be a major source of uncertainty. For example, a standardized approach to estimating forest yield—such as measurement of the growth rate of a few trees, which is then extrapolated across an entire stand—will generate uncertainties when applied to a diverse landscape of varying productivity. Uncertainties are also magnified when a resource cannot be observed directly. For example, it is not possible to count how many fish die of natural causes in the ocean. Natural mortality, therefore, will usually be estimated as a certain proportion of the total fish stock; this estimate will then be applied to modeling fish population dynamics. The estimate is likely to be inaccurate but by an unknown amount.[23]
- *Reporting Uncertainty.* Data used by resource scientists are often reported by the resource users themselves. However, information they provide

about their own activities or the state of the resource may not be accurate. For example, fishers subject to quotas may underreport their bycatch (fish that are not of the species or age category sought).

- *Specialist Uncertainty.* Resource scientists tend to focus on only certain aspects of ecosystems—usually those with economic value. As a result, our knowledge of other aspects will often be incomplete. For example, forest researchers tend to focus on economically valuable species, rendering more uncertain predictions of how the ecosystem as a whole will behave. Even our knowledge of the factors affecting economic components is often uncertain, because of this tendency to specialize. For example, ecologists often describe foresters' predictions of future timber supply as naive because they ignore the ecological impacts of harvesting, including erosion, nutrient depletion, and biodiversity loss.[24]
- *Theoretical Uncertainty.* Knowledge of a resource may be uncertain because available theoretical perspectives provide an inadequate basis for interpreting available information. For example, it is difficult to assess the decline of west coast salmon stocks, or even the number of stocks, because scientists do not agree on the level of genetic distinctiveness needed to define a stock.[25]

Other forms of uncertainty and ignorance relate to characteristics of nature:

- *Noise.* Uncertainties may result from natural variability. For example, reproduction within a fish population, or the productivity of a forest, often changes unpredictably from year to year. These variations may not even be recognized until after they have occurred, and after management decisions have been made that were based on the implicit assumption that this noise did not exist.
- *Unexpected Events.* Resources are often affected by unanticipated and unprecedented events. Entry of an exotic species into an ecosystem is one example. The entry of the zebra mussel into the Great Lakes, and its subsequent spread across eastern North America, has had many unexpected impacts on aquatic ecosystems. Other kinds of ecosystem disruptions, such as forest fires or defoliating insects, can similarly propagate unpredictably across large areas, rendering knowledge of resource conditions more uncertain and creating new realms of ignorance.[26]
- *Novel Conditions.* It is increasingly evident that, contrary to what is commonly assumed in resource management, the future will not be like the immediate past. Climate change will have substantial (but difficult to predict) consequences for forests, fisheries, and other resources. Human activities can result in other kinds of long-term, unpredictable changes. For example, cutting and replanting the temperate rainforests of the Pacific coast of North America constitutes a long-term experiment, the outcome of which, particularly its effects on soil fertility, cannot be predicted.

- *Ecological Uncertainty.* Ecosystems can exhibit chaotic, inherently unpredictable behavior, even as a result of apparently minor environmental changes. In complex systems, these changes can magnify quickly and unpredictably, and, once past a threshold, can cause transformation of the ecosystem, creating havoc with predictions based on the assumption that ecosystems behave in a linear, nonchaotic fashion. Loss of ecosystem resilience—its capacity to maintain its structure and function in the face of change—will make dramatic change more likely. As C. S. Holling has explained, resilience is often lost when resource management prevents normal patterns of ecosystem change. To take a familiar example, preventing forest fires leads to accumulated brush and litter, making a fire of catastrophic intensity more likely.[27]

These uncertainties and areas of ignorance have many consequences. The most significant is that there may be more than one plausible interpretation of available data, and no consensus as to which is correct. In the resulting debate—over how many fish may be caught, or how many trees may be cut—opposing interests will use whatever interpretation best supports their own position. Scientists and managers will also tend to interpret the data in ways compatible with their own expectations and interests.

This was in fact what happened before the cod stocks off Newfoundland collapsed. Scientists were anxious to demonstrate that management was successful; they were also under pressure to justify the high quotas that had been set for the fishery. Both circumstances gave them a strong incentive to interpret the data as suggesting that the cod stocks were healthy. Even as evidence accumulated that stocks were in trouble (in particular, inshore fishermen were finding that some stocks had apparently disappeared), scientific warnings were couched in such uncertainty that they could be discounted by politicians understandably reluctant to close this economically essential fishery. In effect, science was not able to provide the precise, certain information needed to justify closing the fishery. Quotas were instead set on the basis of the most optimistic interpretation, with little margin for error, while uncertainties masked the effects of overexploitation until the damage was severe and perhaps irreversible.[28]

Such outcomes are one reason why resource agencies seek, above all, to eliminate uncertainty, by exerting control over an ecosystem, reducing variation and increasing predictability. In effect, they impose an industrial discipline on nature. Holling has argued that such efforts result in a "pathology of natural resource management" in which the resilience of an ecosystem—its capacity to respond and adjust to change—is eroded. Diminished genetic variation in hatchery fish; fire suppression in forests; agricultural monocultures—these are all examples of resource systems in which variation and therefore resilience are reduced. In effect, management "freezes" the ecosystem, in a highly productive, but also more fragile state. Management of such ecosystems will encounter not less, but more uncertainty, because of a greater tendency for sudden, unexpected, and large-scale change—that is, for "surprises."[29]

Holling has extended this account of changes in nature to the evolution of management attitudes and practices. At first, efforts to control nature and reduce uncertainties may succeed. In response, a management agency will shift from efforts to understand the resource, to seeking instead greater efficiency in performing its standard tasks while ensuring its own survival. The agency will also become ever more isolated, both from the systems being managed (as research focuses only on those components of immediate interest) and from the public (as relationships tighten between the agency and client groups). Harvesting will become increasingly dependent on the continued ability of management to control nature, to ensure a steady flow of resources. Overall, ecosystems, resource agencies, and economic interests will become less resilient in the face of change.

Scientific uncertainties, therefore, pose a variety of obstacles to the sustainable use of resources. But they can also have political consequences, including conflicts between resource users. Uncertainties regarding the state of a resource and the relative importance of diverse human impacts can exacerbate disputes over allocation of the resource, encouraging mutual recriminations between resource users. One example of this was seen in 1994, when a dispute broke out between the major fishing groups—commercial, sport, and native—on the Fraser River in British Columbia. Large uncertainties in salmon population estimates, including discrepancies between population counts near the mouth of the river and at upstream locations, generated arguments over who was responsible for the "missing" salmon, creating tensions that impeded resource sharing arrangements in the river.[30]

A second political consequence of resource uncertainties is the destabilization of management arrangements as a result of the diminished authority of resource scientists. One illustration of how this can occur is provided by the recent evolution of caribou management in northern Canada. During the 1970s Canadian Wildlife Service biologists reported that their population estimates suggested a "caribou crisis": herds had become dangerously depleted, indicating the need for immediate controls on hunting. In the early 1980s more extensive surveys, drawing on additional sources of information, including the experience of Inuit hunters, found the earlier estimates to be highly inaccurate. This experience encouraged an opening up of caribou management arrangements, with greater participation by hunters and less reliance on wildlife service biologists.[31]

Resource Science and Industry

Early in the twentieth century Gifford Pinchot, the first director of the U.S. Forest Service, provided the classic formulation of the "public interest" with respect to natural resources: that resources exist to be used; they should be used for the common good, not just for private gain; both waste and depletion of resources are to be avoided.[32] In Pinchot's day the public interest with respect to forests was clear: ensuring a reliable and affordable supply of timber for industry. Since then, resource science, particularly within public agencies, has been justified in the name of pursuing, through rational, objective research and application, this public interest.

But this image of public-spirited resource science and management has often been criticized. One objection has been that, far from pursuing the public interest, science in fact privileges the interests of the resource industry over those of other resource users and the public. As resource industries, and resource management, have expanded over the last century, they have displaced the resource practices of communities that drew on local knowledge and skills. This erosion of local control has, critics argue, endangered both conservation and equitable access to resources. It has also been suggested that the Forest Service has facilitated this trend, by defining forestry as a scientific matter, removing from the table moral or ethical dimensions of forest use, reducing forestry to the pursuit of efficiency, which, in practice, becomes defined as meeting the needs of the most powerful resource users.

Resource management today is widely seen as a compact between government and industry, with barriers to public participation reinforced by defining management as a scientific matter. Research on resources conducted within public institutions, including universities and government agencies, is often oriented toward industry priorities. This reflects the close industry–public sector–university ties often formed as a result of research funding, consulting and advisory relationships, and the fact that industry will ultimately employ many graduates. Fisheries researchers, for example, tend to view industry as the only legitimate client for their services. Similarly, forestry planning is usually conducted through negotiations between industry and government; the wider community, as well as local interests, are excluded, or have only token influence. In Canada, after decades of activism and evolving public values, public participation remains more symbolic than real, and the basic structure of provincial forest policies has remained essentially unchanged. In practice, real change in resource management only appears possible when the issue becomes politicized and is lifted out of the closed government/industry circle.[33]

This pattern perpetuates the characteristic tripartite pattern of American government: "iron triangles," composed of a public agency, experts, and an interest group (most often, an industry) that share a consensus concerning their objectives and how to achieve them, and that tend to exclude groups not already in the triangle. These triangles are reinforced by the view that only professionals, speaking a common language of technical and managerial expertise and sharing similar assumptions concerning knowledge, values, and priorities, have the competence to participate. Hamish Kimmins, a Canadian forest scientist, summarized an attitude widespread among professionals: "[t]he public, often lacking the appropriate technical knowledge, has frequently not understood either side of the arguments about the environmental impact of forest management."[34] Large companies are also usually viewed as better resource managers, because only they can afford to hire the necessary scientific expertise.

A more subtle, but equally important dimension of contemporary resource management is the tendency of resource professionals to develop a perspective on nature consistent with industry values.[35] Resource science, focused on efficiency and productivity, implicitly assumes that all resources exist to be used, and that those elements of nature that cannot be used should be minimized. For example, the redefinition within forestry science of certain tree species as commodities simultaneously redefines other species as weeds. This is reflected in the language of the science: forestry scientists use terms such as "tree crops," draw an analogy between farming and forestry, and often claim that undisturbed forests will "deteriorate"—that is, become less productive. Kimmins, for example, has noted that "if they remain undisturbed for many centuries, some cool, humid coastal old-growth forests may lose vigour and 'stagnate.'"[36] Such perspectives exemplify the "master narrative" of resource management, in which nature is viewed as a source of raw materials for industry, with experts—the arbiters of the interaction between humans and nature—pursuing its efficient harvest.

Industry values are expressed in many ways in resource science. Forestry research focuses on the efficiency of production: more efficient ways of planting trees, better methods of controlling competing vegetation, improving through breeding and biotechnology the productivity of selected tree species. In contrast, less attention is typically paid to the long-term, ecosystem effects of management practices.[37] Resource values can be reflected even in the categories used to describe nature. For example, foresters often use a "site index," in which soil, slope, rainfall, and aspect are combined into one measurement that can predict how large a tree will grow at that site over a certain number of years. Such an index reduces a forest to its wood content, neglecting other priorities, such as maintaining a diverse forest.[38]

Industrial interests often employ science in their conflicts with other resource users. In particular, historians describe how science has been used to justify displacement of small-scale resource users. On the Pacific coast, fisheries regulators sought to eliminate the coastal canning monopoly's competitors: small-scale fisheries and small-boat fleets, native fishers, seals and sea lions.[39] In Canada, early scientific forestry supported industrial interests through land classification, prohibiting settlers in areas designated for timber production. Small operators were also accused of wasteful practices, a policy that favored large companies, which were perceived as more efficient.[40]

Industry's use of science to support its interests in resource conflicts is also seen in efforts to develop its own expertise as a means of contesting government policies. Industrial fisheries, for example, often no longer rely on government stock assessments, but hire their own scientists to conduct assessments, in part to ensure their interests are taken into consideration in management decisions. Industry-funded "contested stock assessment" is expected to become more common as individual transferable quotas become more widely used. In such situations experts may simply seek whatever information will enable them to act as advocates for their employer. Fishing interests have been described as having instructed their scientific consultants to "just find some holes in the government assessment; this will provide us the opening we need with the politicians."[41] Science becomes, in effect, an instrument used to increase uncertainty concerning resource stocks, thereby reducing pressure for controls on their exploitation.

In many ways, then, science and resource industries form a mutually supportive relationship: scientists receive funding from industry, while industry perspectives on nature are legitimated by science, with the production of commodities attaining privileged status through its accounts of nature (as when, for example, a forest is measured in terms of timber production rather than wildlife habitat). In the resource field as in other areas of environmental politics, interests are less readily challenged if they are considered to reflect the actual order of nature, as revealed through science.

Over the last four decades industrial perspectives on resources have come under heavy attack. Changing public values—including a desire to protect forests and other resources for their wilderness or recreational value as well as for commodity production—have led to demands for wider participation in resource decisions. Resource debates have broadened to involve a wider range of interest groups, including environmentalists, native groups, and communities living in or near forests. This has generated a wider range of expectations regarding resource management. Wildlife management must be concerned not only with game species, but with endangered species and habitats; forest management is no longer only about timber, but about biodiversity, habitats, ecosystem health, and human activities other than harvesting.[42] But as I have noted, resource management has been unable or unwilling to respond effectively to these changing values. Modification of certain management practices has not prevented critics from asserting that commodity production remains dominant, with other goals, such as preserving wildlife habitat or recreational opportunities, seen merely as constraints on this overriding objective.[43] Resource science and its close ties with industry have often been implicated in this failure to respond to change. Forestry science that is focused on efficient timber production may not accord sufficient attention to other environmental components, such as streams or wildlife. Similarly, the pursuit of maximum sustained yield in fisheries management will neglect all values other than simply the quantity of fish.

Certainly, a tremendous amount of work has been done on reinterpreting public values in scientific terms: from understanding the ecological requirements of a healthy wilderness to measuring the economic value of recreational activities, or of a scenic view unclouded by smog. Economic analyses measure environmental values in terms of willingness to pay; for example, the value of a wilderness area may be determined by measuring the costs individuals are willing to incur to visit the site. Another approach is contingent valuation, in which individuals are asked how much they would be willing to pay for a given environmental improvement, such as protection of a natural area. The Forest Service uses these methods to estimate the recreation value of its lands. Such techniques can make it possible to incorporate these values into resource management decisions, ensuring a better balance between consuming and protecting ecosystems. Nevertheless, certain public values, like the intrinsic worth of an old-growth forest, cannot be expressed in scientific terms at all. Nor can arguments framed in terms of "rights" (including those of other species). As a result, scientists tend to dismiss such arguments, viewing them as the last resort of those unable to justify their preference quantitatively (ideally, in terms of cost-benefit comparisons). In general, nonquantitative arguments tend to be rendered invisible within resource debates framed in terms of science. This frame may be narrow indeed, as questions require precise boundaries if they are to be answerable through science. For example, a question about the effects of different widths of streamside buffers is easier to answer than is one about the appropriate use of the watershed for logging or for other purposes.[44] In short, the definition of resource questions in terms of science tends to focus attention on immediate impacts rather than on larger political or social issues.

Interests other than industry, including environmental groups, are aware of the value of expert knowledge and have made considerable efforts to gain access to expertise. However, they usually do not have industry's financial resources, and so are not able to participate as effectively. Few organizations have the expertise and resources necessary for involvement in detailed forest planning negotiations between industry and government.[45] Interest groups have also often found that they are unable to obtain expertise relevant to specific controversies because all experienced scientists are already employed by industry or government.

Conventional resource science can also exclude other forms of knowledge, including that of resource users, as well as indigenous knowledge. This knowledge can be essential. For example, Newfoundland inshore fishermen foresaw the collapse of the North Atlantic cod stocks before many scientists did. However, this knowledge is often discounted by scientists and managers, who view science as objective and universal but lay persons' knowledge as specific to a particular natural or cultural world, and therefore less credible.

Two of the most significant consequences of restricted participation in resource decisions (particularly when this restriction is enforced by science) are that basic assumptions are less likely to be questioned, and wider discussion of the practices and objectives of resource policy simply does not occur. Change can be resisted, even when change is necessary. One illustrative episode took place in British Columbia. For two decades after 1950 a sustained yield policy took hold that ultimately, if unintentionally, laid the basis for the long-term depletion of the province's forests. The province, however, failed to address this predicament effectively, particularly because there was no wider discussion of provincial forest policy. Instead, government, industry, and the University of British Columbia School of Forestry retained tight control over this policy—a classic "iron triangle." Novel scientific ideas, as well as new economic or political priorities, such as tourism or wilderness protection, were resisted. The result, as historian Jeremy Wilson describes, was a "barren" debate in which innovation was limited to improving the efficiency of existing policies.[46]

but what happens when debate is only a smoke screen.

Innovation in Resource Science

"debate but too acknowledgment" "ghost"

This chapter began with the suggestion that resource management is in crisis. But times of crisis can be opportunities for innovation. One such opportunity appeared in 1993 in the Clayoquot Sound region, on the west coast of Vancouver Island. After years of disputes between timber companies, native groups, and environmentalists, the issue boiled over, with mass protests and more than 800 arrests, as well as a political crisis the provincial government could not ignore. The government created a scientific panel to advise on how to resolve conflicts in the region. Two years later, the panel recommended an entirely novel approach to the region's forests, responsive to both evolving scientific knowledge and public concerns. Decisions, it urged, should be guided by the following principles:

- Forest planning should seek, above all, to protect ecosystem integrity; this implied many changes to forestry practices, including an end to clearcutting.
- Forestry plans should adapt to changing conditions and new information, and should employ a precautionary approach.
- Communities and interest groups, and especially native communities, should be involved in forest planning.

To fulfill these principles, the panel offered 120 specific recommendations, collectively overhauling conventional logging practices.[47] Implementation, which began in 1995, has been difficult and contentious. But these recommendations were a major innovation in British Columbia forest planning—an illustration of how innovation can emerge out of crisis.[48] *let's not wait*

Crisis—whether political or ecological—can generate innovation by forcing a questioning, even a discrediting, of conventional resource management, and by creating a demand for new ideas. But for innovation to actually occur these new ideas must be available: intellectual capital to be drawn on when a crisis arises. As the Clayoquot Sound panel illustrated, science can be a source of such capital, contributing new ways of understanding nature and responding to change.

However, one cannot wait until after a crisis has emerged before generating the intellectual capital needed to deal with it. Having such capital on hand requires, rather, the slow accumulation of new knowledge, through basic research in ecology and other fields. Such an accumulation has been taking place over the last several decades. Research in ecology has stimulated changes in both professional and public understanding of old-growth forests, and of the importance of diversity to forest ecosystems generally, including those elements given too little attention, such as soil organisms. The forest management agenda has been expanded by knowledge of the ecological impacts of forest cutting, acid rain, and ultraviolet radiation. Disturbances such as the Mount St. Helens eruption in 1981 and the Yellowstone Park fires of 1988 have become opportunities to understand the significance of disturbance and recovery in ecosystems; this understanding, and its implications for clearcutting and other management practices, has led to new perspectives in forestry.[49] Knowledge of the genetics of endangered species populations is influencing wildlife and fisheries management. Fish populations are now understood not as homogenous assemblages of individuals, but as genetically heterogeneous: Pacific salmon populations are composed of at least several hundred distinct stocks—some now extinct and many more in decline.[50] The importance of long-term environmental change has been demonstrated by studies of the impact of climate change on fisheries and forests.[51]

But applying new information in resource management, or responding to changes in the environment or in public priorities, implies a capacity to learn. Such learning, however, is often obstructed by poor relations between scientists and managers. They usually work in different contexts—in universities, or in agency or industry offices—and rarely communicate directly. Each tends to see communication problems as the fault of the other. Managers complain that scientific research is often not applicable to real problems, that it is too theoretical and too narrow; researchers complain that managers are not using the available science, that managers expect unrealistically simple solutions to complex problems, and that they simply don't understand how science works.[52]

A major problem in linking science to management has been that resource agencies tend to focus research only on immediate management needs, and especially on increasing the efficiency of existing practices. Critics argue that, as a result, resource management institutions are not generating the science needed in an era when change is occurring both in the environment and in public values. And in fact, many recent scientific innovations relevant to resource management have been generated outside conventional resource management institutions. In forestry, the knowledge base needed to consider ecological alongside commodity values has been provided by nontraditional forest research centers, including university departments of biology and environmental sciences, and through the work of researchers in a wide range of scientific and professional disciplines other than forestry. New ideas are often reported not in conventional forestry journals, but in journals such as *Conservation Biology* or in the reports of nongovernmental organizations such as the David Suzuki Foundation in British Columbia.

The innovations in Clayoquot Sound forestry planning illustrate the impact that new scientific ideas, along with changing public values and broader participation, can have on resource management. Since the 1970s the once "barren" debate over forestry in British Columbia has been transformed, with the emergence of new environmental values and doubts concerning the sustainability of forest harvesting. The pool of local experts pursuing research in conservation biology, ecosystem ecology, and other fields sympathetic to environmental values has expanded, in universities and in provincial ministries of the environment and forests. A professional critique of forestry has also emerged within the environmental movement.[53] And as I discuss below, developments in science have alsó generated innovations in resource practice across North America, including adaptive management and ecosystem management,.

But new scientific information is no panacea. While it is often assumed that more knowledge will lead to consensus, in fact it can even exacerbate controversy. Such has been the experience with American forest management. A great deal of research has been done over the last three decades, but the hoped-for outcomes—improved policies, better planning, and an end to forestry conflicts—have often not materialized. According to its critics, while the Forest Service now employs a wider range of knowledge about forests, it still views resource planning as primarily a technocratic exercise, and as a result forestry conflicts continue. Consider as well the experience of the Forest Ecosystem Management Assessment Team (FEMAT), composed of scientists from several federal agencies, convened in 1993 to develop a solution to forest conflicts in the Pacific northwest. FEMAT provided a valuable assessment of the practice of forest ecosystem management. However, it failed to resolve these conflicts.[54] Such experiences illustrate how scientists by themselves cannot resolve resource controversies.

Uncertainty and Innovation

If knowledge alone is not enough, then how can science contribute to resolving resource crises? One can begin to answer this question by considering some novel approaches to dealing with a central problem of resource management: uncertainty. Innovation in dealing with uncertainty begins with the realization that it is inevitable: fish and forests may be measured more precisely, but we can never know exactly how many fish there are, or how fast trees will grow. The task, therefore, is not to pretend that certainty is achievable, but to ensure that scientists are able to provide useful advice, and managers (or the public) are able to make effective decisions, even in the face of uncertainty.

One approach to uncertainty is to reduce the consequences of acting on the basis of erroneous information. This is the essence of the precautionary approach. Its precise implications are not always clear (the approach is discussed more extensively in chapter 7), but the basic idea is that the burden is placed on resource users to prove that a given level of exploitation is sustainable.[55] The irony is that this risk-averse approach is often only implemented after a crisis. For example, in the aftermath of the collapse of the northern cod, the Canadian

Department of Fisheries and Oceans began to pursue a precautionary approach, erring on the side of conservation rather than of maximum harvests.[56] A more radical approach (at least in the context of conventional fisheries management) to precaution is to set aside reserves where no fishing is permitted. A growing number of fisheries scientists see these as effective means of reducing risk when there is uncertainty about the status of fish stocks or about the ecological links between species and their surrounding ecosystem.[57]

Dealing effectively with uncertainty can also involve reconsidering how scientific advice is communicated. Scientists tend to assume that they are the best qualified to assess their own data. They therefore provide their single "best" estimate, with debates over the relative merit of other estimates, and the quality of the data, kept out of the public eye, for fear of confusing the issue.[58] But this approach is now being reconsidered. According to Ray Hilborn and his colleagues, when scientists provide only one estimate, managers are unable to understand what uncertainties are inherent in the scientific advice, and signals in the data that may contradict the estimate are masked.[59] A single estimate also does not acknowledge that resource decisions are never made in a vacuum. In practice, advice provided by a management agency will be weighed against the views of economic interests (with their views often backed up by their own scientific evidence, and usually advocating a higher level of harvest), and a single estimate provides no indication of the consequences of choosing it or the option preferred by these interests. Nor does a single estimate indicate what assumptions were made by the scientists. For example, if scientists do not mention a particular option, such as an alternative harvesting strategy, managers cannot evaluate its implications—they may not even be aware of its existence.[60]

One alternative to a single "best" scientific estimate or advice is to provide several estimates, each accompanied by an explanation of its consequences if adopted. Scientists would describe the range of possibilities that are consistent with the data, and computer models could portray different states of the resource and the different consequences of alternative harvesting strategies. Managers could then experiment with these models, asking "what if?" questions regarding the consequences of different decisions, including the risks inherent in the most optimistic option.[61] A chief benefit of this explicit acknowledgment of uncertainty is that discussion of options, and the connection between the science and the decisions, would thereby be more open and transparent. In addition, debate is shifted from the merits of the scientific advice itself to where it belongs: deciding which resources should be harvested, and when.[62]

These approaches to uncertainty imply a more intensive relationship between scientists, resource managers, and other parties beyond simply passing information along and hoping for the best. Illustrating this, the Clayoquot Sound scientific recommendations were accompanied by changes in the structure of resource management itself, including the relationships between scientists, government, and interest groups—in this case, industry, local communities, natives, and environmentalists. Within this structure, scientists contributed by defining the problems, persuading all parties that a joint approach was necessary, and defining the options available to them.

Many initiatives are now under way that are aimed at achieving greater sustainability of resource use, as well as attention to a wider range of environmental values and interests. Efforts to reshape the role of science are often a major element of these initiatives. New ideas regarding this role are especially evident in three approaches to resource management: adaptive management, ecosystem management, and community-based management.

Adaptive Management

Adaptive management begins with the idea that there are limits to knowledge: in a world of rapid, unpredictable change there will always be uncertainties and incomplete understanding. This implies a need to manage in ways that improve our capacity to learn and adapt to change; it therefore implies a closer relationship between scientists, managers, and resource users: managers and users drawing on scientific knowledge as it evolves, scientists understanding the contexts in which their knowledge is used, and all parties sharing in planning and doing research. In effect, adaptive management constitutes an argument to extend practices of the scientific community—especially experimentation—to the world of resource management.

Since its development in the 1970s, within a community of scientists at the University of British Columbia led by C. S. Holling, adaptive management has been invoked in many contexts. Definitions of adaptive management vary just as widely: from better monitoring of the ecological effects of resource management, and an improved capacity to respond to unexpected changes; to a more formal process involving modeling of the potential impacts of alternative policies, experiments to test these predictions and to obtain new knowledge, and application of this knowledge to management practice, with these steps repeated as an iterative process.[63] The British Columbia Ministry of Forests provides a representative statement of the approach, emphasizing the close relationship between science and management:

> Adaptive management is a systematic process for continually improving management policies and practices by learning from the outcomes of operational programs. Its most effective form—"active" adaptive management—employs management programs that are designed to experimentally compare selected policies or practices, by evaluating alternative hypotheses about the system being managed.[64]

Adaptive management has most often been invoked in aquatic ecosystems, such as the Columbia and Colorado rivers, the Florida Everglades, and British Columbia coastal fisheries.[65] Such systems can be more readily experimented with over shorter time periods. For example, in 1996, 1997, and 2000, scientists and managers greatly increased the volume of the Colorado River for a few days, and then watched closely to see how the river responded, in an attempt to understand how to restore it to conditions closer to those present before the Glen Canyon Dam was completed in 1963. By the following year these experiments had produced useful results. In contrast, adaptive management has been less often invoked in forest ecosystems, where the effects of changing practices may not be apparent for many years.

It is striking, however, that adaptive management has been invoked more often than it has actually been applied. It does, after all, present a variety of challenges, beyond obtaining timely results. It means extending the practices of science beyond the laboratory or the small-scale field experiment, to encompass an entire river, wetland, or other ecosystem. And, just as in scientific research, the results can be ambiguous. Such was the experience in one of the first attempts at adaptive management, on British Columbia's Rivers Inlet, the site of an important salmon fishery. In 1979 the Canadian Department of Fisheries and Oceans began a management experiment intended to rebuild the inlet's salmon spawning runs. It closed the fishery for five years, and then increased it gradually for five years. However, the expected increase in salmon populations failed to occur. There were several possible explanations, but according to the scientists involved, it was not possible to determine which was correct.[66]

Extending scientific practices into the world of resource management is also costly: it requires pulling together existing knowledge, modeling different possible actions to predict their results, conducting experiments (which may include several distinct management practices), and then monitoring and comparing the outcomes across a wide variety of variables and on a much more ambitious scale than is typical in resource management.[67] For example, monitoring the experimental flooding of the Colorado River required measuring everything from sediment accumulation to water temperature to fish populations. Economic interests may resist paying some of the costs of experimentation. These costs extend beyond the expense of the management practices themselves: manipulating the Colorado meant losing some power production; similarly, fisheries experiments may oblige fishers to reduce their catch, without any guarantee of a larger future catch. The intergenerational tradeoff implicit in adaptive management can also be discouraging: the benefits of experiments, in the form of improved information, will mainly benefit the next generation, while the present generation pays all the costs. There are also ecological risks: experimenting on an entire ecosystem may endanger sensitive species, or other valued ecological features.

Given these costs and uncertainties, it is not surprising that resource agencies often resist adaptive management, at least in its more elaborate forms: modeling the outcomes of alternative practices, conducting experiments, monitoring outcomes, applying the lessons. Indeed, while agencies commonly invoke adaptive management, actual practice is often closer to what is vaguely referred to as "learning by doing": following conventional practices while monitoring the outcomes more carefully. Thus, while adaptive management addresses a genuine need for better communication between scientists and those who use scientific information, it also exhibits the challenges involved in applying scientific methods within complex economic and institutional circumstances. Consequently, in situations where there are many interest groups and agencies, it can be difficult to achieve agreement on implementing adaptive management. This is why, as Carl Walters, one of its most prominent practitioners, has noted, adaptive management has so far really only proven effective in simpler political contexts where there are relatively few interest groups and a single resource agency has a clear jurisdictional mandate.

Ecosystem Management

Both science and common sense tell us that a forest is more than trees, and a river more than a school of salmon. But it has been a struggle for resource management institutions and science—both focused on commodity production—to accommodate this basic insight. The last two decades, however, have seen many efforts to address this oversight, and ecosystem management has become probably the most widely invoked innovation in resource management. In 1992 the U.S. Forest Service adopted ecosystem management as policy for its national forests, and other agencies have since followed, including the Fish and Wildlife Service, the National Marine Fisheries Service, and the Bureau of Land Management. By one estimate, ecosystem management has been applied in more than 600 instances in the United States alone.[68] However, there is no consensus on what ecosystem management is, or what it implies.

Some see it as a great innovation: according to the Forest Service, "ecosystem management celebrates the wisdom of both our minds and hearts, and lights our path to the future."[69] Heady stuff. Others, however, view it as simply a repackaging of old ideas—what used to be referred to as "multiple use" management.[70] Certainly, the concept has a longer history than is often acknowledged: Aldo Leopold drew a distinction between "Type A" foresters, who viewed forests as an industrial crop, and "Type B" foresters, who regarded them as ecosystems. Leopold's land ethic has itself been described as an early statement of ecosystem management.[71] Elements, at least, of ecosystem management have also long been practiced by fish and wildlife managers seeking to maintain not simply species populations, but their habitats.[72]

There are many definitions of ecosystem management—indeed, so many that the concept has been criticized as malleable enough to justify nearly any action. This characteristic was already evident when the concept was only discussed among ecologists: they defined an ecosystem as everything from a watershed, to a pond, to a stand of trees, and they examined aspects of these systems as varied as the movement of elements and the relations between prey and predator. During the last three decades, as discussion of ecosystems has broadened beyond the discipline of ecology, definitions have continued to multiply; undoubtedly the concept owes much of its popularity to this capacity to accommodate itself to a diversity of purposes. However, certain common elements can be discerned. Most importantly, ecosystem management signifies a broader range of considerations in resource management, encompassing both scientific understanding of entire ecosystems (and not just the resource of economic interest) and the full range of human values and interests at stake in resource issues. In addition, the concept usually encompasses a recognition of uncertainty, and the need for a cautious approach to managing resources, with management prescriptions considered as working hypotheses, subject to revision as more information is acquired.[73] And finally, ecosystem management shares with adaptive management an emphasis on close links between scientists and those who use scientific information.

Ecosystem management has several implications for how science is used in managing resources. It implies an expanded research agenda, encompassing a broader range of scientific disciplines. In forestry, for example, it implies a broadening of the agenda beyond industry objectives, to encompass such topics as the effects of cutting on stream ecosystems and on soil fertility, the impacts of road building, the relation between forestry and wildlife, the design of parks and reserves, and the protection or restoration of endangered species.[74] Beyond this, there are a range of possibilities for science in ecosystem management. Science may be applied to understanding the factors affecting a particular resource commodity; it may provide the basis for cooperation on meeting diverse human interests relating to resources; or most ambitiously, it may guide a redefining of the goals themselves of resource management, away from human interests and toward those of nature.

For many fisheries scientists, ecosystem management means understanding the effects of all factors within an ecosystem on a particular species of interest. A leading example of this is management of salmon fisheries. As a species, salmon are vulnerable to changes in its ocean and river habitats. On the Pacific coast of North America, researchers have described the impact on salmon populations of both natural environmental changes, such as climate cycles or predation, and human-caused changes, including dams, irrigation, logging, hatcheries, exotic species, and climate change. They have then interpreted the effects of fishing in the light of knowledge of these other impacts.[75] A similar perspective is evident in research on forest ecology, when that research focuses on the effects of forest harvesting on long-term soil fertility, and hence on the productivity of selected tree species. This approach to ecosystem management, therefore, remains focused on production of a specific commodity.

A second form of ecosystem management emphasizes responsiveness to a broader range of human priorities. These encompass not just commodity production, but recreation, wilderness protection, and every other value that has been attributed to nature in recent decades. This form of ecosystem management is primarily a political innovation, in that the goal is to improve the capacity of resource management to respond to public values, including those that can only be provided by healthy ecosystems. It thus implies more communication and collaboration in resource management, so that a variety of groups and agencies are able to affect resource decisions.[76] Many argue on the basis of this perspective that a "New Natural Resource Management Paradigm" has emerged that emphasizes protection of ecosystems and citizen participation in public lands management.[77]

A key challenge in this form of ecosystem management is reaching a consensus among a diversity of interest groups. This requires collaboration among many parties—government, industries, property owners, and other stakeholders— as well as the development of common goals that focus on broader geographic scales and long-term benefits.[78] This implies a critical role for science in identifying goals that can meet the needs of most stakeholders, even if the route taken to achieve these goals is not the one envisaged by the stakeholders themselves. One way in which scientists can respond to this diversity of interests is by identifying the ecological basis for the amenities—such as clean water, sustainable commodity production, or healthy wildlife populations—that are demanded by interest groups. Scientists can also provide a common language to facilitate communication between groups, with (it is hoped) resource conflicts minimized through "information-based collaboration" among experts from diverse disciplines: hydrologists, foresters, landscape ecologists, wildlife biologists, and others.[79]

The third form of ecosystem management is the one most explicitly defined in terms of science. It entails reconsidering the goals of management: rather than thinking in terms of a specific commodity or set of human values, the focus is on the state of the ecosystem itself. Goals such as commodity production or the supply of other amenities are adjusted to be consistent with the preferred state of the ecosystem. Science therefore becomes the essential foundation of resource management, because both its goals and its means are defined in terms of a scientific understanding of ecosystems. According to some ecologists, such an approach requires understanding the dynamics of ecosystems: the cycle of slow accumulation and sudden release and reorganization of biological capital; the roles played by destabilizing forces that maintain diversity and resilience; and the function of stabilizing forces that maintain productivity and nutrient cycles. Informed by this ecological perspective, the goal of management is to maintain not stability, but resilience, while permitting natural variation, rather than insisting on constant conditions. Attention to ecological processes that affect ecosystem resilience—nutrient cycles in forests, variable flow regimes in rivers, a diversity of predators to eat up pests in agricultural systems, for example—becomes essential.[80]

Three observations can be made about these forms of ecosystem management. First, like adaptive management, ecosystem management has been more widely invoked in principle than applied in practice. While American federal agencies have adopted it, the forest industry has, on its own land, tended to maintain a focus on commodity production.[81] Ecosystem management has also yet to penetrate effectively into Canadian forestry, apart from special cases such as Clayoquot Sound. For example, the federal Model Forests Program of the 1990s nominally adhered to an ecosystem approach, but in fact continued to focus on timber production.[82] This gap between principle and practice reflects, in part, the economic costs of ecosystem management, as well as resistance from commodity interests. But it can also be traced to the challenges involved in reorienting resource science toward ecosystems. Management jurisdictions usually do not correspond to ecosystems: forest agencies manage forests, and fisheries agencies manage fisheries. Attention to the impact of, say, forest cutting on salmon habitat requires communication across both agencies and specializations—a challenging task. As a Canadian salmon biologist noted, dozens of scientists study various aspects of salmon and their ecosystems, but "we never really talk to each other."[83] There may also be a lack of basic scientific information about the ecosystem, especially long-term monitoring data, that was left uncollected because it was not considered relevant to the commodity of immediate interest. Breaking out of conventional resource frameworks can be difficult, and ecosystem management is often only adopted through outside pressure, as a result of crisis, new information, or public pressure.

A second observation relates to the contradiction embedded in the rationale for ecosystem management. Like adaptive management, ecosystem management is often said to be an acknowledgment that our knowledge will always be incomplete and uncertain. But it also sets a highly ambitious scientific agenda —understanding the behavior of complex ecosystems—while promoting science to a more prominent role in setting management objectives. This ambition sits uneasily with the institutional obstacles to understanding ecosystems that I have just noted, with the limits of uncertain science, and with the general decline in the authority of science that I discussed in chapter 2. Is it realistic to envisage a larger role for science in shaping the objectives of resource management, when science itself is being increasingly recognized as providing at best only an imperfect understanding of our environment?

My third observation also relates to the elevated status of science within ecosystem management. This status raises significant questions regarding the relative role of science and other factors (such as political, economic or moral interests and preferences) in determining policy. "Ecosystem" originated as a strictly scientific concept, and it has ever since implied a dominant role for scientists in both understanding nature and determining appropriate conduct.[84] Ecosystem management perpetuates this reliance on science, particularly when its goals are defined in terms of resilience or other attributes of ecosystems not readily perceptible by nonscientists. If only scientists are able to understand how ecosystems work, and only scientists can evaluate whether the goals of management are being reached, they must have a dominant role in resource decisions. Other people may be included in the process, but as objects to be studied, managed, and occasionally consulted, not as decision-makers. Ecosystem management therefore sharpens the tension between technocracy and democracy, and more specifically, between the science-based orientation of resource management and interest in a larger role for communities and resource users.[85]

A central role for science in ecosystem management can be problematic on practical as well as political grounds. The ecological determinism it implies can exclude other factors that may be more significant in resource decisions, such as relations between economic interests and policymakers, or modern society's appetite for resources. Scientists are also, as noted in chapter 3, unable to provide easily agreed-upon standards by which to define a healthy, well-managed ecosystem. If, for example, disturbance is a normal feature of ecosystems, what would be the optimal frequency and intensity of these disturbances, given historical variability? The lessons of ecology are often ambiguous—as is reflected in the use by timber interests (to the chagrin of environmentalists) of the ecology of ecosystem disturbances to argue that cutting is no more harmful to forests than are natural fires.

Adaptive and ecosystem management are both approaches to resource management framed in terms of scientific knowledge and its application: the incompleteness of this knowledge and the consequent need for learning; and the requirement to understand resources not in isolation, but as part of complex ecosystems. This framing reflects the origins of both approaches in the scientific community. Both are significant innovations, addressing long-standing inadequacies in natural resource management. Nevertheless, they also imply new complexities for the relations between science and politics: determining how nature will be understood, who has the authority to determine what counts as knowledge, and who is permitted to make decisions on the basis of this knowledge.

Resources, Communities, and the Commons

The model of the tragedy of the commons—that any resource with open access will be overused and degraded—has justified expansion of government regulation, guided by scientific expertise. It has also often been invoked by those who argue for extending property rights to all resources. But with experience showing neither regulation nor privatization to be a panacea for resource degradation, there is renewed interest in the concept of resource commons: discrete resources, such as a forest or salmon river, to which numerous users have access, with this access regulated by the users themselves, cooperating, as members of a community, to ensure long-term sustainability. Sociologists, anthropologists, and other social scientists have devoted much attention to such arrangements, noting their impressive record of stewardship while identifying objections, both theoretical and empirical, to the tragedy model. They have also described how in many instances sustainable and equitable local arrangements for allocating resources have been displaced by government regulation. The result has often been a slide to ruin: unable to regulate resource use effectively, or favoring industrial interests that seek profit over sustainability, conventional regulation has tended to result in de facto open access and a race to exhaust the resource.[86]

Many communities, particularly in the developing world, are now assuming a stronger role in local resource management, in an effort to gain control over their economic and social well-being.[87] Such efforts reflect how people in resource-dependent communities see themselves: as stewards of their local environment, with their livelihoods, their social relations, even their sense of who they are intertwined with their use of local resources. Often they have developed an environmental ethic: a sense of responsibility to leave the resource as good as they found it.[88] Indigenous communities have been especially active in asserting control over local resources. A distinctive feature of such communities is the extent to which resource use and management are integrated into their economy, society, and culture. They often possess considerable cultural capital, in the form of traditional environmental knowledge, gained through long experience of living on the land. In some areas of the world, indigenous peoples have retained ownership or some other form of control over local resources; this authority is now receiving stronger legal recognition, as seen for example in comprehensive land claims settlements in northern Canada. Interest in community management of resources has been given additional impetus through international recognition of both its practical record of sustainability and its contribution to local self-determination, particularly of indigenous peoples. The Brundtland Commission's report in 1987 was a significant step in providing this recognition.

The chief consequences of these developments have been a willingness to consider alternatives to conventional resource management and a proliferation of diverse arrangements for managing the commons: from partnerships between resource users and government agencies, to multi-stakeholder bodies, to more informal collaborative arrangements between scientists and communities, such as participatory action research. In Canada, there is growing experience with community forestry, while across North America various negotiated arrangements for joint responsibility have been made between fishers and government agencies.[89] Such arrangements emphasize local, often informal systems of tenure based on common property arrangements, looser ties to market forces, and a major role for communities in long-term stewardship of the resource. They also challenge the view that resource management is the purview of apolitical, objective experts, independent of resource users. Collaboration with communities has, like ecosystem management, moved into the mainstream for resource professionals.[90]

There are several potential advantages to community-based management of the commons. Because those regulating resource use will be most directly affected if the resource is damaged, sustainable use is more likely. Individuals are more likely to cooperate in restraining their use of the resource, or in resolving conflicts, when they participate in managing it. Because of this, struggles asserting the rights of communities (particularly indigenous peoples) to control over resources are often tied to campaigns that have more strictly environmental objectives. Community-based management is also viewed as more responsive to alternative uses of resources, including those for which there is no formal market; it may also be more flexible in managing and allocating these uses. Above all, such arrangements provide a means by which resource management can respond to local circumstances and priorities, while links with national or regional resource management agencies can help ensure that resource decisions take into consideration larger phenomena, such as climate change.

Knowledge and the Commons

Community-based management of resource commons poses a challenge to industrial resource management, resource science, and the worldview they jointly legitimize: reliance on formal rules, standardization of nature in the interests of efficiency, and a primary role for the state and the market in determining how resources should be allocated. Community-based management, in contrast, usually relies on more informal systems of resource allocation and management, with a large role for resource users and their knowledge.

These systems can take many forms. The degree of authority a community wields can vary widely, from merely being consulted to having effective control over the resource. Co-management is probably the most common arrangement; in this model a community has some, but not complete, responsibility for managing the resource, working in cooperation with a government agency. Research and monitoring are often central to these arrangements, and they too vary widely. A limited approach can involve a community monitoring resources under scientific guidance, with people from the community gathering data and reporting their own use of the resource. There are several advantages to a community and a resource agency sharing responsibility for research and monitoring: more reliable information from a wider array of sources, as well as the incorporation of social and cultural values into data collection and decisions. Those who live within a community and use the resource often have a broader understanding of the environment, drawing on observations over a longer period of time, than do scientists. For example, fishers with years of experience can build up a detailed knowledge of changes within the marine environment, and they constantly experiment, and so provide a more holistic and flexible way to assess stocks. In contrast, biologists' focus on one species at a time may be seen as remote from the practical realities of the sea.[91] As one author notes: "Self-management and co-management, particularly in the area of data collection, can allow a more efficient harvest: local data collection which draws upon local knowledge, and incorporates academics' knowledge as well, produces superior data which can be used to generate more specific, more flexible, and more timely responses to management opportunities."[92]

Indigenous systems of resource management, while sometimes characterized as "traditional" (implying constancy), in fact often exhibit substantial flexibility and capacity to adapt to change. For example, the Cree of northern Quebec have learned to take the unexpected into account in their unpredictable subarctic environment. As Fikret Berkes found, their resource management practices are adapted to characteristics of their ecosystem, including low productivity and high variability, and are also closely integrated into their social system and culture.[93] While their fishing techniques seem to violate every rule of conventional resource management, they are nevertheless sustainable, apparently because the resilience of the fish populations is maintained. Their arrangements exemplify how many indigenous communities have recognized that change, both gradual and rapid, occurs in the environment, and so have accumulated a knowledge base to guide their responses to these changes.[94] Indigenous resource management can also accommodate limits to knowledge. For example, because it is more difficult to count how many fish are being caught than it is to know what methods are being used, indigenous communities often regulate fishing methods rather than quantity of fish caught.[95]

Knowledge of the resource can play several roles in managing a commons. Involving resource users in gathering information can encourage compliance with limits on resource use. Fisheries managers have found that fishers, not surprisingly, are also more likely to comply with management strategies they helped create, that draw on knowledge they gathered. Shared knowledge can also provide a basis for negotiation, agreement, and cooperation on resource management priorities. By developing a consensus on what is known, through monitoring, mapping, and other strategies, users of a resource can develop a consensus on how the resource should be used. Based on this insight, many efforts are underway to build decentralized, collaborative management arrangements that operate on consensus and can offer long-term solutions to local problems, enhance local expertise, and customize national laws to local conditions.[96] This puts a premium on scientific information that can be readily communicated and that is viewed as trustworthy and legitimate. Finally, knowledge gathering can be an essential means by which communities respond and adapt to change. Local institutions tend to learn about and respond to signals from the environment, such as users' perceptions of declining resource stocks, more quickly than can centralized agencies.

Questions regarding science and the management of commons inevitably bring into focus the relations between communities and larger scales of jurisdiction, particularly national or provincial/state government agencies. These relations can have both negative and positive implications for the local management of commons.[97] While centralization of authority within government agencies impedes local management, some actions by the state can also strengthen local institutions: recognition of their legitimacy, support for their cultural or political revitalization, or other assistance in developing local capacities. It is especially through science, however, that these relations make their significance apparent. In the first place, scientific information demonstrates that these relations are functionally necessary, that local resources are embedded within a larger environmental context—after all, salmon live most of their lives in the ocean, and forests may be affected by acid rain generated hundreds of miles away. Research on larger scales is therefore necessary to understand fully the status of a resource at the local level. On the other hand, the case for local action can also be derived from science. For instance, awareness that there are genetically distinct salmon stocks within each of hundreds of streams on the west coast of North America has demonstrated the need for managing each of them separately: information on the health of each stock will be lost if they are viewed as a single coastal population. Because scientific knowledge, especially when framed in terms of general theory, can be insensitive to local variations in environmental conditions, as well as to the knowledge, rights, and interests of local resource users, community-based management provides a means by which such knowledge can be adapted to specific local conditions. Often, these different forms of knowledge can complement each other: scientists can create excellent synchronic data sets, assembling information across large areas, while local resource users can provide accurate diachronic data, representing the history of resource conditions in one location. Both sets of data can be integrated for a full understanding of the resource.[98] In general, research and monitoring must provide a basis for understanding resource stocks on a variety of scales: not just local, but regional and global. The capacity to learn from experience in many places is also important, and this requires communication between, as well as within, communities. This can be a challenge. Resource users are often unable to communicate their knowledge effectively: much of it is tacit, intuitive, and hard to express. It is also a challenge to transform knowledge relevant in one context into knowledge applicable elsewhere.[99]

Scientific knowledge can also play a political role in relations between government resource agencies and local communities. A theme of this chapter is that this knowledge has often served as a means to assert control over resources. Thus, government and industry have argued for decades that they, not communities, have the scientific expertise necessary to manage resources. The political implications of such arguments have been seen, for instance, in northern Canada, where wildlife management by the Canadian Wildlife Service displaced local systems of management and government science came to be seen as a tool for the control of both resources and people.[100] Many communities, in contrast, have argued that their knowledge of the local environment, gained through daily experience, is superior to conventional science because it is more relevant to local conditions, and often more accurate. In particular, indigenous communities have argued that their knowledge—gained over many generations of living on the land, passed down as oral knowledge, and tied to cultural or spiritual beliefs—justifies their control over resources. They also argue that fish and wildlife are important not just as material resources, but for their contribution to social well-being and cultural identity. Hunting and fishing are not just about gathering protein—the activities themselves are essential to keeping a community together and reaffirming who they are. Reasonably enough, therefore, they insist that study and management of these resources should be under local control. A community's knowledge of its resource therefore serves as an instrument of empowerment—cultural capital that a community can use to further its interests.

The effective use of science in community-based management therefore requires supportive relationships between the local and larger scales of resource activity. One approach is for resource agencies to provide funding or scientific advice to support research and monitoring activities that the communities themselves direct. This can help ensure that scientific expertise is applied to local resource issues while enabling communities to learn from experience elsewhere. One example is the Wildlands Project, which provides technical support to regional groups, linking conservation biologists and activists. In such arrangements opportunities for communities to use their own forms of information are important, as are ways of linking this information with scientific knowledge.[101] More informal means of assisting communities can also be important, including those promoted not by institutions, but by committed and innovative individuals. In British Columbia, Herb Hammond has served for many years as an advocate of "holistic forestry." He works with communities and native groups, providing technical advice, including landscape ecology analysis, to develop a local vision of community-based, ecologically sound forestry. This helps empower communities to assume control over their forests, through forest boards or other mechanisms.[102]

Conclusion

Adaptive management, ecosystem management, and community-based management can be best understood as responses to the three chief challenges faced by natural resource management: our uncertainty and ignorance regarding a complex and changing environment; the need to understand not just the resources themselves but the ecosystem within which they are embedded and the diverse values that have become attached to resources; and the growing demands for a role for users and communities in managing resources and resolving conflicts. In practice, distinguishing between these approaches can sometimes be merely a matter of emphasis: adaptive management commonly takes an ecosystem approach, while community-based approaches usually take a broad, ecosystem-level perspective and exhibit a capacity for adaptation.

A broad if sometimes reluctant shift in resource management is also evident: from restricted circles of managers and scientists, primarily within government and industry, to more inclusive circles involving a wider range of expertise, resource users, and interest groups. Resource management is being recognized as a political as much as a technical activity. Neither conflicts over resources nor the global crisis of sustainability itself can be resolved merely by doing more research, and solutions must involve more parties than government and industry alone.

Science is implicated in all dimensions of contemporary resource crises: sharing the blame for resource depletion, hindering fair consideration of all interests, restricting participation by "non-experts" in resource decisions, and supporting a view of nature as primarily a repository of resources for humans. Thus, the evident need for change in resource science: to consider a broader range of environmental factors, to be more open to public ideas and knowledge, and to draw on a wider range of knowledge, about both society and nature. Most crucially, science must provide a basis for trust, consensus, and willingness to cooperate. As Geoff Cushon argues, if resource management can be best viewed as a conversation among many points of view, then the "role of the scientist, or technician, or professional forester becomes one of enlightening the conversation by offering options, by providing an understanding of nature's capacity to respond to our needs," not by dictating one definitive solution. Scientists contribute to this conversation, but they do not dominate it: rather, their role involves outlining options and consequences, recognizing the importance of practical knowledge, and being aware of the motives and aspirations of others.[103]

CHAPTER 5

Science and the Global Environment

❧

No one has ever seen the greenhouse effect. But most agree that carbon dioxide and other trace gases trap the sun's heat, and unusually hot summer days are no longer just the weather, but harbingers of a changing climate. Such has been the recent impact of climate science on our attitudes. Nor has anyone ever looked through a hole in the stratospheric ozone layer. But all agree that CFCs (chlorofluorocarbons) catalyze the breakdown of ozone, allowing ultraviolet radiation to reach the earth's surface. Negotiations on eliminating CFCs began soon after scientists had confirmed this phenomenon. These perceptions and responses illustrate how significant science has become to how we understand the global environment.

Environmental science can make its influence felt in unexpected ways. Recently my insurance agent came by my office with papers for a house I'd just bought. He stayed to chat about pollution and the planet (polls may identify the economy or security as our chief concerns, but the environment never seems far behind). He had no doubt the earth's climate was changing. A big rainstorm back in June 2002 had cost the local insurance industry $2 million in claims (backed-up sewer drains were the big problem); this was a portent, he was convinced, of an ever more unpredictable, and more costly, global climate. Global environmental science may be an arcane business of satellites and super-computers, but its political implications can be as immediate as sewer drains and other mundane matters.

It is a cliché that pollution knows no boundaries. But it has also become a dominant theme in environmental affairs. Awareness of our capacity to affect the global environment dates back to the early cold war and concerns regarding nuclear testing and the transport of radioactive fallout to distant areas, such as the Arctic, once considered pristine. Since then, scientific views of the world as a single system have developed, through research on the cycling of elements, weather patterns, and other physical processes. Today, much environmental research examines the entire globe, attacking problems on scales of time and space beyond the perception of any individual. A series of global issues—ozone depletion, the transport of contaminants across hemispheres, and, especially, climate change—have captured the attention of environmentalists and scientists.

The emergence of global environmental science has been paralleled by formation of a transnational scientific community, pursuing not just knowledge, but influence. Scientists now participate in environmental negotiations and international institutions, such as the Intergovernmental Panel on Climate Change (IPCC), helping to determine which knowledge becomes accepted as authoritative. Their research has generated a great deal of political activity, such as ongoing climate change negotiations and an agreement for the elimination of CFCs; both issues emerged on the international agenda because of warnings from scientists. Their authority as the only credible source of knowledge about the globe has been won even as their products, such as global climate models and satellite images of stratospheric ozone concentrations, bear no relation to daily experience.

The importance of global environmental science reflects a widely held view regarding the relation between science and politics: that scientists describe the natural world, and political actors receive this knowledge and take appropriate action. According to this view, science has a major role in environmental politics but is nevertheless distinct. Scientists have encouraged this view, stressing both the relevance of their work and the boundary between science and politics.

But the relation between global environmental science and politics is more complex and ambiguous. Each has developed over the last several decades in close association with the other: science justifies development of global institutions, and these institutions in turn provide essential support for further research. Scientific ideas underpin the basic conceptions of nature on which global environmental politics is based, including the very notion of a global environment.[1] (That climate change is defined as a global issue is not inevitable, but a product of the recent history of the science and politics of the environment. There are, as I note below, other ways of imagining the issue.) That science is our chief way of understanding global problems and their solutions is itself a proposition rife with political implications because it implicitly devalues other ways of understanding the world. Scientific knowledge also serves as a significant political resource, strengthening or undermining negotiating positions.

But contrary to these close ties between global science and politics, recent events have suggested that in fact these ties are quite tenuous. In spite of scientific consensus, political bodies have been slow to take effective action on climate change, with even the modest requirements of the Kyoto Protocol appearing too ambitious. Links between science and politics must be weak indeed if after decades of research the global community is still reluctant to take decisive action.

Efforts to understand the apparent political ineffectiveness of global climate science often focus on uncertainty: that there are still enough uncertainties in what we know and can predict to justify delaying action. And clearly, these uncertainties do raise difficult political challenges, such as weighing uncertain consequences against the costs of avoiding them, or understanding the difference between uncertainties about fundamental matters and areas of minor disagreement. There are also obstacles to action that have little to do with the science, including opposition from economic interests and resistance to environmental or global initiatives as a matter of ideological principle.

But it can also be suggested that the structure and conduct of climate science itself might be an obstacle to effective action. In fact, an approach to climate science that emphasizes phenomena at the local or national level may be more effective than the predominant global perspective. The causes of climate change are deeply embedded in modern industrial society—it is, after all, the product of millions of individual economic decisions and a multitude of national and local policies. Addressing these causes demands a similar diversity of actions: from encouraging people to choose bicycles over sport utility vehicles, to developing "smart growth" approaches to urban planning, to encouraging greater industrial efficiency. Why, then, should study of the phenomena privilege a global perspective?

The Science of the Global Environment

The principles of the greenhouse effect have been understood for many years. In 1863 John Tyndall identified water vapor as a greenhouse gas, and in 1898 Svante Arrhenius described the relation between carbon dioxide and atmospheric warming. Arrhenius went on to sketch the relation between industrial pollution, carbon dioxide, and world temperatures. During these decades, the study of weather and climate became an arena of international cooperation, initially as a result of efforts by scientists, but eventually usurped by governments, once the practical implications of the scientific knowledge had been recognized. The International Meteorological Association was formed in 1873 and served as a foundation for cooperation (interrupted by wars) on climate issues.

Study of the global atmosphere accelerated after the Second World War. Civilian and military imperatives prompted the establishment of weather stations around the globe, as meteorological data became essential for transportation, agriculture, and other purposes. The International Geophysical Year of 1957–58 quickened international cooperation. Such initiatives served political as well as scientific and economic purposes: cooperation in politically neutral sciences such as meteorology rationalized and justified international political initiatives and the building of a postwar system of international governance.[2] Meanwhile, the cold war encouraged research on the global environment, including studies of the movement of radioactive contaminants.

By the late 1960s a global perspective had also emerged within environmentalism, reinforced by images of Earth brought home by astronauts and expressed through events such as the 1972 Stockholm conference on the global environment. Concerns about human population added their own impetus, motivated by Malthusian arithmetic and computer models demonstrating the limits to growth in a finite world. Several conferences, such as the Study of Critical Environmental Problems in 1970, and the Study on Man's Impact on Climate the following year, codified evolving attitudes toward climate change that defined it not as a promising development (as had once been the case), but as a danger. By the 1970s scientists in universities and government, mostly in wealthier nations, were developing climate research programs, coordinated by institutions such as the World Weather Watch, the Global Atmospheric Research Programme, and the World Meteorological Organization. By the 1980s they had generated some consensus regarding how climate should be studied—using models, analysis of historical data, and other methods—and about the dangers of a warmer world. A conference at Villach, Austria, in October 1985 exhibited this consensus and also marked the beginning of organized efforts by scientists to generate a political response, such as an international convention on climate change. Several scientists, including Stephen Schneider, had already made a case for recognizing climate as an issue that should be of concern to society.[3] By 1988 climate had indeed become a significant political issue, and that year a conference in Toronto produced a call for a 20 percent reduction in greenhouse gas emissions. The same year also saw formation of the Intergovernmental Panel on Climate Change, an organization with the mandate of building a scientific consensus on climate. As a political counterpart to the IPCC, a series of negotiations led to the Framework Convention on Climate Change in 1992, and subsequently to the Kyoto Protocol of 1997. As climate change gradually became defined as both a political and a scientific issue, matters of method and interpretation of data once of interest only to scientists became the focus of broader debate.[4]

A growing store of scientific knowledge was essential to the emergence of climate change as a global environmental issue. Monitoring initiated by C. D. Keeling at Mauna Loa in the 1950s (originally for a different purpose) indicated increasing atmospheric concentrations of carbon dioxide (allowing for seasonal variation), eventually confirming Roger Revelle's claim that the oceans would not absorb carbon dioxide and so prevent its buildup in the atmosphere.[5] Figures portraying a stepwise increase in carbon dioxide also communicated effectively the relentlessness and irreversibility of atmospheric change. Information regarding the importance of other greenhouse gases such as methane and CFCs broadened the discussion, reinforcing the view of climate change as an issue touching almost every human activity while adding a greater sense of urgency, once it became apparent that these other trace gases might have an effect equal to that of carbon dioxide.[6]

As these examples suggest, the impact of scientific information has been felt especially through shifts in perspectives on the global environment and humanity's position in it: from the view of human activity as globally insignificant (it had been known for centuries that humans could affect regional climates) to awareness of the global scale of human impacts; from assuming that such changes would be compensated for by the oceans to recognizing that they would not; from the prospect of climate change as something to be welcomed, even encouraged, to a view of it as both uncertain and dangerous; from the view of climate change as a distant possibility to seeing it as a phenomenon already underway.

In chapter 3 I noted that changing environmental values and perspectives cannot be attributed only to new scientific information. This has also been the case with climate change. Even as climate science evolved to form the foundation of a new political issue, environmental attitudes were emerging that would also affect our ideas about climate. Malthusian visions of humanity outgrowing a finite earth; the discovery of radioactive fallout, pesticides, and other contaminants in the most remote areas of the globe; and a revolution in air and space travel reinforced impressions that the world had shrunk and was thus more vulnerable to manipulation. The transformation in attitudes toward climate change, from viewing it as useful (as reflected in the many experiments in weather modification conducted during the 1950s and 1960s) to seeing it as a hazard, reflected a new view of the global environment: as a fragile system in which any change would have uncertain, and probably unfortunate, consequences. This was in part a manifestation of the emergence of environmentalism in the 1960s; it was also a product of experience with climate disasters in the 1960s and 1970s, including droughts in Ethiopia and floods in Bangladesh. By the 1970s these attitudes had encouraged a shift in scientific research toward understanding the causes and consequences of long-term trends in climate. In a similar way, unusual weather in the late 1980s, including a long, hot summer in 1988, raised the visibility of climate as both a political and a scientific issue.

Just as evolving attitudes toward the earth have both influenced and been influenced by scientific knowledge, so too has there been a complex relationship between science and global scientific institutions. Ever since the formation of the International Meteorological Organization the histories of global environmental science and of these institutions have been intertwined. The institutions, however, have been motivated as much, or even more, by economic and political imperatives—transnational trade, communications, empires and alliances—as by evolving scientific knowledge. During the cold war ecological research was closely associated with security concerns, as evident in studies of the environmental impacts of fallout and nuclear war. Study of the global atmosphere was also related with security in its contributions to formation of the postwar order of stable international governance. International scientific organizations like the IPCC, as well as national climate research initiatives like the U. S. Global Change Research Program, have had political as well as scientific objectives from their beginnings.

The relation between climate science and politics can be best understood, therefore, not in terms of one inspiring the other, but as a co-evolution of scientific and political institutions and ideas, each influencing the other. At the same time there has been a tension in global climate science and politics between the consensual efforts of the IPCC and the domestic and international politics of climate change, expressed through adversarial negotiations between nations, as well as with other parties.

Contemporary Climate Science

Climate science today uses a variety of methods, chief among which are analysis of historical data and computer modeling of the global climate system. This variety is itself a product of the recent history of global environmental science: methods originally developed for other purposes, such as study of the movement of elements in the environment or weather forecasting, have been adapted to understanding how changes in composition of the atmosphere can affect the global climate. Climate science is also the product of years of nego- tiation among scientists about appropriate methods and perspectives: regarding the merits of modeling versus other strategies, of considering the entire globe versus change within specific regions, or of focusing on gradual or sudden change. Various assumptions regarding how science is supposed to be done, and how it can best relate to politics, have also shaped contemporary climate research.

Study of climate history draws on records of both temperature and atmo- spheric composition. Temperature records extend back to the mid-nineteenth cen- tury; once corrected for changes in method and local conditions they indicate a rise in the global average temperature of about 0.6° C over the last 150 years. Scientists have also studied longer records of global temperatures, using other forms of evidence, in hopes of identifying a statistical "fingerprint" of a shift in climatic patterns.[7] Trends in atmospheric carbon dioxide concentrations, in- dicating an increase of more than 30 percent since 1850, can also be deduced from historical evidence. This record can be extended back many hundreds of years, using indirect evidence of changes in temperature or atmospheric com- position, such as tree rings, expansion and contraction of glaciers, and analysis of Greenland and Antarctic ice cores. Analysis of these cores can demonstrate that past ice ages coincide with lower levels of carbon dioxide, indicating a cor- relation between atmospheric composition and climate but not confirming a causal relation.[8]

These historical data carry considerable political significance. First, when linked to recent experience, the record tends to substantiate popular perceptions of warming encouraged by hot summers and mild winters. This perception is aided by the ease with which the historical record can be presented in simpli- fied form by the media: for example, that seven of the ten warmest years ever recorded occurred in the 1990s, or that the warmest year ever occurred in 1998.[9] Second, the correlation between increasing temperatures and increasing green- house gases, especially carbon dioxide, strengthens the common-sense assump- tion that there is a connection between changing temperatures and a changing atmosphere. And finally, the demonstration that the earth is now warmer, and carbon dioxide concentrations higher, than at any time over the last ten centuries suggests (if not proves) that recent trends are not the product of natural variability, but the effects of human activity.

But while the historical record is important, climate scientists rely more on computer simulation models. Known as "General Circulation Models," these are distant descendants of weather forecasting models: sets of equations representing the physical laws that govern behavior of the atmosphere and oceans and their interaction with other phenomena such as solar energy, clouds, and ice.[10] Highly complex, constructed from multitudes of submodels, they demand very large and expensive computers. There are probably fewer than fifty GCMs in the world, many sharing elements. [11] GCMs can also be coupled with models of other features that affect the climate, such as land surfaces and sea ice, to become "earth systems" models that can simulate all major elements of the earth's climate system.

The chief purpose of models is to project future climate conditions on the basis of various scenarios of changing concentrations of greenhouse gases. Most often, they are used to project the consequences of an atmosphere with twice the concentration of carbon dioxide as in preindustrial times. These "equilibrium models" forecast what the world would be like if the atmosphere suddenly jumped to that concentration and then remained at that level. Not too realistic, but a useful indicator. With faster computers, however, "transient models" have become possible that simulate the effects of greenhouse gas concentrations that change over time. These models are more realistic because they can capture, for example, the delay caused by the slowness of the world's oceans to warm. They may also be more politically effective, as they provide a graphic demonstration of the unfolding consequences of increasing greenhouse gases. (Skillful presentation of the output of such a model with related ecological predictions can, as I've witnessed, elicit gasps from a lay audience.)

Climate scientists use a variety of techniques to increase their confidence in models, including demonstrations of the models' ability to simulate the effects of factors with which we already have experience, such as volcanic eruptions, seasons, and changes in greenhouse gases over the past century. But the projections of different models still vary, and there are still large uncertainties. This makes models and their results vulnerable to dispute, as does their reliance on a variety of assumptions, including those relating to components of the climate system that are not yet entirely understood. Accordingly, much of the research on improving the capacity of these models focuses on assessing those processes thought to be important, such as uptake and release of carbon dioxide by plants, so that they can be incorporated within the models. However, predictions of climate models also depend on the credibility of emission scenarios: that is, on predictions of how much greenhouse gases will be produced in the future. And these, in turn, depend on a range of assumptions about political and economic developments.

In addition to study of the past (through the historical record) and study of the future (using models), a third major area of climate research is study of the potential impacts of climate change on ecosystems and human society, and the possibility of adaptation to these impacts. Considerable effort is devoted to developing "integrated assessment models" that apply projections generated by GCMs to understanding the impact of a changing climate on specific regions. One approach is to begin with some projected future climate and to then examine what it would mean for the environment and for society. For example, assessments of climate change in California have generated predictions of a variety of consequences for weather and ecosystems, and from these consequences, have traced the implications for water supply, agriculture, power demand, air pollution, and other conditions directly relevant to California.[12] Assessments of regional impacts serve both to render meaningful the effects of climate change, thereby encouraging action, and to guide adaptation efforts. Regional studies, as have also been done for the American Gulf Coast and for the Great Lakes Region, are often conducted by nongovernmental organizations such as the Union of Concerned Scientists that seek to "bring home" the consequences of global climate change.

Integrated assessment models are also used to evaluate the consequences of various policy scenarios and alternatives, such as mitigation strategies. As such, they constitute efforts to bridge the gap between scientific models and those who use scientific information in decision-making. The integrated assessment approach is one response to demand for policy-relevant information, especially for comparing the potential damage from climatic change with the costs of policies to prevent or to adapt to change. Climate scientists can try out different policy scenarios and climate forecasts; and the models are ultimately simple enough for policymakers to try out different policies on their own computers, to give them a "feel" for different climate policy options.[13] With ever faster computers, regional models have been able to achieve finer resolution of geographic features. However, different models can still vary considerably in their forecasts of regional conditions.

Several observations can be made about climate science. The first I have already noted: that computer models have become the dominant approach to understanding and predicting climate change, with other approaches, such as analysis of historical data, playing supplementary roles. Their position atop the "knowledge pyramid" of climate research has been justified in scientific terms: models provide a way to "experiment" with a system that is too large, in both space and time, to manipulate experimentally; in addition, because models simulate physical mechanisms they do not just describe climate change, but are also able to determine its causes. They can therefore go beyond the mere correlations of atmospheric composition and temperature indicated by historical data. Models can also be justified politically as the only practical way to test the implications of different emissions scenarios. The authoritative status of computer science, as among the "hardest," most technology-intensive forms of research, also contributes to the status of models.

The dominance of models has had several consequences. One is that climate science tends to be centralized, with much of the funding devoted to a relatively small number of "centers of excellence" that house the powerful computers needed to run models. While climate science is ostensibly a global effort, the models at the center of this activity are definitely not: the six major models used up to 1992 were all located in American institutions, and subsequent models have been based on principles the original models established.[14] Another consequence is that models function as a kind of common language for the scientific disciplines involved in climate research, and also between scientists and society—in effect, a common ground constructed out of all the disparate forms of knowledge about climate. This does not imply, however, that communication between climate science disciplines is always effective. For example, communication between modelers and other climate scientists can be largely in one direction: scenarios generated by models are applied to assessing the impacts of climate change, but information from these assessments is not necessarily fed back into improving the models. Nor will scientists working within one domain always fully understand the work being done within another. In particular, scientists assessing climate impacts may not be fully aware that modeled scenarios are uncertain and require knowledge and judgment to interpret properly; for their part, scientists developing the scenarios may not be well enough aware of what kinds of information those studying the impacts of future climate change actually need.[15]

Another consequence of the dominant role of models is that only those aspects of reality they can represent are likely to be viewed as possible. As it happens, models are much better at simulating gradual change than at simulating sudden and inherently unpredictable large shifts. This means that gradual change will be assumed to be more likely. Perhaps the classic instance of the consequences of this assumption was the delay in discovering the ozone "hole" over the South Pole. Since the mid–1970s satellites had been collecting data consistent with a thinning of the ozone layer; however, the computer programs used to analyze these data rejected this evidence because it fell outside of expectations. Only in the mid–1980s, when unusual levels of ultraviolet radiation reaching the earth's surface were detected, were the data reexamined, eventually leading to the "sudden" discovery of the hole.

Other methods indicate what may be lost by this privileging of gradual change. Historical studies suggest that sudden change is possible: ice core data tell of large shifts in climate occurring over short periods of time—as much as five degrees Celsius in less than a century. Such records hint at the thresholds, both known and unknown, that may be encountered as the global climate changes. Changes in greenhouse gas concentrations may produce a small effect at first, and then, beyond a certain point, much greater warming. Another threshold may be crossed if Arctic permafrost melts, releasing large quantities of methane, thereby accelerating the greenhouse effect. There is a remote possibility of dramatic change in ocean circulation patterns, or of disintegration of the West Antarctic Ice Sheet. But such possibilities are very difficult to model. As a result, as the National Research Council concluded, "climate models typically underestimate the size, speed, and extent of those [abrupt] changes," and the significance of such changes is too little appreciated by climate scientists.[16] Taking their lead from models, discussions of scenarios and policy options tend to focus on gradual change, and do not consider events deemed to be unlikely. Nor do they consider the possibility of social or political transformations, effectively sidelining the problem of how society might go about reducing its vulnerability to sudden, nonlinear change. In short, as Schneider and Kuntz-Duriseti note, "[a]lthough researchers recognize the wide range of uncertainty surrounding global climate change, their analyses are essentially surprise free."[17]

As products of history, the current structure and practices of climate science are contingent on the particular combinations of disciplines, ideas about science, and political imperatives that have attended its development. Other approaches to climate study could be imagined, especially if models were not assumed to be the most reliable pathway to knowledge. For example, study of the impacts of climate change need not be based only on model results. Another approach is forecasting by analogy: studying how society might be affected by future climate change by examining how it has responded to unusual climate in the past, such as the drought and Dust Bowl conditions in North America during the 1930s.[18] Such a method indicates not just that there are alternatives to models, but that the physical sciences are not the only possible foundation on which to build an understanding of climate change. I return below to the possibility of alternatives to global models as ways of understanding climate change and its implications.

Certain assumptions regarding the relations between science and politics are also embedded in the practice of climate science. These are evident in the work of the Intergovernmental Panel on Climate Change. The IPCC structure includes three working groups. The first assesses the impacts on climate of the accumulation in the atmosphere of carbon dioxide and other trace gases. The second evaluates the potential impacts of climate change on ecosystems and humans, and the possibilities of adapting to change. The third considers strategies for limiting greenhouse gas emissions and examines other policy responses to the scientific results. In addition, the Task Force on National Greenhouse Gas Inventories has developed and encouraged use of standard means of measuring and comparing greenhouse gas emissions. These working groups do not conduct research themselves; they assemble, weigh, validate, and synthesize the accumulated results of climate scientists, establishing the consensus view of the research community. Scientists from about 120 countries produce comprehensive reports on various aspects of climate change and its policy implications; they are backed by about 2,500 scientists who review these reports and certify their rigor and reliability.

The IPCC process has demonstrated the capability of the scientific community to transcend its disciplinary divisions and converge on a consensus view of the world's climate. This process of convergence has been demonstrated through reports published by the Panel in 1990, 1995, and 2001, in which it provided ever more precise prognoses of climate change and its implications. By 1995 IPCC scientists had agreed that "the balance of evidence suggests a discernable human influence on global climate," and by 2001 they had concluded that "most of the warming observed over the past 50 years is attributable to human activity."[19] Model predictions have also converged on a rough consensus: an increase in average global temperature of 1.4 to 5.8° C is expected over the next century; this range is in part the product of different scenarios of greenhouse gas emissions. Studies of the historical record have also found substantial evidence of unprecedented warming, beyond what can be explained by natural variation. This consensus has generated a sizable political reaction: by the IPCC's own account the 1990 report led two years later to the Framework Convention on Climate Change, and the 1995 report laid the basis for the 1997 Kyoto Protocol.[20] It has also generated intensive debate within and between many countries.

Climate Science and Politics

Climate research is expensive. In 2002 the U.S. Global Change Research Program (GCRP) alone had a budget of nearly $1.7 billion, split almost evenly between scientific research and space-based observations.[21] This expenditure can be justified, in part, by the intrinsic scientific interest of the phenomena studied. Its chief rationale, however, is the role scientific knowledge is expected to play in developing policies. The GCRP is presented as providing scientific information that, while "policy-neutral," will "support informed public debate and decision making on climate change and other global environmental issues." The U.S. Climate Change Research Initiative, announced in June 2001, emphasizes a particular focus on "decision-relevant information."[22]

Climate science fulfills several roles in policy. First, it describes the problem: how much climate change has already occurred (as indicated by the historical record), how much is likely to occur (as forecast by climate models), and what the impacts are likely to be on humans and ecosystems (as estimated using models as well as ecological and other forms of information). The political significance of such information is considered to rest on its capacity to motivate action, by demonstrating a global scientific consensus, leading to international negotiations and, ultimately, to agreements such as the Kyoto Protocol. By identifying the impacts of change on specific nations or regions, the science is also expected to build a political constituency for action, one nation at a time.

Second, this research provides a theoretical underpinning for observations and forecasts by explaining the physical processes through which climate change occurs: the sources of greenhouse gases; their behavior in the atmosphere; the interactions between the atmosphere and the oceans, land, and other components of the global climate system; the significance of variations in solar radiation; and so on. Such explanations can seem closer to basic than to applied science, but they nevertheless play an essential political role, by rendering predictions of climate change more persuasive, particularly by grounding the "virtual" results of climate models in a physical reality. This political role is evident in how organizations advocating action often introduce their case with an explanation of the physics of the greenhouse effect. This approach is effective because it is simple and is based on a widely accepted physical fact: greenhouse gases must have an effect, or else our planet would be as cold as space. The accompanying argument that more gases mean more warming has a persuasive logic that is able to cut through uncertainties.

Third, climate research provides not only motivation, but a guide to how to respond to the prospect of climate change. By identifying the major greenhouse gases, their relative importance, and their sources, policymakers can set priorities for their control. Assessments of the impacts of climate change on specific regions are viewed as not only motivating participation but guiding efforts to adapt to whatever changes in climate may be underway. The relative effort devoted to avoiding or adapting to climate change depends on evaluations of the prospects of stabilizing levels of greenhouse gases.

These are the roles, then, that justify investing very large sums in research: they add up, in effect, to raising awareness of climate change—its likelihood, magnitude, and effects—thereby encouraging action. These roles imply a particular relationship between science and politics. In it science has authority as objective knowledge, distinct from political interests and intrigues. This relationship between science and politics is often discussed in terms of an epistemic community: a network of individuals or groups able to make an authoritative claim to policy-relevant knowledge, and that share ideas about the practice of science, the appropriate relation between knowledge and policy, and, often, the nature and urgency of particular environmental problems.[23] Members of an epistemic community need not agree on every detail, but the political authority and influence of that community depends on consensus. An epistemic consensus, theorists have argued, compels action: as evidence of global warming becomes ever more conclusive, nations will respond rationally, becoming ever more willing to make sacrifices to avoid it. Conversely, a lack of consensus, and scientific uncertainty, will be an obstacle to action.[24]

Participants in the IPCC—leaders, authors, and reviewers—constitute the epistemic community seeking to establish a scientific consensus on climate change, and thereby, a compelling rationale for political initiatives. Underpinning this community are shared ideas about the practice of science (such as the value of models and the appropriate inferences to be made on the basis of historical data) and about the appropriate relation between science and politics.

The epistemic communities approach to understanding the relation between science and politics is based on the view that knowledge itself can form a foundation for action: that once scientists form a consensus, others will find their case compelling and will rally around it, creating the institutions, such as a climate treaty, needed to implement it. However, as I noted above, the history and sociology of science have shown how knowledge can be as much a product as an instigator of particular institutional arrangements. For example, forestry scientists—constituting their own epistemic community—create a perspective on forests as economic commodities jointly with the government agencies and corporations that employ them. Similarly, the knowledge that ecologists create regarding ecosystems has been shaped by the institutions within which they work, even as they use this knowledge to justify creation of new kinds of institutions. The key point, as Clark Miller notes with regard to climate science, is that ideas do not act as independent agents: they both help shape and are the products of the institutions within which they are formed.[25] The science of climate change has helped bring the politics into existence, and vice versa.

Climate science today is deeply embedded in political debates. It is invoked by those who seek to mobilize support for controls on greenhouse gases: campaigns of organizations such as Greenpeace and the World Wildlife Fund commonly resemble seminars on the science of global warming (emphasizing the aspects of the science about which certainty is greatest), exemplifying their view that this knowledge is the most persuasive resource they have. On the other hand, scientific evidence is also invoked by those seeking to delay action on climate change; they, however, emphasize its uncertainties. I will discuss the role of science in these debates below. For now, I will simply note the inevitability that science would become embroiled in political debate, given both its political authority and the possibility of challenging this authority, as I discussed in chapter 2. These political roles played by climate science—both encouraging and delaying action—perpetuate the pattern of scientific debates serving as proxies for political and economic conflicts.

Climate science has many other political implications. It is invoked in debates over matters ranging from the appropriate roles of economic incentives (such as carbon taxes and emissions trading) as instruments of environmental governance; the design of energy policies, such as that of the Bush administration; and, in Canada, the division of jurisdiction over natural resources between federal and provincial governments. Scientific representations of the global climate have even been used as the basis for calls for radical change in the global economic and political order, implying a questioning of basic principles of governance, such as the sovereignty of national governments.[26]

The political significance of science is also evident in its role in the pursuit of national interests in climate negotiations. For example, when researchers elsewhere identified India as a major source of methane, the Indian Methane Campaign conducted its own studies and concluded that India's contribution to global methane emissions was in fact much lower.[27] The difference, India's researchers argued, stemmed from closer attention to the specifics of local farming practices and soil characteristics. This result diminished the apparent contribution of India to greenhouse gas emissions, and therefore its obligation to control its emissions. Similarly, Canadian scientists have conducted much research on the role of forests, wetlands, and other ecosystems as carbon sinks, measuring and modeling their rate of carbon sequestration and assessing possibilities for increasing this rate. They have done so to support Canada's view that it should receive credit (as permitted under the terms of the Kyoto Protocol) for the contribution these ecosystems make to removing carbon dioxide from the atmosphere. Because this negotiating strategy is highly controversial (it is uncertain whether carbon sequestration is truly permanent, and some critics view the strategy as simply a way to avoid real reductions in greenhouse gas emissions), research can be essential to imbuing it with enough credibility to be taken seriously in climate negotiations.[28]

Political implications are also evident in how science reshapes how we think about the world. Although often considered the closest we can get to understanding the entire global environment, climate science really focuses on only part of it: changes in concentrations of trace gases, and the implications of these changes for ecosystems and humans. Climate change is also defined as a global issue. Thus the environment becomes defined as the global atmosphere. Creation of the concept of the global environment has changed the meaning of "climate" itself. Displacing the conventional view of climate as a local phenomenon tied to the prevalent weather (a "desert climate" or an "Arctic climate," for instance), scientists, and their models, now define climate as a global phenomenon composed of the physical processes linking atmosphere, oceans, land, and life. This redefinition of weather and climate reminds us how science entails not merely accumulating knowledge about the world, but redefining the conceptual categories by which the world is understood.

The crucial point is that how the world is defined has political implications. First, viewing climate as a global scientific concept implies that it must also be viewed as a global political issue, requiring global treaties and initiatives. This is consistent with a long-standing tendency to define the most critical environmental problems as those that affect the entire world. As Simon Shackley argues, the dominance of global models in climate science reflects their consistency with the logic of globalization and global environmental management. I return to this point below. Second, the redefinition of global environmental change in terms of climate has led to redefinition of many other environmental problems. National and international agencies, as well as environmental organizations and business groups, have seized on climate as the organizing rationale for a range of issues. Initiatives as diverse as insulating homes, curbing urban sprawl, and renewed investment in nuclear power have all been justified in terms of climate change.[29] Whereas in the 1980s tropical deforestation was most often discussed in terms of species extinction or the well-being of the human communities (particularly indigenous peoples) that depend on them, these forests are now more often considered as sources of or sinks for carbon dioxide.[30] Thus, climate change has influenced how we think about a range of environmental issues, even those with no immediate link to the global environment.

Defining environmental change in terms of the global atmosphere has other political implications. It determines who is qualified to make decisions about, or even discuss, the issue. Since only scientists can measure and evaluate the significance of changes in the atmosphere, the environment becomes defined not as a phenomenon accessible to all through untrained observation, but as a strictly scientific matter. The emphasis on developing a "sound scientific basis" for action exemplifies this view of science as the primary means by which the environment is understood, and as the foundation for political initiatives. The privileged status of scientific experts is reinforced by the distinction between the science and the politics of climate change: while scientific information is able to drive the policy agenda, political concerns are not considered to affect research, and the global environment is understood in isolation from its social and political contexts.[31]

This technocratic orientation is evident in the work of the IPCC, which is viewed by its participants and by observers as a primarily scientific organization. The social sciences are also drawn on (but narrowly, with economics predominant), particularly in the work of the third working group on approaches to mitigating climate change.[32] Non-scientists, including representatives from government, business, and nongovernmental organizations, as well as social scientists, are considered important participants because they can enhance the credibility and political relevance of the scientific conclusions while indicating how society will respond to them.[33] Their role, however, is to respond to the scientific conclusions, while the social sciences are subordinate to the natural sciences: they provide information on human activities that affect natural processes, or they work out the social consequences of model predictions. In effect, non-scientists and social scientists are attached to a primarily scientific organization, seeking an understanding of the global environment that is defined in scientific terms.[34]

Such a perspective legitimizes the technocratic assumption that the problem should be addressed by experts rather than through political debate. As Stewart Cohen and his colleagues argue, in as much as a narrow scientific focus on climate change addresses an undifferentiated global "we" and relies exclusively on the authority of science in doing so, "we" are more likely to be spectators than participants.[35] In addition, the perspective commonly adopted in climate science, in which forecasts extend over the next century with little gesture to the shorter timeframes of the political world, implies that the issue is best kept separate from the political sphere.

An Unequal World

In July 1997 the United States Senate voted 95–0 to reject any climate treaty that did not impose obligations on the developing world. The vote expressed one of the most strongly held objections to the Kyoto Protocol, at least in the United States: that it requires only the wealthier nations of the world to cut greenhouse gas emissions. For a decade climate negotiations have been marked by this persistent division: the United States and some other industrialized countries insisting that every nation take responsibility for reducing emissions, with developing nations responding that the problem would not even exist if it were not for industrialized nations' overconsumption of fossil fuels and that therefore the industrialized nations must take responsibility for solving it. Developing countries also argue that wealthier nations can more easily afford to reduce emissions, since much can be attributed to "luxury" purposes, such as excessive use of inefficient motor vehicles. Poorer nations are also disproportionately vulnerable to the consequences of global warming: agriculture accounts for a higher proportion of national income, large numbers of people in coastal areas are at risk from rising sea-levels, and greater poverty implies less capacity to adapt to change. Ultimately, developing nations argue, climate change can be traced to global economic and political inequalities; refusing to acknowledge this smacks of environmental colonialism. Global justice therefore demands that wealthier nations take responsibility for addressing the problem.[36]

Climate science is deeply implicated in these matters of justice and responsibility. In the first instance, of course, these matters arise only if the scientific case for climate change is accepted. In addition, scientific assessment of the relative importance of sources of greenhouse gases—fossil fuel combustion versus other sources, such as clearing of tropical forests, or agriculture—also underpins debate regarding the relative responsibility of developed and developing nations. One early indication of the terms of the debate was provided by a controversy instigated in 1991 by a report of the World Resources Institute that presented the relative contribution of nations to global greenhouse gas production in terms of their net emissions. According to India's Center for Science and the Environment, not only were the figures of questionable accuracy, but they ignored the contexts in which greenhouse gases are produced.[37] Calculating emissions in terms of per capita production, rather than net emissions, would give a fairer sense of relative responsibility. The episode provided an effective demonstration of how statistics that scientists had thought were quite straightforward in fact can have significant political implications.

Such debates relate, more generally, to the challenge of reconciling a single global perspective on climate change with the reality of a world divided by disparities in wealth and power. According to Anil Agarwal, this scientific perspective remains biased toward the concerns of the industrialized nations and further reflects the dominant role played by scientists from these countries. Scientific evidence has been used to exaggerate the responsibility of developing countries by projecting that increases in their greenhouse gas emissions will obviate the benefits of reductions by industrialized nations. This, Agarwal argues, fails to distinguish between the survival emissions of the developing world and the luxury emissions of industrialized nations. According to the dominant scientific perspective, the origins of greenhouse gases are inconsequential: every molecule of carbon dioxide has the same effect, whether produced by a cooking fire in Africa or an idling sport utility vehicle in America. The global perspective of climate models also implies a single, global environmental problem: a common threat to, and the shared responsibility of, an undifferentiated humankind—ignoring inequities, and unequal responsibilities for and vulnerabilities to climate change. Finally, Agarwal notes that relatively little research has been done on the impacts of climate change on poorer countries, even though these countries are much more vulnerable to these impacts.[38]

These features can be traced to how, notwithstanding its global aspirations, climate science is largely funded by wealthier nations, conducted by scientists from these nations, and dominated by their interests and perspectives. Early in the work of the IPCC one critic summarized these concerns:

> With due respect to the work of the IPCC, it must be observed that the developing world is not completely at ease with the contributions of that organization. This is only natural, given the fact that the IPCC reflects the prevailing dominance of the Western countries in the field of scientific observation and study. Western scientists with access to adequate finances and communications are often on the same wavelength, due to frequent intercommunications and meetings. Scientists from developing countries lack these facilities and opportunities. Hence, we hope that the future work of the IPCC will reflect a more balanced composition.[39]

Such sentiments exemplify the suspicion with which developing nations view climate science—suspicion that is often grounded in specific aspects of how the science is applied to climate negotiations. For example, mechanisms intended to provide industrialized nations with more flexible means by which to meet the Kyoto Protocol, including emissions trading and the Clean Development Mechanism (the CDM provides credits to industrialized nations that invest in programs to reduce greenhouse gas emissions in developing countries), fail to address all the concerns of poorer nations. In particular, African countries would be sidelined by the CDM, because they burn so little fossil fuels that there are few opportunities to reduce emissions. Research into flexibility mechanisms therefore addresses the interests of wealthier nations more than those of these poorer nations. In addition, according to critics, studies of the cost of reducing greenhouse gas emissions have ignored differences between the economies of wealthy and poorer nations.[40]

As I have noted, science can be a significant resource for nations pursuing their own interests in climate negotiations. As Miland Kandlikar and Ambuj Sagar note, this is especially evident for a nation like India, a major greenhouse gas producer that is also vulnerable to climate change. India has a large scientific community, but inadequate resources limit its participation in climate science: there is too little access to computers, and there are also obstacles to forming research teams and pursuing a diverse research agenda. A large fraction of Indian research tends to reflect foreign donors' priorities rather than a specifically Indian agenda. For example, studies of greenhouse gas abatement options have been favored over studies of the impacts of climate change and strategies for adaptation, although the latter may be more relevant to India's interests.[41] Globally, the barriers to entry into climate science—both expense and access to expertise—are set very high, placing developing nations at a significant disadvantage. Nongovernmental organizations from the developing world face similar barriers, hindering their participation in climate negotiations.[42]

By funding, and thereby controlling, most climate science, the industrialized nations are able to define their concerns as global priorities. Thus, as Vandana Shiva argues, the "global" in global climate science does not represent universal human interests, but rather a "particular local and parochial interest which has been globalized through the scope of its reach."[43] This distracts attention from the environmental problems of greatest concern to poorer nations: while they affect millions, lack of clean drinking water or decent housing are nevertheless defined as "local" problems. Invisible to simulation models and satellites, such problems are displaced by the single imperative of reducing greenhouse gas emissions. And finally, a reliance on scientific accounts of the global environment steers attention away from the political and economic dimensions of the international environment, such as the impacts of debt and aid, and the exploitation of the environments of poorer nations for the benefit of the wealthy, through trade in toxic wastes, export of unsafe or polluting industrial facilities to poorer nations, and production of cash crops for markets in industrialized nations.

The IPCC has responded to these concerns by subsidizing participation by scientists from developing countries, in an effort to achieve geographical balance among its contributors. Since 1995 the Panel has also focused more attention on regional as well as global consequences of climate change and on understanding national differences in vulnerability and adaptive capabilities. However, critics still suggest that these initiatives fail to overcome a widening gap in climate research between developed and developing countries.[44] At the same time, industrialized nations continue to see attention to political and economic inequalities as part of an agenda that has little to do with climate change. Their preferred focus on proximate causes—that is, on greenhouse gas emissions themselves—will likely continue to be reinforced by scientific research that defines political and economic issues as beyond the scope of investigation.

How Effective Is Climate Science?

Viewed from one perspective, climate science has been quite successful: it has generated conclusive evidence of a warming trend and ever more definitive predictions of climate change and its consequences. The IPCC's success in generating scientific consensus has been impressive: its systematic approach to preparing and reviewing reports has made it a model of rigor, transparency, and credibility. Without its work, public perceptions of changing weather—hot summers, mild winters, drought, and so on—would likely be only scattered observations, lacking significance or influence.

But the purpose of such research is not just to answer interesting scientific problems, or to modify public perceptions, but to assist society in dealing with the complex challenge of climate change. The question to ask, therefore, is one of effectiveness: why has scientific consensus not yet generated a substantial political response? On the one hand, as both national initiatives and international negotiations suggest, scientific knowledge has certainly put the issue on the political agenda. In December 1997 the world's industrialized nations agreed to reduce their emissions of greenhouse gases by 5.2 percent by 2010. But the Kyoto Protocol is still the only international agreement on climate change. It is no more than a modest first step: scientists have suggested that a 60 percent reduction may be necessary to stabilize the global climate. In 2003 there was still doubt that the Protocol would even be ratified, let alone that ratifying nations would fulfill their obligations—and this, after the IPCC had been operating for fifteen years, generating three assessment reports. While the scientific consensus on climate has been widely invoked to justify international negotiations, the specific details of this consensus appear to have been ignored.

As the recent history of climate politics demonstrates, there are many obstacles to effective action, reflecting deep divisions of ideology, economics, and politics. Developing nations remain on the sidelines, and industries and other interest groups continue to resist action. Although in 1996 the United States expressed willingness to take action (a position attributed to the case made by the IPCC in its Second Assessment Report), the Bush Administration's intransigence, resisting even voluntary measures while expanding subsidies for fossil fuel production, suggests that it is no closer to reducing its emissions than it was a decade ago.[45] The irony, of course, is that the United States also funds the world's largest climate research program. This suggests, at least, that the connection between science and action is anything but direct.

The key question, therefore, is why climate science has not yet been politically effective.[46] Most often this has been attributed to uncertainty: scientists have not been able to provide the reliable, precise evidence or predictions that could overcome entrenched resistance to action. Instead, scientific uncertainty has been used as an excuse to wait for more definitive results.[47] As a result, Eugene Skolnikoff, among others, has described reducing uncertainty as essential to addressing the problem, both because uncertainty can be used to justify inaction and because accurate forecasts of climate change and its impacts are needed to plan adaptation and mitigation.[48]

The widespread belief that convincing evidence of climate change, with minimal uncertainties, is necessary for action implies that the best approach would be more research: refining the historical record of climate change, adding details to models, constructing ever more precise predictions. But it is also essential to recognize that uncertainty cannot simply be solved through more science. There are several reasons for this. First, given the complexity of the global climate system, there will always be scientific uncertainties. As I noted in chapter 4, there are many sources of uncertainty in environmental science, some stemming from characteristics of nature and some from how we study nature. In the case of climate research, these uncertainties range from the quantities of greenhouse gases produced (especially from diffuse sources of carbon dioxide such as forest fires; or from rice fields, livestock, and other sources of methane); to doubts concerning the statistical significance of observed increases in temperature; to ambiguities relating to how much of this increase can be attributed to greenhouse gases and not to other phenomena such as cloud cover, ice patterns, or the sun's output of energy. Uncertainty is also unavoidable in predictions of the scale and timing of future climate change. Model outputs are sensitive to small changes in initial conditions or assumptions; different models can yield different regional patterns of climate change, even if they are based on the same scenario of greenhouse gas emissions.[49]

The ecological and economic consequences of climate change are also uncertain.[50] Simply changing the discount rate with which the present value of future outcomes is calculated can dramatically affect estimates of the costs and benefits of reducing greenhouse gases. It is also not possible to predict how society, either collectively or as individuals, will respond to change. For example, there is no consensus regarding the capacity of farmers to adapt. Some experts, including economists, argue that they will adapt very readily, and that the costs of doing so will be minor; others, like some ecologists, suggest there are large obstacles to changing farming practices, and high costs. The disciplinary perspectives underpinning these divergent assessments illustrate how varying assumptions can affect predictions. A similar point can be made regarding contrasting assessments of impacts: while economists tend to view these as minimal, ecologists are usually more pessimistic.[51] And finally, predictions of how society will respond to climate change remain wrapped in uncertainty. Will the United States embrace energy conservation? Will the Chinese continue to rely on coal? Will those nations that have ratified Kyoto live up to their commitments? Will they someday agree to even deeper cuts?

These diverse forms of uncertainty compel recognition that it is not something that can be eliminated through research. It is, rather, an intrinsic property of the varied perspectives relating to climate change (and to environmental issues generally), generating different standards of evidence, different levels of willingness to make decisions, and different interests and preferred outcomes, causing some to minimize and others to emphasize uncertainty.

This also means that we can question the view that uncertainty is the chief obstacle to climate action. Many argue that the evidence is now strong enough to justify action: on this point environmentalists, the nations that have ratified the Kyoto Protocol, and many actors in the private sector, including the insurance industry and even some energy companies, agree. Polls indicate that a majority of citizens in many countries do as well.[52] But as recent political developments have indicated, it is also always possible to identify enough uncertainties to justify a "wait and see" approach, if there are political or economic motivations for doing so. Since 1989 the industry-funded Global Climate Coalition has sought to portray climate science as highly uncertain, particularly by publicizing the ideas of a small number of dissenting scientists.[53] The attention given to contrarian scientists also illustrates how the media, wittingly or unwittingly, can collude with determined efforts to emphasize uncertainty. Opponents of climate action have also sought to discredit climate science generally, denying that models are able to yield objective knowledge or suggesting, as has the Global Climate Coalition, that the IPCC has corrupted the peer review process.[54] On the other hand, while opponents emphasize scientific uncertainties, they attribute greater certainty to predictions, particularly by economists, of the damaging consequences of controlling greenhouse gases.

One response to claims of uncertainty is to exclude from climate studies those factors that are most uncertain, such as economic projections, the outcome of climate negotiations, or the impacts of climate change on specific regions. However, this risks making the science less relevant to political and economic concerns. Ever more precise knowledge of the physical dimensions of climate change—the areas in which greatest precision is possible—does not reduce uncertainties in more contentious and politically relevant dimensions, such as the impacts of change on particular economic interests. In other words, that about which we can be most certain is not necessarily what we need to know to achieve political effectiveness.

More generally, there will never be a time when the scientific evidence is so certain that it can on its own compel decisive action. Unlike simpler challenges, such as the elimination of CFCs, the climate change conundrum will be with us indefinitely—indeed, as long as we have fossil fuels to burn. Scientific uncertainties will also continue to be magnified: as the arguments made by the Global Climate Coalition demonstrate, those opposed to action on climate view it as more effective to question the science than to defend their interests directly. On the other hand, those advocating climate action tend to minimize scientific uncertainties, not least by emphasizing that the greenhouse effect is itself a physical fact. In effect, science serves as a surrogate for political and economic conflict, imparting authority to positions on either side, but at the expense of becoming fully embroiled in these conflicts.

Efforts to reduce uncertainty through more research rely implicitly on the assumption that uncertainty is an objective characteristic of scientific information, that, once reduced below a certain threshold, will cease to obstruct decisive action. But the manipulation of scientific uncertainty—whether by magnifying or minimizing it—suggests a different way of thinking about it: as a concept constructed at the intersection of science and practical politics, framed in the language of science, but shaped by political preferences and values. Nations and other interests interpret scientific information, including its uncertainties, in ways consistent with their own interests. As greater certainty develops in one area of knowledge, debate may simply shift into other areas where uncertainties persist. One demonstration of this was provided by the debate that took place before the Canadian government ratified the Kyoto Protocol in December 2002. The context of this debate was a broad consensus among most parties regarding the science of climate change (even opponents of ratification agreed that climate change was a "real" problem). But this consensus failed to generate agreement on action; rather, the debate simply moved from science to economics, where uncertainties about the costs and benefits of action provided ample opportunities for continued debate.[55]

Recent developments in climate politics have demonstrated how tenuous, in fact, is the link between uncertainty and willingness to take action. It is becoming more difficult to argue that climate change is a mirage; interestingly (if unexpectedly), this growing consensus has now been employed to support arguments opposing action. Bjorn Lomborg's book, *The Skeptical Environmentalist*, attracted much attention when it was published in 2001. Lomborg argued, to the delight of many conservatives, that scientific evidence proved the environment is much cleaner than environmentalists were willing to acknowledge, and that extensive additional efforts to protect it were no longer necessary. With respect to climate change, he argued not that it was unlikely or uncertain, but that it was inevitable, even if the Kyoto Protocol were ratified, and that the costs of cutting emissions would be greater than the costs of adapting to a warmer world.[56] The episode illustrated how, far from encouraging consensus, scientific knowledge can actually strengthen resistance to action, when it is employed as a strategic resource in a political debate. It has even been suggested that predictions of climate change, once accepted as certain and inevitable, may induce not merely a reluctance, but an inability to act. The view of global warming as an unavoidable threat creates a sense of paralysis, as scenarios of a hotter, drier, more disease-ridden world take on the role of an "end of the world" cultural narrative, with society powerless to resist.

Issues of scientific uncertainty and effectiveness have, of course, been brought to the fore by recent American climate policies. Early in 2001 there took place a stark exhibition of science seemingly having no political impact. In January the IPCC stated definitively that the world's climate is warming, at least in part as a result of human activities. Only two months later George W. Bush, newly appointed as president, repudiated the Kyoto Protocol, refusing to commit the United States to reducing greenhouse gas emissions. The inability of a strong statement by most of the world's climate experts to overcome political opposition within the nation that supports the largest climate research program demonstrated how scientific knowledge, no matter how widely accepted, need not compel a response—that it need not, in other words, be politically effective.

But can this failure be attributed to science? It might be argued, as many have, that no scientific advice could overcome entrenched economic or ideo-logical opposition to action. President Bush did invoke shortcomings of science in justifying reluctance to act, citing "the incomplete state of scientific knowl-edge of the causes of, and solutions to, global (climate) change."[57] In response, it was noted that Bush's statement neglected the existence of a substantial sci-entific consensus; it implied, incorrectly, that knowledge of climate change will someday be "complete"; it neglected the opportunity costs associated with fail-ing to act; it also failed to consider how policy decisions are often in fact made on the basis of imperfect evidence.[58]

Inaction, then, can have more to do with how science is manipulated than with the science itself. It is, however, worth considering whether research can be framed so as to forestall invoking uncertainty to justify lack of action. It is possible that if research had proceeded in a different way, focusing not just on reducing uncertainties but on identifying and overcoming the many barriers to action, then action on climate change could have occurred more readily. For ex-ample, the first steps to be taken—the easiest and cheapest actions—could be identified, even if they are imperfect or incomplete. The key point is that when opponents of action invoke uncertainty as a reason for delay, simply seeking to reduce uncertainty is not necessarily the appropriate response.[59] Governments and other parties have failed to take action not because they are waiting for more accurate predictions, or for conclusive evidence that recent warming is anthro-pogenic, but because they perceive that such action would affect their interests, by reducing economic growth or through impacts on specific industries. Focus-ing on uncertainty may therefore be counterproductive if the real obstacles are elsewhere and uncertainty is simply a resource useful in distracting attention from these obstacles.

Scientific certainty, therefore, is not necessarily the linchpin of political effectiveness, and developing a strictly scientific basis for action will be insuf-ficient, even counterproductive. More generally, the model of the policy pro-cess that underpins the IPCC—consensual science generating a rational political response—is unrealistic, because it neglects the extent to which scientific knowl-edge, including uncertainties, will be interpreted to serve specific interests.[60] On the other hand, uncertainty can be a virtue: while knowledge of the general nature and direction of change is valuable, advice that avoids exact predictions may be less susceptible to challenge on the details. Ambiguity can also be help-ful in that it holds imperfectly defined exactly who may gain and who may lose as a result of climate change, helping to make the challenge a unifying rather than a divisive force.[61]

One constructive approach to dealing with uncertainty about the future climate is to address directly perhaps its largest source: emission scenarios. In-stead of attempting to predict the most likely scenario, the IPCC presents the consequences of climate change through a variety of scenarios, based on differ-ent rates of economic and human population growth and on several possible gov-ernment policies affecting greenhouse gas emissions. This approach has not received a great deal of public notice, but it could provide the basis for more open discussion about which scenarios should be pursued, and which avoided. Such an approach would be a step toward choosing a preferred policy option, rather than attempting to forecast which option will actually be followed. And, as in resource management, it can be most beneficial for climate scientists to communicate not just their assessments, but their uncertainties, including estimates of the probabilities of various outcomes, and an account of areas of ignorance, where these probabilities cannot be determined.[62] In the absence of explicit information about uncertainties, users of scientific information may assume (incorrectly) that there is a single possible outcome, not a range of possibilities. Or, more likely, they will draw their own conclusions regarding uncertainties and probabilities, without direct knowledge of the underlying data.

But if more certain evidence and ever more precise predictions are not likely to be politically effective, then what is? Some insights can be drawn from experience with the science and politics of the stratospheric ozone layer. By the late 1980s the scientific community had achieved some consensus: that CFCs catalyze the breakdown of ozone molecules, that ozone depletion could be expected to occur over the next century, and that the likely effects of increased ultraviolet radiation included more cases of cancer and damage to ecosystems. But as Karen Litfin explains, agreement on these broad outlines was accompanied by an absence of consensus on the details: several plausible interpretations of the scientific evidence were available. Nevertheless, an agreement on eliminating CFCs was achieved. Science contributed to this not just through the accumulation of evidence, but by linking this evidence to the imperative of taking action before the worst consequences became evident. The delayed discovery of the ozone "hole" played a key role in forming this link. The fact that the hole was not predicted by models precipitated a sense of crisis, opening the door to framing knowledge in terms of the precautionary approach. It was not, in other words, scientific consensus, but scientific ignorance—that is, models that failed—that set the stage for international cooperation.[63]

Another lesson can be drawn from the debate provoked by publication of the *Limits to Growth* study in 1972. A simple computer model predicted the consequences of increasing human population and resource use: environmental degradation, resource exhaustion, eventual collapse. The model was criticized on a variety of scientific grounds. In political terms, however, it was highly effective, not because of any specific predictions, but as a heuristic tool demonstrating the dangers of exponential growth in a finite world.[64]

The limits to growth debate in the 1970s and the ozone debate in the 1980s demonstrated how science can be politically effective even in the absence of precise predictions or complete consensus. Science may shape policy not through specific predictions, but by influencing attitudes and perspectives, encouraging an appropriate framing of the problem in terms of, for example, the precautionary principle.[65]

How can these ideas about scientific knowledge and political effectiveness be applied to climate change? We can start to answer this by understanding public attitudes toward the environment. According to the anthropologist Willett Kempton and his colleagues, these attitudes should be understood not just in terms of specific concerns and issues, but in terms of "cultural models": perspectives on nature that help people make sense of the world. Underlying the environmental values of many Americans, even when their government is hostile toward environmental protection, is a cultural model of nature as an interdependent, balanced, often delicate system, vulnerable to "chain reactions" triggered by human activities. Such a model implies a cautious approach to such activities because of their potentially unpredictable, irreversible consequences.[66] It is also consistent with evolving scientific views of global environmental problems—from a focus on the impacts of specific human activities to a broader concern about modifying systems: terrestrial ecosystems, the ozone layer, or the climate.[67] (It also underlies resistance to proposals to respond to human modification of the environment by modifying it even more—to counter climate change, for example, by fertilizing the oceans to increase carbon dioxide uptake.)

Cultural models can be especially important in times of crisis, because they are used to help make sense of apparently capricious events. Such events— a severe El Niño, drought, bad hurricane season, even an especially hot summer—can be highly effective, in terms of motivating action, so long as there is a cultural model, grounded in science, that is available to link these events with long-term global change. This was demonstrated in 1988, when many interpreted a very hot summer as an early warning of climate change, encouraging at the Toronto conference that year the first significant political commitment to climate action. (Interestingly, this commitment emerged at a time when the predictions provided by climate modeling were far more vague than those obtained more recently.) Similarly, the political persuasiveness of expectations of more hurricanes or severe weather as a result of climate change may well depend more on awareness of their destructive power and knowledge of the increasing costs of weather-related damage (as tallied by the insurance industry) than on exact predictions of how many hurricanes, and of what severity, will occur. (In fact, the actual evidence that hurricanes have themselves increased in number [as opposed to the trend of increasing damage] is very weak.) In short, the political effectiveness of climate science may depend more on how well it relates to cultural models of the environment, and to popular experience with severe weather, than on precise predictions of the future global climate.

These attitudes toward climate, and toward "unusual" weather, also illustrate the different perspectives of the scientific community and the wider public on what makes for effective science. To scientists, computer models are most effective, for several reasons: they make possible "experiments" on the global climate system, they generate predictions of the future climate, they integrate data from several disciplines, providing the foundation for scientific consensus. In contrast, anecdotal evidence, say of robins and other temperate species observed for the first time above the Arctic Circle, have no such impact. Often, however, it is exactly those kinds of observations that can be most persuasive to the public. Things in places they do not belong suggest there is something strange going on—a suggestion that fits well with cultural models of a fragile nature, and with humans' predilection to be wary of things out of place. Thus, while computer models predicting a warmer climate a century from now can also be important, the impact of such models on public attitudes may depend more on isolated observations than the low scientific status of those observations might warrant.

While a cultural model portraying a fragile nature implies that Americans are open to action on climate change, the resistance of their government indicates that other barriers must be surmounted before climate science can be politically effective. One major barrier is concern for the economic costs of reducing greenhouse gas emissions, especially given that the benefits are apparently more distant and uncertain. This barrier can be surmounted by identifying benefits to climate action that are both more immediate and more certain. This, of course, is the basis of the often invoked "no regrets" approach to climate action: the identification of actions that will deliver definite, measurable benefits even if climate change proves to be illusory. A leading example is energy conservation. Conserving fossil fuels results in less carbon dioxide released, but it has other benefits as well: less acid rain, diminished health impacts from air pollution, less dependence on imported energy, greater energy efficiency, more competitive industry. An advantage of the "no regrets" approach is that it establishes a link between the long-term, global perspective provided by science and actions on smaller, more politically tangible scales. Home energy conservation, for example, cuts fuel bills and makes for a more comfortable house, and yet it is also effective in reducing carbon dioxide emissions. While climate change may be a planetary problem, larger cuts in greenhouse gas emissions may be achieved through countless local actions than through comprehensive global agreement. Ironically, research into alternative energy technologies has dropped considerably in recent years, and this is likely to result in fewer options for addressing climate change. Robert Margolis and Daniel Kammen note the promise of "mundane science": the linking of public support for technological research and development with the need for clean, efficient sources of energy, by supporting not only research, but dissemination and use of new technologies.[68] The International Research Institute for Climate Prediction is pursuing another approach, focused more on bridging the boundary between science and politics by providing guidance for appropriate decisions in the context of climate change.[69]

This distinction between local solutions and global action is one way in which discussions about climate have diverged from discussions about sustainability—an area of environmental discourse that has developed in parallel with, but separate from, global change. The *Our Common Future* report (1987) argued that creativity at the local level would be essential to achieving sustainable development, and this emphasis on local solutions has persisted in sustainability discourse.[70] Such an approach would also be helpful in dealing with climate change, and yet emphasis on local innovation has been given little support or inspiration by climate science perspectives that insist on encompassing the entire globe.

The promise of local action suggests it may be necessary to reconsider how we transfer our scientific understanding of the climate issue to the political sphere. One assumption widely evident in discussions of climate change policy is that science has provided not just a description of the problem, but a template for action. As a recent discussion began: "[c]limate change is a global problem, and dealing successfully with this problem will require the efforts of many nations. Although some climate policies can be implemented unilaterally, international coordination of national efforts is crucial to addressing climate change in the most effective and equitable manner."[71] The description provided by science of the problem is commonly taken as unproblematic; for example, Jonathan Wiener explains that "[r]egulating a global problem is difficult because the institutions of governance are not matched to the spatial scale of the problem."[72]

More generally, the view that action must follow the scientific description of climate as a global issue appears to be based on the assumption that effective policy must be derived from how the problem is understood scientifically, and on the assumption that policy responses to scientific evidence should be generated through processes of rational analysis analogous to those employed in science. As Wiener argues, "through careful analysis an effective and efficient global regulatory regime for climate change can be constructed. A comprehensive, incentive-based, and adaptive regulatory design can be matched to the causal, spatial and temporal complexities of global climate change." He goes on to argue that a global, comprehensive approach to climate change action "attempts to match the regulatory design to the complex environmental system being regulated."[73] But there is much reason to doubt that such an approach will be politically effective. Perceptions of climate change as a global challenge can actually discourage action, if it is believed any initiatives that are less than global will be inconsequential and will put the initiator at a disadvantage. This was the lesson of the 95–0 vote by the U.S. Senate in July 1997. During the floor debate on this resolution, its co-sponsor, Senator Robert Byrd, argued that climate change is a global problem requiring global action.[74] This view has since been reiterated by President Bush. Defining the problem as global imposes a requirement for near unanimity before effective action can begin. It also implies that any domestic initiatives should be national in scope, given the national government's responsibility for foreign affairs, and, more generally, for representing the nation to the world.

Rather than modeling political responses on science, a more effective approach might be to seek a closer match with how environmental problems are understood by non-scientists. This means paying attention to questions of cultural models and scale: thinking of climate in terms of how it is actually experienced—as weather to which we are vulnerable on a daily basis, not long-term trends. This implies shifting the focus of research from reducing long-term uncertainties to reducing our vulnerability to weather events—everything from my insurance agent's backed-up sewer drains to hurricanes.[75] And it also means responding to how environmental solutions are commonly achieved: not through comprehensive approaches, but step by step. The risks involved in incremental-ism include the possibility that the problem may simply be shifted from one me-dium to another, as has occurred with separate laws for air, water, and land pollution, resulting in an endless search for the "ultimate sink."[76] But such an outcome merely indicates how necessary it is that all the consequences of any action be considered. The optimal approach would be to seek comprehensive solutions while encouraging local initiatives and experimentation, acknowledg-ing that greenhouse gas emissions are the products of countless decisions made both locally and on larger scales, both at the time emissions are produced and in the past.[77]

The promise of local initiatives, meaningful both politically and environ-mentally, underlines a central problem of global science. While research has made it possible to look into the next century, it is also necessary, when considering political initiatives, to climb down from this global, long-term approach, to make climate change meaningful at the local level, narrowing the gap between how scientists think of climate (in terms of a global system) and how the public sees it (in terms of the local weather). Most important is the need for local-level in-novation and experimentation, both in adapting to climate change and in reduc-ing emissions, whether through energy efficiency, new technologies, or changes in behavior. This highlights the value of knowledge of the local environment: its climate and ecology; as well as knowledge of local institutions and social and political values.[78] Community nongovernmental organizations most often have just this kind of knowledge, and so can provide an effective link between global politics and local realities, promoting energy conservation, use of public transit, and other initiatives that reduce greenhouse gas emissions. Organizations such as the International Council on Local Environmental Initiatives can also play an essential role in facilitating communication and sharing ideas between communities. This emphasis on local initiatives (and local benefits) also fits well with willingness at the local political level to take action. In Canada, Toronto and Vancouver responded promptly to the call by the 1988 climate conference for a 20 percent reduction in greenhouse gas emissions: both cities adopted this as a goal. In contrast, the national government took nearly fifteen years before tentatively committing to a less ambitious goal, thereby demonstrating how not just misleading, but ineffective it is to define climate change as a global (or na-tional) problem. The many local and state climate initiatives in the United States tell a similar story.

Climate change demands credible science. But it also requires treating sci-entists with less deference, discarding the notion that they alone can identify both the problem and its solution. Instead of isolating climate science from the political process, both those who use scientific knowledge and those affected by decisions made on the basis of science should be brought into the practice of science itself, both in setting its priorities and in considering its conclusions. Linking climate science with the practicalities of everyday life might be the best way of assuring that knowledge of global change is used effectively in creating, and not merely forecasting, our future.

CHAPTER 6

Science in a Risky World

A changing climate raises expectations of hotter summers, flooded coastlines, disrupted agriculture, tropical disease. It is a worrying prospect, but a distant one. Other hazards can seem far more immediate—indeed, as near as the next person coughing. In 2003, many countries experienced such a hazard, in the form of a new illness—Severe Acute Respiratory Syndrome (SARS). The experience can tell us much about the science and politics of risk.

SARS first appeared in November 2002 in Guangdong Province, China, perhaps transferred from a farm animal. Highly contagious, often deadly, it spread rapidly. In late February 2003 a doctor visiting Hong Kong passed it to other hotel guests, who then spread it to Vietnam, Canada, Singapore, and elsewhere. On March 15 the World Health Organization (WHO) issued a worldwide alert, even as Chinese authorities downplayed concerns. By May outbreaks in several countries appeared to be contained. Within China itself, however, the number of new cases and deaths continued to climb, provoking a belated, but massive response: hospitals quarantined, thousands of schools closed, travel severely restricted.

As the scale of the outbreak became evident, scientists mobilized. They made rapid progress: by mid-April the agent had been identified as a new variety of coronavirus, and by May its genetic structure had been worked out and published. Such information was considered essential to developing diagnostic tests, treatments, and, eventually, a vaccine. Health experts became media figures; the phenomenon testified to how scientists can briefly become stars during a crisis.

But rapid scientific progress generated new uncertainties, demonstrating how much remains to be understood about viruses. Many SARS patients apparently lacked the coronavirus. It appeared to come in several strains, and it exhibited different patterns of transmission and effects. Some patients developed a relatively mild illness, but others died, and it was hard to know why, or whether outcomes had something to do with overall health. For some reason children appeared to have greater resistance. Experts disagreed: when in April 2003 the WHO recommended avoiding all but essential travel to Toronto, other experts, in Canada and elsewhere, suggested instead that travelers simply take precautions, such as washing hands frequently.

Translating evolving and uncertain scientific knowledge into practical advice presented one of the toughest challenges. Consider, for example, the problems involved in identifying cases. Was the presence or absence of the coronavirus a reliable indicator? Should anyone from an affected area be considered infected? Or anyone with a fever? How could people distinguish between a case of the sniffles and something more serious? In the absence of solid information many people used ethnicity as the basis for evaluating the hazard and avoided Chinese restaurants and neighborhoods.

But while drawing on scientific knowledge, the crisis also became a political issue. It required not just accurate scientific information, but finding ways of applying it effectively and distributing it in trusted, accessible formats, ensuring that people would take the necessary precautions without panicking. In Vietnam authorities responded promptly, screening, identifying, and isolating everyone potentially infected. Vietnamese health officials showed how a political response was as necessary as advanced science; as one WHO official said: "What you do need is a very high level of political commitment, and that was there from the beginning." In contrast, Chinese authorities' initial failure to acknowledge the problem created a crisis of public confidence. Some officials were fired, including the health minister and the mayor of Beijing. Chinese citizens themselves questioned their leaders' priorities; many asked why China's public health system had been allowed to fall apart, or why leaders apparently valued complacency over effectiveness. Journalists even noted a parallel between SARS and the 1986 Chernobyl explosion: perhaps this crisis would force greater openness in China, as had occurred in the Soviet Union.[1] This deceptively simple virus also raised more general political questions: about the compromise between protecting civil liberties and protecting public health; or about the meaning of globalization in an era when not just ideas and commodities, but unknown diseases, can leap oceans, and someone half a world away is vulnerable to unsanitary conditions in a Guangdong meat market.

SARS does not immediately come to mind as an environmental issue. But the matters of science and politics it raised—the importance of expertise, the implications of scientific uncertainties, the difficulties in translating scientific information into usable form, the many ways (both scientific and political) in which a risk may be viewed—parallel those encountered in efforts to regulate environmental hazards. More than four decades ago Rachel Carson sketched in *Silent Spring* much of the agenda of environmental regulation: the protection of humans from toxic chemicals in air, water, and food, and from the other hazards of industrial society. Ever since, in the "pursuit of safety" the Environmental Protection Agency and other agencies have used risk as an organizing principle, justifying regulatory initiatives in terms of hazards, their effects, and the costs of addressing or ignoring them.[2]

The emergence of risk as an organizing principle in regulating hazards has been tied to three trends in environmental politics. The first has been increasing concern regarding the novel hazards of modern industry. These hazards are seen as novel for several reasons: they affect whole ecosystems; they affect not just specific places, but the entire globe; and they can affect all humans, not just those within a specific group.[3] Together these hazards epitomize the contradictory nature of modern science and technology: as both a source of dangers and a chief means by which we can detect and understand these dangers. The second trend has been the priority attached to protection of human health. While in the 1960s environmental activism and regulatory responses were most often aimed at protecting all species and ecosystems, since the 1970s most American environmental lawmaking and much of the federal environmental research effort has been focused on human health.[4] And finally, there has been the increasing demand, particularly when economic stakes are high, to set priorities by comparing the costs and the benefits of regulating risks.

And indeed, the stakes are often high. Environmental regulations can require substantial investment by industries. The costs of inaction can be as high, or higher—the impacts of air pollution in the United States alone include thousands of lives, and billions of dollars in health costs each year. The indirect costs can be still higher. In the late 1990s decisions made by the British government regarding the risks posed by BSE (mad cow disease) threatened not only citizens' lives, but the viability of entire sectors of the economy, including agriculture and rural tourism. Risk decisions can either damage or restore trust in the competence of government to protect public health and safety. This can have economic implications; it can even affect the perceived legitimacy of a government.

One of the consequences of these high stakes is that risk regulation has come to be defined as a scientific matter. For more than thirty years, scientists have been called on to measure and explain risks and to provide the authority for regulatory action. The objective of risk science is to evaluate potentially hazardous activities and substances; the evaluation produced is to provide the basis for rational decisions. Does, for example, the risk posed by the presence of a potential carcinogen in drinking water justify the expense of modifying treatment processes to remove it? Does the risk of equipment failure or accident at a nuclear power station justify additional safety features? Determining the answers to such questions has come to be defined as the task of experts—toxicologists or engineers, for example—who are considered able to evaluate hazards rationally and objectively, working in a realm that is, ideally at least, free of political distortions.[5] Risk has become the most active arena of environmental science, employing ever more sophisticated techniques for identifying and evaluating risks—analytical equipment that measures contaminants in the parts per billion;

epidemiological studies of large populations extending over many years; computer models that predict the movement of contaminants in the environment—all to meet the heavy demand for expert advice on environmental risks. Since the 1970s quantitative risk assessments have proliferated in environmental and health agencies, becoming the chief means by which regulatory actions are justified, and, as such, the primary link between scientific expertise and political decisions. In countless controversies, science has held the promise of objective, rational solutions, defining the common ground between opposing economic interests and political values.[6]

The status of risk assessment as an objective perspective on environmental hazards is reflected in suggestions that it serve not only to justify regulatory decisions, but to set the regulatory agenda itself. By comparing risks—their urgency, their consequences, and the costs and benefits of addressing them—it would be possible, it has been claimed, to set appropriate priorities for regulatory action, ensuring that resources are spent on the most significant hazards.[7] For example, the National Air Toxics Assessment, the EPA's ongoing evaluation of air pollutants—sources, concentrations, human exposure, and health risks—is intended to ensure that the EPA focuses on the worst hazards first.[8] Using comparative risk assessment as a tool for setting regulatory priorities has had influential champions, including former EPA administrator William Reilly. Some environmentalists also see it as a useful means of insulating regulatory priorities against political pressure.[9] While comparative risk assessment has usually been presented as complementing, not replacing, more explicitly political means of determining priorities, experts usually play the largest role in these exercises.[10]

But the hope implied by this activity—that risk decisions would become matters not of politics, but of rational science—has not been realized. Instead, risk remains an arena of intense political controversies. The science itself of risk has often been at the center of controversies: about the role of expertise in decisions affecting the public or economic interests; about how certain forms of knowledge are defined as authoritative and others as unreliable; and about the interests served by expert knowledge. The view of risk assessment as an expert-driven undertaking in which science is the final arbiter, and in which questions of fact remain distinct from moral or political questions, has often been criticized as inadequate, because it fails to acknowledge that science cannot be separated from questions of values and politics. Risk controversies involving science raise tough questions about the implications of environmental regulation and the appropriate balance between private interests and the public good. Such questions cannot be solved simply through more research.

Risk Assessment as Science

Explanations of risk as a scientific concept often begin with a definition: risk is determined by the absolute hazard posed by a substance, technology, or activity, and by the likelihood of exposure to this hazard. In short, risk equals hazard multiplied by probability. Thus, a significant hazard to which relatively few people are exposed (say, highly toxic conditions within an isolated industrial facility) may turn out to be equivalent, in terms of risk, to a small hazard to which many people are exposed (for example, a low concentration of contaminants in the water supply of a large city). This definition also serves to emphasize the quantitative nature of risk.

Risk assessment can be broken down into four interrelated elements: hazard identification, dose-response assessment, exposure assessment, and risk characterization.[11] To illustrate each of these, we can consider what questions may be asked when assessing the risk posed by a potentially toxic substance.

- *Hazard identification*: What hazard does the substance pose? Is it carcinogenic, or does it have some other impact on human health, or on other species?
- *Dose-response assessment*: What is the quantitative relationship between exposure to the substance and its effects? Does this relationship exhibit a threshold below which there is no effect? Is there a correlation between amount or length of exposure and toxicity?
- *Exposure assessment*: Which populations, or species, are exposed to the substance, for how long, and under what conditions? Is the substance found in particular workplaces? Are residents near an industrial facility exposed? By what routes might the toxin enter the human body? Is the substance in the drinking water of some communities? Is the substance in the air, rendering certain sectors of the population—those exercising, or suffering from asthma, or children, most exposed?
- *Risk characterization*: What conclusions can be drawn from this information? Are there regulatory implications? Should certain individuals be advised to modify their activities? Who should be protected, and why?

Risk assessors use a variety of methods to answer these questions. These methods are in constant evolution, as new techniques—from toxicological assays to molecular epidemiology to population health surveys—are developed. However, they can be described in general terms.

For more familiar hazards, historical data are usually available. Using these data, the risks of traveling by automobile, train, or airplane, for example, can be estimated precisely, because complete statistics are kept on the use of each form of transportation and the frequency of accidents and deaths. When, on the other hand, historical data are lacking, estimates of risk must be derived indirectly. To assess the likelihood of failure of a complex technological system, such as a space shuttle or nuclear reactor, "event trees" can be used. These involve determining what events would need to take place for a failure to occur, and then determining the sum of these probabilities. This is the basic idea of "probabilistic risk assessment," developed decades ago as a way of predicting the effects of failures of small components on the operation of complex aerospace systems such as rockets (it was eventually also applied to nuclear systems).[12]

This type of assessment depends, especially, on the assumption that the probability of failure of any one component is independent of the probability attached to any other component.

Other methods are used in assessing the risks posed by hazardous substances. Computer models simulate movement of contaminants in the environment, in order to predict exposure of human populations. The EPA, like other regulatory agencies, uses complex models able to track the movement of several pollutants, along pathways through a variety of media, as tools to support its regulations. Epidemiology—the analysis of records of illness and mortality in human populations—is used to identify potential health risks and their distribution. Epidemiological studies have determined, for example, that certain occupations and lifestyles pose higher risks for certain diseases, including cancer. Given the multitude of factors that affect human health, epidemiological studies commonly employ highly conservative standards of proof. As a result, the impact of a contaminant or other hazard must be large indeed for it to be visible in epidemiological terms. As David Ozonoff of Boston University notes, "A public health catastrophe is a health effect so powerful . . . that even an epidemiological study can detect it."[13]

Risk information can also be obtained by exposing animals to a hazard and then extrapolating the observed effects to humans. Several sources of uncertainty are inherent in basing risk assessments on animal trials: the extrapolation from animals to humans, which entails assumptions relating to physiological similarities between humans and other species; extrapolation from the high doses usually administered in trials (intended to make any effect more readily apparent) to the low doses usually experienced by humans; and extrapolation from short-term to long-term exposures. When regulations are being set, these uncertainties are usually addressed through the use of safety factors that allow for the possibility of the actual risk being greater than that estimated. For example, the World Health Organization and the Food and Drug Administration apply a 100-fold safety factor to data obtained from animal trials: a safe level of exposure is defined as 1/100 of the level at which no adverse effects are observed. This figure is derived from the assumptions that humans may be up to 10 times more sensitive than experimental animals to a chemical's toxic effects, and that within human populations there may also be up to a 10-fold difference in sensitivity.[14] The use of such safety factors, difficult as they are to justify in strictly empirical terms, exemplifies the importance of expert judgment in risk assessment.

When evaluated scientifically, risk is most often defined narrowly: that is, in terms of human health; and, more narrowly still, in terms of the risk of death or of cancer. The probability of mortality is seen as a measure of risk that cuts across the diversity of human experience and circumstance; it is also something on which the most reliable data are available, in the form of actuarial tables, hospital records, and so on. This focus also parallels the preeminence of health risks in environmental politics that has developed since the 1970s. From toxic contaminants in Great Lakes water and fish, to the risk of pesticide residues in food, to electromagnetic fields generated by electric power lines, the focus of activists and regulatory agencies alike is on human health. As one activist noted: "We are about protecting ourselves, not birds and bees."[15] This also reflects a legal mandate: most American statutes relating to risk, such as the Food and Drug Act and the Toxic Substances Control Act, either encourage or require attention to human health, often specifying cancer.

Obviously, this focus on human health, or on cancer alone, does not capture the range of possible impacts of hazards. Therefore, broader definitions of risk have been devised. In 1990 the EPA's Environmental Science Board suggested that not one, but four types of risk be considered in risk assessment: human mortality and morbidity, and ecological and welfare effects in the broader environment.[16] Since then, this view has received considerable elaboration, as codified in documents such as the EPA's *Guidelines for Ecological Risk Assessment*, released in 1998.[17] This view of risk acknowledges that human health means more than avoidance of death, that protecting human health will not necessarily protect the health of other species, and that ecological risks merit attention alongside those that affect humans. Scientists have suggested that risk assessment can be profitably applied to complex ecological problems, such as the decline of Pacific salmon.[18]

Nevertheless, the application of risk assessment to ecology has been, at best, only tentative. There are several obstacles, even beyond the preoccupation of risk science and politics with effects on humans. One is incomplete knowledge: while there remains much we do not understand regarding factors that affect human health, still less is known of risks to other species or to ecosystems. This reflects both the complexity of ecosystems and the heavy emphasis risk science has traditionally placed on human health—illustrating how research choices can generate areas of ignorance.[19] And in contrast to human health risks, there is less consensus regarding ecological risks: if, as I note in chapter 3, many kinds of change in nature are normal, and there is no scientific consensus on what change counts as damage, then how can these risks be evaluated? Faced with these ambiguities, ecological risk assessment in practice often uses the health of selected species as surrogates for a broader concept of ecological health.[20]

Applying Risk Science

Risk assessment is conventionally understood as part of a broader decision-making process that links scientific information with its regulatory implications. This process, known as risk analysis, is made up of three stages: the science of risk assessment itself, risk management (combining the results of a risk assessment with nonscientific considerations, such as political or economic priorities, in order to make whatever decisions will minimize the risks and maximize the benefits of the technology, substance, or other entity being assessed), and risk communication (the transmittal of the results of this process to the public).[21] The crucial point is that risk assessment is considered as distinct from risk management—a distinction codified in the early 1980s.[22] Thus, while risk assessment seeks to answer a question of fact (what is the risk?), risk management seeks to answer a question of values (what should be done about this risk?). Risk assessment is therefore the province of experts, insulated from the pressure of interest groups, while risk management, as a political activity, involves a wider range of participants. Risk communication, in turn, is viewed as necessary because public understanding of risks is often based not on science, but on subjective perceptions; education therefore will help ensure that the public is aware of actual risks and will make the appropriate rational decisions. As a professional activity, risk communication developed because it was considered necessary to determine how expert assessments could best be communicated so that people would rely on the "true" estimates of risk provided by experts, and not simply on their perceptions. While criticisms of risk communication are common, it retains a substantial following in industry and government.[23]

Underpinning the practice of risk science are certain ideas concerning knowledge: that risk is an objective property of the physical world; that it is therefore amenable to measurement and can serve as a measure of environmental quality; that people everywhere perceive environmental hazards in the same way; and that this way can be revealed by science, overriding historical and cultural differences. In sum, as Carlo Jaeger and his colleagues note, as "approaches for objectively quantifying risk, actuarial analysis, probabilistic risk assessment, and epidemiology/toxicology all assume that risks can be assigned a value of harmfulness independent of the social, economic, political, or cultural context."[24] These ideas have significant implications. First, since knowledge of risks is drawn from science, these risks only exist if they have been described scientifically. Second, the definition of risks as scientific implies that they are manageable: that they can be measured by experts and controlled by regulatory agencies. Thus, failure to manage them can only reflect a deficiency of either knowledge or political will.[25]

The problem with all this, however, is that many risk challenges clearly cannot be reduced to failures of knowledge or will. Defining risk strictly in terms of science hinders efforts to understand this, because it forestalls drawing on our knowledge of the complexity of the science and politics of the environment. That environmental hazards have come to be defined in terms of risk science is less a product of the nature of these hazards than of the political context in which they became matters of concern. Risk assessment developed because it was consistent with the needs of institutions and interest groups involved in environmental issues. For agencies such as the EPA, it promised a means of wrapping its decisions in the authority of science: as the product of objective science, these decisions would be less likely to be overruled as arbitrary and capricious. Thus risk assessment came to be seen, particularly in the United States, as the foundation for rational decision-making: by determining "acceptable risk," administrators of environmental regulation could define their work as a scientific matter isolatable from political controversy.[26] Defining environmental problems in terms of risk also made the problems seem more manageable: the costs of acting or not acting could be more readily compared, rendering the choice of priorities more defensible.

The authority of risk science itself, in turn, was rooted in postwar confidence in scientific expertise, as expressed in a reliance on administrative rationalism across many areas of government activity. And underpinning this attitude was the notion of "objectivity": that facts could be separated from values, and that it was possible, at least in principle, to observe the world undistorted. This constituted, in effect, a territorial claim for the authority of science.[27] This territory was especially firmly held in the United States, where a distrust of institutions, combined with confidence in formal processes, encouraged reliance on the objective, mathematical assessment of risks.

This reliance on expertise in dealing with risks was reinforced in the 1980s, when the Reagan and Bush administrations challenged the very notion of regulation. Environmental agencies were pressured by the "hard look" doctrine of this era to justify regulatory decisions as necessary and reasonable. They did so by accumulating scientific evidence regarding risks, by quantifying uncertainties, and by emphasizing cost-benefit analysis and comparative risk assessment— in short, through formal, quantitative scientific and economic analysis.[28] The result, as Sheila Jasanoff notes, was a paradox: "policy-making in this most open and transparent of political cultures has come to depend most aggressively on abstruse, technical and distancing expert discourses."[29]

Interest groups have had their own reasons for endorsing risk assessment. Defining an issue in terms of risk science enforces a narrow view of it, discouraging those who wish to raise broader political or moral concerns. As a result, industry has seen a clear benefit to basing risk regulation on science: regulatory debates can thereby be more readily influenced, even controlled, by deploying expertise. For example, Monsanto has argued strongly that its controversial products, such as "Round-Up Ready" crops, genetically engineered to tolerate doses of the herbicide Round-Up (also produced by Monsanto), should be evaluated strictly according to scientific criteria. From Monsanto's perspective, allowing nonscientific matters to be raised in the regulatory approval process would raise the cost of getting products approved while shifting the debate beyond areas in which it has developed considerable expertise.[30] Similarly, advocates of free trade have found that defining risk in terms of science can be a useful weapon. For example, the United States has demanded that the European Union accept the import of genetically modified food products unless it can be proved scientifically that they pose an unacceptable risk.[31] Scientists as well have generally supported the use of risk assessment, because of its professional benefits. The view it implies of science as value-free and objective reinforces their own status within environmental administration and within society generally.

Risk Assessment as Controversy

Risk assessment promised a pathway out of political controversies, enabling rational evaluation of hazards and authoritative support for regulatory decisions. But this is not how it has turned out. Across many recent issues, from nuclear power to genetic engineering to synthetic chemicals, risk has become ever more controversial, resisting resolution through science. Risk assessment itself—the supposed antidote to controversy—has been an area of heated dispute, with opposing experts facing off as relentlessly as in any other area of environmental controversy. Originally advocated as the means to restore consensus and legitimacy to public policy, risk assessment now, ironically, undermines the legitimacy of decisions based on it.

One reason for this shift is the inescapability of uncertainty and ignorance. These are rooted, in part, in risk science itself: in the extrapolation from animal trials to human health, in the difficulties inherent in isolating individual risk factors on the basis of complex epidemiological data, or in the challenges involved in understanding hazards whose effects may not be apparent for decades, or may impact humans through multiple pathways. New research results render the scientific basis of regulation chronically unstable.[32] All these sources of uncertainty generate opportunities to challenge the results of risk assessment.

Pervasive uncertainties and ignorance also reflect the nature of contemporary environmental hazards. Highly complex, seemingly intractable, these hazards are often referred to as "wicked" problems: not only is no solution readily apparent, but it is not clear where to look for a solution, or even how to define the problem. Endocrine disruptors are one example of such a problem: widely distributed in the environment and found in many industrial products, such as pesticides, plastics, and detergents, these synthetic chemicals can affect animals, and possibly humans, in minute quantities, disrupting development and fertility in subtle ways.[33] Another example is the safeguarding of high-level radioactive waste. The long controversy over a waste depository at Yucca Mountain, Nevada, has provided many opportunities to demonstrate the challenges involved in assessing the risks of such a facility, not least of which is foreseeing and preparing for changes in geological and hydrological conditions over many thousands of years. Ignorance is inescapable, given the possibility of earthquakes or volcanic activity.[34] A third case is agricultural biotechnology, especially genetically modified organisms, and the risks associated with releasing them into the environment. The variety of possible consequences, both for other crops and for ecosystems generally, render it essentially impossible to predict the outcome of this ongoing experiment.[35] It is no coincidence, of course, that these intractably wicked problems have also been among the most controversial of the last two decades.

Faced with uncertainties and complexities, scientists must exercise judgment in interpreting the information available to them. When they do so, their experience, values, and assumptions—both professional and personal—come into play, shaping, among other things, how the problem is structured: which substances are chosen for analysis, which effects are considered significant, which priorities are expressed in assessment protocols, and so on. Differences in inference guidelines, which specify how missing data should be inferred on the basis of known information, can be important. These guidelines can vary widely between agencies, resulting in substantially different assessments of the same hazard.[36] Disciplinary differences can be significant: epidemiologists may be more reluctant to attribute effects to a given substance (given the difficulties in generating conclusive evidence from their studies) than would toxicologists convinced on the basis of animal trials.

Evaluation of risk can also be affected by whatever stake an expert may have in the outcome of the assessment. For example, an assessment of the risk of a nuclear power plant failure by an expert supportive of nuclear power (perhaps because he had a role in developing it) might include the assumption that the plant was built properly and that its operators will not make any errors. In contrast, an expert critical of nuclear power might take into consideration the possibility of defects or occasional mistakes on the part of plant operators. Disagreements between experts can often be attributed to employment or professional affiliations, with industry scientists tending to apply more risk-tolerant assumptions than do government or academic scientists. For example, toxicologists in industry tend to see chemicals as more benign than do their counterparts in academia and government, and they are less inclined to agree that evidence that a chemical has caused cancer in animals indicates a cancer risk for humans.[37] The importance of these affiliations is reinforced by the long-term relationships often maintained between a regulatory agency and a particular set of consultants or industry experts; as a result, risk assessments by that agency may be disproportionately influenced by the perspectives of these outside experts.[38] In practice, experts tend to underestimate risks associated with specific technologies, simply because they are often closely associated with development and dissemination of that technology. Most nuclear experts work for the nuclear industry, most experts in genetic engineering work for biotechnology corporations, and so on.

Risk assessments of genetically modified crops illustrate the significance of prior assumptions in shaping conclusions. Assessment is focused not on the entire plant, but only on what is produced from the specific gene that has been modified to produce the preferred characteristic (say, resistance to herbicides). The protein produced by that gene is grown by bacteria into which the gene has been inserted; this protein is then purified and fed to rats for a few days. Such a test is founded on the assumptions that insertion of a new gene into an organism will affect only the single protein produced by that gene, and that the gene will produce the same protein even in different genetic or cellular contexts. Both assumptions are contrary to what is known about the complexities of gene expression, including the capacity of a single introduced gene to modify the genetic expression of an entire cell.[39] In general, regulatory science relating to genetically modified products has been typified as rife with such assumptions and values, albeit framed in scientific terms. According to the joint EU–US Biotechnology Consultative Forum, "differences of opinion (on GM risks and benefits) frequently occur in areas where there is a lack of substantial scientific data and evidence, often more as personal interpretations disguised as scientifically validated statements."[40]

Thus, expert judgments and the biases (both scientific and nonscientific) that shape them together refute the notion that risk assessment is based strictly on objective "facts." As Sheila Jasanoff explains, one implication of this is that regulatory agencies are able to shape the outcome of risk assessments by selecting scientists who are more likely to deliver the preferred judgment.[41] Industries can pursue a similar strategy, and they devote considerable effort to identifying and supporting scientists likely to provide assessments consistent with their interests.[42] Divergent expert views are also magnified in an adversarial legal system that pits experts against experts, contradicting each other's assessments, eroding, as I described in chapter 2, the authoritative status of science as objective knowledge. The ultimate outcome is the most incisive criticism of risk assessment: that its claim to be strictly scientific is specious because it relies on so many assumptions and offers so many opportunities for judgment.

Another illustration of how professional perspectives, economic interests, and institutional and disciplinary ties can influence risk assessments is provided by the controversy concerning lead that extended over much of the twentieth century (and which we briefly encountered in the first chapter). When chemical and automobile corporations announced in 1922 that they were starting to put tetraethyl lead into gasoline, some public health officials warned of dangers, and urged delay and study. For several decades, however, a lack of convincing evidence of harm was used to justify postponing elimination of lead from gasoline. Much of the controversy involved not just differences concerning what conclusions should be drawn from uncertain evidence, but disagreements pertaining to the relative value to be placed on industrial production as against public health, and on the level of proof considered necessary before action would be required. Differences over these questions reflected, in part, institutional affiliations: those urging stronger controls were located predominantly in hospitals, while those taking the opposing view were usually found in industry. Disciplinary affiliations were also significant: those who specialized in understanding how lead can be consumed in food, or through inhalation; specialists in occupational health or in biogeochemical cycles; and clinical pediatricians or laboratory researchers, all tended to exhibit different perspectives on the risks posed by lead.[43]

Uncertainties, areas of ignorance, the need to exercise judgment, and disagreements between experts have together generated ample opportunities to challenge risk assessments and the scientific arguments on which they are based. The potential for challenge can perhaps be illustrated most effectively by noting the curious fact that risk assessment has been criticized both as being too cautious and as not cautious enough. Some critics, and particularly those who speak for industry, argue that risk assessment exhibits a bias toward regulation. Certain interpretive assumptions are said to exaggerate risks: that the relation between dose and response is linear, and that there is therefore some risk at any level of exposure (rather than that there is a threshold below which exposure does not result in harm); that human responses will resemble those of the most sensitive animals tested; or that tumors induced in rats or mice must imply a risk of cancer for humans.[44]

On the other hand, those advocating stronger regulations often view risk assessment not as an ally, but as an obstacle. Risk assessments impose a narrow definition of risks. They may fail to consider all the pathways by which the public is exposed to contaminants, the synergistic effects of multiple contaminants, or the greater vulnerability of certain groups, such as children or those with pre-existing medical conditions. Because of their rarity, the significance of singular events may be underestimated, even though such events have been responsible for accidents in the past.[45] Effects are also narrowly defined, often limited to cancer, ignoring such other aspects of human health as chronic illness, let alone effects on other species. Information provided by non-experts, such as members of a community affected by an industrial facility, may be disregarded. Assumptions regarding the level of proof needed to justify action, or the requirement that the benefits of a regulation must be demonstrably greater than its costs (even though benefits are often difficult to measure), may discourage a cautious approach toward suspected hazards.[46] As Frank Fischer notes, one consequence of a bias against regulation is that, typically, a risk conflict entails a government or industry study showing a low level of risk being contested by environmentalists or the public.[47]

These challenges to risk assessment have led many critics to dismiss it as biased and untrustworthy: a specious practice, founded on an uncritical and incorrect view of science as neutral and value-free, and a poor basis for decisions on regulations that affect the health of millions. According to Peter Montague, editor of *Rachel's Environment & Health News*, all "risk assessments are fiction, shot through with assumptions, guesstimates, judgments, and biases—all disguised disingenuously as 'good science.' The only thing that allows risk assessors to hold their heads up in public is that most people don't have the faintest idea what risk assessors do for a living or the consequences their work entails."[48] Some go even further, arguing that risk assessment has been a disaster: "scientifically indefensible, ethically repugnant, and practically inefficient."[49] Even many risk assessors have doubts about their work; one eminent practitioner has noted an emerging consensus within the profession that "risk numbers generally are not credible."[50]

Uncertainty, expert disagreements, loss of credibility—these are serious concerns. For many, however, the problem is not just the science itself, but its political implications. Many critics and commentators have emphasized that risk controversies are usually matters as much of politics as of science, and raise questions extending beyond specific risk assessments.

One of these questions relates to determining how to respond to the conclusions of a risk assessment. How much proof of harm is necessary to justify action? Should the proof be as stringent as is commonly applied in science? Or, as Kristin Shrader-Frechette argues, should other standards of proof apply, since the consequences of not taking action on a real risk may be greater than those encountered if something is done about a hazard that turns out to be exaggerated?[51] How, and by whom, should the precautionary principle be applied to uncertain hazards?

Another essential question relates to determining the appropriate role of risk assessment. Should it be limited to assessing hazards, or can it also contribute to setting priorities for regulation, as advocates of comparative risk assessment have proposed? Many view such a proposal as both unworkable and politically inappropriate. One objection is that it gives more power to agencies and interests that have more access to expertise and diminishes the weight given to public concerns and values (including those of people most affected by a hazard). As such, it is viewed as indicative of the undemocratic tendencies of risk assessment. With participation in risk assessment limited to those able to amass the necessary expertise, environmental and community groups have often felt disenfranchised, excluded from decisions that affect them directly.

Sharpening the concerns of activists and scholars regarding the undemocratic nature of risk assessment is awareness that its political agenda—always present, even if disguised under a cloak of objectivity—may differ from that of the general population. Regulatory agencies have often been perceived to be concealing political choices behind the apparently objective pronouncements of experts, using risk assessments to rationalize decisions already made on other grounds. More generally, as Ulrich Beck argues, the scientific apparatus of risk assessment serves to conceal the political attitudes and choices embedded in modern technology while intimidating citizens.[52] According to this interpretation, risk science, as employed by government and industry, supports the status quo, justifying to the rest of society the preferences of these institutions, often limiting the options considered to those that can be represented in expert terms. More subtly, risk science enforces a particular way of looking at risks, channeling power in society, ruling out other ways of thinking about hazards. It encodes tacit normative and political judgments, not least the notion that choices about technologies can be regarded as value-free and morally neutral, and therefore the appropriate province of specialists.[53] It also implies a single way of viewing the world, and a hierarchy of participation, in which experts are given priority over other citizens. One manifestation of the undemocratic nature of risk assessment is the history of the professional practice of risk communication. Its original aim was not to provide accurate, objective information, still less to encourage informed debate about new technologies; rather, it was to encourage public acceptance.[54] Early risk assessment and communication efforts that focused on nuclear power, such as the 1975 study by the Nuclear Regulatory Commission, Reactor Safety Study: An Assessment of Accident Risk in U.S. Commercial Nuclear Power Plants (more often referred to as the Rasmussen report, or WASH 1400), are now considered to greatly underestimate the risk of a nuclear accident, and so (especially in the light of the 1979 Three Mile Island accident) to be more intent on asserting than investigating the safety of this technology.[55]

A more specific concern relating to the politics of risk assessment is that it implies a kind of environmental triage: some hazards will be addressed, but others may not, especially those for which action cannot be justified through cost-benefit analysis. Such an approach can be considered objectionable on several grounds. It implies that only those aspects of the risk that can be expressed in economic terms will be considered, and that no consequences are beyond comparison or negotiation.[56] But while certain hazards may not be calculated to be significant enough to warrant action, they may nevertheless be of real concern to certain communities, who may view the need for attention to them as beyond argument. At the local level concerns regarding industrial hazards and risks are also evaluated against economic priorities, particularly implications for employment, as well as whatever other values people attach to living in the community; the complexity of these considerations may simply be missed in a risk assessment.[57]

It is well known that poor and minority communities are disproportionately affected by industrial or waste facilities, in large part because these communities, marginalized politically and economically, are less able to protect their own interests. These inequalities can be reinforced by risk assessment processes that privilege expertise and that only consider economic costs and benefits. The failure of risk assessment to consider how risks are imposed on vulnerable populations therefore raises questions of environmental justice. Another concern is that only certain components of the environment, or certain species, will be considered by a risk assessment calculus to be worthy of protection. Such a view is antithetical to an environmental ethic that values all species and ecosystems. Finally, it can be argued that using risk assessment to justify regulatory action places too much emphasis on managing environmental hazards and tends not to explore the possibility of eliminating them entirely.[58] Together, these objections undermine the legitimacy of risk assessment; indeed, critics go so far as to argue that using risk assessment in human health decision-making is "premeditated murder," because it accepts the premise that some people will be permitted to die prematurely in order to achieve certain net benefits.[59]

Attitudes regarding risk assessment are commonly linked to ideas regarding the appropriate relation between government and economic activity. While some see regulation as a reasonable investment in the public good, others consider it an unacceptable infringement on private activities. In the 1980s, and again since 2001, the view that regulations hinder economic activity and infringe on personal rights has been prevalent in the United States, at least within more influential interest groups. This view has also reduced the credibility of regulation and its technical justification. Some argue that risk assessment can reduce the costs of meeting regulations, while others argue that it inflates them (citing the Superfund experience, in which the expense of cleaning up hazardous waste sites has expanded far beyond original estimates). Ideological objections to government have been expressed through insistence that all regulations be subject to cost-benefit analysis—a practice considered likely to justify eliminating many regulations as too costly.[60]

According to Ulrich Beck, these political dimensions only hint at the pervasive importance of risk. Beck has described the contemporary world as a "risk society" in which concerns regarding material scarcity have been displaced (at least in wealthier nations) by a pervasive anxiety regarding the novel implications of industrial technology.[61] Economic inequalities have been superseded by a rough equality in exposure to risks, with even the wealthy no longer able to avoid them: where once they could simply move away, the pervasiveness of modern risks has eliminated that option. The politics of knowledge is central to Beck's perspective. He identifies a growing tension along the "fault line" of the risk society: between those who have and those who lack scientific knowledge. But as scientific expertise has become ever more essential to managing risks, there has also emerged a skepticism toward both science and those institutions that invoke the authority of science. As the public has recognized that environmental problems are the result of corporate and state decisions, including choices regarding the application of science, this has led to a questioning of the nature of technological society, generating tensions between experts and the public. In this context of "reflexive modernization," Beck argues that the claim that science can provide essential guidance breaks down, because it is based on assumptions that cannot be tested through experience: "Science's rationality claim to be able to investigate objectively the hazardousness of risk permanently refutes itself. It is based on a house of cards of speculative assumptions, and moves exclusively within a framework of probability statements, whose prognosis of safety cannot even be refuted by actual accidents."[62] Science cannot even demonstrate the safety of a technology without imposing it, without consent, on society. Having lost so much authority, science, Beck suggests, must become more self-critical, more willing to examine its own assumptions and biases.

Several critiques have been made of Beck's thesis of a risk society. Some stress the problem of generalizing on the basis of a concept that reflects specifically German ideas about risk, government, and society. The skepticism toward scientific authority Beck describes mirrors the diminished status of science in Germany, while his view of risks as pervasive and inescapable reflects the social equality characteristic of northern Europe but not necessarily the rest of the industrialized world. In the United States, where inequality and poverty are more common, disadvantaged communities are more likely to be exposed to hazards (such as lead); and with injustice a common part of local environmental landscapes, the notion that all, regardless of class, are exposed to the most serious risks becomes commensurately less convincing.[63] Frank Fischer, following Brian Wynne, notes another objection to Beck's thesis: that the notion of a new political consciousness generated by pervasive risks still relies, in spite of Beck's comments regarding a reflexive approach to knowledge, on the assumption that these risks actually exist and can be described objectively by science.[64]

A chief consequence of these political dimensions of risk is that debates about the science—for example, over what inferences can be made from the available evidence, or how much proof is enough—may be merely surrogates for debates that should take place about the real issues but often do not. Risk disputes will resist resolution through science because risk is not an objective feature of nature, but a product of its context; with the concept of "risk" itself contested, attempts to regulate it solely on the basis of expert knowledge will inevitably fail. Those questioning the conclusion of a risk assessment (say, those living near the site of a waste facility that has been assessed as safe) may reject not only the technical findings, but the way in which the problem itself was defined and understood. Such objections reflect a recognition that scientific work is unavoidably bound up with its practical consequences, and that how a question is posed usually affects its answer. Parties to a risk dispute are therefore unlikely to be persuaded merely by efforts to enhance the scientific credibility of the assessment.

Experts and the Public

Risk controversies exhibit striking differences between experts and the public in how each understand risks. Paul Slovic in particular has drawn attention to how the public sees some forms of technology and some activities as riskier than do experts. Contrasting views of nuclear power are the paradigmatic case: while nuclear engineers view it as relatively safe, the public has consistently viewed it as risky, even after years of information campaigns designed to build support for it. In contrast, experts view other potential hazards, such as medical x-rays or swimming, as riskier than do non-experts.[65] Other studies have corroborated this difference across the expert/public divide, even allowing for the ambiguities involved in defining who, precisely, are expert in particular risks. As I have noted, it is a pattern repeated in countless risk controversies: official pronouncements of safety, backed by panels of technical experts, are resisted by citizens who insist that the hazard is greater than the experts acknowledge.

To some, this state of affairs suggests a confused or ignorant public that prefers unfounded fears of modern technology to solid scientific information; as Cass Sunstein asserts, "[w]hen they disagree, experts are generally right, and ordinary people are generally wrong."[66] If only, it is thought, citizens had a better understanding of the scientific method, and of the technical details of risk issues, then they might be less susceptible to irrational fears. Perhaps, some have suggested, people resist expertise simply because of the authority it represents, or because they naively wish for a world of zero risk. This view of public concerns has been evident in recent controversies over biotechnology: proponents of genetically engineered food have presented themselves as the victims of smears about "frankenfoods" and "out-of-control" science. The public has been portrayed as ignorant about where food comes from, and therefore as easily taken in by fearmongering industry critics.[67]

In the practice of risk assessment, dismissal of public "irrationality" and "ignorance" have tended to be cloaked in the distinction commonly drawn between "real" risks, as measured objectively by experts, and "perceived" risks, as experienced subjectively by the public.[68] But the implication is the same: only experts are able to understand the actual risks of modern technology. This framing of the expert/public distinction formed the foundation of the fields of risk perception research and risk communication, established to understand the basis of public attitudes toward technology and to determine how the public could be encouraged to respond more appropriately to—that is, to be more readily accepting of—technological innovations. Such attitudes on the part of experts and their employers, whether expressed pejoratively or in the more subtle language of reality versus perception, have rightly been criticized as patronizing and dismissive of genuine public concerns. The result, as Douglas Powell and William Leiss note, has been a breakdown in trust and communication: "experts bemoan the public's irrationality while being repaid with the public's contempt for their indifference and arrogance."[69]

But over the last two decades a more subtle perspective on experts and citizens has been developing, one that views their relationship not as a clash between knowledge and ignorance, or between rationality and emotion, but as an encounter between two very different ways of understanding risk, each with its own set of commitments. While both actively employ science, they do so in different ways, with different objectives and different sets of understandings of how scientific knowledge relates to other forms of knowing the world.[70] We can, following Frank Fischer and other scholars, understand these divergent perspectives in terms of the contrast between technical and cultural rationality.[71]

Technical rationality pursues the ideal of risk decisions being made on the basis of empirical evidence, gathered and evaluated by experts and expressed in universal, quantitative terms. Quantifying risks implies taking a narrower view: asking, for example, about the risk of death, but less often about impacts on human welfare or on other species. It also makes it difficult to account for more complex issues not readily reduced to numbers. Thus, when considering a technology, technical rationality implies asking primarily if it will work, while larger questions—about the need for the technology, for instance, or about whether the institution operating it should be trusted—go unasked. In other words, the political and moral dimensions of risk are taken for granted. However, by avoiding explicit attention to these dimensions, this perspective perpetuates the political and moral commitments of those institutions—in both government and industry—that usually underwrite risk analysis.

In contrast to technical rationality, cultural rationality, sometimes also referred to as an "expanded vocabulary of risk," implies a different way of thinking about the world and the choices it offers. It suggests that people do not calculate risks the way experts do—that is, by evaluating the expected consequences of a course of action and multiplying them by the probability of their occurrence. Instead, they proceed more intuitively: recognizing patterns, classifying alternatives in terms of clusters of values, applying rules of thumb.[72] In doing so they take a broader view of environmental hazards, a view that encompasses aspects of the hazards themselves and how they are encountered. One aspect is whether the risk is voluntary or involuntary: tolerance for chosen risks (such as recreational activities) tends to be higher than for risks imposed by an authority. Another is familiarity: the less known about a risk, because it relates to a technology with which the public has little experience (such as biotechnology) or because the link between the hazard and its consequences is unclear (because of a long period of latency, for example), the less likely it will be considered acceptable. The degree to which the risk involves catastrophe is important: an airplane crash arouses greater concern than do traffic accidents. So is the identity of those affected: risks affecting children will be seen as more significant. Aspects of the risk event itself can be significant: whether undue stress is involved, or if there is a stigma associated with the event.[73]

A perspective grounded in cultural rationality also weighs the broader contexts of a risk: whether the benefits of a technology are shared equitably among those exposed to it, thereby raising questions of environmental justice; or if certain species are especially affected, raising questions of environmental ethics. Whether the benefits and costs can be compared fairly is also important: are they measurable, or too far in the future, or too intangible? Other considerations include appropriate standards of proof, disagreements between experts (which suggest that the assessment of evidence may not be objective, and so encourage a discounting of expert views entirely), the availability of opportunities to participate in risk decisions, and whether options are limited to those that can be represented in expert terms—in short, whether political choices are shielded behind the spurious objectivity of expertise. More generally, cultural rationality is shaped by attitudes regarding authority, whether exercised by scientists, governments, industry, or other powerful actors; and by other symbolic and cognitive elements of culture, including shared values, beliefs, and social practices.

These contexts are also historical: past experience with risks, and with the institutions that create and manage them. This history reflects the importance in its evaluation of not only the information itself, but its source. The public's experience with how experts have tended to dismiss public concerns or to engage in deception has generated considerable distrust. Major institutions, including governments and industry, have a record of denying knowledge of risks, often at the expense of worker safety, public health, or the environment. The tobacco industry's denial of links between smoking, addiction, and disease; the concealment by industry and governments of evidence associating exposure to asbestos with lung disease; obfuscation regarding the risks of nuclear energy—these and other experiences have justified skepticism toward the claims made by powerful interests. So have their responses to those who have raised awareness of hazards, from the dismissal of Rachel Carson as "hysterical" to the biotechnology industry's failure to address concerns about genetically modified organisms. In sum, experience has reinforced expectations of deception, and this influences how the public perceives risk: having heard it before, the public responds skeptically to claims of minimal risk made by government or industry. In contrast, while x-rays and other medical technologies may pose significant health risks, these risks are usually more readily accepted, because people usually trust their own doctor (although experience with malpractice litigation demonstrates how this trust has also been eroded in recent years). In the face of official claims about risks citizens turn to their own experience, asking, as Frank Fischer describes, questions like: What has been our experience with these people? Why are they telling us this? Is there a hidden agenda? Whose interests are at stake? Cultural rationality, constructed from experience, tells citizens who they can and cannot trust; thus a great deal of history can be encapsulated in decisions about risk advice.[74]

With the trustworthiness of institutions in doubt, one outcome can be a reluctance to accept any risk whatsoever, and to deny to experts any status as arbiters of what is and is not acceptable. In contrast, assessments by experts usually take trust in institutions for granted, and so from their perspective risk judgments based on lack of trust can appear irrational; they may even be puzzled by how a risk controversy that appears readily solvable in technical terms nevertheless resists political resolution.[75]

The distinction between technical and cultural rationality demonstrates how risk controversies are not just about risks alone, but about their contexts and implications: their psychological dimensions, the distribution of costs and benefits, experience with institutions (and what this experience teaches about trust and authority), and the relative importance of health and other considerations. Similarly, "perceived" risk is not a simplified or distorted version of "objective" risk, but a more inclusive view that includes objective risk as a component but also includes considerations of value and alternative ways of thinking, as well as sensitivity to aspects of hazards not readily encompassed in technical risk assessments.

Given these diverse cultural and political factors and forms of rationality, perceptions of risk will inevitably vary. This variance has several implications. One is that it renders the role of the expert ambiguous, since different experts may have different views of risk, depending on their ideologies and institutional affiliations, with no straightforward way of demonstrating that one is superior over another. Another is that communication should be oriented toward not merely transmitting quantitative expressions of risks and benefits, but creating shared meaning and trust. Making decisions about risks means finding ways to build common ground through open dialogue. In making these decisions, identifying an "objective" level of hazards and benefits may be less important than ensuring that all views are considered and all parties treated fairly.[76] A third implication is that even after discussion, competing views may still conflict, sometimes for good reasons, such as irreconcilable differences in worldview. It is necessary to acknowledge this diversity rather than argue (as conventional risk assessment does) that there is only one rational way of understanding the world.

In short, "risk" is not just something to be measured, but a political entity demanding discussion. A recent joint American/European study of biotechnology illustrated these complexities, noting that

> judgements about risk cannot be reduced to scientific assessment alone. There are legitimate concerns for which science, at least natural science, cannot provide answers. Such concerns may cover issues of distribution of power and influence, risks of concentration of knowledge and expertise to a few very large corporations, relations between different social groups and classes, between ethics and social values, between large corporations and small companies, between small-scale subsistence farmers and family farmers and the agro-industrial complex, between developed and developing countries. As is true of all technologies with the potential for far-reaching benefits, the societal consequences are far-reaching as well.[77]

No wonder, then, that risk controversies can be so protracted. Often their polarization is accentuated by the different parties' contrasting views of these risks: as scientific or as political. Such polarization has been especially evident in the ongoing dispute between the United States and the European Union regarding the export to Europe of genetically modified foods—an ironic outcome, considering the consensual view adopted by the transatlantic study I just quoted.[78]

Within these controversies, scientific knowledge has no special status: it is simply one of many considerations, and how it is received reflects awareness that there is no such thing as a neutral fact. Instead, people interpret knowledge in the context of their own experience and values, constructing their own understanding of hazards.[79] Cultural rather than technical rationality will be especially relied on in situations where the credibility of government or industry is in doubt, because when citizens expect to be deceived or manipulated the conclusions of a technical risk assessment will, predictably, be viewed with skepticism.[80] Rejection of a technical risk assessment may mean that the quality of the assessment itself is only a secondary concern; the chief issue, rather, is likely the political and cultural assumptions inherent in, but often unstated in, such assessments. In particular, when risk assessment is used as a means of bypassing democratic participation in a decision, the controversy will only be aggravated.

There have been many instances of such an outcome. A classic case was Shell's proposal in 1995 to sink and dispose of its Brent Spar drilling rig, used in the North Sea oil fields. Shell conducted an extensive technical analysis of the implications of sinking it in the Atlantic Ocean, demonstrating, to its own satisfaction at least, that this was the optimum solution. And in strictly technical terms, including the possibility of contaminating the ocean environment, it may have been. However, this analysis failed to consider many political concerns, such as expectations of opportunities for consultation and discussion, suspicions encouraged by secrecy and the possibility of collusion with regulatory agencies, questions regarding scientific uncertainties (including how much contaminants were still in the rig), concerns that a precedent would be set (there are still more than 400 rigs in the North Sea, and all will eventually require disposal), demands that the cumulative impact of disposal of all rigs be considered, and a general sense that the ocean should not be a disposal site for industrial waste. After much controversy, in which Greenpeace played a leading role, Shell was obliged to find another solution.[81] Such an outcome is common when governments or companies apply a narrow technical perspective to risks, ignoring broader concerns, including awareness that this perspective itself incorporates tacit political and moral assumptions.

The Brent Spar case also illustrates how a chief objective of environmentalists and other activist groups can be not simply to question the technical risk assessment, but to redefine the issue itself as political and therefore as requiring debate. One example of this is the work of the Council of Canadians, a nationalist public interest group led by Maude Barlow, to promote a broader view of the debate over biotechnology in the food industry. The Council argues that many public objections to biotechnology, grounded in moral and political concerns not readily reducible to numbers, have been disregarded by regulatory agencies.[82] This strategy has been especially prevalent in recent debates regarding genetic engineering.

In the extreme case, risk controversies can be transformed when what Sheila Jasanoff describes as a "civic dislocation" occurs: a complete breakdown in trust between authorities and the public. Britain experienced this in 1996, when in the face of fears regarding BSE (bovine spongiform encephalopathy, otherwise known as mad cow disease), the British government managed to eliminate its own credibility through repeated assurances (later retracted) that there was no reason for concern. Statements expressing breezy confidence conflicted with people's skepticism toward government pronouncements, compounded by a general awareness that things are rarely so straightforward, and an uneasy feeling that feeding animal byproducts to cows is simply too at odds with the natural order of things for there not to be some consequence.[83] In the context of scientific uncertainty about BSE, the public was also as able as the experts to take sensible precautions (by eating less beef, for example).

There are, in sum, many complexities inherent in the use of science in risk controversies: it provides authoritative descriptions of hazards, but it is also accompanied by awareness that this authority serves certain interests, and that scientific conclusions reflect far more than simply the facts of nature. Risk issues can also be of a complexity irreducible to the terms of a technical risk assessment, with hazards neither of equal concern to all parties, nor understood and assessed by all in the same way. How, then, can science, in all its contested authority, assist society in navigating among these hazards?

Implications for Risk Practice

Reliable scientific knowledge is obviously important in understanding and managing risks. But risk controversies cannot be resolved simply through more information—in fact, more information will often only reinforce opposing views. What is necessary, rather, is to consider other approaches to risk controversies that explicitly acknowledge their political nature, and the value of both technical and cultural rationality. This involves a new kind of relation between experts and the public.

There is no consensus today as to what that relation should be, and continuing controversies over risk illustrate how these diverse views are still being negotiated. Some continue to see risk as a strictly scientific notion and view the public with contempt regarding its ability to understand rational decision-making. Others agree that risk is a scientific concept, but they believe the public will be able to understand and contribute to decisions involving risk if regulatory agencies are able to communicate effectively. Finally, there are those who share the increasingly accepted view of risk as something not measured by science, but constructed by society, of scientific information and other kinds of knowledge as well.

The first requirement of this third view is effective communication: for the meaning of scientific risk assessments to be presented clearly to the public, and for public concerns to be known and respected by risk experts. Scientific information, including uncertainties and probabilities, as well as knowledge gaps and efforts to close these gaps, should be explained in ways that can build trust and credibility. Scientists should also understand how the public frames risk issues, and should address directly citizens' concerns and questions, acknowledging that these are often quite different from those of the experts. It is also necessary to provide the means by which the public can acquire the information and skills necessary to participate in risk decisions.

The importance of communicating scientific information effectively testifies to how science, although not the only requirement for decisions, is certainly essential to the process. To be sure, members of the public do make decisions that by any reasonable calculation appear irrational, and so might benefit from greater awareness of the results of risk assessments. For example, the popularity of sport utility vehicles must have something to do with the perceived safety advantage of surrounding oneself with an extra ton of steel. This perception, however, contradicts data indicating that occupants of SUVs are statistically less safe than those in smaller cars (not to mention, of course, the involuntary risks imposed on occupants of cars that collide with SUVs). In this situation, information about actual risks would appear to be an urgent requirement, not least to counter automobile manufacturers' efforts to reinforce this perception of greater safety.

But effective communication alone is not enough. The view of risk assessment as a political and cultural as well as a scientific phenomenon implies two things: that (as in any other political issue) there may well be disagreement over what actions to take in response to a risk; and that the public has a right to participate in risk decisions. Both imply a need for open discussion of risks. Experience with both success and failure have helped bring about an evolution in attitudes. For example, the lesson learned from a successful effort to locate a hazardous waste treatment facility in Alberta was, according to one observer, that to "assume that the problems to be solved are mainly technical, to undertake a siting program that is mostly technical . . . can also be considered a blunder."[84] In this effort, rather than simply having experts identify the one "best" site (an approach often referred to as DAD: "decide, announce, defend"), the problem of identifying the site was defined as requiring a collaborative approach. Technical information regarding the facility was trusted because it was presented within a transparent process, in which there was ample opportunity for negotiation.[85] On the other hand, Britain's BSE crisis, Jasanoff has explained, showed how "lay questioning, however ignorant or ill-founded, might have led to deeper reflection on the limits of expert knowledge and, in turn, to more collaboration among citizens, scientists and government about how to manage the multiple uncertainties of mad cow disease."[86]

Such lessons have received official imprimatur. In 1996 the National Research Council Committee on Risk Characterization called for redefining traditional risk assessment, combining scientific approaches to hazard identification and characterization with deliberative strategies involving all interested and affected parties. The next year the Presidential/Congressional Commission on Risk Assessment and Risk Management acknowledged the need for public deliberation in defining risk questions, collecting information, and characterizing risks, particularly in situations of complexity and uncertainty: "Increasingly, risk management is being conducted outside of government arenas, by individual citizens, local businesses, workers, industries, farmers, and fishers. This decentralization has resulted in part from the growing recognition that decision-making is improved by the involvement of those affected by risk problems ('stakeholders')."[87] Such pronouncements reflect a shift over the last two decades, especially evident when these views are compared with the National Research Council's 1983 report, *Risk Assessment in the Federal Government*, which viewed public attitudes toward risk as primarily a problem of education.[88] Overall, many risk regulators and scientists have developed an awareness that if risk controversies are to be resolved, and the public is to have confidence that risks are being managed appropriately—that is, that industrial society is no more dangerous than it must be—then risk must be framed in terms of cultural rationality.

There is evidence to suggest that even in the most complex areas of technology the public can play an important role. For example, public knowledge of the risks of nuclear power has been found to complement expert perspectives, encouraging more careful examination of accepted ideas. Long before nuclear experts began to disagree with one another in public, many citizens were questioning expert assumptions about this technology, and this questioning eventually led experts themselves to follow suit. As Fischer notes, expert dissent can be encouraged by public doubt and disaffection.[89]

Playing such a role is, in part, a matter of access to and control over knowledge. Environmental and community groups have found that they can participate most effectively in a controversy by applying their own knowledge and experience to challenging expert advice. Workers have made critical contributions to identifying industrial hazards, as has the general public, including residents living near potential hazards.[90] By mapping and monitoring their own environments, using the Internet and other resources to learn about issues, and developing relationships with sympathetic experts, citizens can intervene more effectively in controversies, challenging how authorities, and their experts, define risk issues and insisting that the tacit judgments that arise in science—about which questions should be studied, what methods should be used, how scientific uncertainty should be interpreted, and so on—be opened up for discussion.[91]

This challenge can extend to the practice of science: instead of relying on specialized expertise, community groups emphasize broad participation, with a close relation seen between democratic access to knowledge and empowerment, equity, and environmental justice.[92] A prominent example is the Center for Health, Environment, and Justice (formerly the Citizens Clearinghouse for Hazardous Waste), which grew out of the Love Canal controversy of the 1980s and now provides community groups with advice on the technical dimensions of hazardous waste. Science, in short, is being held accountable.

"Popular epidemiology" has emerged as a prominent exemplar of democratic access to expertise and of knowledge as an instrument of community empowerment. A form of participatory research, it involves using surveys and other strategies to gather information about local patterns of health and hazards, addressing questions defined by the people, not just by epidemiologists. Woburn, Massachusetts, is the site of a classic instance, in which scientists and citizens assembled information about childhood leukemia, the distribution of water wells, and other environmental conditions to back up their concerns about toxic waste. By drawing on local knowledge of hazards, economic conditions, and patterns in health (such as clusters of disease in some neighborhoods), studies in popular epidemiology are better able than conventional studies to identify links between health and specific occupations or neighborhoods. Not just the results but the process itself is important, as a strategy for political mobilization and for pressuring officials and industry to respond. Without sacrificing scientific rigor, the inescapably political nature of risk assessment is openly acknowledged, making it possible to shape the assessment so as to respond to the community's priorities. Ideally, it can be a transformative, empowering experience.[93]

These experiences—governments finding that privileging authority and expertise only makes risk controversies more difficult, interest groups asserting broader perspectives on risk issues, communities learning about local hazards and becoming empowered to do something about them—have together gener-ated an awareness that risks require not just research, but deliberation. Dealing with risks is best viewed as a collective process in which all interested parties participate in negotiating the definition of the problem, learning more about it, and coming up with solutions, thereby evolving beyond reliance on centralized organizations for regulating risks. Instead, authority is distributed across a wider range of institutions.

In such a process science and politics are intertwined from the start, and both public and expert knowledge and perspectives are considered relevant. This has several advantages: access to a wider range of information (including knowl-edge about local conditions and preferences about which scientists may be un-aware), awareness of a broader range of possible solutions, and, perhaps most crucially, opportunities to build trust among all parties. It also acknowledges that risk is not just a physical entity amenable to expert measurement, but a po-litical phenomenon, constructed out of the diverse experiences and values of ex-perts, other authorities, and the public, that can be understood in many ways. And finally, there is a certain democratic logic: once given the opportunity to discuss their concerns and to gain more information, people have a better idea than do scientists as to which risks are acceptable and which are not; it makes sense, then, for scientists to orient their work to respond to public views, not the other way around.

Such a process needs continuing support—scientific, legal, and political—from higher levels of government, particularly to avoid being captured by local interests. It must also be carefully designed and managed to ensure that all par-ties, especially those that have been historically marginalized, are able to par-ticipate effectively. Questions of representation and due process inevitably arise, and they can erode trust as quickly as can over-reliance on expertise.[94]

PART III

Seeking Effective and Democratic Science

CHAPTER 7

Credible and Effective Science

❧

The preceding chapters have presented a contradictory image of scientific knowledge. On the one hand, this knowledge is clearly essential: we need to know about the world and what we are doing to it if we are to protect ourselves and other species. Without this knowledge we would still be harvesting forests oblivious to the impact on endangered species, heedlessly producing CFCs that erode the ozone layer, and spewing countless contaminants—invisible, but toxic—into lakes and rivers. Investments in environmental science over the last several decades, and the accumulation of environmental laws invoking scientific knowledge, testify to this view of science as the essential basis for environmental policy.

But there is also ample reason to doubt this view of science. As I discussed in chapter 2, there have been many challenges to the authority of science as objective and compelling knowledge, needed to ensure a protected environment. Yes, it can tell us about the ecological impacts of forest harvesting—but many still see the forest industry as a destructive force. Yes, science warned us about CFCs—but we remain unable to address other impacts on the atmosphere, especially the accumulation of greenhouse gases. Yes, we have controlled some contaminants—but there is still ample reason for concern about our toxic environment. And science seems often enough implicated in these unhappy situations: in the form of a narrow managerial ethos expressed through industrial forestry, or in climate science that is unable to overcome barriers to decisive action, or in continuing scientific controversies about contaminants and the risks they present. Many see science not as objective truth, but as an instrument in the service of its patrons, or as a realm in which, in all but the simplest situations, the claims of opposing experts cancel each other out. Deprived of any special status, scientific knowledge is not able to demonstrate why it should have any priority over, say, the clash of competing interest groups in shaping environmental policy.

In the face of these opposing positions—between the view of science as objective knowledge and the view of science as merely politics by other means—one response is to deny that such a conundrum exists. In December 2000, participants gathered for the first National Conference on Science, Policy, and the Environment. With the contested Bush-Gore presidential election a very recent memory, participants might have been expected to reflect on the political nature of numbers. Instead, they merely emphasized in their recommendations the need for more investment in scientific knowledge and for greater efficiency in its transfer to "policymakers" and the public. This was seen even when the discussion turned to very controversial areas of environmental politics, such as the urban environment, biotechnology, and natural resource management. Such recommendations, stressing translation and delivery, exhibit a desire to view scientific knowledge as somehow above politics.[1]

It may be more productive to embrace rather than ignore the political nature of science, by asking how we can ensure that our decisions and policies include appropriate regard for what we know about the world, even as we are aware that this knowledge is often uncertain and bound up with our values and interests. In other words, if science is not simply a source of objective facts about nature, how can it nevertheless play an appropriate role in environmental politics, ensuring, as numerous recent writers phrase it, that institutions and society are able to learn and to act effectively?

When we think about the problem in terms of effectiveness, our attention is drawn to two aspects of the relation between scientific knowledge and society. The first is credibility: the extent to which science is recognized as a source of reliable knowledge about the world, and not simply as, say, random observations, or an expression of the preferences of a particular interest group. The second is influence: whether science is actually able to affect the decisions and actions of those involved in environmental issues. Together, these two aspects constitute the necessary conditions for an effective role for science in environmental politics. They are themselves dependent on other aspects of science, such as relevance and effective communication.

In Search of Credibility

If we want to understand how science can be so important and yet so ineffective in environmental affairs, the best place to start is any controversy in which opposing interests face off against each other, wielding competing scientific assessments. These assessments should immediately alert us to a problem: when a controversy is defined as a matter of competing scientific views, the underlying political, economic, or ethical issues—that is, what the controversy is really about—will be neglected. Instead of discussing whether a certain forest should be preserved in its natural state or harvested for timber, opponents face off over competing assessments of the ecological impacts of timber cutting. Rather than debating the role of fossil fuels in our energy supply, attention is stuck on uncertainties in climate models. Questions of who should take responsibility for industrial hazards take a back seat to the search for weak points in opposing risk assessments. In each situation, scientific knowledge deployed by one interest is portrayed by its opponents as not credible. This exemplifies, as I discussed in chapter 2, the particular challenge to scientific knowledge in adversarial contexts. Opposing interests highlight uncertainties in the evidence, discrepancies and ambiguities in interpretations, ties between scientists and economic or political interests, and any other technical aspects of the problem that can provide an opportunity to question the credibility of scientific practice. Ultimately, resolution of the controversy may occur not through agreement on the most reasonable or acceptable course of action, but through the ability of one interest to impose its preference on the other.

Such situations illustrate how reasonable argument and agreement on a course of action are impossible in the absence of facts accepted by all parties. This does not imply that complete consensus is necessary on every detail; however, without at least a core of facts and ideas that all consider credible, albeit subject to revision as new information is gained, productive conversation simply cannot begin. In the absence of such agreement, debates about issues with scientific content will tend to devolve into unproductive disputes about whether the science itself is credible. How, then, can the credibility of science be assured, particularly in those contexts in which it is challenged most vociferously?

The strategy most often used involves offering assurance that knowledge has been produced through procedures considered credible by the scientific community itself. This strategy is peer review. Its foundation is the notion that scientists know things about the practice and products of research that nonscientists—politicians, interest groups, or the public—do not, and that they are, therefore, best able to evaluate its quality. Only scientists, by this view, know what kinds of questions about scientific method and reasoning need to be asked when reviewing a piece of research. For example, does the research meet accepted standards of objectivity, completeness, reproducibility, accuracy, and precision? Are the data, methods, arguments, and other components sound and reliable? Are the conclusions clearly expressed and related to existing knowledge of the topic?

We can trace the practice of peer review back to the first formal scientific journals: the *Philosophical Transactions of the Royal Society* and the *Journale des Sçavans*, both of which first appeared in 1665. Since then, peer review has become the sine qua non of scientific journals: each article submitted is sent to two or more scientists knowledgeable about the topic, who consider whether the methods are appropriate, the data interpreted correctly, the conclusions reasonable, and so on. Peer review is used not only in evaluating the products of research, but in setting the research agenda: grant applications to funding agencies such as the National Science Foundation are commonly evaluated by individual scientists or by committees; each application is ranked according to both its intrinsic merits and the likelihood of the research contributing meaningfully to the progress of the discipline. Peer review thus constitutes a chief mechanism by which the scientific community asserts its status as a self-governing entity, able to set its own priorities and standards and willing to police the boundary between professional and amateur. Within this community, peer review also commonly serves to ensure that new knowledge fulfills the requirements regarding methods, evidence, and forms of reasoning that are specific to particular disciplines.[2]

What is noteworthy, however, is how the practice of peer review, pervasive in basic research, has over the last three decades been transferred into the realm of science-based environmental regulation. The logic is straightforward: just as peer review is considered to be an efficient means of assuring the quality, and therefore the credibility, of basic research, so too, it is believed, can it be applied to certifying the credibility of science in environmental affairs. This view is widely held, within both regulatory agencies and interest groups. As Sheila Jasanoff describes, a consensus emerged within the Environmental Protection Agency, in the wake of frequent challenges to its regulatory decisions, that the scientific community should play a larger role in assuring the credibility of the agency. This would be accomplished by subjecting the scientific basis for regulations to systematic peer review.[3] Agency accounts of its science now commonly stress that all research activities and results are peer-reviewed. Peer review is also widely applied in natural resource management: the Magnuson Stevens Fisheries Conservation and Management Act calls for the use of peer review in sorting out disputes over fisheries harvest levels, while the Forest Service supports peer review of forest management decisions. Peer review is also central to efforts to reform the Endangered Species Act.[4] Internationally, an elaborate and formal process of peer review has become a foundation for the work of the Intergovernmental Panel on Climate Change, where it is considered essential for assuring not just the scientific credibility and authority of the panel's reports, but their political acceptability as well. Indeed, the IPCC's peer review practices have gone beyond the relatively informal routines of the scientific community: it employs strict and explicit rules for the review of results, in keeping with the policy community's expectations of formal procedures.[5]

As the experience of the IPCC implies, much of the impetus for peer review has come from outside the scientific community. This extends to domestic issues: for example, one survey found at least sixty groups, representing a range of interests, expressing support for subjecting applications of the Endangered Species Act to scientific review. Such attitudes stem from the view that peer review can be a means of ensuring that decisions are more objective, less under the control of one particular agency, and less vulnerable to litigation.[6] Indeed, a decision by an agency may only be accepted by interested parties once it has been certified as credible by scientists from outside that agency. An agency can also enhance its reputation for expertise, and its overall scientific credibility, by supporting basic research: in effect permitting some of its scientific work to be conducted in response to priorities set through disciplinary peer review, rather than in response to immediate political or regulatory pressures.[7] And environmental organizations such as Greenpeace and the World Wildlife Fund also use peer review to help assure the credibility of their arguments.[8] In contrast, research that is not subjected to peer review can be especially vulnerable to criticism. Some of the most effective attacks on the credibility of industrial research emphasize that, as proprietary knowledge, it is inaccessible to review by independent scientists.

On the other hand, the capacity of peer review to assure the credibility of science has also been questioned. Studies of peer review have judged it a failure as a dependable indicator of research quality: the likelihood of agreement between referees on the quality of an article is usually only slightly better than chance.[9] And in addition to problems with quality assurance, misconduct and fraud have been encountered within research institutions that live by the ethos of peer review, forcing the realization that it is far from foolproof as a method for ensuring credible science. Peer review cannot reliably detect fraudulent research. Nor can it detect the influence of government and corporate funding of research. As I noted in chapter 2, industry-sponsored studies are more likely to generate results favorable to the sponsor than are non-industry studies. This is not necessarily because such studies are of lower quality, perhaps because of inappropriate methods or large numbers of errors (shortcomings that are detectable through peer review), but because there are many opportunities to design research questions and techniques in ways that subtly favor the desired outcome.[10] The inability of peer review to detect this influence is tacitly acknowledged by recent initiatives by several biomedical journals to require authors to disclose financial relationships with the producers of the therapeutic products, particularly pharmaceuticals, they are assessing.

The shortcomings of peer review stem from several factors. Most obviously, the quality of a review depends on the competence and care of the reviewer. Not all scientists can do it well, or will devote the necessary time, or will be able to complete the task satisfactorily under the pressure of controversy or tight regulatory deadlines. Personal and political factors can affect a review, particularly in smaller research communities in which anonymous review cannot always be assured (and many publications inform reviewers of the identity of the author). Peer reviewers often fail to be objective, giving preferential treatment to authors they know. Such problems reflect a breakdown of the trust inherent in the peer review process—that scientists will adhere to a code of professional ethics that mandates a fair and conscientious effort. Peer review can also tend to discourage publication of innovative, unusual, or challenging ideas, instead favoring studies that confirm existing beliefs.[11]

The fundamental assumption of peer review—that there exist certain objective standards of quality that most scientific peers are able to enforce—can also be questioned. It may hold when there is agreement about theories, methods, and goals, but it breaks down when there is not. When the knowledge base is contested, disciplinary divisions are deep, and there is no agreement on what questions should be asked, let alone what the right answers would look like—in short, when there is no consensus on what is "good" science—deciding whether a particular piece of work is acceptable becomes a matter of negotiation and compromise.

Difficulties with peer review can be especially significant in political and administrative contexts, when decisions regarding regulations or management must often be made quickly, on the basis of knowledge that lies at or beyond the margins of scientific consensus, where clear guidelines for evaluation are not yet available, and where non-scientific considerations play a large role. Differences in the cultures of research science and regulatory science make it unlikely that peer review can provide an authoritative, indisputable check on the science used in making decisions, or that these decisions can through review be somehow lifted beyond politics. Scientists are also often reluctant to participate as reviewers in these contexts: there may be little professional benefit, and there are disincentives to becoming involved in what may be a highly politicized process. The result can be that a disproportionate number of the scientists who choose to become involved also have some particular interest in the issue. And, given the numerous opportunities for bias in expert assessment of risks (as in other areas of environmental science), these biases can be perpetuated through the application of peer review to regulatory decisions. Peer review can thus be readily manipulated: it may be selectively invoked by a party seeking to challenge a decision with which it disagrees, or the process may be co-opted, and the outcome shaped, by stacking the deck: selecting reviewers with the appropriate disciplinary and professional backgrounds, to examine evidence and arguments themselves carefully chosen to render more likely the evaluation sought.[12]

A further difficulty inherent in applying the peer review process within political contexts is the implicit assumption that environmental issues are entirely scientific in nature. Of course they are not; but subjecting decisions to scientific review can make it more difficult to weigh appropriately their non-scientific dimensions. The consequence can be confusion and continued disputes, as Deborah Brosnan notes has occurred in various controversies involving endangered species and habitat conservation. For example, in Tongass National Forest independent reviewers made various recommendations regarding how the forest should be managed that were based on scientific evidence alone. These recommendations differed from those provided by a team of internal reviewers, and the difference only undermined public confidence in whatever decisions might eventually be made. The Oregon Department of Forestry encountered a related problem: when it asked twenty-three independent scientists to review a habitat plan, the result was not one, but several views of the plan's merits, which only deepened confusion.[13] These outcomes parallel those of other efforts to define and resolve environmental controversies in strictly scientific terms. One such effort was experiments in the late 1970s with a "science court": a panel of scientists that would apply the rigor of science and the practices of the courtroom, including rules of procedure and cross-examination, to the review of technical arguments behind conflicting policy or regulatory proposals. The effort foundered when too few participants accepted that truly impartial scientists could be found to serve as judges.[14]

The common elements in these experiences are two assumptions that underlie the application of peer review in the political sphere: that science can provide a single "right" answer to complex questions, once appropriate quality control is applied; and that science can be the instrument by which these questions can be lifted above clashing interests and perspectives—that is, above politics. As the experiences of numerous agencies confirm, these assumptions are fallacious.

Nevertheless, peer review can fulfill a vital function in science and politics. The success of the Intergovernmental Panel on Climate Change in providing a widely accepted understanding of this complex problem demonstrates this. As Paul Edwards and Stephen Schneider argue, the key is to acknowledge that peer review is fallible: it cannot function as a kind of "truth machine," able to prevent all error, to encourage every useful idea, to foster a convergence on the scientific truth, or to indicate the correct path for society.[15] What it can do is enhance the accountability of science by fulfilling a "witnessing" function: improving the quality of scientific work by catching errors and questioning assumptions; and moderating the influence of personal, social, and political factors, encouraging scientists to consider unfamiliar but relevant ideas and approaches while building a scientific community that shares certain core principles and beliefs. I have drawn a similar lesson from my experience as a journal editor. Receiving peer reviews for nearly 200 papers over the last three years, I have found that reviewers often disagree on whether a paper should be accepted or rejected. Rather than considering this outcome as invalidating the process (as a view of peer review as a "truth machine" might imply), I have found it more productive to draw on the useful counsel usually found in both negative and positive reviews, and to advise the author accordingly as to how the paper might be improved. Particularly in interdisciplinary or political contexts (often these are found together), this function can imply reconsidering the structure of peer review itself: rather than relying on individual reviewers, groups of experts with diverse skills, as independent as possible of whatever interests are at stake, may be more likely to fulfill this witnessing function impartially.[16]

In environmental controversies involving, as they often do, substantial political or economic stakes, the credibility of scientific knowledge will depend not just on the imprimatur of peer review, but on perceptions of the relations between scientists and interest groups. This can apply to either side of an environmental issue. For example, in the acid rain controversy of the 1980s, some scientists were accused of politicizing science by tying it closely to their advocacy of action on the problem. On the other side of the issue, a 1987 report by the National Acid Precipitation Assessment Program was criticized for providing a distorted view of the science, because its advice mirrored too closely the preferences of an American government that wished to avoid taking action.[17]

More recently, governments involved in, or supporting research in, economically promising areas such as biotechnology have been seen as less credible sources of information about those areas.[18] Contract research conducted for economic interests will often be viewed as less objective and less credible than research done by independent scientists. As I noted in the previous chapter, the ties between researchers and economic interests involved in risk controversies often generate suspicion and distrust of the science itself. In particular, research done by industry scientists is often considered the least credible because of the perception that such research is shaped by the interests of that industry—a perception backed up by a lengthy record of manipulation of research by industry.[19]

In contrast, research conducted by university scientists and funded by independent granting agencies such as the National Science Foundation or the Natural Sciences and Engineering Research Council of Canada is more readily considered credible. This is a product of not just the peer review these agencies employ, but their broader image of independence from economic interests. Expert panels organized by the National Academy of Sciences and by other institutions enjoy a similar level of credibility, derived at least in part from their reputation for independence. For their part, industry interests have, as I noted in chapter 2, often sought to reinforce the credibility of their research by creating research institutions that, while still funded by industry, can maintain at least the appearance of independence. One example of such an institution is the National Center for Food and Agricultural Policy. While it receives much of its funding from the biotechnology industry, and has demonstrated a willingness to shape its research so as to generate results consistent with industry interests, it has nevertheless been described in the media as a "nonpartisan" independent research agency.[20]

While perceptions of ties between science and interests can mean a loss of credibility, that does not mean that preserving credibility requires scientists to avoid expressing any political position, to instead maintain a stance of pure objectivity. After all, Rachel Carson exerted tremendous influence in the 1960s with a message that effectively combined science and its political implications. Since then, numerous scientists have taken political positions, on the national or international stage, or by participating in local controversies, with their clout as scientists recognized by other actors. For example, during a recent controversy regarding suburban development in Toronto, activists opposing development assembled a petition of support signed by 450 scientists. They did so because, as one activist put it, "[i[t's easy for politicians to say 'oh yeah it's just a bunch of environmentalists,' but now to get scientific specialists on board carries a lot more weight."[21] The emergence and influence of "movement scientists" demonstrates that credibility, and therefore influence, is not determined by some naive notion of objectivity. While some have argued that scientists who take a political position abuse their public trust in doing so (an argument likely made most often by those who oppose that position), such arguments are balanced by the assertion that scientists should not be disenfranchised as citizens simply because of their status as experts, or even that they have a moral responsibility, as possessors of essential information, to participate politically.

Nevertheless, scientists do put themselves in a vulnerable position when they draw political conclusions from their research, because it provides an opening opponents can use to cast doubt on the credibility of the scientific knowledge itself. This doubt can be more persuasive if the conclusions can be portrayed as not only derived from the knowledge itself, but shaped by the institutional affiliation of the scientist—whether it is a contract between the scientist and a corporation, or the scientist's membership in an environmental organization. Such affiliations diminish the credibility of research because opponents can claim that its conclusions were not subjected to critical examination, and will not be open to revision if new results arrive. In other words, loss of credibility engendered by ties between science and interests can be based not only on the possibility that the science was shaped by these interests, but that these ties prevented open, independent review. One response to this would be to acknowledge openly, as did Carson, that certain values informed the interpretation of the science. As its opening fable made clear, *Silent Spring* was as much a celebration of the wonder of life, and an evocation of fear over its fate, as it was a presentation of scientific evidence. And such frankness can be the strongest guarantor of trustworthiness.

An alternative approach to demands for credible scientific knowledge is represented by numerous recent proposals for independent scientific institutions. William Leiss, among others, has proposed that rather than rely on in-house and industry-based expertise for knowledge about risks, regulatory agencies should instead draw on the expertise of scientific bodies that are independent of government and industry (perhaps based in universities), and that would make public all their scientific conclusions. Such an arrangement would, in effect, enforce an institutional separation between science and politics, allowing a clearer distinction between knowledge and its regulatory implications, forcing the process of drawing these implications to become more transparent. This transparent process would, Leiss argues, give governments less "wiggle room" in their decisions about risk.[22] Canadian fisheries scientists made a similar proposal after the collapse of the Newfoundland cod fishery, which they attributed to political interference with the science. They argued that the credibility of fisheries science could best be restored by creating a research institution that would be independent of the resource management agency.[23]

Such proposals emulate existing institutions created to provide a single, unified source of expertise in a particular area, a source that could reduce manipulation and conflicts regarding knowledge. Examples of this type of structure range from the Intergovernmental Panel on Climate Change to the International Council on Radiation Protection. The creation in 2002 of the European Food Safety Authority testifies to the widely perceived need on that continent for independent scientific expertise, after several years of intense controversy over BSE and genetically modified foods.[24] Another example, in the United States, is the Health Effects Institute: it conducts research on air pollution, receiving funding from both government and the auto industry, while maintaining its independence. The interests that support this institute do so because they see value in a single knowledge base, insulated (but not isolated) from the regulatory process, and considered scientifically credible (through peer review of research) by all parties.[25]

However, such arrangements are not a panacea for every controversy. Several conditions must be met. All parties must agree that the issue itself requires research, and that their interests (particularly of those parties able to fund their own research) are not served better through proprietary relationships with scientists. (It is difficult to conceive, for example, of the biotechnology industry entering freely into an arrangement whereby its present dominance over research in this field would be diluted.) Nor are such arrangements necessarily always successful in developing a consensus on "the facts." Samuel Hays notes several failed efforts to develop a comprehensive scientific understanding of a contentious issue, including the National Coal Policy Project, and the Timber, Wildlife, and Fish (TWF) process in Washington State.[26] Such outcomes reflect, among other factors, the diverse criteria by which different interests and institutions assess the credibility of research: varying standards of proof, methodological preferences, or approaches to weighing economic and environmental priorities can make it very difficult for a single inquiry to satisfy all interests.

Another problem is that research arrangements supported by several interests may nevertheless fail to represent all interests, and might, in fact, advance only one perspective on a contentious issue. This has been the experience with research on salmon aquaculture in British Columbia. While several research programs have been developed through the cooperation of industry, governments, and universities, they nevertheless privilege one option: continued expansion of the aquaculture industry, rather than alternative approaches to managing and protecting salmon. As a result, these programs have failed to gain the confidence of fishers, communities, and salmon consumers.[27]

What lessons can we draw from the capacity, partial at best, of peer review and independent research institutions to assure the credibility of science? One lesson, perhaps, is that credibility is determined not just within the scientific community, or within the institutions that apply scientific knowledge, but within society itself, among the interest groups and communities that define the terrain of environmental politics. Within this context, scientific credibility is often determined not so much by the merits of the scientific information itself as by scientists' attitudes toward other forms of knowledge, and particularly the knowledge of people most directly affected by or aware of the problem or issue. Charles Lindblom and David Cohen provide a useful definition of this lay knowledge: "knowledge that does not owe its origin, testing, degree of verification, truth, status, or currency to distinctive . . . professional techniques, but rather to common sense, casual empiricism, or thoughtful speculation or analysis."[28]

How scientists respond to this knowledge—with arrogance or with open

minds—is crucial. When scientists dismiss lay or local knowledge, they risk losing credibility among those who hold this knowledge. Conversely, openness toward it will enhance their credibility. There are pragmatic reasons for this: such
knowledge can be essential to understanding and solving environmental problems, given that such problems (for example, health concerns provoked by a hazardous waste site) often gain their significance as a result of local conditions
that only residents may be fully aware of. Relying only on scientific knowledge
excludes experiential and other forms of knowledge held by the public that can
be a valuable and relevant source of insights.[29] More generally, awareness of
this knowledge is necessary in order to understand how people view and think
about their environment—that is, their cultural rationality. A common feature
of local knowledge is the capacity to manage within the context of an irregular
and varying environment: exercising an ability to be flexible, to be open to uncertainty, to adapt rather than attempt to standardize environmental conditions.[30]
Such attributes suggest a need to challenge the assumption that knowledge that
can be "generalized" and applied to any situation is always of higher value than
the specific, local knowledge of citizens. Acknowledging and understanding local
knowledge is also essential to maintaining or restoring trust and mutual respect
between scientists and citizens. And finally, this acknowledgment can be part
of scientists' becoming more aware of how their knowledge fits in relation to
other ways of understanding the world. According to Sandra Harding, scientists
could become more credible by acknowledging that all scientific knowledge is
the product of a particular perspective: what one sees is shaped by where one
stands. Greater awareness of this, and a serious effort to understand alternative
perspectives, could then enable scientists and their patrons to view their own
science more objectively.[31]

Brian Wynne demonstrates the damage that can be done to scientific credibility by a failure to recognize local knowledge in his study of the relations
between experts and sheep farmers in England's Lake District after the Chernobyl
reactor explosion sent radioactive contamination across western Europe. The
farmers noticed immediately how ill-informed the experts sent to advise them
were about both sheep farming and the local environment, and how they also
failed to acknowledge that the farmers themselves had a great deal of knowledge about these topics, as well as a broader familiarity with how to make decisions in this ever-changing environment, by seeking not certainty and control,
but to adapt to uncertainties. The farmers, predisposed already to distrust authority because of the history of secrecy surrounding the nearby Sellafield
nuclear station, quickly came to be skeptical of, and even to ridicule, these outside experts. In effect, both scientists and farmers recognized as credible only
those claims made within their own cultural style: either standardized general
knowledge, or familiarity with and adaptability to the local environment.[32]

Part of the challenge of developing mutual credibility between scientists
and citizens is that scientists have tended to emphasize the differences between
these forms of knowledge, and their own status as holders of distinctive, superior

knowledge. As I noted in chapter 2, efforts to assert the authority of scientific knowledge have often been based on the argument that, being rational, objective, and universal, it is inherently different from other forms of knowledge more closely associated with the contexts in which they are produced. On the other hand, we have in recent years gained an understanding of how science is shaped by its own contexts, as manifested in its techniques, disciplinary structure, practical and political roles, and other characteristics that are mediated by its institutions. Conversely, local knowledge has come to be more widely recognized as the product of careful observation, common sense, and local values and beliefs, as well as an essential resource in solving problems and managing local environments. This appreciation of science and local knowledge as more similar than was once believed can provide the basis for professional practices, such as those already discussed in relation to managing natural resources and environmental risks, that combine general scientific knowledge and particularized local knowledge, enhancing the credibility of both.

Scientific credibility therefore is affected not only by characteristics of the science itself, but by how research is supported and directed (including the relative roles of government, industry, universities, and other institutions) as well as by how scientists relate to the rest of society, including other perspectives and forms of knowledge. Credibility is thus a highly flexible term, constructed by different individuals or groups, in a variety of contexts; existing, like uncertainty, at the intersection of science and politics. Its position at this intersection has generated yet another set of efforts intended to ensure the credibility of science: the creation of institutions able to straddle this intersection by combining scientific and political perspectives. These "boundary organizations" are able to internalize within themselves the ambiguous border between science and politics, moderating the tendency of conflicting interests to dismantle the scientific claims of their opponents (especially in legal and other adversarial fora), in effect stabilizing this border so that scientific claims are better able to meet the criteria of both political and scientific credibility.[33] The Intergovernmental Panel on Climate Change is one example of such an organization: it seeks to maintain credibility within both scientific and climate policy communities, not least by retaining within itself (as much as it is able) debates about climate science and policies, so that it is able to present a more unified, and therefore more credible, case to the rest of the world. It also, like other boundary organizations, focuses much of its work on the elaboration of "boundary objects": forms of scientific practice and communication that serve both scientific and political objectives. In the case of the IPCC, these are objects like climate change models and satellite data sets that serve scientific and political bodies as a means of communication and a support for the credibility of their claims.[34] The success of the IPCC as an authoritative source of climate knowledge testifies to the potential of boundary organizations to safeguard scientific credibility.

Overall, experience with these efforts—peer review, formation of independent institutions for research, and development of boundary organizations that combine science and politics—demonstrates how the credibility of science is determined not by applying universal norms of scientific conduct, but through a process of negotiation that is highly context-dependent. These negotiations must take into consideration local interests and concerns—with "local" encompassing anything from sheep farms in England's Lake District to global climate negotiations.

Seeking Effective Science

The effectiveness of science is the extent to which scientific knowledge is used appropriately to address society's concerns and priorities with respect to the environment. Of course, such a definition skips over some complex matters, such as what is meant by "appropriately," as well as who in society gets to define these concerns and priorities. However, this definition can provide a starting point for examining effective science: what it is, how it can be assured, what obstacles it may encounter. It is also, appropriately, broader than the definition used in some recent work on the role of science in environmental politics. In particular, the Social Learning Group chose to define effectiveness in terms of the impact of science not on individual decisions (since examples of such impacts have been, the Group concluded, elusive at best), but on advancing the overall policy agenda: the extent to which science was able to help identify new options, remove unhelpful options from the table, and so on.[35]

In the often-invoked model of a rational policy process, the effectiveness of science is understood in terms of the efficient operation of basic and applied research. Scientists conducting undirected research identify an environmental problem—say, a new class of contaminant—describe its implications, and explain it in terms of our general understanding of how the world works. The problem is then matched with an optimal solution through a process of rational analysis, guided by policymakers knowledgeable about both science and the relevant regulatory or policy tools. These policymakers may also apply more focused research—studies of the toxicity of the contaminant, for example—to any technical obstacles impeding this solution. The solution is then applied, and the situation is monitored to see if any additional measures are needed.

Obviously, this model describes an ideal process rarely encountered in the real world of environmental politics. In the first place, the distinction between basic and applied research, each performing its assigned role of either identifying environmental problems or developing solutions, breaks down quickly once examined more closely: basic research often has immediate practical applications, while applied research can generate new theoretical knowledge. More fundamentally, the model pays little heed to the complexities of science within the political process, including the apparently simple issue of whether, in fact, anyone will listen to what the scientists have to say. Unfortunately, the political effectiveness of science is too infrequently considered in discussions of the relations between science and environmental politics. One problem, as Jonathan

Wiener notes, is the assumption, routine in most analyses, that the optimal form of regulation, once identified through some rational means, will be imposed autocratically on all actors.[36] Such an assumption takes the effectiveness of science for granted. Alternatively, it is sometimes argued, especially by those who insist that environmental decisions be based on "sound science," that the chief problem is that people simply don't pay enough attention to science, especially because it is too often drowned out by emotion and by overreaction to exaggerated hazards, with the Alar controversy of the late 1980s often taken as the paradigmatic case of public fears sweeping aside calm, rational science.[37] This too is a simplification. How, then, might we get beyond either caricature—of science quietly fulfilling its role in a rational policy process, or submerged under a tide of public fears—and develop instead a more realistic conception of how science is used in environmental politics?

A good place to start is by identifying just how, precisely, science affects decisions and actions. I will do this by attempting to enumerate the various political roles of environmental science. The following list is probably not comprehensive, but it indicates, at least, how these roles go far beyond the simple distinction between basic and applied research; that is, between identifying and solving problems.

- *Identifying and Anticipating.* Many emerging environmental problems have been identified and placed on the public agenda through research. Examples abound, and include detection of the unexpected effects of various pollutants, such as the impact of chlorofluorocarbons on the stratospheric ozone layer; disruption of wildlife reproductive biology by synthetic hormones; and the environmental significance of a wide range of medications.[38] Such results constitute, in effect, the discovery and exploration of areas of ignorance that were once not even known to exist. This role may be fulfilled serendipitously through basic research, and the importance of this research in identifying hitherto unknown problems testifies to the danger inherent in focusing studies on already evident environmental concerns. Such research often proceeds entirely out of the public eye, generating extensive debate among scientists before the larger community becomes aware of the problem. Monitoring is also often important, generating data that gradually develop in significance, such as the long-term records at Mauna Loa that indicated increasing atmospheric carbon dioxide. Like basic research, monitoring (often itself inseparable from basic research) cannot, if it is to fulfill this anticipatory role, be too closely tied to specific environmental perspectives or problems: monitoring systems that eventually generated information highly relevant to climate change and ozone layer depletion were originally set up with quite different purposes in mind.[39]

- *Prescribing Action.* Occasionally, research is able to provide such a convincing, authoritative account of a problem that it immediately galvanizes the public and politicians, sweeping away obstacles, demonstrating in its most direct form the link between knowledge and action. One example was the demonstration in the late 1960s of the importance of phosphorus to nutrient enrichment and eutrophication of the lower Great Lakes, which quickly led to controls on phosphorus in detergents and to the 1972 Great Lakes Water Quality Agreement. A second, more famous case was the identification of the hole in the ozone layer over the Antarctic in the mid–1980s, which quickly led to the 1987 Montreal Protocol. Significantly, this information gained its impact not because, like the role of phosphorus in lakes, it was conclusive knowledge, but because of the opposite: it demonstrated how incomplete our knowledge of the ozone layer remained. (Both examples also indicate how the capacity of science to prescribe action can depend on more than just the evidence itself, including the availability of an economically and politically feasible solution.)

- *Building Theory*. Considerable ecological and environmental research is not necessarily relevant to specific problems, but it generates theoretical knowledge that may eventually influence environmental attitudes. For example, ecological studies have undoubtedly helped change perspectives toward wetlands: from stagnant swamps fit only for draining, to diverse ecosystems worth preserving. This change of perspective was then expressed in countless local controversies involving endangered species, natural area protection, and resource management, not necessarily by prescribing a certain course of action, but by influencing attitudes and values in more subtle ways.

- *Framing Issues*. Sometimes research results are presented in such a way that they reshape attitudes not only about a specific environmental issue, but about how issues and decisions are framed generally, encouraging debate, activism, even new institutions. *Silent Spring* is the classic instance: a presentation of scientific information about pesticides, paired with a discussion of political and ethical implications, that had an impact far beyond that issue. In the 1970s, information about limits to growth had an analogous impact: encouraging, at least temporarily, the framing of population and resource issues in terms of a finite world. Knowledge of the ecology of acid rain is a third example: it shifted concerns regarding air pollution from a preoccupation with human health to an emphasis on ecosystem impacts.

- *Supporting Management*. Considerable environmental research is focused on meeting specific managerial or regulatory goals: fisheries stock assessment, research on tree harvesting, evaluation of the toxicity of specific contaminants, to cite three examples. Such research, usually conducted by a resource management or regulatory agency, or by industry, seeks not to question the objectives of these institutions, but merely to ensure their efficient implementation. More generally, this research serves to enhance the credibility of regulatory agency decisions, im-buing them with the authority of science (although they often encompass political and economic calculations as well) and certifying that the agency's approach is balanced, its conclusions based on objective evidence.[40]

- *Questioning Management.* Some research that is relevant to managerial and regulatory goals fulfills its role not by advancing but by questioning these goals and the techniques by which they are achieved. Examples include studies of the ecological impacts of forest harvesting and of the shortcomings of single-species approaches to fisheries management. Such research usually takes a broader perspective than do studies focused on supporting management, encompassing species of no direct economic value, as well as impacts that may be beyond the jurisdiction of the management agency. The results may indicate that management must address a broader range of factors to be sustainable, or that it must respond more effectively to evolving public priorities, or to changing conditions, such as a warming climate. Sometimes the implications can include substantial revision of accepted practices, such as expanding beyond reliance on population dynamics in fisheries management to include approaches that acknowledge the ecological complexity of the oceans, such as marine reserves.[41]

- *Supporting Arguments in Adversarial Contexts.* Since the 1970s considerable research has been framed in terms of generating evidence that can be used in controversies and legal proceedings and that can meet the requirements of the adversarial culture of American environmental regulation. Such research commonly takes a reductionistic approach, emphasizing aspects of the environment and methods of study that can generate results considered credible and relevant even in the face of cross-examination. To meet these requirements results should be comprehensible in simplified terms, should draw on only the strongest conclusions, should avoid areas of uncertainty, and should focus on those impacts that can be expressed in economic terms or that are of special public interest.[42]

- *Maintaining Expertise.* Regulatory agencies commonly conduct scientific research that fulfills its role not only through the knowledge produced, but by maintaining the agency's scientific capabilities. Agencies need these capabilities in order to be able to evaluate and use effectively information arriving from outside (as provided by regulated industries, for example). A certain amount of research activity that is not tied directly to the agency's regulatory mandate can also be necessary to attract and retain competent scientists, who might otherwise seek more interesting research opportunities elsewhere.

- *Building a Community.* Environmental research can play a role not only through the knowledge it produces, but through the process itself: scientists and other parties build a community of common interest around an issue by doing research and sharing the results. This might entail construction of an advocacy coalition or an epistemic community, such as that surrounding climate change, or, on a regional scale, the community of scientists involved in studying and advocating protection of the Mediterranean Sea.[43] This role can also be seen in the building of a sense of common interest within a community of citizens, through surveying local wildlife habitats threatened by development, or through the practice of popular epidemiology.

- *Symbolizing or Avoiding Action.* Finally, research may be used not to encourage nor to guide action on an environmental problem, but to provide a basis for avoiding action. Like research that maintains expertise or builds a community, this research fulfills its role not through the knowledge it generates, but through the process itself. Prominent examples include acid rain research by the Reagan Administration in the 1980s and research on climate change by the Bush Administration after 2001. In both cases scientific uncertainties have been used to justify additional research, although many observers have argued that the evidence was or is sufficiently firm to compel action. This can be a long-term strategy: for three decades, beginning in the 1940s, the Ontario provincial government used research as a substitute for imposing controls on sulfur dioxide emissions from nickel smelters, even after considerable evidence of forest damage had accumulated. The research was viewed as a way of appearing to be doing something about the problem without actually interfering with the industry.[44] A related role of such research is to suggest an agency's commitment, at relatively low cost, to environmental protection. One instance was the former Atomic Energy Commission's support for ecological research: this served an important rhetorical function as a demonstration of the Commission's environmental values, while deflecting any questioning of the Com-mission's commitment to atomic energy.[45] Another manifestation of research fulfilling this role are studies conducted or sponsored by industries that aim to divert attention toward risks for which they have less responsibility.[46] Studies by coal producers of the natural sources of acid rain and studies by fisheries interests of consumption of fish by seals or other predators illustrate this phenomenon.

Several observations can be made about these roles. First, they underline the complexity of the contributions of science to environmental politics. Obviously, we cannot see effective research as being either simply science-driven (with scientists setting their own priorities) or policy-driven. And just as we need to adopt a pluralistic perspective on the roles of science, so too must we employ several models for understanding how science influences knowledge and action in the public and private spheres. At times, science can fulfill an "enlightenment" function, shaping general attitudes toward nature, but with less impact on specific decisions. In other situations, science can be more closely implicated in environmental decisions, particularly when the evidence is compelling or when there are close ties between those who study the environment and those who make the decisions. In other circumstances again, science may encourage delay and inaction. Such complexities remind us that our knowledge about the environment, and the actions we take on the basis of this knowledge, reflect not only some objective reality, but our political concerns, economic priorities, and values, and that science is therefore closely implicated in the process of working through the relationship between nature and society.

In turn, these diverse relations between science and action reflect different models of the role of scientific expertise in politics: as a kind of early warning system, anticipating problems facing an otherwise unaware society; as a source of authoritative guidance, sweeping away competing political or economic priorities; as a provider of general knowledge, accessible to all, that may or may not be heeded; or as an instrument of power, available mostly to those able to pay for it and who use it to assert their interests over their adversaries. Each model provides a piece of the puzzle of the relations between science and politics.

These roles can also be interpreted in terms of the steps by which an environmental problem travels from first encounter to solution, and in terms of the forms of science that may be most important at each step. Basic research in the natural sciences may be most important in first identifying a problem, recognizing it more effectively than would research more closely tied to immediate managerial or regulatory priorities. (Recent studies of the development of global environmental risks have emphasized this role by describing how these risks, before they gained political visibility, were treated for long periods largely as scientific issues.[47]) At some point, the work of individual scientists may be overtaken by more formal efforts by governments to focus research on the problem. The role of basic research, however, declines in subsequent steps in the policy process, when solutions are proposed, argued over, and eventually implemented, often with the guidance of engineering or economic expertise. For example, while climate change entered the agenda of the scientific and policy communities originally through basic research on carbon cycling and global models, development of policy options demands more economic and technological expertise, to create cost-effective strategies for reducing greenhouse gas emissions and to overcome objections to these strategies.

Of course, this sequence, while useful in reminding us of how the relation between knowledge and action may evolve over time, can be only a rough guide. The complexity of the relations between science and politics has encouraged competing efforts of explanation: from the view that problems, once identified, encourage a search for solutions, to the opposite view that a preferred solution (say, a new source of energy) may appear first, with its champions then casting about for problems that can justify its application. A third perspective sees the search for both problems and solutions as enmeshed within the pursuit by interested parties of agendas that have only a tenuous relation to either. As John Dryzek notes, these models of science and politics can even provide competing explanations for the same phenomena: while Peter Haas describes the 1987 Montreal Protocol as an example of policymaking driven by science, Karen Litfin identifies a discursive shift, motivated only in part by scientific knowledge, as most important, and Jeffrey Berejikian underlines the importance of actors pursuing their own economic interests with science providing only a backdrop.[48] The point is that no single model can provide a full account of how and why science can be effective, even in a single instance of policymaking, let alone across the whole of environmental politics.

The Contexts of Effective Science

So far I have emphasized how the character of the science affects its role and effectiveness in environmental politics. However, effectiveness often has little to do with the science itself. Critical events, whether natural or political, can affect the perceived significance of scientific information. Unusual weather—the hot summer of 1988, or storms occurring outside their normal season—makes scientific claims about global warming more effective. The sudden loss of fish from favorite lakes in the Adirondacks and in Ontario's Muskoka Lakes region—"cottage country" for affluent and influential Torontonians—sharpened the impact of acid rain research. Events and crises like these testify to how steady attention to an issue can be less significant than bursts of controversy, even though these may emerge and then recede more quickly than any strictly rational model of the policy process can account for. The political climate may shift just as quickly, requiring a politician to demonstrate his or her "green" credentials by introducing policies, accompanied by scientific rationales that may have been available for some time but that now serve as an antidote to charges of opportunism. Conversely, election of a leader hostile to environmental protection, as Reagan was in 1980, will ratchet down the political effectiveness of science for reasons that have little to do with the merits of the science itself.

The effectiveness of scientific information depends as well on other aspects of its context. It will have a greater impact if it has a significant human element, particularly involving children, or if it relates to the personal interests or concerns of a significant number of citizens, or if the phenomenon described is not written off by the public as a freak occurrence.[49] How well scientific information fits within preexisting cultural models of nature can also be important, confirming or disputing views of nature as resilient or fragile.[50] More general attitudes regarding the relations between government, industry, and other interest groups also shape the effectiveness of science. Their significance is especially evident in terms of the oft-noted contrast between the legalistic, often adversarial approaches to environmental affairs in the United States and the more flexible, cooperative, often corporatist arrangements common in Europe. These contrasting "policy styles" have several implications in terms of which forms of science are considered more relevant and credible.

One implication of the importance of these contexts is that we must be careful not to attribute too much significance to the role of science in defining environmental problems. In particular, it has often been suggested that something can only become an environmental issue through science: that science and technology are "best considered necessary but not sufficient conditions for the emergence of issues."[51] In fact, many issues are defined and attract attention without any direct reference to science: logging threatens a forested valley, valued for its beauty or recreational opportunities; a dam forces people from their homes, endangering their livelihood and sense of well-being; a tanker breaks up and oils a coastline, eliciting a reaction grounded more in aesthetics and animal welfare concerns than in knowledge of ecological impacts. The contribution of science to policy is episodic: sometimes it is important, other times other factors are more significant. (One may even hypothesize that scholarly studies of the role of science in politics have tended to exaggerate this role because they most often focus on issues originally identified and framed in terms of science, such as climate change or the ozone layer.) Nor can environmental problems be solved merely by applying science. It is important, in summary, to keep in mind that environmental policies are rarely the product of a rational process in which problems are precisely identified and then matched with optimal solutions. Most policies emerge haltingly and piecemeal through bargains and compromises between government agencies, industries, environmental organizations, communities, and other interest groups. While a policy generally requires some warrant from the scientific community, this requirement is contingent on many other factors.

These contingent factors also affect the relation between credibility and effectiveness. At first glance, it would appear self-evident that scientific knowledge must be credible if it is to be effective. If scientists lack confidence in this knowledge, why would anyone else pay attention, particularly those opposed to whatever policy or decision that knowledge is intended to support? But the connection between credibility and effectiveness is not always so direct. As I discuss below, knowledge that is widely accepted within the scientific community may have no political impact. The converse can also occur: scientific information may not be considered credible, but may nevertheless be effective, at least in influencing attitudes. For example, Bjorn Lomborg created a sensation with his book, *The Skeptical Environmentalist*. While the book was presented as a factual, science-based account of "the real state of the world," most scientists found Lomborg's claims to be dubious at best. Nonetheless, his book received a great deal of positive attention, particularly in the conservative media. A similar disconnect between credibility and effectiveness is evident in the small number of scientists who have won wide attention for their skeptical view of climate change, far out of proportion to their credibility within the scientific community. Scientific information may also be presented in ways that are less credible, but more effective. Critics of "alarmist" responses to environmental risks often complain that more sensational, but less credible, scientific claims of hazards have a disproportionate influence on regulatory priorities and that when more credible evidence arrives it is ignored.[52] A more subtle effect can result from how raw data are translated into meaningful terms for both scientific and non-scientific audiences. For example, satellite images representing ozone over the South Pole portray continuous gradations in its concentration in terms of a color-coded ordinal scale, conveying the erroneous, but highly effective, impression of an actual "hole" in the atmosphere.[53]

Communication and Relevance

There is nothing simple about effective science: how it can be achieved and what obstacles it faces. One way to begin examining the challenge of effective science is in terms of communication: by understanding what factors determine whether scientific information will be accessible and meaningful to those in a position to use it. Much has been written about communicating science to the public, particularly through the media. It is often emphasized that information must be presented in ways consistent with how the media approach communication generally: by using graphic or evocative verbal and visual imagery, de-emphasizing complex or obscure theory in favor of concrete information relevant to peoples' own lives and concerns, and so forth. The history of popular communication of environmental science is punctuated by powerful images and metaphors: a "silent spring," "acid rain," the ozone "hole," or the "greenhouse" effect. All are effective because they establish a connection between subtle changes in the atmosphere and more immediate or familiar images: dead birds, dying lakes and forests, fears of cancer, the hot stuffiness of a greenhouse. Similarly, information regarding biodiversity loss or biotechnology becomes more meaningful when linked with charismatic species—as demonstrated by the attention given to evidence that genetically modified crops could harm the Monarch butterfly. Probably no other insect could elicit such concern.

But to be truly effective, communication must involve an actual dialogue, in which scientists move beyond the notion of citizens as simply empty buckets, ready to be filled with scientific facts (as is often implied in studies of scientific literacy). Scientists should not only disseminate information, but learn about the knowledge and concerns of citizens, so that they are able to relate their research results to how non-scientists see the world. In such a dialogue, science is communicated in ways consistent with peoples' specific concerns and with their general cultural models of nature and the world.[54] Building trust is an essential element of such a dialogue.

This approach is also relevant to the persistent complaint that scientists too rarely provide the information needed to develop policy and make regulatory or managerial decisions. Such problems—the product of differing expectations and cultures—are often expressed in deeply practical ways. From the perspective of policymakers and regulators, scientists are often unable to deliver useful conclusions in a timely way, or work on the basis of imperfect data, or communicate their results without qualifications or conditions; they are also too reluctant to participate in the regulatory process, preferring to communicate with their peers. In my own research on environmental science in northern Canada, I found a deep dissatisfaction among policymakers and managers regarding science and scientists. Their concerns were expressed through statements such as "[c]ommunication of results is very difficult, as few scientists have requisite skills to develop management perspective on findings, or provide a 'so what' to the public"; or, as another expressed it, "[c]ommunication would be improved if academic researchers were less concerned about getting results into scientific journals, and made more effort to communicate it in [a] meaningful way to regulators in a position to do something about impacts."[55] This failure to communicate, with scientists working in isolation from those supposedly in a position to apply their results, is a common experience: as William Clark and his colleagues in the Social Learning Group found, "most assessments have been undertaken with no clear understanding of whose choices or decisions they were seeking to illuminate."[56]

Such difficulties stem both from failures to communicate and from the divergent priorities of scientists and those who use scientific information. The consequences of this divergence were illustrated by the experience of the National Acid Precipitation Assessment Program (NAPAP), created in 1980 to study and report on the causes, effects, and possible responses to acid rain. While its assessment was, in scientific terms, of excellent quality, it was not, according to one scholar, accompanied by an adequate explanation of how to make the difficult policy choices implied by the research. It was therefore much less effective than it might have been in influencing public debate and decisions.[57] The NAPAP experience can be generalized: there has been a persistent trend in assessments of global environmental risks, at least in the United States, toward emphasizing their scientific dimensions, and a reluctance to examine political, economic, or social implications.[58] Assessments of climate change have tended to define the issue in terms of parts per million carbon dioxide or methane, and not, say, in terms of society's vulnerability to the consequences of a warmer world. This has occurred because consensus—viewed as the most reliable indicator of scientific truth and credibility—is more readily achieved by focusing on the "hard" sciences. The options considered will tend to be the most conventional, the "safest," those most likely to be acceptable to all parties. But such assessments are also then less relevant to the hard decisions and tradeoffs that must be made with respect to climate change and other global risks. If, as it is reasonable to assume, the issues that most need examination are those on which there is least consensus, then the absurdity of this tendency is obvious. In effect, efforts to enhance the credibility of assessments often, ironically, reduce their relevance and therefore their effectiveness. This can also be the outcome when a preference for conclusive, credible proof linking cause and effect leads those assessing research to discount evidence of more subtle indirect or multiple causes of environmental impacts.[59]

In contrast, both the Environmental Protection Agency and the Food and Drug Administration have learned how to participate more effectively in controversies, or have been able to avoid controversies altogether, through more intensive communication between scientists and those who use their results. This has provided a basis for ensuring that scientific assessments are sensitive to political realities, and for avoiding decisions that will not be accepted as scientifically legitimate.[60] The value of dialogue between those producing scientific knowledge and those who may apply it, with each side willing to modify its activities in response to the concerns of the other, has also been demonstrated in international negotiations.[61]

Andrew Webster, a British scholar of science and politics, used a wonderful ecological image to express the challenges of communicating scientific information. He called for abandoning the "notion that knowledge is a pool of information in which other scientists and industry fish for new ideas. The more appropriate image might be a marsh or delta, where knowledge of the local terrain is vital, where what lies in the murky waters is uncertain while attempts to channel the flow are expensive and often to the detriment of the local ecology."[62] "Knowledge brokers" can play an essential role in guiding users of scientific information through this marsh. These are individuals (or institutions) that understand both the science and the political or administrative realities and can function as translators between them. Rachel Carson may be seen as the paradigmatic case: her effectiveness stemmed from a deep understanding of the science of pesticides, as well as knowledge of how that information could be related to people's concerns and to the political context in which decisions about pesticides were being made. One of the more elaborate analyses of the role of knowledge brokers was provided in Karen Litfin's examination of the science and politics of stratospheric ozone. Knowledge brokers facilitated the crucial step toward an agreement by linking uncertain evidence of an eroded ozone layer with the precautionary principle. By making this link, and thereby shifting the discourse of ozone science and politics, they were ultimately more influential than either politicians or scientists.[63] Penelope Canan and Nancy Reichman also emphasize how individuals, characterized as "institutional entrepreneurs," contributed to the implementation of the Montreal Protocol by creating the conditions necessary for productive and collegial working relationships.[64] The roles of nongovernmental organizations as knowledge brokers in climate negotiations—gathering and disseminating information, linking it to the concerns of small island states or other parties vulnerable to climate change—can also be noted.[65]

Knowledge brokers can also play a significant role within an agency. Sheila Jasanoff has described how the most valued individual in an advisory process can be the one able to transcend disciplinary boundaries, synthesizing knowledge from several fields, while also understanding the limits of science and how those limits relate to the issues facing the agency.[66] Such a role is often filled by an employee, usually of long standing, who accumulates a store of tacit knowledge of the organization and so becomes known as the one who knows most about what people are doing, about who knows what and how it all fits together. This role may be taken on informally, never appearing on any organizational chart. Consulting firms also can play such a role, through the assessments they generate for their clients (who may include regulatory agencies): collecting and synthesizing the accumulated scientific information regarding an issue and explaining its significance.[67] Such firms can be especially important in the aftermath of government cutbacks, when an agency may have lost too many of its more experienced employees to fulfill this brokerage function itself. More generally, researchers in government, industry, or consulting firms, who (unlike many academic scientists) have built their careers by addressing immediate regulatory or managerial priorities, are accustomed to viewing effective communication of scientific information (emphasizing its practical political and economic consequences) as a chief criterion by which their performance is evaluated. They often have had more practice in communicating with non-scientists, and may have developed informal ties with policymakers. However, their communication is often limited to their immediate clients, especially since funding support for management-related research does not usually extend to publication in scientific journals or to communicating with the wider public.

Can Institutions Learn?

Effective communication of scientific information, including explanation of how it relates to other attitudes and priorities, while necessary, is not on its own sufficient for science to play an effective role in society. The capacity of society, and particularly of institutions, to receive this information and to learn and change in response to an uncertain and changing world must also be considered. This requirement, however, comes up inevitably against the tendency of bureaucratic organizations to resist learning, to prefer (in the spirit of administrative rationalism) efficiency, standardization, and accountability over innovation. In fact this is a choice American regulatory agencies are required to make, in order to demonstrate that their decisions are not arbitrary, but consistent with prior practice. Such a requirement, however, is incompatible with the novel and tentative knowledge generated through basic research.[68] Instead (as is noted in chapter 4 with reference to resource management agencies), a persistent pattern is observed, in which, once a program is put in place to deal with a problem, innovation becomes less important, is displaced by adherence to rules, regulations, and standard operating procedures. Bureaucratic needs lead to the "capture" of scientific information, and learning becomes focused on more efficient delivery of standardized programs and services, not on understanding unexpected consequences or seeking alternative ways of fulfilling mandates. Information that furthers existing objectives is preferred over any that questions them. In addition, the demand for administrative efficiency can itself be inimical to innovation: learning (including experimenting with alternative ways of achieving objectives) is difficult to achieve in an institution that is always stretched to capacity.

Other obstacles to learning are created by the placement of expertise within organizations. Most often, expertise is scattered throughout an organization, and no individual has a comprehensive understanding of any one complex issue, such as climate change, genetically modified foods, or a fishery. And in practice, the knowledge most grounded in experience is usually located in the peripheries of an organization: in the field offices where employees have daily contact with both the ecosystems and the people most affected by the actions of the agency. These employees will be most aware of the practical consequences of these actions, but they are also likely to be distant geographically from headquarters and to be many rungs down the organizational ladder, with commensurately little contact with the senior officials who set policy.

Obstacles to learning are evident outside government as well. Industries will resist, indeed often suppress, information that questions accepted practices or endangers profitable products. Biotechnology firms, for example, have invested far more in developing and promoting genetically modified food products than in examining their broader implications. As a result, we still know remarkably little about the consequences of releasing genetically engineered organisms into the environment—even with this technology now being used on tens of millions of acres. Nor are basic questions about the science being asked: as Jonathan Porritt notes, enormous effort is being devoted to engineering pest resistance into crops, seeking benefits that may well be illusory: "it is astonishing that serious scientists can be so childishly enthusiastic at the prospect of swapping today's chemical treadmill for tomorrow's genetic treadmill, all in pursuit of the unattainable dream of pest eradication."[69]

Environmental groups too can be less than receptive to information that contradicts the organizational imperative of emphasizing the seriousness of environmental problems (although this tendency may be balanced by a desire to highlight "good news" stories as a way of spurring others to action). In these groups as well, learning will tend to be instrumental: focused on how to achieve goals that have already been set. When there are several institutions or groups with a common interest in an area of policy—an advocacy coalition or policy network—the preference will be, again, for information that will further their common objectives, and they will resist information that suggests these objectives are invalid or unattainable.[70] Disagreements will be seen, and settled, as technical problems, not as opportunities to raise more fundamental questions.

The difficulties involved in instilling a capacity to learn in organizations are indicated by two phenomena. One is that some scientists and managers, having found it difficult to get the attention of their own organization from the inside, choose to be whistle-blowers, publicizing through the media the organization's errors or shortcomings, in an effort to create external pressure for change.[71] A second indication is the fact that the most dedicated critics of large organizations are often individuals on the outside, including retired scientists and other employees.

Opportunities for learning can be the product of both chance and design. They may arise unexpectedly, as a result of a crisis. This can be, as I noted in chapter 4, a crisis in the environment itself, such as the loss of a major fishery. But a crisis can also occur within institutions or society. In particular, a major disagreement or controversy can provide an opportunity for learning if it politicizes what had previously been a technical dispute, giving previously excluded groups from the wider community a chance to gain entry to the issue.[72] The entry of new people can bring forward alternative perspectives; it can also provide an opening for parties already on the inside, including government, to distance themselves from their traditional views of an issue.[73]

The premise of adaptive management, as discussed in chapter 4, is that it can provide a way through these various obstacles to learning: experimenting with different courses of action, evaluating them by observing their consequences, building (it is hoped) greater resilience into institutions in the face of evolving, unpredictable environments, both political and natural. It is, essentially, a means of applying the ability of science to generate knowledge to the development of new policies and management practices. Generalized as a strategy for evaluating the consequences of alternative policy options or decisions, adaptive management may also be applied beyond natural resource management. For example, climate models test, through scenarios, the consequences of alternative policy options—providing a virtual counterpart to the real-world experiments of adaptive managers. A variation on this are decentralized "policy teams" that can generate and test a variety of alternative policies, on regional or local scales, and over relatively short time periods. It would thus be an alternative to global approaches to environmental problems, seeking instead actions on smaller scales: not comprehensive solutions, but incremental changes. Such change would not only enable more effective "learning by doing," it would be better able to take into consideration local political, social, and ecological conditions, including the knowledge that people have of their surroundings. These arrangements are also more consistent with the collaborative partnerships between governments, business, and other groups that are often seen as necessary to deal effectively with complex environmental problems.

Such partnerships can be especially important in ensuring that science can play an effective role even in the presence of uncertainty and ignorance. These are an inescapable part of science in environmental politics, stemming (as noted in chapter 2) from several factors: the complexity and chaos of nature, the novel ways in which humans have affected nature, characteristics of the scientific community, and the nature of environmental politics, including the preference of some interest groups to emphasize uncertainty in scientific evidence. Uncertainty and ignorance do not simply exist in nature; they are created, constructed, and manipulated. When questions of their interpretation arise, scientists must work closely with those making decisions, explaining the ambiguities in the information.[74] The Health Effects Institute, for example, has had to deal with this basic dilemma, of maintaining scientific credibility through a degree of separation from the pressures of regulatory decision-making while still remaining relevant to policy.[75]

One conclusion to be drawn from the need for a capacity to learn within institutions is that proposals to enhance the credibility and hence the effectiveness of science by enforcing a separation of scientific from policy institutions are more likely to result in science becoming less rather than more effective. Indeed, the notion is unrealistic, given that scientific and policy conclusions affect each other so closely. Returning to the example in chapter 4 of the cod fishery off Newfoundland (the collapse of which led to calls for a separate fisheries research institution), the sequence of events demonstrated the need for timely scientific advice in managing the fisheries, including making sense of the uncertainty created by contradictory information. This implied a need for closer integration of science and management, not separation. In contentious issues, an "independent" scientific institution, far from providing an authoritative resolution to debates, would likely be just one more voice added to the cacophony.

Awareness of the limits of uncertain science has also encouraged the emergence within American regulatory agencies of what Sheila Jasanoff has described as the "science policy paradigm." This paradigm has three elements: that agencies should be permitted to make regulatory decisions on the basis of imperfect knowledge; that a decision made on the basis of scientific evidence may be regarded as valid even if the scientific community doesn't universally accept it as such; and that when experts disagree, an agency should have the authority to resolve the dispute in a way consistent with its legal mandate.[76] Regulatory decisions in the context of this paradigm clearly require close interaction between scientists and regulators; this continued to be the case even as the paradigm was challenged, as courts became less willing to defer to agencies in matters involving scientific judgment and so exercised greater oversight over their decisions.

It is possible for science to be effective: to help ensure that decisions draw appropriately on scientific evidence, even in the presence of uncertainty and ignorance. To do so, however, requires a great deal of mutual awareness on the part of both scientists and policymakers as to what each can provide. This awareness has only gradually developed over time, as manifested in innovations such as adaptive management, boundary organizations, and knowledge brokers. This process of learning is also sometimes evident in evolving regulatory requirements, as evidenced in the recent history of air and water pollution control in the United States. Implementation of the 1970 Clean Air Act posed a technical challenge, because models used to relate emissions to air quality necessarily involved considerable judgment and the possibility of error. Accordingly, in 1977 the regulations were revised to require emitters to meet not an ambient air standard, but certain technological standards—a requirement that could be verified with far less uncertainty. Similarly, given the uncertainties involved in relating pollution discharges to the quality of receiving waters, the 1972 Clean Water Act also specified technological standards.[77] In both cases, the issue was to determine whether pollution control would be based on the quality of the receiving environment (which is, after all, what pollution controls are all about) or on the technology: a less direct, but also a less uncertain factor. Faced with the need to defend their regulatory decisions, often in an adversarial arena, institutions have learned to rely on less uncertain forms of evidence, based on technology, rather than on ecology.

Such a strategy might be the only effective one when actions are closely scrutinized and firmly resisted. But it can also limit the capacity of a regulatory agency to draw on new knowledge. One illustration of this was the national goal of reducing emissions of sulfur dioxide by 10 million tons, as specified in the 1990 Clean Air Act. While this number had only a distant relation to the science of acid rain, it nevertheless demonstrated a remarkable "stickiness," persisting even as ecological knowledge was accumulating that could have provided a more effective link between controlling emissions and protecting the environment. This knowledge, in the form of the "critical-load" concept (identifying how much acid rain ecosystems could absorb without significant damage), had been developed by scientists in the 1980s and was widely applied in Europe, where it was seen as having several advantages, not least that of flexibility.[78] In the United States, however, this concept failed to displace the goal of limiting emissions, likely because the adversarial nature of American environmental politics hindered construction of the community of trust and common values on which such a concept would rely. Regulations founded on keeping emissions below an ecosystem's critical load would be simply too vulnerable to challenge. In general, as American regulatory agencies learned to defend their actions by drawing on only the most certain forms of science, ecological knowledge—often the most uncertain science of all—tended to be marginalized, regardless of its potential contribution to ensuring that the environment really is protected.

In recent years no approach to acting on the basis of uncertainty has generated more debate than the precautionary principle. The concept itself is quite straightforward—indeed, it is common sense: when in doubt, better to be safe than sorry, and absence of evidence of harm does not constitute evidence of absence. A more elaborate formulation of the principle, now codified in many official statements, is that when there is the possibility of a significant or irreversible hazard to human health or the environment, lack of conclusive proof should not be used to justify not taking appropriate action to forestall this hazard. Uncertainty would not be an excuse for postponing action. This implies shifting the burden of proof from those advocating protection against potential harms onto those urging a wait-and-see approach. For example, a chemical product or bioengineered food crop could not gain approval on the basis that no harm from it had been proven; rather, it would need to be demonstrated to be safe. The precautionary principle has been invoked in many controversies: from CFCs and the ozone layer in the 1980s, to climate change, to biotechnology, to persistent contaminants—whenever, in short, there is the possibility of significant but uncertain risks.[79] Indeed, in recent years the precautionary principle has come to signify not simply caution in the face of uncertainty, but an insistence that decisions be made within an inclusive, transparent process, taking into consideration the many factors—political, social, ethical—that are excluded when issues are defined in strictly scientific terms.[80]

As its common-sense formulation implies, the principle has a long, if informal history, encoded in folk wisdom and everyday practice. Codification in environmental law has been more recent, beginning, perhaps, in America with the Delaney Clause of the Federal Food, Drug, and Cosmetic Act of 1958, which prohibited in foods any residues found to cause cancer in animals or humans. It received more explicit formulation in the Vorsorgeprinzip ("foresight" principle) of the German Clean Air Act of 1974, which has gone on to occupy a prominent place in German environmental regulation. The precautionary principle has also become a cornerstone of European environmental policy, and it is being invoked by many local governments in the European Union.[81] An early appearance in international law was in the European Union's Ministerial Declaration on the Protection of the North Sea (1987): "In order to protect the North Sea from possibly damaging effects of the most dangerous substances, a precautionary approach is necessary which may require action to control inputs of such substances even before a causal link has been established by absolutely clear scientific evidence."[82] The declaration of the 1992 United Nations Conference on Environment and Development included a statement of the precautionary principle (Principle 15), and it has since been incorporated into numerous international treaties and conventions, most recently the Cartagena Protocol on Biosafety (2000) and the Stockholm Convention on Persistent Organic Pollutants (2001).[83]

However, the precautionary principle has been received less favorably in North America. It does appear in some legislation, such as the Canadian Environmental Protection Act (relating to the screening of new substances for regulation); but in the United States it has been less readily adopted, the Delaney Clause notwithstanding. The American government has actively opposed its incorporation in international agreement.[84] At least when exports are at stake, the American government views the principle as simply trade protectionism, dressed up as a high-minded concern for future generations and the environment. Accordingly, U.S. government opposition to European restrictions on the import of genetically modified foods (of which the United States and Canada are major producers) has often targeted Europeans' use of the precautionary principle to justify these restrictions.

To understand these transatlantic differences, we need to go beyond cultural distinctions. After all, Europeans appear to be no more averse to risks than Americans (driving on Italian highways certainly confirmed this for me, at least). Rather, as the current flashpoints for the precautionary principle—genetically modified food and the Kyoto Protocol—suggest, specific economic and political factors are likely more important than general "European" or "American" attitudes toward risk. In the first issue, export promotion, and in the second, a reluctance (for many reasons) to embrace energy conservation, can better explain American resistance to precautionary action. In addition, the American regulatory system, through its own inflexibilities, discourages a precautionary approach. Detailed regulations (reflecting a reluctance to grant them too much discretion) provide little scope for agencies to take action on threats outside their specific mandates, the slowness of the "notice and comment" regulatory process precludes swift precautionary action, and the distribution of responsibilities for regulating risks among numerous agencies makes broad-based precautionary responses virtually impossible. Perhaps most important is that regulatory decisions must be constructed so as to be defensible to other levels of government and robust enough to withstand legal challenge. This places a premium on strong scientific evidence while discouraging the judgment involved in applying the precautionary principle.[85] In contrast, European regulations, constructed through more informal, consultative processes, are less subject to adversarial review and so are not as obliged to be justified "by the numbers," thereby providing some latitude for non-scientific considerations, including the precautionary principle.

While economic concerns evidently drive much of the debate about the precautionary principle, the debate itself is often framed in terms of the appropriate use of uncertain scientific information. On the one hand, critics argue that the principle constitutes a "retreat from reason": a rejection of rationality and science. Instead of relying on science-based risk assessment, with its promise of objectivity, the principle substitutes moral values and preferences. Aaron Wildavsky presents this view in considerable depth, with many case studies of what he describes as persistent overreactions to small risks.[86] Industry groups and their consultants have engaged in an extensive campaign aimed at discrediting the precautionary principle. As a Dow Chemical official explained: "Application of the precautionary principle has many in industry very concerned, because it is viewed as starting down a 'slippery slope' that could result in public policies based on theories, fear, and innuendo rather than sound science."[87] The precautionary principle has been described as inherently biased against innovation: protecting against theoretical risks while ignoring risks we already experience that could be mitigated or eliminated by new products.[88] The precautionary principle might open the door to non-scientific considerations playing a larger role in regulatory decisions—a prospect that industry, preferring to keep issues and controversies more narrowly defined and therefore more controllable, would rather not chance.

Advocates of the principle agree that, indeed, it does imply relying on more than science. This is necessary, because questions regarding the weighing of evidence, burdens of proof, the determination of what constitutes sufficient grounds for action, are as much political as scientific. These questions relate to determining which risks should be regulated and which are up to individuals to deal with, and balancing innovations and their unknown risks against what is tried and true. More broadly, they relate to whether it is appropriate to consider our environment and society as a kind of testing laboratory for new products. The precautionary principle also implies reconsidering how uncertain scientific evidence is evaluated, and whether strategies used in basic research can also be effective for policy-relevant questions. The principle says not: that while the priority in theoretical science is to avoid false positives (identifying an effect when there is none), in policy-relevant areas the aim should be to avoid false negatives, given the consequences of missing a problem as potentially serious as an unknown environmental hazard. A 95 percent confidence level may be appropriate when it is only a theory being tested, but will be less so when a potentially dangerous risk is being considered.[89] Advocates of precaution also note that risk assessment itself, far from being strictly science-based, comes with its own set of commitments: an implicit preference for higher levels of proof and for new technologies, as their benefits are usually more readily apparent than their potential harms.

The relevant question regarding the precautionary principle, therefore, is not whether environmental decisions should be based on science or on political values, but whether the political dimensions of these decisions should be openly acknowledged or concealed beneath spurious invocations of scientific objectivity. Ultimately, the principle's contribution to the effectiveness of science may be not in terms of providing firm rules for dealing with difficult questions, but simply in asserting that being scientific does not mean always being certain and that it is appropriate to consider carefully the uncertainties and areas of ignorance that surround complex issues. This can justify a more reasoned pace in which adequate time is taken to study the consequences of innovations before they are rushed into production.[90]

These elements—effective communication of science, institutions able to make use of this knowledge, appropriate frameworks for determining whether science provides a basis for action, such as the precautionary principle—are all important to effective science. But they do not address the most crucial piece of the puzzle: the science itself. What are the characteristics, in terms of choice of problems and conduct of research, of effective environmental science? One answer to this question, most often expressed through periodic efforts to develop research programs that target specific environmental challenges, is that the agenda for science should reflect the environmental agenda, and we cannot afford to rely on undirected basic research that may or may not be relevant to these problems.

Relevant research is clearly important: managers and regulators need timely information, for decisions on everything from setting fisheries quotas to approving new pesticides or other potentially hazardous products. But such research cannot on its own fulfill all the roles of science I have enumerated, and good basic science (also known as research science) is not the same as good policy-relevant science (regulatory, or mandated science): each is evaluated according to different criteria.[91] Building general theory is not the same as applying knowledge to specific problems; indeed, it can impose contradictory requirements. As Richard Levins explained in the 1960s, a scientific model cannot be at the same time general (applicable to all situations), realistic (representing the actual processes occurring in nature), and precise (providing quantitatively exact predictions).[92] While theory-building may demand generality and realism, practical decision-making insists on precision. Both approaches are relevant in different ways to environmental policy.

The problems created by defining relevance too narrowly were well illustrated by Brian Wynne and Sue Mayer's account of Great Britain's reliance on a "sound science" model of environmental inquiry. Hobbled by conservative standards of proof and an inflexible approach to complex problems, research on the possible impacts of pollution produced only a few observable results, such as mortality and disease, with proof of impact depending on demonstration of direct cause-effect relations. This excludes the possibility of indirect effects, in effect burying larger uncertainties and sources of ignorance and thereby expressing a built-in bias against environmental protection. By seeking precise, hard answers, the methodology precludes a richer understanding of the system. In contrast, a "greener" science would be more open to the possibility of multiple interactions and would not discount complex interactions simply because they cannot be precisely described.[93]

The problem of relevant science has recently attracted much attention from scientists themselves. In February 1997 ecologist Jane Lubchenco, in her presidential address to the American Association for the Advancement of Science, presented one solution to this problem: a new social contract for science. Global environmental problems, and their pervasive impacts on ecosystems and humans, she argued, are of such urgency and impose such demands for new research and communication efforts as to require "a commitment on the part of all scientists to devote their energies and talents to the most pressing problems of the day, in proportion to their importance, in exchange for public funding."[94] New approaches to education, organization of research, reward systems for scientists, and better bridges between science, policy, and management would also be required.

While Lubchenco presented this proposal as strikingly novel—the first substantial revision in the social contract between American science and society in half a century—it is less sweeping than it first appears, and indeed, less ambitious than many other experiments in revising the relationship between science and society. The emphasis on fundamental research as the basis for American science remains, research goals are still chosen by scientists themselves, and even Lubchenco's account of the environmental crisis facing humanity privileges the scientific perspective, in emphasizing change at the global and not the local level. If, she implied, science must change to become more effective in the face of a global environmental crisis, it will nonetheless be scientists who determine this change, and improving the ties between scientists and society means, essentially, rendering more efficient the one-way communication between them.

Lubchenco and other commentators (mostly from the scientific community) who stress the need for basic research are making an important point. Several roles of science in environmental politics, such as anticipating emerging problems, framing issues, and questioning "standard" management attitudes, imply a need for studies that are not directed toward immediate concerns, but follow instead the logic of basic research, in which scientists set their own priorities and are able to pursue long-term projects, building a cumulative understanding of some aspect of nature without demands for immediate practical justification. Such research, and the ideas and theories it generates, must also be protected against overly critical standards of testing, such as that encountered in legal and other adversarial contexts, in order to allow promising possibilities to be pursued before conclusive evidence has been accumulated to support them.[95] This form of science often achieves its effectiveness quietly: framing problems, generating a climate of ideas that affects policymakers' thinking in subtle ways. It often as well proves itself in times of crisis, when a long-developing environmental issue suddenly reaches the public consciousness, a scientific problem is redefined as a political issue, established institutions are challenged, and intellectual capital patiently accumulated is suddenly in demand.

The histories of numerous environmental issues have demonstrated the value of basic research: identifying the significance of acid rain, in part through observations of rainwater chemistry at the Hubbard Brook Ecosystem Study in New Hampshire and elsewhere (a research model now applied at two dozen other sites, through the National Science Foundation's Long Term Ecological Research program); accumulating awareness of the unexpected role of synthetic chemicals as disruptors of endocrine systems in wildlife; developing knowledge of the importance of biodiversity in maintaining the health of forests; or broadening understanding of the health impacts of air pollution, from the acute effects of local, high-level exposures (such as the London fog of December 1952, and the "killer smog" at Donora, Pennsylvania, in October 1948) to the chronic effects of lower concentrations, as well as the possibility of transport of air pollutants over long distances.[96] Collectively, these episodes demonstrate how complex environmental problems are not simply "discovered," but constructed over time, through long-term research often guided as much by serendipity as by carefully plotted research plans. Research focused strictly on issues already identified would have hindered understanding of all these problems.

But as I suggest throughout this book, more is needed for effective science than simply more basic research, communicated more effectively. It is not enough to leave it up to scientists to ensure that all problems—known and un-known—are covered. They will not on their own generate all the forms of knowledge required to fulfill the many roles of science in environmental policy. There should also be mechanisms to ensure that science is directed toward immediate, identified problems. What is required overall, therefore, for effective research is a pluralistic array of research strategies, addressing both basic and applied, long-term and immediate priorities.

The many disciplines within environmental science constitute one dimension of this pluralism. Across the field of environmental research, disciplinary specializations have developed, often isolated from each other and presenting accounts of nature that often contradict each other. Indeed, differences among scientists regarding the significance of environmental problems can often be traced to disciplinary perspectives: foresters and ecologists have different views of the impact of timber harvesting, and epidemiologists and toxicologists will disagree on the hazard posed by a toxic chemical. Failures of scientific creativity in dealing with environmental concerns—when, for example, foresters focus on the biology of trees but fail to address the impacts of harvesting on other species; or when atmospheric scientists, most trained in physical meteorology, are slow to recognize problems with the atmosphere's changing chemistry, such as acid rain (as occurred in Canada)—have often stemmed from a kind of disciplinary monoculture within environmental agencies.[97] In contrast, the diversity of views offered by a variety of disciplines can provide opportunities for creative responses to problems. In some cases, the crucial innovation can come through the work of scientists outside the mainstream disciplines. The discovery by Mario Molina and Sherwood Rowland of the effects of CFCs on the ozone layer is a classic instance. Provided the context is not overly adversarial, the competition of ideas between disciplines can promote a constructive querying of assumptions, and the identification of possibilities that might otherwise be missed. For this to happen, however, researchers need opportunities to collaborate across disciplines and across borders. For example, recognition of acid rain as a significant issue occurred as a result of researchers working in several countries whose research on topics ranging from atmospheric chemistry to botany to lake ecology were only gradually realized to be touching on aspects of one big problem.[98] That case illustrates how some of the most effective scientific work has been done by combining a variety of disciplinary perspectives, within research organizations of various kinds: from individuals to large interdisciplinary teams. In summary, a diverse network of expertise, representing a variety of disciplines and institutions, can provide a more effective basis for the negotiations that lead to new knowledge about nature.

In tying the effectiveness of science to a pluralistic perspective we can also take a cue from philosophers of science, who have argued persuasively against the risks of following only the most promising or profitable paths in research. Not only is it impossible to predict which paths are most likely to lead to useful knowledge, but, as James Brown explains (drawing on Paul Feyerabend), pursuing several theories and multiple methodologies—in short, cultivating a pluralistic attitude—is more likely to generate a better understanding of nature, because more theories and methods generate a more diverse array of evidence against which we can test our ideas.[99]

Environmental expertise has diversified enormously over the last several decades, with knowledge now dispersed across many agencies and other actors. Many American federal agencies now have expertise relating to the environment, as do the larger state governments, giving them the capacity, on occasion, to challenge federal positions, as when California has set the national agenda in automobile emissions control, or, more recently, with numerous state initiatives on climate change that seek to fill the vacuum created by federal inaction. This dispersal and fragmentation of expertise is also evident in forest management, where professional forestry, once dominant, has been challenged by experts in wildlife, fisheries, hydrology, and other fields. This expanded view of the expertise deemed relevant has been driven by public concerns regarding the impact of forestry practices and by insistence that new forms of knowledge be used to address these concerns. Beyond government as well there has been a broadening of interests involved in environmental research, with environmental organizations, as well as citizens themselves, developing expertise and networks through which to share their knowledge. Industry has also developed expertise with which to participate in controversies and influence decisions. This diverse participation has been especially evident at recent international climate negotiations. That more than 500 nongovernmental organizations attend these negotiations, representing both environmental and industrial interests, testifies to the potentially wide-ranging impacts of climate change and efforts to mitigate it.

Environmental organizations provide some of the most compelling demonstrations of how broader participation in environmental research can enhance its political effectiveness. In the 1980s Friends of the Earth, by conducting a survey of forest health, was able to help reshape British debate over acid rain. Their results obliged the government, skeptical of hypotheses of forest damage, to take the problem more seriously.[100] Another illustration is provided by Greenpeace—an environmental organization that has pursued scientific work as intensively as any. In the 1980s dioxin became a significant public concern in Canada, particularly in connection with the pulp and paper industry, which produced dioxin during the bleaching of pulp and released it into the environment, and also produced paper products that had dioxin residues. In 1987 Greenpeace tested the environment near pulp and paper mills in Howe Sound, just north of Vancouver, British Columbia, and found dioxin and furans in sediment and shellfish. This gained immediate public attention, and the notice of the federal minister of the environment, even though scientists in the minister's own department had already found even higher levels of contaminants (the department's findings never received much notice). Greenpeace also prepared an extensive report detailing the science of dioxin in relation to the pulp and paper industry. This was the first of a series of assessments communicating science to a wide audience, through which Greenpeace transformed the dioxin debate in Canada. The reports were readable, scientifically credible, and extensively referenced. Industry and government, in contrast, failed to communicate their views effectively: while the chemical industry scrambled to respond to each new Greenpeace report, governments kept silent or retreated into scientific research.[101] As a result, Green-peace became the most authoritative source of knowledge, effectively calling attention to this potential hazard.

While a pluralistic approach is necessary for effective science, it may also be at risk. In both Canada and the United States the corporate sector has become an increasingly significant actor in funding university research. The Natural Sciences and Engineering Research Council of Canada (the main funding agency for university research) ties an increasing fraction of its support to researchers' ability to obtain matching funds from industry. In both Canada and the United States, industry has also become an increasingly important direct contributor to university research. As universities and industries develop ever more intimate ties, accompanied by tighter rules imposed on scientists with respect to confidentiality and new pressures to patent rather than publish results, less commercially promising areas of science may suffer. Such a pattern has been most evident in agricultural research, where support for biotechnology has far exceeded that for alternative forms of agriculture, such as organic farming, that present fewer opportunities for commercialization.[102] In addition, government environmental research now appears to be subject to an unprecedented degree of political manipulation, wielded through appointments to advisory committees, choice of research topics, and controls on publication. All these developments raise concerns about the capacity of science to examine the consequences of new technologies openly and critically, and to fulfill the diverse roles expected of it.

Experience demonstrates that science can fulfill its roles most effectively through a variety of strategies: from basic research, guided by the priorities of the scientific community, to research focused more directly on immediate environmental issues and problems. This diversity must extend as well to the actors pursuing or supporting research, strategies for communicating results, and the institutions that link science and politics.

CHAPTER 8

Democratic Environmental Science

❧

In *Silent Spring*, Rachel Carson indicted not just pesticides and their "unthinking bludgeoning" of the environment, but the institutions that allow this violence.[1] Too often, she argued, decisions were made not by those with broad knowledge of their consequences, or by citizens, but by experts in the Department of Agriculture and the chemical industry, especially economic entomologists, who refused to consider even the possibility of alternatives. It was time, therefore, for everyone else to have their say: for the "millions to whom beauty and the ordered world of nature still have a meaning that is deep and imperative" to pay attention.[2] And she acknowledged the many who had already spoken out against pesticides, "who are even now fighting the thousands of small battles that in the end will bring victory for sanity and common sense in our accommodation to the world that surrounds us."[3]

Carson's themes—the dangers of insular expertise, and the need for citizens to take action—became central to the environmental movement of the 1960s, expressed through challenges to the authority of science-based resource and regulatory regimes and through efforts to assert the value of more open, democratic approaches to making decisions. At the root of these challenges and assertions was the question of the place of expertise in a democratic society. More than forty years after *Silent Spring*, this question continues to resonate in environmental controversies.

The most difficult, but most essential environmental questions are not scientific, but political. They concern the question of what might be an appropriate relationship between humans and other species, balancing of individual freedoms against the collective good, and the responsibility of present communities to the future. Finding the best answers to those questions depends not on more sophisticated analytical apparatus or scientific theories, but on refining the processes by which communities can debate their differences and arrive (if possible) at a consensus.[4] Determining how the environment, and preferred environmental futures, can be defined and measured scientifically—whether in terms of sustainability, or climatic stability, or ecosystem integrity, for example—must be informed by, and contribute to, these political processes. What must be imagined, then, are processes that are both scientific and political.

The Environment and Democratic Politics

Back in the 1970s (and occasionally since then), several writers suggested that environmental crisis will eventually enforce limits on democracy. According to William Ophuls, Robert Heilbroner, Laura Westra, and Rudolf Bahro, environmental degradation and resource depletion will compel a turn to more authoritarian forms of government able to impose necessary reductions in resource use and economic activity. New institutions, like Bahro's "Environmental Council"—experts armed with overriding power—will ensure that economic policies adhere to environmental limits.[5] Such views have since become unfashionable, with scholars and activists alike urging more, not less, democracy: access to information, public participation, and all the other apparatus of open government.[6]

Nevertheless, a reluctance to embrace democracy is still often seen in discussions and actions relating to the environment. It is evident sometimes in impatience: environmentalists recite the litany of environmental challenges facing the world and bemoan how "politics" obstructs effective action. Some environmentalists tend to be suspicious of liberal democracy, viewing as problematic the absence of prior commitments to environmental values, its focus on the pursuit of economic and other anthropocentric interests, and the likelihood that bargaining over conflicting interests will result in tradeoffs that ignore the complexity of nature.[7] Splitting the difference between interests by, say, protecting one half of a watershed and cutting the other half may seem a reasonable compromise, but to grizzly bears or salmon half a forest may be as useless as none at all. Although amply refuted, the "tragedy of the commons" model still exerts some authority, buttressing fears that the pursuit of self-interest inevitably leads to environmental decline: because people are unable to consider the larger consequences of their actions they require expert regulation. And finally, skepticism toward democracy may be encouraged by the delays involved in achieving public awareness of environmental problems (often long after they have been described by scientists) and the fickleness of their attention once gained (a phenomenon captured decades ago in Anthony Down's issue-attention cycle). As Down's cycle suggests, and data provided by the Social Learning Group also illustrate, public attention to environmental problems tends to lag years behind scientific developments, and, when it does arrive, tends to come in short bursts.[8] This pattern may be viewed as incompatible with the sustained, steady attention necessary to understand fully and to resolve problems.

In addition, as Robert Paehlke describes, various features of environmental problems themselves provide grounds for doubt as to whether they can be addressed democratically. These include the need to find ways of limiting economic activity so as to be sustainable within a finite world, even as politicians stand or fall on their ability to encourage economic growth; the incremental nature of most environmental problems that makes them poorly suited to attracting attention in political systems addicted to urgency; ambiguous scientific information that is often unable to make a compelling case for action, especially given competing political priorities; and the disconnect between political boundaries and the natural world, with environmental problems rarely fitting well within democratic jurisdictions.[9] Those responsible for environmental problems may not be those who experience its impacts, either because the problems themselves cross borders (like depletion of the ozone layer or global climate change) or because economic activities in one place can have consequences in distant parts of the world (as evident, for example, in the trade in endangered species or the production and disposal of toxic waste).[10] In the Canadian Arctic indigenous people must deal with toxic contaminants in the caribou and other species that remain an important part of their diet. These contaminants originate in industrial and agricultural activities thousands of miles to the south, rendering nonsensical any notion that these people have "democratic" control even over their food supply.[11] And of course, future generations affected by decisions today cannot vote.

Given these challenges, it could be suggested that, whatever democratic principles one may espouse in theory, obstacles to applying them are such that democracy need not be a crucial element of effective environmental policymaking. This may be especially apparent in global environmental issues. Indeed, the recent study of such issues by the Social Learning Group chose to frame its analysis in terms of an "elite" discourse of professionals and political leaders, in part because "the general literatures on agenda setting, issue framing, and policy making suggest that accounting for lay perspectives is unlikely to be essential for explaining many of the questions that most concern us here."[12] If public perspectives and actions need not be considered in understanding how society has responded to these issues, does that suggest that democracy is dispensable?

Certainly, environmental policy and administration, even at the domestic level, are far from some democratic ideal. In practice, democratic politics is commonly seen within agencies as interfering with rational, efficient administration. Policymaking is highly political, done not by a single decision-maker, but through a complex process in which contending interest groups advance their interests. While there are now more actors than several decades ago, institutions with longer histories and greater resources, including regulatory agencies and industries, remain dominant. There is more public participation in setting agendas, evidenced by the highly visible role played by public interest groups in drawing attention to environmental problems. However, these groups, lacking resources and institutional ties, are still underrepresented in regulatory and policy proceedings. Many issues are still the product of "inside initiation," in which business groups with access to decision-makers initiate a policy or development and resist any move to contest it in public or to shift it beyond closed negotiations with the regulatory agency.[13] Once broad policy goals are set, there are many opportunities for significant decisions to be made by this restricted set of participants, with few opportunities for outsiders to influence them.[14] Any learning is likely to be restricted to drawing lessons about the effectiveness of existing arrangements, not the possibility of new arrangements. While these administrative structures are often portrayed as objective, they in fact include among their bases certain consistent value choices.

However, demands for democratic decision-making have been a central feature of the environmental movement, especially evident in controversies involving resource management and risk management. In response, innovations intended to improve environmental protection have often been designed in terms of more open political and administrative processes: public hearings, access to information and right-to-know laws, citizen panels, access by interest groups to regulatory proceedings, and so on. Most professionals now advocate, at least publicly, public input in setting policy goals and objectives. Their point is not to deny the value of experts, but to diminish the privileged status of those experts and to ensure that citizens also have opportunities to contribute to decisions on issues that affect them.[15] Thomas Beierle and Jerry Cayford summarize this view: rather "than seeing policy decisions as fundamentally technical with some need for public input, we should see many more decisions as fundamentally public with the need for some technical input."[16] Picking up on this, some recent efforts to sketch a transformed environmental politics emphasize the promise of democratic procedures and grassroots participation. In particular, William Shutkin sees environmental problems as local, demanding community-based solutions, achieved through "civic environmentalism": an ideal of local democracy and community solidarity.[17]

To be meaningful, democratic environmental politics must entail working through the essential environmental challenge: balancing the rights of individuals to determine their own use of the environment with the many environmental matters that must be determined collectively, while acknowledging that, in return, these collective decisions often shape the choices available to individuals. (For example, a decision to favor highways over public transit affects the choices available to individuals, as well as the collective environment.) Democracy should also entail providing a means for working through political conflicts fairly and peaceably, when agreement is not possible. There are several dimensions of democracy: transparent decision-making, people being able to define their interests for themselves, equal rights and equal access to power with which to pursue these interests—in short, affirmation that citizens are equal. As John Dryzek explains, the extent to which a system of government fulfills these may be evaluated in terms of three criteria: franchise (how many individuals are able to participate); scope (the range of issues accessible to democratic control); and authenticity (the extent to which people are able to make a substantive and informed contribution to decisions).[18]

Many compelling arguments have been made in favor of democratic politics, beyond basic issues of rights. Pragmatically, people know best what is consistent with their own interests and values. Adhering to democratic principles also makes government appear more trustworthy and its decisions more legitimate, while making people better, more informed citizens. Better decisions are also more likely, since people possess knowledge that is relevant to both framing and applying public policy.

The specifically environmental virtues of a democratic politics are also many and varied. The terrible environmental record of authoritarian regimes in the former Soviet bloc, and today in China, is well known. Even within democratic societies, approaches to environmental affairs that bypass democracy often show themselves to be inadequate. Resource management that excludes public participation focuses too much on commodities and the interests of certain industries, not enough on the broader public interest. Expert-driven risk management ignores public concerns regarding certain types of risks. The history of cities is full of expert efforts to reshape them through plans that failed to take into consideration how people actually want to live. This observation was the basis for Jane Jacobs's indictment of professional planning: that expertise of spurious objectivity has succeeded only in imposing an orderly view of cities in which there is no place for people's own ideas and aspirations.[19]

Some of the strongest arguments for democratic environmental politics are from history. Countless initiatives, indeed the emergence of environmentalism itself, can be attributed not to information provided by experts, but to the involvement and commitment of citizens. Advances in environmental protection, when they required overcoming obstacles to change, have most often been as a result of actions pursued through open and participatory forms of decision-making. One analysis of twenty-four "success stories" of environmental policy found that in every case public awareness or public pressure was important.[20] Democratic systems at least offer the prospect of learning from experience and improving policies.[21]

Experience also indicates that democratic approaches can produce better environmental decisions. These approaches make it possible to take into account all interests, concerns, and sources of knowledge, to balance divergent views, including alternative approaches to an issue, and to consider environmental values that would otherwise be neglected. Democratic processes also reduce the temptation to define decisions and problems in technical terms, thereby diverting attention from the real issues at stake. Instead, the political or moral dimensions of decisions can be addressed directly. As numerous scholars have suggested, environmental protection will be most effective through democratic approaches that are able to balance environmental values against other values such as social justice, economic prosperity, and national security.

Public participation in environmental governance, and the civic benefits that this can generate, relate to democratic pragmatism: solving problems through reasoned debate. According to the pragmatic perspective, as outlined by John Dewey and others, it is best to begin with the assumption that with complex social or political issues there is no single "right" answer or moral position, and that no such answer can be found simply through analysis by experts or through the state functioning as the arbiter of competing interests. Instead, finding the best approach should be an exercise in problem-solving, to be achieved through experimentation, guided not by experts, but by ordinary knowledge. This requires a pluralistic approach, with participants providing a range of perspectives, from both within and outside government. These perspectives can, through reasoned public debate, be cobbled together into a workable solution: a convergence, in effect, on a common understanding of the public interest.[22] Participants in the process will agree that this understanding is to be tentative and provisional, subject to revision as problems and knowledge continue to evolve and to be discussed.

Recent experience has corroborated the notion that democratic approaches can produce better solutions to complex problems. Across a range of issues, people have shown that they are capable of grappling with complex problems, including those with considerable scientific content. This has been demonstrated by AIDS activists, who have accumulated a great deal of scientific expertise and have used it to influence the direction of research.[23] A similar demonstration has been provided by experiments in citizen involvement in policy deliberation, particularly in northern Europe.[24] Such outcomes illustrate how, as Aaron Wildavsky in particular argues, one need not have advanced education in order to contribute to interpreting scientific evidence or to making a reasonable decision on science-based policy issues.[25] Understanding such issues, ultimately, is no more difficult than what the average citizen does in running a small business or balancing the conflicting demands of work and family. People have in particular shown considerable sophistication when it comes to the politics of science, often exceeding that demonstrated by scientists themselves. This includes awareness of the relations between science and interest groups, as well as of how decisions can be made with uncertain information.[26] People are also able to consider a broader range of concerns than is implied by viewing them simply as calculators of their own self-interest. As Mark Sagoff argues, they can view environmental issues both in terms of personal advantage, and as citizens concerned with the wider public good.[27]

Given these capabilities, the challenge is to ensure that people have opportunities to exercise them, overcoming the widely noted signs of apathy (low voter turnouts, a decline in civic society). According to some observers, apparent ignorance and lack of interest in politics reflect more than anything a lack of opportunities to participate, and to develop the skills needed to participate effectively.[28] In other words, citizens have noted a lack of opportunities to influence policy, and have come to the logical conclusion about where to expend their efforts. In contrast, opportunities to participate, and an immediate concern or threat, will generate citizens' efforts to gather information and make their views known.[29] Thus, beyond specifically environmental benefits, a democratic environmental politics can generate a citizenry more engaged in the life of their community, perhaps counteracting the decline in civic life that Robert Putnam identifies. As Melody Hessing and Michael Howlett argue:

> As an educational tool, more direct and decentralized forms of decision-making would contribute to community cohesion, produce a well-informed electorate, and foster an environmentally informed citizenry. Participation in arenas such as consultative tribunals would not only educate citizens in the substantive areas of concern, such as pesticide hearings, but also teach them about the functions and processes of state agencies and environmental law. The expressive effects of participation further contribute to the development of individuals' capabilities of self-expression.[30]

As people's competence to participate in environmental decisions has become more apparent, the consensus has developed that they have a right to opportunities to exercise these capabilities. As a result, the process by which an environmental decision is made has become as important as the decision itself, at least in terms of its acceptability. A decision that is simply announced will be received less warmly than if all interested parties have been involved in arriving at that decision, regardless of the merits of the decision itself. Decisions will not be considered legitimate unless they have included opportunities for citizen involvement, both in defining the problem and in searching for solutions, through an open and fair process. This applies not just at local and national levels, but in international environmental affairs, where participation by organizations representing diverse interests can open up otherwise closed negotiations, imparting some assurance of transparency and accountability, and thereby legitimacy, to the process.[31]

A more democratic environmental politics can entail modifying the conventional state-centered view of democracy, incorporating awareness of a wider range of concerns and interests. It can also be something more ambitious, with not simply representatives acting on behalf of citizens, but citizens themselves participating, individually and in groups, together expressing a vibrant, healthy civil society. As Martin Jänicke suggests: "it is not primarily the institutional set-up of representative democracy which is advantageous for positive policy outcomes, but rather the constitutional civil rights of western democracies—the participatory, legal and informational opportunity structures available to proponents of environmental interests—which appear to be most decisive."[32] Even at the international level, positions are formed and negotiations proceed not merely through nation states, but within a large and diverse community, composed of environmental organizations, the private sector, scientific bodies, and other actors. In summary, a democratic politics would address environmental challenges through a variety of means: by ensuring representation, to enable collective decisions that reflect the general will; by allowing interests of all kinds to define and pursue their own objectives, separate from, but able to influence, the state; and by providing the means by which conflicts can be resolved, through fair processes of negotiation.[33] Finally, it includes determining the limits of democracy. Some technical decisions are best made by experts (and other kinds of decisions are the expression of basic rights, and so should also not be subject to the popular will). But defining an issue as technical is itself a political matter, requiring open, democratic deliberation.

Is Science Democratic?

One argument sometimes heard is that science is not really relevant to these questions of democratic politics. According to this view, science is neutral, neither pro- nor anti-democratic: research generates useful knowledge that may be applied for good or evil, but it is up to society to decide which. By this view, it is hard to see how science could be a threat to democracy; indeed, if the knowledge is widely accepted as valid and useful (a question that is up to non-scientists to determine), then it even has a kind of democratic authority.[34]

In practice, however, science is closely implicated in these questions. Science and democracy have often been considered akin, dependent on the same conditions: freedom of thought, speech, and association, the free flow of information, with individuals able to question authority and discover their own truths. Ancient Greece fostered both an early democracy and substantial scientific activity, while the inseparability of genius and challenges to oppressive authority is a standard theme in scientific biography, from Galileo to Darwin to the physicists who escaped Nazi oppression. John Dewey expressed the relation succinctly in 1939, arguing that "freedom of inquiry, toleration of diverse views, freedom of communication, the distribution of what is found out to every individual as the ultimate intellectual consumer, are involved in the democratic as in the scientific method."[35] Many practicing scientists today would endorse such a view— indeed, the relation of science to freedom is one of the more pervasive tacit assumptions within the scientific community, and exceptions to this relation— Lysenkoism and Nazi science, to take two examples—are considered an unnatural deviation from the normal order. By this view, science and democracy share the same virtues and similar hazards. Obstacles to the conduct and application of science, such as a lack of open communication or the subjugation of knowledge to economic authority, are viewed as parallel to the problems that bedevil democracy.

The legitimacy of science also depends on researchers conducting themselves in ways consistent with democratic principles. This implies transparency, reasoned deliberation, and participation by diverse interests and perspectives, both in research itself, and in applying science to political and regulatory decisions.[36] These requirements stem, of course, from awareness that scientific knowledge is not simply a mirror of reality. Given the lack of a clear boundary between science and politics—between ideas about what the world is like, and what it should be like, as evidenced by the roles of science in the policy process, in interest groups' use of science to pursue and justify their goals, in the existence of uncertainties and other opportunities for interpretation of evidence, and in awareness that other forms of knowledge can be as valuable as conventional science—it is becoming more widely accepted that democratic norms should be applied to environmental science. Failure to do so generates skepticism and doubt regarding the legitimacy of knowledge, rendering it ineffective.

One of the chief advantages of a more democratic science is that it can provide a way of sorting through the ambiguous relation between what the world is and what we would like it to be—in other words, determining which questions are truly scientific and which raise other (perhaps political or ethical) issues. As I have noted in previous chapters, defining issues as scientific is a highly political exercise: interests that have a substantial investment in expertise will prefer to define questions as scientific, so as to restrict non-experts, and their political, economic, or social concerns, from the debate. Perceptions that this is occurring will encourage mistrust and doubt regarding the legitimacy of the process.

Finally, a more democratic science is necessary in order to question directly the often unexamined imperatives embedded within science: to reshape the world, to impose a standardized perspective, to pursue efficiency above all else. Once they examine it openly, people may choose to reject this imperative, opting instead for a less dominating, more flexible, adaptive relationship with the world.[37] Citizens can also question how experts frame an issue, by identifying unexplained assumptions and tacit value choices and by suggesting alternative approaches to ambiguous data. However, alternative perspectives can only be considered if the dominant scientific approaches themselves are opened up to public scrutiny. Without this scrutiny it will be assumed that the public's values are identical with those of scientists.[38] This can extend across borders: the formation of an international research and environmental community can provide a check on the influence of any single scientific imperative, or government or corporation promulgating a particular perspective.

The value of opening to scrutiny the assumptions embedded in scientific practice is illustrated by how issues can sometimes only be resolved through questioning and rejecting these assumptions. For example, in the 1950s and 1960s weather modification was considered a promising technology. It was eventually discarded, not because of new information, or because it didn't work, but because of changing attitudes toward uncertainty and risk and the evolving view that manipulation of the environment on such a scale was inherently problematic.[39] A similar story can be told regarding the need for wider oversight of the assumptions that guide resource management science and risk science. What is essential, if scientific knowledge is to reflect changes in social attitudes—to avoid, say, researchers continuing to study weather modification long after it has become unacceptable to society—are effective links between the scientific community and the rest of society, including opportunities to question the assumptions that guide scientists.

However, while science can benefit from adopting democratic principles, science is also widely viewed, in practice, as contrary to these principles. First, the scientific community sees itself not as a democracy, but as a self-governing meritocracy. It sets itself apart from other ways of knowing nature, reinforcing this separation through boundary work. Nor are scientific authority and the advice that scientists provide open to the usual compromises of democratic politics.[40] Second, while science may flourish in a democracy, the way its application to society is sometimes portrayed can imply that democracy is dispensable. Indeed, alternatives to democracy have often been framed in terms of expertise. Consider Plato's concept of guardianship: that in a complex world people need to be governed by someone smarter and more rational, a philosopher-king able to see beyond appearances into the real nature of things, who can apply the science of ruling. In the 1600s Francis Bacon proposed a utopian society, run by an elite able to use scientific knowledge to assure an efficient, orderly, progressive governance. This vision of expertise as an alternative to democracy has been picked up on ever since, suggesting how readily democracy and expertise have been seen as contradictory imperatives. Indeed, it has become a cliché of modern times that the past century has witnessed a paradox: citizens now have greater rights to govern themselves, but in a society being reshaped by science and technology beyond the capacity of most citizens to understand. Confidence in the ability of expertise to identify appropriate goals for resource management was a central belief of the progressive conservation movement. By this view, expert knowledge was neutral: a tool to achieve efficiently the purposes of the people. It thus did not threaten, but assisted democracy. Such a view has been perpetuated in administrative rationalism: that the public interest is not something for the public to debate, but for experts to determine, through techniques such as cost-benefit analysis. Many public officials appear still to believe that expert understandings of risks are superior to those of the public: more rational and objective, based on evidence rather than emotion.

The scientific character of many environmental issues might be invoked as rationale for exempting them from democratic principles. Perhaps when non-scientists make science-based policy it is simply the tyranny of the ignorant, analogous to allowing people to vote on whether creationism or evolution should be taught in high school biology classes, or on which medical treatments are best. Skepticism regarding the public's capabilities are implicit in the "deficit" model of public understanding of science as promulgated by, among others, Great Britain's Committee for the Public Understanding of Science.[41] According to this model, the lay mind is an empty bucket into which the facts of science can be poured. Aaron Wildavsky provides a more subtle perspective: that concerns regarding the environment must be science-based, that many public concerns reflect an ignorance of science and a readiness to be stampeded by irrational fears, but that citizens, once educated, are able to understand the science.[42] This view is sometimes backed by surveys of "scientific literacy" in which members of the public are asked to define terms such as "eutrophication" or to explain the chemistry of acid rain or the difference between ozone depletion and global warming. The problem with this approach to measuring "scientific literacy" is that it denies the importance of context in the interpretation and use of scientific knowledge. People may ignore scientific knowledge if it is seen as irrelevant to their lives or if it is unaccompanied by any opportunity to actually do something with it. Critics also note that this deficit model adheres to a prescriptive, top-down view of public affairs in which scientists are seen as having all the knowledge.[43] Research purporting simply to demonstrate public ignorance can imply its own political prescriptions.[44]

Expert framings of issues emphasize abstraction and rationality, excluding public concerns, which are rejected as emotional or non-rational. The political impact of this is often evident at public hearings, where experts typically present their conclusions in an impersonal, technical format, reinforcing the impression of professional neutrality. The experts' framing becomes the authoritative one, and public attempts to resist it by bringing in nontechnical issues or by becoming angry or confrontational, can be dismissed as "emotional." In effect, democratic participation is discouraged, except on the terms defined by the experts.[45] This can be especially problematic because it can be difficult to determine when experts go beyond their areas of knowledge to express covert political views. To assert, therefore, that science is an objective, nonpolitical basis for policy is to make a political statement.

Environmental science restricts participation in other, more specific ways. Scientists tend to impose a standardization and aggregation of knowledge that is insensitive to local conditions, variations, and forms of knowledge. For example, in the aftermath of the Chernobyl accident, and amid concerns regarding radioactive contamination, scientists in England's Lake District ignored farmers' knowledge of the local environment. As a result, the farmers felt that their social identity as specialists, with an adaptive, informal cultural idiom, had been dismissed by ignorant but arrogant experts.[46] Such a pattern has often been encountered, particularly in natural resource management.

One of the most significant impediments to participation is access to scientific information. There are numerous constraints, including restricted access to government information and the fact that much information simply doesn't exist, because of inadequate research and monitoring. Information collected by industry that relates to specific development applications or resource extraction activities is often private property.[47] Corporate funding of research creates a culture of secrecy, with restrictions often imposed on publication of research results. When results are not to a sponsor's liking, it may suppress them, even at the expense of the public interest.[48] Much of the information about environmental impacts, such as the nature of the pollution, the impacts of regulation, the state of the resources, and so on, are often only available to the industry, and not to the government, let alone to the public. Lack of access to scientific information, then, poses a fundamental problem for democracy, analogous to that posed by secrecy.[49] Ultimately, access is wrapped up in the same structures of power that shape environmental politics generally. The experience of the Cree people of northern Quebec was telling. In the 1970s Hydro Quebec (the provincial power utility) announced plans for massive hydroelectric power developments in their territory. Although they had lived in the region for centuries, the Cree were obliged to express their concerns regarding the developments not in terms of their own knowledge of the landscape, but in scientific terms. However, they found it difficult to find scientists who were not dependent on funding from either Hydro Quebec or the provincial government; most scientists in Quebec were reluctant to offer views contrary to the interests of these powerful institutions.

As the experience of the Cree suggests, these problems of access extend to determination of the research agenda itself. Scientific information, even if available, may only be in forms that are useful to industry and say little about overall trends in the environment. For example, data collected in the course of resource management activities may only reflect economic values, not ecosystem or aesthetic concerns. Industry funding of research can affect entire areas of knowledge. As Dan Fagin and Marianne Lavelle note, weed science is mostly funded by industry, and is generally devoted to justifying the use of herbicide.[50] Close ties between science and particular interests—whether represented by government agencies or industry—can hinder the pursuit of research in the public interest. Instead, research is focused on narrower industry priorities. For example, research on salmon aquaculture on Canada's west coast has tended to focus on industry priorities, leaving societal concerns, such as the viability of wild salmon stocks, relatively unexamined. The most prominent instance of this, however, is the orientation of agricultural research toward genetically engineered food crops. The potential consequences of this technology on ecosystems and on other interests have been neglected, as has the potential of other approaches to sustainable agriculture, such as integrated pest management or organic farming. The impoverishment of public debate is evident when government agencies provide promotional materials for the technology, in the guise of "public information," and superficial and tendentious studies by industry-funded groups such as the National Center for Food and Agricultural Policy are lauded as comprehensive and insightful analyses.[51]

When an issue is defined in scientific terms it narrows the choices to those that can be measured, excluding those that require discussion. For example, debates regarding biotechnology are often framed in terms of science, forcing what should be a political discussion into an inappropriate scientific framework. Evaluating biotechnology in terms of its measurable risks and benefits avoids the need to consider a variety of questions: whether it is the appropriate solution to agricultural problems, and whether its risks and benefits can be accurately calculated and fairly compared. It also discourages consideration of other forms of agriculture, and it neglects the great complexity of agricultural ecosystems and the social and political systems within which they are embedded. Finally, it ignores other concerns regarding the science of biotechnology, including the relationships between research institutions and government and corporate sponsors, as well as its implications for the corporate control of agriculture, in which expertise is shifted from farmers to the corporations that provide the seeds and other technologies, effectively shifting farmers closer to "bioserfdom"—mere reproducers of the corporations' intellectual property.[52] Such concerns cannot be debated without those directly involved; and this must extend to participation in decisions about the biotechnology research itself, both because its results will affect them directly and because knowledge about the local environment in which this technology is to be applied is necessary. Similar observations can be made about the science and politics of natural resources management, or responses to climate change, or risk issues. In each case, citizens have played an essential role in opposing the definition of political questions as matters of science, instead insisting that these questions be taken out of the hands of the scientific community and their patrons and opened up to wider discussion.

Another obstacle to democratic decisions is evident in the tendency of environmental science to impose a global view (epitomized by the definition of climate change as "the" environmental problem of our times), driving a shift in environmental affairs to the international level, which is less accessible to democratic governance. Within governments, foreign affairs are traditionally seen as less accessible to democratic mechanisms, a view expressed by the adage that "politics ends at the water's edge." International public policy processes, such as trade negotiations, are far from open and participatory.[53]

Science-based environmental administration can also be interpreted as contrary to democratic principles because it implies that experts should determine priorities and how they should be implemented, once citizens have spoken on the broad objectives of policy. This approach, consistent with the permissive consensus model (that citizens give policymakers latitude in pursuing environmental policy, so long as they are seen as acting within the general consensus that environmental protection is important), is problematic because the actual outcomes of policies are often determined during their implementation.[54] The insulation of environmental administration from democratic oversight is reinforced by defining it as a process based on science. The policy process has an enormous appetite for information, not only because of the belief that better information leads to better policy, but because information confers political advantage.[55] In this context, science is no more neutral than it is infallible: it is part of the economic and institutional advantages that economic interests and state actors have over other participants in the policy process. When an agency or industry is the principal source of information, it is able to shape issues, to release or withhold information, or to choose to pursue or foreclose certain lines of research. The overall result is to restrict democratic participation in environmental decisions. When issues are defined in scientific terms—when, say, a controversy over the future of a forest is considered strictly in terms of modeled projections of forest growth and the costs and benefits of harvesting, or global environmental change is defined in terms of changing concentrations of trace gases—then those who lack expertise will be discouraged from participating. Instead of a broadly based, accessible process for evaluating policies, participation in the process is defined very narrowly. This extends to the institutions that support environmental administration. Reviewing several leading American university programs in environmental studies, Timothy Luke concluded that they perpetuate a view of the environment "as a highly complex domain far beyond the full comprehension of ordinary citizens or traditional naturalists. Because it sustains economic growth, ecology becomes something to be managed by expert eco-managerialists armed with coherent clusters of technical acumen and administrative practice."[56]

Relying on expertise in environmental administration therefore endangers two foundational principles of democracy: the neutrality of the state and the equality of citizens. The state, as both a chief patron of experts and dependent on them, will find it difficult to remain neutral in the face of the value commitments inherent in expert advice.[57] While democracy may depend on open debate, the imperatives of the state and its experts will always be lurking in the background, affecting evaluations of what is reasonable and feasible. At the same time, expertise privileges its possessors with powers that violate the conditions of rough equality presupposed by democratic accountability.[58] Again, therefore, the image of reasoned debate amongst equals is limited by the exercise of unequal resources of expertise.[59] These patterns apply to the environmental movement as well. Although the movement has been associated with democratic ideals, environmental groups, especially at the national level, can tend to follow something like the permissive consensus model, in which their activities are disengaged from their own membership and they develop instead a close relationship with the industries and agencies they are seeking to influence.[60] The definition of environmental administration as a scientific activity reinforces this tendency. To build up the expertise they considered necessary for participation in national environmental affairs, mainstream groups in the United States had, by the 1990s, turned away from their grassroots origins, seeking instead closer ties to corporations, foundations, and national agencies. In their place, a dense array of local and regional organizations formed, much more closely tied to particular communities and constituencies.[61] The significance of expertise in separating national and local organizations, serving even as a symbol of cultural and political distance, is evident in Lois Gibbs's account of a meeting she organized between them: "It was hilarious. . . . People from the grassroots were at one end of the room, drinking Budweiser and smoking, while the environmentalists were at the other end of the room eating yoghurt. We wanted to talk about victim compensation. They wanted to talk about ten parts per billion benzene and scientific uncertainty."[62]

An important example of how expertise can have consequences that are neither democratic nor environmentally sound is provided by the nearly sixty-year history of the World Bank. By design, it is not a democratic institution: policy is determined not by those affected by its projects but by its largest funders, led by the United States. It is also a highly technocratic institution, reliant on economic expertise and, to a much lesser extent, environmental expertise in making decisions regarding projects that will have environmental impacts. The consequence, as many critics have described, has been countless projects destructive both to the environment and to the welfare of many millions of people.[63]

Building Democratic Science

Describing a system of government as democratic doesn't necessarily help very much when it comes to determining which decisions are best made by the people, which by elected officials, and which by the courts or by experts. The diversity of possibilities inherent in democracy have similarly varied implications for the role of science. Representative democracy has certain advantages, but also limitations. One argument for it is that the substantial scientific content of many issues gives the advantage to this approach over more direct approaches to democracy. Only representatives engaged full-time in governing are able to devote the necessary effort to gathering information and thinking through complex issues.[64] Such a view of representative democracy parallels the permissive consensus model of governing: citizens express a general preference for environmental protection, but then delegate to their representatives, and their advisors, the details of how this preference will be implemented.

However, representative democracy has definite limits, as the proliferation of more participatory approaches has made clear. If policies are to be responsive to public concerns, then those concerns must be presented in the negotiations that generate these policies. Bargaining between competing resource interests, public debates over a proposed development or the future of a natural area, and legal actions against industries accused of polluting illustrate the diverse formats in which this takes place. Those presenting concerns must have access to the scientific information needed to support their claims, in the face of adversaries who will have their own sources of information. This requirement has varied implications for scientific expertise. Participatory processes may be limited to elites, who may be defined in terms of expertise (such as science advisory boards) or because they represent certain interests, especially those of more powerful economic actors. They may also involve a broader range of actors, as when, for example, citizens work on building consensus regarding options for a region, through round tables or stewardship committees, sharing information as a basis for building cooperation and a common vision. Alternatively, information may be used not to develop a consensus, but by one group to assert their position against their adversaries in a controversy, explicitly linking expertise to specific interests. One important dimension of democratic science is ensuring that groups have the capacity to challenge the science-based claims made by more powerful actors (including industry and government). For example, to query the basis for regulating agricultural biotechnology requires much scientific expertise, in order to examine the assumptions used in designing tests of genetically modified crops, and also to consider these assumptions, and the science itself, in terms of the economic, political, or ethical implications of the technology.[65]

Access to information can depend on access to expertise. Often in controversies citizens are assisted by a volunteer expert, perhaps from the local university, who answers their own questions on their own terms.[66] However, volunteer arrangements present their own problems, given that controversies demand a substantial time commitment. Access to funding can therefore be necessary, to hire expert witnesses, conduct research, disseminate the results, prepare presentations, and complete all the other tasks implied by participation in the policy process. When financial support is not available, it can tend to encourage perceptions that the process is open only to those able to afford expertise; in practice, that means those parties, particularly industry, that have a direct economic stake in the issue.

Many environmental organizations, recognizing that scientific knowledge is a prerequisite for participating in the policy process, devote considerable effort to obtaining and disseminating it, demonstrating a strong commitment to and capabilities in science. Many groups are highly pro-knowledge: seeking relevant, useful information, and seeking to revalue and re-legitimate forms of knowledge that professional science has excluded. Smaller environmental organizations obtain advice from local scientists and engage in community-based monitoring of environmental resources, or in health surveys that follow the tenets of popular epidemiology, while larger organizations have the resources to bring their own scientists to negotiations or to commission scientific research. In international environmental negotiations on topics such as climate change and hazardous waste, environmental organizations have used science as a basic resource: conducting research, assembling information, applying it to framing environmental issues as problems requiring a political response.[67] One arena in which these capabilities have been demonstrated is global climate negotiations. Environmental organizations play key roles in disseminating information and advising negotiators, including those from smaller or poorer states, such as the Association for Small Island States, that would otherwise lack the resources to defend their interests.

One intriguing example of the political significance of scientific information was the Canadian Coalition for Acid Rain, established in the 1980s to lobby the American government for action on acid rain. The coalition recognized that rather than acting directly, it could be most effective by providing information to domestic American interests advocating action on the problem. Accordingly, it became an information broker, providing scientific knowledge about acid rain to any who requested it, establishing itself as a credible, nonpartisan source. In effect lobbying at arm's length, the coalition made itself less vulnerable to political attack, and so more effective than if it had set out to lobby directly.[68] The success of the coalition also illustrated how some organizations can have advantages over government when it comes to using scientific information, bringing it to bear on immediate, pragmatic goals: public information, lobbying, or participating in legal or other adversarial contexts, playing an essential role in converting scientific information into politically useable forms.

This coalition's activities also highlight the role of environmental organizations generally in global issues. The point about the coalition's use of science is that it enabled representation in decisions by those outside a political jurisdiction in which decisions are made, but within the ecosystem affected by those decisions. In effect, science was employed to expand democracy beyond political borders, to define polity according to ecological borders instead. Other situations in which borders have been redrawn using science include Scandinavians' use of science in the 1970s to place acid rain on the European environmental agenda, and nongovernmental organizations' use of scientific information to build a cross-border consensus on environmental protection in the Great Lakes region. Some theorists are now arguing that it is time to move beyond viewing democracy as necessarily linked to nation-states, and instead to consider postnational models of democracy that do not rely on the traditional "ties that bind" but on "making institutions, elites, and governments accountable to a plurality of voices often joined together by issues, interests, or causes."[69]

Not only established environmental groups, but citizens themselves pursue access to environmental information, through research, networking, and the Internet, learning about issues so that they are able to intervene skillfully in environmental controversies. A vast number of individuals have arisen who, while not technical experts, are knowledgeable about the role of such expertise and where it can be found. Often citizens themselves become experts, and knowledge is shared within networks of amateur and professional specialists. Clearinghouses for technical information have also been formed, with technically trained people keeping in touch with research, serving as vehicles for transferring information to a wider audience.[70] A well-known example is the Center for Health, Environment, and Justice mentioned in chapter 6.

As all this makes clear, environmentalists are most often pro-knowledge, gathering and using it in advocating protection of the environment and humans, seeing it, if used appropriately, as an instrument of democratic action. Experience has shown that if a scientific issue has a direct impact on a community, people will quickly acquire technically sophisticated information, enough to challenge professional expertise.[71] When there is apparent resistance to knowledge (as is sometimes suggested when environmentalists are portrayed as preferring emotion over reason), this likely stems from distrust over how the science is directed and used, and from concern as to whether the knowledge will be used to hinder citizens from influencing decisions. As Benjamin Barber argues: "Give people some significant power and they will quickly appreciate the need for knowledge, but foist knowledge upon them without giving them responsibility and they will display only indifference."[72]

Public access to scientific information is also necessary for helping people make appropriate decisions as individuals. As Wildavsky has argued, citizens must be able to evaluate critically claims regarding environmental hazards, so that they will be able to choose correctly which ones they should be concerned about. This should also include making informed choices in the marketplace: providing information about hazards themselves and about how and where they are encountered. Information about genetically modified foods, for example, should accompany labeling of the products on supermarket shelves. The danger with knowledge used to inform individual actions, however, is that it implies that a healthy environment is a matter of individual choice, not a problem demanding political or institutional change. This apolitical message can be especially attractive to public agencies—evident in efforts to solve a garbage crisis by exhorting individuals to reuse and recycle. It is especially evident in public information provided by agencies. For example, the Environmental Protection Agency provides timely and accessible information on local air quality through its "AIRNOW" web site.[73] This information is accompanied by advice on "What you can do" that emphasizes not, say, how to identify large polluters in one's neighborhood or tips on political action, but how to modify one's personal habits: by driving less often, for example. Official information, viewed as an instrument by which citizens can make effective decisions, can be especially problematic if it only serves to disseminate a dominant viewpoint.[74]

A democratic environmental science can also encompass a new way of defining "good science." The chief implication is a broadening of the evaluation criteria, beyond scientific excellence (the appropriate province of peer review) and relevance to immediate regulatory or managerial goals. These criteria should encompass not only the content of the science, but the context in which it is performed, including funding and other possible relationships with sources of authority, as well as the legitimacy of the uses to which the scientific knowledge is put. Attitudes displayed toward nonconventional knowledge are also important: people will mistrust a process if they perceive that the information they are providing is not considered equal in value to that provided by scientists.[75] One concept that captures how these diverse criteria can be applied is that of the extended peer community: composed not only of scientists, but also of others concerned or knowledgeable about an issue and prepared to help assure the quality of the relevant science. Participants would include experts and lay people, especially those with local knowledge.[76] The community thus convened would negotiate a common definition of good science, seeking agreement on such matters as appropriate research topics, approaches to handling uncertainty, the reliability of various sources of information, and other contentious elements of environmental science. The participation of non-scientists is essential; indeed, often it has been environmental organizations lacking a scientific background that have been more critical of scientific opinion and expert judgment, and that have more readily understood how science can be manipulated by authorities.[77]

While environmental organizations come closer to an ideal of participatory democracy by broadening participation in policy and the application of scientific expertise, they also fall short, as the most disadvantaged members of society are at once least likely to be mobilized and most affected by environmental problems. Many organizations tend to speak for upper-middle-class concerns more than for the concerns of those with less resources, while even expert public interest groups, such as the Natural Resources Defense Council or the Environmental Defense Fund, can only compete in a few arenas.[78] This applies on the global scale as well, with poorer nations, and their citizens, having much less access to expertise. Thus, exercising the right to participation requires correcting unequal access to information and the effective disenfranchisement of those lacking such access. More equitable access to scientific knowledge can be provided through, for example, technical assistance to communities, to enable them to understand better their environment and the impact of human activities. It can also imply wider access to scientific careers, to make the scientific community more nearly representative of the general population.

Access to scientific information implies that knowledge is a public right, not private or privileged property. A prerequisite for this is that ample opportunities exist for research that does not address only private interests, and that research results are not proprietary. This means, at least, maintaining the capacities of universities to conduct basic research, as well as maintaining the independence of granting agencies such as the National Science Foundation and the Natural Sciences and Engineering Research Council of Canada (NSERC). Such research—guided by many factors, including disciplinary priorities, the interests of researchers, and general societal concerns—while not of itself sufficient to fulfill effectively all the roles of science, is important in helping to insure that a variety of possibilities are pursued.

However, enhancing access to science, whether through official programs or through the initiatives of environmental organizations or citizens themselves, has a significant limitation. In essence, it entails grafting conventional research practices onto community activism. It does not, therefore, contribute to helping people speak for themselves—a key requirement of participatory democracy.[79] This is essential, if the assumptions embedded in scientific practice are to be examined openly, and if necessary questioned or rejected. For example, Wildavsky's argument that citizens merely need access to scientific information in order to make informed decisions tacitly assumes that science provides an objective view of risks, thereby closing off inquiry into the assumptions that may underlie the research.[80]

To address such concerns, some scholars and activists have called for more participatory methods of conducting research that would allow wider participation in shaping the research agenda, especially from interests other than industry or government. These are commonly referred to as civic science, or citizen science. One essential element of them is funding for research that can challenge dominant perspectives on issues. For example, relatively little research has been done on the potential hazards of genetically modified crops, reflecting a preponderance of research on developing this technology, not on assessing its hazards.[81] There might be some advantage in encouraging expression of more diverse interests in the development of technologies, including interests other than those seeking saleable products. In short, therefore, democratic science implies wider examination of what questions are being asked, why they are important, what counts as answers, and how these answers might be used.[82]

Perhaps most crucial is opening up the identification of research priorities to a wider range of interests and perspectives. For example, as I noted in chapter 4, environmentalists have often advocated research on a broad range of objectives relating to forests, while industry and government have tended to focus on narrower objectives, such as greater productivity and harvesting efficiency, that are consistent with the view of forests as primarily wood producers. Local and regional groups have played an important role in forestry controversies, getting to know their own forests, establishing monitoring systems to keep track of harvesting activities and road construction. In these episodes expertise developed in citizen groups confronted the Forest Service with detailed knowledge that it could not ignore.

Organizations like Greenpeace, and many others that support scientific research perform a useful role as a counterweight, by funding research that is unappealing to dominant actors in industry and government.[83] With a wider variety of interests influencing the research agenda, it becomes possible to ask new questions—to consider why so little research is devoted to the concerns of minority communities living near hazardous waste or industrial facilities, or why, as Friends of the Earth asked, when they surveyed the health of British forests (as noted in chapter 7), evidence of acid rain could not also include signs of multiple stresses on forests, and why action could not be justified even without conclusive proof of harm.[84] Wide participation in research—monitoring, field experimentation, evaluating restoration projects, and so on—is another step toward a civic science. Civic science, however, is not just about citizens doing the procedures of science with the help of scientists; rather, it involves scientists as citizens and citizens as lay scientists in an interactive process between experts and non-experts, based on trust and mutual respect.[85]

Deeper involvement of citizens in science can also entail greater transparency in the funding of science, exposing ties between economic and political interests and research. It should also provide opportunities for non-scientists to interpret, evaluate, and challenge scientific knowledge, as well as to incorporate non-scientific knowledge into authoritative accounts of the world. The objective, in short, would be to ensure that science serves less as an instrument in the service of powerful interests than as a means of empowering those not now able to protect their own interests, while pursuing objectives more readily identifiable as being in the public interest.

The importance of expertise to community empowerment is illustrated by a variety of experiments in improving access and participation. Among the most widely known are "science shops," linking community groups with university experts. Originating in the Netherlands, these "shops" have since been established in many countries, under different names, and they are now receiving support from the European Commission. In Canada, the "Community University Research Alliance" program of the federal research granting councils fulfills a similar role. In the United States the "Science for Citizens" program established in the late 1970s was also intended to fulfill this role, providing an independent source of information and analysis.[86] Its elimination by the Reagan administration illustrated the political vulnerability of such programs. However, since then a small but growing "community-based research" movement using collaborative research methods has emerged in the United States.

"Participatory research" constitutes a more radical vision of democratic science. It has been defined as "scientific investigation with education and political action," and it entails experts working cooperatively with people in a community, helping them to understand and confront realities and choices that affect their own interests, emphasizing empowerment and self-help. This type of research became especially prominent in developing countries during the 1970s, in the face of recognition of the failure of conventional development.[87] Participatory research has also evolved in the context of struggles against hazards in communities and workplaces. Rather than providing technical answers that are intended to bring political discussions to an end, participatory research assists citizens in efforts to examine their own interests, gain access to information, design research that meets their needs, and make their own decisions. The expert acts as a "facilitator": posing questions and presenting information to assist citizens in their own efforts, and in their own language, to examine interests and to answer questions on their own terms, and to plan appropriate courses of action.[88] Participatory research emphasizes "common sense," or "ordinary knowledge," drawing a distinction between formal knowledge and informal, contextual, local knowledge, often organized in narrative form and told as stories. Not only can such accounts provide local information; they may also uncover insightful, often counterintuitive surprises. The challenge is to combine, perhaps in a dialectical process, formal expert knowledge with the knowledge of ordinary citizens to produce a deeper understanding of a situation. One interesting model of participatory research has emerged in northern Alberta, through the efforts of the Arctic Institute of North America. Researchers and residents collect indigenous knowledge and integrate it into forest management practices, helping to ensure that communities gain a meaningful role in forest decisions. Over the last decade natives have become increasingly involved in northern Alberta forest management, and in 1997 the Alberta-Pacific Corporation, one of the largest pulp and paper companies in the region, committed itself to in-corporating their knowledge and concerns in its forestry planning process.[89]

Such arrangements imply more than a reorientation of research; instead, they entail a questioning, even a transformation, of the practice of science it-self, in order to access more diverse sources of information. Achieving this di-versity also entails opening up the process by which research funds are allocated, directing them toward priorities set by a wider array of interests, while giving more attention, and credibility, to alternative forms of knowledge. It involves wider participation in decisions about how the results of research, including new technologies, are to be used, perhaps through greater public ownership of the products of research. Widening access to the products and process of research can enhance both its effectiveness and its legitimacy: it would be seen less as an instrument in the service of powerful interests, and more as a means of de-fining and achieving the public interest. It also implicitly challenges traditional scientific values of detachment and objectivity. Cutting across the varied ap-proaches to participatory research is the view that people can define their own reality. Local organizations can be important alternatives to the top-down model of knowledge-making and diffusion, through access to local experience and to alternative models of environmental health or sustainability.[90] These arrange-ments constitute a redrawing of the boundaries that demarcate government, the private sector, and communities, asserting, in effect, that essential knowledge is not to be entrusted only to authoritative institutions, or to be considered private property, but that access to knowledge as a prerequisite for participation in po-litical life is a right.

Participatory research can be especially significant in terms of its rela-tion to environmental justice. One of the most innovative aspects of the envi-ronmental justice movement has been the emergence of efforts to confront scientific information about risk and to enable communities to collect and in-terpret their own information with which to press their concerns. This has given rise to a new kind of public expertise.[91] Environmental justice activities often include developing community scientific expertise, placing scientific practice within, rather than prior to, the political process. The "right to know" move-ment has used scientific information to force industry and government to re-consider conventional practices involving toxic contaminants and to mobilize residents and workers anxious about risks, thereby redefining power in the work-place as well as fostering a new sense of citizenship among its participants. In short, information is used to educate and empower workers and citizens.[92]

These political dimensions of science have other implications as well for environmental politics. One is the capacity of a participatory research process to contribute to politics on scales beyond the local. Community-based organi-zations can link up with global politics in many ways: by supplementing gen-eral scientific theories of the global environment with local knowledge, by disseminating environmental information to local audiences, by identifying short-comings of this knowledge, and by reframing dominant policy paradigms to take account of social and scientific uncertainty. In such ways these organizations can serve as creative initiators of policy, not just passive agents of policy directives from senior levels of government. As I noted in chapter 5, this can be an essential element of an effective political response to climate change.

Deliberative Democratic Science and Politics

What if environmental politics were a conversation, with no one interest dominating, but all parties able to have their say, including scientists, who would be there not simply to provide the "answer" but to help define the questions, working with all other parties? This is the essential promise of deliberative democracy. Its conversations could influence both policy and scientific research, acknowledging that policy implications do not flow automatically from scientific results and that science does not exist in an objective vacuum.

In recent years deliberative processes—discussions on topics or problems of interest, as a means of understanding public preferences, resolving conflicts, or developing policy—have received much attention. (We have encountered elements of deliberative democracy in earlier chapters: in some forms of ecosystem and community-based management of natural resources, and in the study and negotiation of neighborhood risk issues.) Ideally, these processes can provide a forum for examining and questioning both political and value preferences and scientific information, identifying underlying assumptions, and exposing both fundamental disagreements and opportunities for consensus. The key idea is that the public interest is best served by creating an open political process in which contending interests have equal opportunity to argue for their priorities. Good policy lies not in delegating authority to neutral experts, but in procedures that give all parties open access.[93]

Deliberation signifies people collectively shaping their own politics through persuasive argument, in effect widening distribution of responsibility for determining the relationship between society and nature. Consensus on the public interest is achieved not through voting (because peoples' choices would not be informed by knowledge of the preferences of others), but through dialogue. Through an iterative process, people would seek not simply to assert their own interests or preferences, but to learn about the preferences of others, about the world, and about available options. Peoples' preferences might then change as they gain more knowledge; the hope driving this process would be that a consensus would develop regarding the future. It is democracy as a process of education. As Simone Chambers explains it: "deliberation is debate and discussion aimed at producing reasonable, well-informed opinions in which participants are willing to revise preferences in light of discussion, new information, and claims made by fellow participants."[94]

Several writers have discussed democratic deliberation at some length: William Shutkin, presenting a vision of civic environmentalism; Robert Reich, with his notion of the "civic discovery" of common goals through public discussion of policy; and John Rawls, with his argument that policies that represent an "overlapping consensus" of interest groups are likely to be fair, effective, and resilient.[95] These and other visions of democratic deliberation may vary in the details, but they all entail making institutions and their decisions accountable to a broader range of interests and groups: democracy is grounded in an uncoordinated civil society composed of a multiplicity of voices.[96]

If policies are to be legitimate, they must be articulated, explained, and justified in public, so that there is ample opportunity for a wide range of actors to examine and critique them. Deliberation has several preconditions, but perhaps the most essential is open, transparent agencies, able to facilitate discussion and critical examination of policies and issues and to encourage citizens to gather their own information and make known their preferences.[97] Deliberation also presents significant challenges, including ensuring that all interests, and not just the more powerful or more eloquent, are able to contribute. Scientific information is inevitably a significant resource in deliberative processes, and ensuring participation in these processes means ensuring broad access to science. Deliberation is usually considered a supplement to, not a replacement for, representative democracy or pluralist bargaining.

There has been much discussion of various means of deliberation: panels, round tables, citizen juries. One example is the "consensus conference," developed in Denmark in 1987 and since experimented with in many countries. In this format a panel of about a dozen citizens, chosen to be representative of a community, engage for several days in intensive study, discussion, and consultation with technical experts, culminating in a public forum and a report summarizing their conclusions.[98] The hoped-for outcome is that reasoned debate will generate agreement on a common conception of the public interest. Somewhat similar processes, often extending over longer periods of intermittent meetings, have been applied to developing options in local and regional resource and environmental management. This vision of deliberative democracy does raise unsolved problems, including the challenge of moving beyond the local level to consider societal-level questions. Experiments in deliberative institutions also tend to involve small numbers of participants, with everyone able to fit into a single meeting room, and so raise questions regarding their legitimacy as representative of larger populations.

At first glance, the status of science within a deliberative process can seem problematic, given that it is contrary to the basic idea of equality that underpins deliberative democracy, in which all participants are seen as having something to contribute. However, scientific knowledge can make several contributions. The deliberative process involves more than just sharing ideas amongst participants; it also includes receiving information from experts, ideally generating a genuine collaboration between researchers and society, in which each party would have things to offer the other.[99] Research activities can themselves facilitate discussion and partnerships, perhaps serving as the first step toward more extensive political cooperation. Research activities can also provide common ground for discussion, as well as a common language for negotiation. For example, scientific models of regional systems have been described as a promising basis on which to build a consensual understanding about the environment and in which to develop appropriate policies.[100] Philip Kitcher suggests that, as part of his concept of "well-ordered science," the priorities for science could also be determined through the consensus of ideal deliberators formed after the tutoring of preferences. In practice, according to Kitcher, genuinely deliberative institutions would be too inefficient and time-consuming. However, more conventional institutions for research could be adapted to generate similar results.[101]

Deliberative processes can also improve the effectiveness of science in political processes. They can avoid the magnification of scientific uncertainties (and erosion of scientific authority) that often occurs in adversarial bargaining. Instead, collaborative consensus building can make it possible to focus more on those areas of knowledge in which agreement is possible. Such processes can also provide opportunities to negotiate the often contrasting commitments of scientists and non-scientists regarding how knowledge can be used: whether it is appropriate or legitimate to control nature, the significance of general versus local knowledge, how to deal with uncertainty—in general, negotiating what counts as good science, as well as the appropriate boundaries between science and politics. This in turn implies science evolving into a more explicitly interdisciplinary undertaking, able to serve as a tool for a more open, participatory culture of decision-making. This entails consulting multiple sources of knowledge, rather than relying on a single set of experts, so that all parties are able to verify or challenge the claims of others. While this might be considered inefficient, it can be useful in assuring that all parties have confidence in the information as accurate and legitimate. Because access to scientific knowledge can function as a form of political power, only when this access is relatively equal can dialogue proceed on an equal basis, achieving the democratic ideal in which only reason has force.[102]

Most important in the use of science in deliberative settings is to ensure that it is used not to determine, but to inform, discussions about policy options. Such determinations can occur in several ways. The options to be considered can be framed so as to exclude those that are unacceptable to the sponsoring institution. That these options exist may not even be apparent to outsiders, perhaps because they were determined beforehand to be technically infeasible. For example, forecasts of increasing demands for electricity, or for highway capacity, or for water, have been employed to portray a predicted trend as inevitable, rather than as only one possibility. In either case, science, in the form of forecasts, is used to legitimate particular political choices. As an alternative, there are, as the National Research Council noted, a variety of tools available whose role is "not to predict the future, but rather to structure and discipline thinking about future possibilities in the light of present knowledge and intentions."[103]

This educative aim can be pursued through a variety of tools, such as integrated assessment models and scenarios. Each of these provides a means of assessing the consequences of particular policy choices—in effect, ensuring that scientific knowledge informs, rather than dictates, the development of options.

One early effort to find ways to push decisions about alternative futures out of science and back into the political realm generated the concept of "backcasting." The basic idea is to propose, after deliberation, a desirable endpoint in some future year, and then determine through study whether and how it is feasible to reach that endpoint. In this way, it becomes possible to address explicitly the assumptions implicit in scientific knowledge about what is and what is not possible. Scientists provide scenarios of alternative futures, their likelihood and consequences, which, used interactively, enable participants to test the implications of different views and preferences, both their own and those of others.[104] These alternative futures would not be considered forecasts of what will happen, but scenarios of what could happen if certain decisions were made. Instead of focusing attention on the science, making its predictions ever more accurate, participants would focus on policy—on determining what future would be most preferable. One example of such an exercise is the Urban Lifestyles, Sustainability, and Integrated Environmental Assessment (ULYSSES) project, which uses integrated assessment models along with focus groups and policy exercises. Another is QUEST: the Quite Useful Ecosystem Scenario Tool, developed at the University of British Columbia. It is designed to be used interactively by lay people to explore possible futures.[105] Yet another example is the Scenario of Canada in 2030.[106] Such a study can be done more easily in the context of a specific geographic area, drawing on local knowledge while placing this regional analysis in a global context. However, as noted in chapter 5, scenarios of global climate change in relation to various policy options, as developed using integrated assessment models, provide opportunities to expand deliberation about possible futures to the global scale.

Theorists of deliberative democracy argue that its most important contribution is its capacity to encourage people to consider not just their own interests, but those of others, and so develop and pursue a vision of the common good—to instill, in other words, a measure of civic virtue. Since environmental issues relate so often to this common good, including protection of common spaces—the atmosphere, the oceans, public land—this makes deliberation especially relevant, because deliberation tends to encourage people to think in terms of the collective good. Perhaps, therefore, the crucial feature of a deliberative environmental politics is its potential to go beyond balancing and resolving divergent views, to formulate a common interest in the environment that can transcend individual interests—to ensure that people think not just as consumers, but as citizens. This vision has implications for science, including a demand for knowledge about the state of common spaces, freely distributed, available to all parties. Overall, deliberation implies a vision of science closely integrated with the political system, with research and deliberation as complementary approaches to understanding the world, forming knowledge and agreement simultaneously, allowing for mutual learning.[107] Such a vision is closer to how knowledge is viewed by people outside the scientific community: tied to its social, political, economic, and cultural contexts, with the notion of "independent expertise" considered contrary to everyday experience.[108]

CHAPTER 9

Achieving Effective and Democratic Science

❧

*T*he problem might be stated as a riddle: How can science be part of the political process, and yet separate? To restate in a slightly expanded form: How can we ensure that scientific research provides the information we need to pursue our environmental values and priorities (whether these relate to exploitation or to protection) without science itself becoming subject to the conflicts and controversies of environmental politics? We know, at least, that science cannot contribute simply by isolating itself, dispensing insights into environmental problems while remaining fixed on the objective pursuit of truth as defined by scientists. There are no such easy truths in the environmental arena: there is no quick answer to lead contamination in a complex urban environment, no obvious connection between ecological knowledge and protection of a rural watershed, and science alone will never tell us all we need to know about climate change. Science that fails to relate to these or other issues risks irrelevancy. Science too closely enmeshed in politics—becoming merely an instrument by which actors pursue their interests—risks becoming itself the focus of dispute, distracting attention from genuine political, economic, and moral differences.

Practical experience and study are now leading us in a different direction: toward a more modest view of the capacity of expertise. According to this view, science can provide valuable information, but so can non-scientists. Scientists can assist in identifying problems we should be concerned about, but others as well have drawn attention to pressing issues. Often enough, it has been non-scientists who have demonstrated the shortcomings of scientific worldviews. While science remains essential to understanding and solving environmental problems, so do other perspectives grounded in other forms of knowledge and experience. In short, context is everything. This modest view is even evident in the titles of recent studies of science in society, such as *Muddling Through*, by

Mike Fortun and Herbert Bernstein, and Clinton Andrews's *Humble Analysis*.[1] These authors explore, from different perspectives, the implications of realizing that scientists are able neither to provide a quick, direct route to the "truth," nor to gain useful knowledge without working with those who approach nature from other directions.

The difficulties involved in defining how science can be at once effective and respectful of democratic imperatives has been reflected in countless controversies, and in failures to deal with environmental challenges such as exhaustion of natural resources, climate change, and the spread of toxic contaminants. There appears, on the other hand, to be a tacit consensus developing among many scholars and practitioners regarding how we might solve the riddle of environmental science: how, that is, science could be part of, yet distinct from, politics. This consensus is in two parts.

The first part relates to how we evaluate science. Twenty years ago William Clark and Giandomenico Majone described four criteria (adequacy, value, effectiveness, and legitimacy) that, if applied to policy-relevant science, could ensure that new knowledge and the process by which knowledge is created are acceptable to all interested parties.[2] More recently this scheme, in modified form, has been applied in large research projects to knowledge of the global and American environments.[3] The four criteria have also been reduced to three. Robin O'Malley and his colleagues summarize succinctly these criteria and how they can contribute: "For information to be used and useful in a broad policy arena, and not itself be the subject of debate, it must meet three standards: It must be policy relevant, technically credible, and politically legitimate."[4]

The second part of the consensus on effective, democratic science relates to its institutional context. Science should not be in isolation, remote from practical decisions regarding the environment; nor should scientists necessarily always be available, "on call" in case their advice is required. Rather, institutions for science are most likely to be able to produce knowledge that is relevant (or salient), credible, and legitimate if they seek to stabilize the evolving boundary between science and politics, ensuring effective communication, translation, and mediation between all interests and scientists. Such institutions, ideally, provide opportunities for true competitions of ideas to take place; this, in turn, contributes to decisions and policies that will be more robust, because less susceptible to challenge on the basis of unexamined information or perspectives, and because of a greater confidence that it was not only "tame" expertise or interests that were consulted.

A great variety of efforts are underway to find ways to navigate, and even redraw, the boundary between science and politics. These are motivated most often by practical experience. They range from "boundary organizations" such as the Health Effects Institute and the Intergovernmental Panel on Climate Change, to adaptive management strategies within resource agencies, to, most informally, daily interaction between experts and resource users, interest groups, and other citizens. The great problem is that while lessons are being learned through these experiments in effective, democratic science, these lessons are not being disseminated to others who may be in a position to apply them. This is not unexpected: scientists gain little credit from reporting how they have interacted with communities or the policy process, while interest groups or others using science are usually and understandably too focused on immediate concerns to report how and why they were able (or not able) to use science effectively. While scholars from a variety of disciplines have provided accounts of many of these experiments, there are still unexamined opportunities to compare experiences. For example, research on global issues can learn from experience gained in adaptive management of natural resources. On the other hand, research on the risks posed by contaminants can learn from institutional innovations developed for global research. Countless other comparisons could be made, demonstrating how across the wide realm of environmental politics still persist the essential challenges and opportunities of democratic knowledge.

NOTES

CHAPTER 1 *Encountering Science and Politics*

1. Michael Klesius, "The State of the Planet," *National Geographic,* September 2002, 102–115. The scientists included Richard Barber, Theo Colborn, Wes Jackson, Jane Lubchenco, Hal Mooney, Sherry Rowland, and E. O. Wilson.
2. Quoted in Frank Fischer, *Citizens, Experts, and the Environment: The Politics of Local Knowledge* (Durham, N.C.: Duke University Press, 2000), 87.
3. New York City Department of Health and Mental Hygiene, *Lead Poisoning Prevention Program, Annual Report 2001* (New York, December 2002), 24.
4. Samuel Hays, "The Role of Values in Science and Policy: The Case of Lead," in *Explorations in Environmental History* (Pittsburgh: University of Pittsburgh Press, 1998), 291–311.
5. Jane Brody, "Even Low Lead Levels Pose Perils for Children," *New York Times,* 5 August 2003.
6. Kirk Johnson, "For a Changing City, New Pieces to a Lead-Poison Puzzle," *New York Times,* 30 September 2003; and "Looking Outside for Lead Danger," *New York Times,* 2 November 2003.
7. Rutherford H. Platt, Paul K. Barten, and Max J. Pfeffer, "A Full Clean Glass? Managing New York City's Watersheds," *Environment* 42, no. 5 (2000): 8–20.
8. Gretchen C. Daily, ed., *Nature's Services* (Washington, D.C.: Island Press, 1997).
9. Mark Sagoff, "On the Value of Natural Ecosystems: The Catskills Parable," *Politics and the Life Sciences* 21, no. 1 (2002): 16–21.
10. Jane Jacobs, *The Death and Life of Great American Cities* (New York: Vintage, 1961), 13.
11. Quoted in Ric Burns and James Sanders, *New York: An Illustrated History* (New York: Alfred A. Knopf, 1999), 516.
12. Kirk Johnson and Andrew Revkin, "Contaminants Below Levels for Long-Term Concerns," *New York Times,* 11 October 2001.
13. Kirk Johnson, "With Uncertainty Filling the Air, 9/11 Health Risks Are Debated," *New York Times,* 8 February 2002.
14. Sheila Jasanoff, "NGOs and the Environment: From Knowledge to Action," *Third World Quarterly* 18, no. 3 (1997): 579–594.
15. Gary Lease, "Introduction: Nature under Fire," in *Reinventing Nature? Responses*

to Postmodern Deconstruction, ed. Michael E. Soulé and Gary Lease (Washington, D.C.: Island Press, 1995), 4.

16. John Dewey, *The Public and Its Problems* (New York: Swallow, 1927).

17. Fischer, *Citizens*, x.

18. Sheila Jasanoff, *The Fifth Branch: Science Advisers as Policymakers* (Cambridge: Harvard University Press, 1990), vii; Brent S. Steel and Edward Weber, "Ecosystem Management, Decentralization and Public Opinion," *Global Environmental Change* 11 (2001): 119–131.

19. See Oran R. Young, *The Institutional Dimensions of Environmental Change: Fit, Interplay, and Scale* (Cambridge: MIT Press, 2002).

20. Stephen Bocking, *Ecologists and Environmental Politics: A History of Contemporary Ecology* (New Haven, Conn.: Yale University Press, 1997).

CHAPTER 2   *The Uncertain Authority of Science*

1. Stephen J. Pyne, *World Fire: The Culture of Fire on Earth* (Seattle: University of Washington Press, 1995); Edmund Russell, *War and Nature: Fighting Humans and Insects with Chemicals from World War I to Silent Spring* (Cambridge: Cambridge University Press, 2001).

2. James Brown, *Who Rules in Science? An Opinionated Guide to the Wars* (Cambridge: Harvard University Press, 2001).

3. Richard H. Grove, *Green Imperialism: Colonial Expansion, Tropical Island Edens and the Origins of Environmentalism, 1600–1860* (Cambridge: Cambridge University Press, 1995); Christopher C. Sellers, *Hazards of the Job: From Industrial Disease to Environmental Health Science* (Chapel Hill: University of North Carolina Press, 1997); Joel B. Hagen, *An Entangled Bank: The Origins of Ecosystem Ecology* (New Brunswick, N.J.: Rutgers University Press, 1992); Bruno Latour, *Pandora's Hope: Essays on the Reality of Science Studies* (Cambridge: Harvard University Press, 1999).

4. Social Learning Group, *Learning to Manage Global Environmental Risks*, vol. 1: *A Comparative History of Social Responses to Climate Change, Ozone Depletion, and Acid Rain* (Cambridge: MIT Press, 2001), 276–277; vol. 2: *A Functional Analysis of Social Responses to Climate Change, Ozone Depletion, and Acid Rain* (Cambridge: MIT Press, 2001), 72–73.

5. Theodore M. Porter, *Trust in Numbers: The Pursuit of Objectivity in Science and Public Life* (Princeton, N.J.: Princeton University Press, 1995).

6. Stephen Bocking, *Ecologists and Environmental Politics: A History of Contemporary Ecology* (New Haven, Conn.: Yale University Press, 1997), 63–88; Sellers, *Hazards.*

7. Quoted in Brown, *Who Rules*, 106.

8. Peter Novick, *That Noble Dream: The "Objectivity Question" and the American Historical Profession* (Cambridge: Cambridge University Press, 1988), 296.

9. Yaron Ezrahi, *The Descent of Icarus: Science and the Transformation of Contemporary Democracy* (Cambridge: Harvard University Press, 1990).

10. Thomas F. Gieryn, *Cultural Boundaries of Science: Credibility on the Line* (Chicago: University of Chicago Press, 1999).

11. Karen T. Litfin, "Framing Science: Precautionary Discourse and the Ozone Treaties," *Millennium: Journal of International Studies* 24, no. 2 (1995): 251–277.

12. Grove, *Green Imperialism.*

13. Jeffrey A. Hutchings, Carl Walters, and Richard L. Beamish, "Is Scientific Inquiry Incompatible with Government Information Control?" *Canadian Journal of Fisheries and Aquatic Sciences* 54 (1997): 1198–1210.

14. Max Weber, "Bureaucracy," in *From Max Weber: Essays in Sociology,* ed. H. Gerth and C. Wright Mills (New York: Oxford University Press, 1946), 196–244.

15. Hugh Heclo, "The Sixties' False Dawn: Awakenings, Movements, and Postmodern Policy-making," *Journal of Policy History* 8, no. 1 (1996): 34–63; Bruce A. Williams and Albert R. Matheny, *Democracy, Dialogue, and Environmental Disputes: The Contested Languages of Social Regulation* (New Haven, Conn.: Yale University Press, 1995), 11–17.

16. Stephen Turner, "What is the Problem with Experts?" *Social Studies of Science* 31, no. 1 (2001): 123–149.

17. Ted Greenwood, *Knowledge and Discretion in Government Regulation* (New York: Praeger, 1984), 252.

18. Robert V. Percival, "Global Environmental Accountability: The Missing Link in the Pursuit of Sustainable Development?" in *The Moral Austerity of Environmental Decision Making: Sustainability, Democracy, and Normative Argument in Policy and Law,* ed. John Martin Gillroy and Joe Bowersox (Durham, N.C.: Duke University Press, 2002), 201.

19. Samuel Hays, "Value Premises for Planning and Public Policy: The Historical Context," in *Explorations in Environmental History* (Pittsburgh: University of Pittsburgh Press, 1998), 27–30.

20. Michel Foucault, *Power/Knowledge: Selected Interviews & Other Writings, 1972–1977* (New York: Pantheon Books, 1980).

21. Rachel Carson, *Silent Spring* (New York: Houghton-Mifflin, 1962); D. Fleming, "Roots of the New Conservation Movement," *Perspectives in American History* 6 (1972): 7–94.

22. Sheila Jasanoff, "NGOs and the Environment: From Knowledge to Action," *Third World Quarterly* 18, no. 3 (1997): 579–594.

23. John Dryzek, *The Politics of the Earth: Environmental Discourses* (Oxford: Oxford University Press, 1997).

24. Elisa Ong and Stanton Glantz, "Constructing 'Sound Science' and 'Good Epidemiology': Tobacco, Lawyers, and Public Relations Firms," *American Journal of Public Health* 91, no. 11 (2001): 1754.

25. Sheldon Rampton and John Stauber, *Trust Us, We're Experts! How Industry Manipulates Science and Gambles with Your Future* (New York: Tarcher/Putnam, 2001), 54–55.

26. Williams and Matheny, *Democracy, Dialogue, and Environmental Disputes*, 105.

27. Dorothy Nelkin, "Science Controversies: The Dynamics of Public Disputes in the United States," in *Handbook of Science and Technology Studies,* ed. Sheila Jasanoff, Gerald E. Markle, James C. Petersen, and Trevor Pinch (Thousand Oaks, Calif.: Sage Publications, 1995), 444–456.

28. Dryzek, *Politics of the Earth*, 16–18, 112–117.

29. R. Pound, R. Wilson, and N. Ramsey, "Memorial Minute—Kenneth Tompkins Bainbridge," *Harvard University Gazette,* 7 May 1998, *www.news.harvard.edu/gazette/1998/05.07/MemorialMinute-.html.*

30. Jeffrey R. Stine, *A History of Science Policy in the United States, 1940–1985* (Washington, D.C.: Government Printing Office, 1986).

31. David Harvey, *The Condition of Postmodernity* (Cambridge: Blackwell, 1989), 13.
32. David H. Guston, *Between Politics and Science: Assuring the Integrity and Productivity of Research* (Cambridge: Cambridge University Press, 2000).
33. David Halberstam, *The Best and the Brightest* (1972; New York: Ballantine Books, 1993); Jane Jacobs, *The Death and Life of Great American Cities* (New York: Vintage, 1961).
34. Heinz Center, *The State of the Nation's Ecosystems: Measuring the Lands, Waters, and Living Resources of the United States* (Cambridge: Cambridge University Press, 2002).
35. National Research Council, *The Science of Regional and Global Change: Putting Knowledge to Work* (Washington, D.C.: National Academy Press, 2000), 10.
36. Stephen R. Dovers and John W. Handmer, "Ignorance, the Precautionary Principle, and Sustainability," *Ambio* 24, no. 2 (1995): 92–97.
37. J. R. Ravetz, "Uncertainty, Ignorance and Policy," in *Science for Public Policy,* ed. H. Brooks and C. Cooper (Oxford: Pergamon Press, 1987), 77–93.
38. Paul Sillitoe, "The Development of Indigenous Knowledge: A New Applied Anthropology," *Current Anthropology* 39, no. 2 (1998): 241.
39. Christina Chociolko, "The Experts Disagree: A Simple Matter of Facts Versus Values?" *Alternatives* 21, no. 3 (1995): 18–25.
40. Brian Wynne, "Public Understanding of Science," in *Handbook of Science and Technology Studies,* ed. Sheila Jasanoff, Gerald E. Markle, James C. Petersen, and Trevor Pinch (Thousand Oaks, Calif.: Sage Publications, 1995), 361–388; Bocking, *Ecologists and Environmental Politics.*
41. Michael Thompson, "Policy-Making in the Face of Uncertainty: The Himalayas as Unknowns," in *Water and the Quest for Sustainable Development in the Ganges Valley,* ed. G. P. Chapman and M. Thompson (London: Mansell, 1995), 25–38; Brian Wynne, "Misunderstood Misunderstandings: Social Identities and Public Uptake of Science," in *Misunderstanding Science? The Public Reconstruction of Science and Technology,* ed. A. Irwin and B. Wynne (Cambridge: Cambridge University Press, 1996), 19–46.
42. Wynne, "Public Understanding."
43. Fikret Berkes, *Sacred Ecology: Traditional Ecological Knowledge and Resource Management* (Philadelphia: Taylor & Francis, 1999).
44. Scientists often save their critiques for the science used in regulatory contexts, comparing it unfavorably with science as it is done within the scientific community and highlighting especially the absence of peer review in the regulatory version.
45. Sheila Jasanoff, *The Fifth Branch: Science Advisers as Policymakers* (Cambridge: Harvard University Press, 1990), 53–55.
46. Jasanoff, *Fifth Branch*, 39–40. Several scientists have confirmed that examination by legal counsel is much more critical than anything they experienced within their profession; see Brian Wynne, "Establishing the Rules of Laws: Constructing Expert Authority," in *Controversy: The Politics of Technical Decisions,* ed. Dorothy Nelkin, 3d edition (Newbury Park, Calif.: Sage, 1992), 38). For a specific case of the effect of these legal demands on ecological research, involving a power plant on the Hudson River, see Bocking, *Ecologists and Environmental Politics*, 106–109.
47. Wynne, "Establishing the Rules," 37.
48. Greenwood, *Knowledge and Discretion*, 1–2.
49. Mary Richardson, Joan Sherman, and Michael Gismondi, *Winning Back the Words:*

Confronting Experts in an Environmental Public Hearing (Toronto: Garamond Press, 1993), 106.

50. Dorothy Nelkin, "Science, Technology, and Political Conflict: Analyzing the Issues," in *Controversy: The Politics of Technical Decisions*, ed. D. Nelkin, 3d ed. (Newbury Park, Calif.: Sage, 1992), xviii–xix; Nelkin, "Science Controversies."

51. Frank Fischer, *Citizens, Experts, and the Environment: The Politics of Local Knowledge* (Durham, N.C.: Duke University Press, 2000), 92–105; Jasanoff, *Fifth Branch*, 7–8, 20.

52. Rampton and Stauber, *Trust Us*, 222–230.

53. Jasanoff, *Fifth Branch*.

54. Following Bruno Latour's notion that "All of culture and all of nature get churned up again every day"; see Alan Irwin, "Business as Usual? Re-assessing Scientific Institutions and Global Environmental Challenges," *Global Environmental Change* 8, no. 3 (1998): 279–283.

55. William Leiss, *Ecology versus Politics* (Toronto: University of Toronto Press, 1979), 264.

56. Samuel Hays, "The Future of Environmental Regulation," in *Explorations in Environmental History* (Pittsburgh: University of Pittsburgh Press, 1998), 121–123.

57. Eyal Press and Jennifer Washburn, "The Kept University," *Atlantic Monthly*, March 2000, 39–54.

58. James Brown, "Privatizing the University—The New Tragedy of the Commons," *Science* 290 (2000): 1701–1702.

59. Justin E. Bekelman, Yan Li, and Cary P. Gross, "Scope and Impact of Financial Conflicts of Interest in Biomedical Research: A Systematic Review," *Journal of the American Medical Association* 289, no. 4 (2003): 454–465; Joel Lexchin, Lisa Bero, Benjamin Djulbegovic, and Otavio Clark, "Pharmaceutical Industry Sponsorship and Research Outcome and Quality: Systematic Review," *British Medical Journal*, 31 May, no. 326 (2003): 1167–1170.

60. Dan Fagin and Marianne Lavell, *Toxic Deception: How the Chemical Industry Manipulates Science, Bends the Law, and Endangers Your Health* (Secaucus, N.J.: Birch Lane Press, 1996).

61. Bekelman et al., "Scope and Impact."

62. *Nature*, "Is the University-Industrial Complex out of Control?" *Nature* 409, no. 6817 (11 January 2001): 119; Press and Washburn, "Kept University."

63. George Davey Smith and Andrew N. Phillips, "Passive Smoking and Health: Should We Believe Philip Morris's 'Experts'?" *British Medical Journal* 313 (1996): 929–933.

64. William Leiss, "Between Expertise and Bureaucracy: Risk Management Trapped at the Science-Policy Interface," in *Risky Business: Canada's Changing Science-Based Policy and Regulatory Regime,* ed. G. Bruce Doern and Ted Reed (Toronto: University of Toronto Press, 2000), 49–74.

65. Fagin and Lavell, *Toxic Deception*, 80–118.

66. Fischer, *Citizens*, 101.

67. Fagin and Lavell, *Toxic Deception,* 46–47.

68. Fischer, *Citizens*, 101.

69. Press and Washburn, "Kept University."

70. See: *www.nserc.ca/programs/indus2_e.htm*.

71. Brown, "Privatizing the University."

72. Fagin and Lavell. *Toxic Deception*.
73. Nature, "University-Industrial Complex"; Press and Washburn, "Kept University."
74. Andrew C. Revkin, "Exxon-Led Group Is Giving a Climate Grant to Stanford," *New York Times*, 21 November 2002.
75. Global Climate & Energy Project, "Project Details: Frequently Asked Questions," *http://gcep.stanford.edu/project_detail/faqs.html*.
76. Quoted in Ray Moynihan, "Who Pays for the Pizza? Redefining the Relationships between Doctors and Drug Companies. 1. Entanglement," *British Medical Journal* 326 (May 31, 2003):1189–1192.
77. Melody Hessing and Michael Howlett, *Canadian Natural Resource and Environmental Policy: Political Economy and Public Policy* (Vancouver: University of British Columbia Press, 1997), 192.
78. Mark R. MacDonald, "Socioeconomic versus Science-Based Regulation: Informal Influences on the Formal Regulation of rbST in Canada," in *Risky Business: Canada's Changing Science-Based Policy and Regulatory Regime,* ed. G. Bruce Doern and Ted Reed (Toronto: University of Toronto Press, 2000), 156–181.
79. Fischer, *Citizens*, 31.
80. Ibid., 81.
81. Simon Shackley and Brian Wynne, "Integrating Knowledges for Climate Change: Pyramids, Nets, and Uncertainties," *Global Environmental Change* 5, no. 2 (1995): 113–126.
82. Alan Irwin and Brian Wynne, "Introduction," in *Misunderstanding Science? The Public Reconstruction of Science and Technology*, ed. Alan Irwin and Brian Wynne (Cambridge: Cambridge University Press, 1996), 8–9; Wynne, "Misunderstood Misunderstandings," 21.
83. Wynne, "Misunderstood Misunderstandings," 19–20.
84. Hays, "Value Premises," 25.
85. Fischer, *Citzens*, 178.
86. Grove, *Green Imperialism*; Arthur McEvoy, *The Fisherman's Problem: Ecology and Law in the California Fisheries, 1850–1980* (Cambridge: Cambridge University Press, 1986); Donald Worster, *Rivers of Empire: Water, Aridity, and the Growth of the American West* (New York: Oxford University Press, 1985).
87. Brian Balogh, *Chain Reaction: Expert Debate and Public Participation in American Commercial Nuclear Power, 1945–1975* (Cambridge: Cambridge University Press, 1991), 62–64.
88. James Fairhead and Melissa Leach, "Webs of Power and the Construction of Environmental Policy Problems: Forest Loss in Guinea," in *Discourses of Development: Anthropological Perspectives,* ed. R. D. Grillo and R. L. Stirrat (Oxford: Berg, 1997), 35–57; Julie Guthman, "Representing Crisis: The Theory of Himalayan Environmental Degradation and the Project of Development in Post-Rana Nepal," *Development and Change* 28 (1997): 45–69.
89. Frédérique Apffel-Marglin, "Introduction: Rationality and the World," in *Decolonizing Knowledge: From Development to Dialogue,* ed. Frédérique Apffel-Marglin and Stephen A. Marglin (New York: Oxford University Press, 1996), 1–39.
90. Vandana Shiva, *The Violence of the Green Revolution: Third World Agriculture, Ecology and Politics* (Penang: Third World Network, 1991).
91. Fischer, *Citizens*, 206.
92. Ibid., 27.

93. Quoted in ibid., 109.
94. Piers M. Blaikie, "Post-modernism and Global Environmental Change," *Global Environmental Change* 6, no. 2 (1996): 81–85.
95. Ulrich Beck, *Risk Society: Towards a New Modernity* (London: Sage, 1992).
96. Helen Watson-Verran and David Turnball, "Science and Other Indigenous Knowledge Systems," in *Handbook of Science and Technology Studies,* ed. Sheila Jasanoff, Gerald E. Markle, James C. Petersen, and Trevor Pinch (Thousand Oaks, Calif.: Sage Publications, 1995), 115–139.
97. Guston, *Between Politics and Science*, 87.
98. Jasanoff, *Fifth Branch*, 93.
99. Heclo, "The Sixties' False Dawn."
100. Williams and Matheny, *Democracy, Dialogue, and Environmental Disputes*, 156.
101. Douglas Powell and William Leiss, *Mad Cows and Mother's Milk: The Perils of Poor Risk Communication* (Montreal: McGill-Queen's University Press, 1997), 159–178.
102. Jasanoff, *Fifth Branch*, 8.
103. Maurie J. Cohen, "Science and Society in Historical Perspective: Implications for Social Theories of Risk," *Environmental Values* 8 (1999): 153–176.
104. Guston, *Between Politics and Science*, 28.
105. Charles Herrick and Dale Jamieson, "The Social Construction of Acid Rain: Some Implications for Science/Policy Assessment," *Global Environmental Change* 5, no. 2 (1995): 105–112.

CHAPTER 3   *Science and Environmental Values*

1. Carolyn Merchant, *The Death of Nature: Women, Ecology, and the Scientific Revolution* (New York: HarperCollins, 1980).
2. See, for example, Evelyn Fox Keller, *Reflections on Gender and Science* (New Haven, Conn.: Yale University Press, 1985); N. Katherine Hayles, "Searching for Common Ground," in *Reinventing Nature? Responses to Postmodern Deconstruction,* ed. Michael E. Soulé and Gary Lease (Washington, D.C.: Island Press, 1995), 56.
3. Merchant, *Death of Nature*.
4. Clarence J. Glacken, *Traces on the Rhodian Shore: Nature and Culture in Western Thought from Ancient Times to the End of the Eighteenth Century* (Berkeley: University of California Press, 1967), 510–512; Donald Worster, *Nature's Economy: A History of Ecological Ideas* (Cambridge: Cambridge University Press, 1994), 31–55.
5. Samuel P. Hays, *Conservation and the Gospel of Efficiency: The Progressive Conservation Movement 1890–1920* (Cambridge: Harvard University Press, 1959).
6. Donald Worster, *Rivers of Empire: Water, Aridity, and the Growth of the American West* (New York: Oxford University Press, 1985), 143.
7. Vandana Shiva, "Western Science and Its Destruction of Local Science," in *The Post-Development Reader,* ed. Majid Rahnema and Victoria Bawtree (London: Zed Books, 1997), 161–167.
8. Jonathon Porritt, *Playing Safe: Science and the Environment* (New York: Thames & Hudson, 2000), 24–35.
9. William Leiss, *The Domination of Nature* (1972; Montreal: McGill-Queen's University Press, 1994), 122–123.
10. Worster, *Nature's Economy*.

11. Richard H. Grove, *Green Imperialism: Colonial Expansion, Tropical Island Edens and the Origins of Environmentalism, 1600–1860* (Cambridge: Cambridge University Press, 1995).

12. Jean-Pierre Goubert, *The Conquest of Water: The Advent of Health in the Industrial Age*, trans. Andrew Wilson (Cambridge: Polity Press, 1986).

13. Christopher Hamlin, *A Science of Impurity: Water Analysis in Nineteenth Century Britain* (Berkeley: University of California Press, 1990); Joel Tarr, *The Search for the Ultimate Sink: Urban Pollution in Historical Perspective* (Akron, Ohio: University of Akron Press, 1996).

14. Thomas Dunlap, *Saving America's Wildlife: Ecology and the American Mind, 1850–1990* (Princeton, N.J.: Princeton University Press, 1988).

15. Roderick Frazier Nash, *The Rights of Nature: A History of Environmental Ethics* (Madison: University of Wisconsin Press, 1989).

16. George Perkins Marsh, *Man and Nature: Or, Physical Geography as Modified by Human Action*, ed. David Lowenthal (Cambridge, Mass.: Belknap Press, 1965).

17. Michael Smith, *Pacific Visions: California Scientists and the Environment 1850–1915* (New Haven, Conn.: Yale University Press, 1987).

18. Douglas R. Weiner, *Models of Nature: Ecology, Conservation, and Cultural Revolution in Soviet Russia* (Bloomington: Indiana University Press, 1988).

19. John McCormick, *Reclaiming Paradise: The Global Environmental Movement* (Bloomington: Indiana University Press, 1989).

20. Sheila Jasanoff, "Image and Imagination: The Formation of Global Environmental Consciousness," in *Changing the Atmosphere: Expert Knowledge and Environmental Governance,* ed. Clark A. Miller and Paul N. Edwards (Cambridge: MIT Press, 2001), 309–337.

21. Wolfgang Sachs, "Sustainable Development and the Crisis of Nature: On the Political Anatomy of an Oxymoron," in *Living with Nature: Environmental Politics as Cultural Discourse,* ed. Frank Fischer and Maarten A. Hajer (Oxford: Oxford University Press, 1999), 35.

22. J. E. Lovelock, *Gaia: A New Look at Life on Earth* (Oxford: Oxford University Press, 1979).

23. Stephen Schneider and Penelope Boston, eds., *Scientists on Gaia* (Cambridge: MIT Press, 1993).

24. Barry Commoner, *The Closing Circle: Nature, Man, and Technology* (New York: Alfred A. Knopf, 1971).

25. See, for example, David Graber, "Resolute Biocentrism: The Dilemma of Wilderness in National Parks," in *Reinventing Nature? Responses to Postmodern Deconstruction,* ed. Michael E. Soulé and Gary Lease (Washington, D.C.: Island Press, 1995).

26. The case was put most prominently in Paul Shepard and Daniel McKinley, eds., *The Subversive Science: Essays toward an Ecology of Man* (Boston: Houghton Mifflin, 1969).

27. Marilia Coutinho, "Ecological Metaphors and Environmental Rhetoric: An Analysis of The Ecologist and Our Common Future," *Environment and History* 3 (1997): 177–195; John Dryzek, *The Politics of the Earth: Environmental Discourses* (Oxford: Oxford University Press, 1997), 155, 167.

28. Dunlap, *Saving America's Wildlife*; J. Baird Callicott, "The Scientific Substance of

the Land Ethic," in *Aldo Leopold: The Man and His Legacy,* ed. Thomas Tanner, 87–104 (Ankeny, Iowa: Soil Conservation Society of America, 1987).

29. Aldo Leopold, *Sand County Almanac* (New York: Oxford University Press, 1949).
30. Richard L. Knight and Suzanne Riedel, eds., *Aldo Leopold and the Ecological Conscience* (Oxford: Oxford University Press, 2002).
31. Rachel Carson, *Silent Spring* (New York: Houghton-Mifflin, 1962), 64.
32. Ibid., 293.
33. Ibid., 297.
34. Ibid., x.
35. Worster, *Nature's Economy*; see also Eugene Odum, "The Strategy of Ecosystem Development," *Science* 164 (1969): 262–270.
36. Peter Crowcroft, *Elton's Ecologists: A History of the Bureau of Animal Population* (Chicago: University of Chicago Press, 1991), xiv.
37. Richard West Sellars, *Preserving Nature in the National Parks: A History* (New Haven, Conn.: Yale University Press, 1997), 204–266.
38. John O'Neill, "Deliberative Democracy and Environmental Policy," in *Democracy and the Claims of Nature: Critical Perspectives for a New Century,* ed. Ben A. Minteer and Bob Pepperman Taylor (Lanham, Md.: Rowman & Littlefield, 2002), 268.
39. Jocelyn Kaiser, "Ecologists on a Mission to Save the World," *Science* 287, no. 5456 (2000): 1188–1192.
40. David Takacs, *The Idea of Biodiversity: Philosophies of Paradise* (Baltimore, Md.: Johns Hopkins University Press, 1996); see also Heather Newbold, ed., *Life Stories: World-Renowned Scientists Reflect on Their Lives and the Future of Life on Earth* (Berkeley: University of California Press, 2000).
41. Michael E. Soulé, "The Social Siege of Nature," in Michael E. Soulé and Gary Lease, *Reinventing Nature? Responses to Postmodern Deconstruction* (Washington, D.C.: Island Press, 1995), 138.
42. Edward O. Wilson, *The Future of Life* (New York: Vintage Books, 2003), 41.
43. Ibid., 134.
44. Ibid.
45. Edward O. Wilson, *The Diversity of Life* (Cambridge: Harvard University Press, 1992), 351.
46. Carolyn Merchant, *Radical Ecology: The Search for a Livable World* (New York: Routledge, 1992), 93–100.
47. George Sessions, "Ecocentrism, Wilderness, and Global Ecosystem Protection," in *Deep Ecology for the Twenty-First Century,* ed. George Sessions (Boston: Shambhala, 1995), 371.
48. George Sessions, *Deep Ecology for the Twenty-First Century* (Boston: Shambhala, 1995); John Barry, *Rethinking Green Politics: Nature, Virtue and Progress* (London: Sage Publications, 1999), 23.
49. Barry, *Rethinking Green Politics,* 29–30.
50. Donald Alexander, "Bioregionalism: Science or Sensibility," *Environmental Ethics* 12, no. 2 (1990): 161–171.
51. Michael Vincent McGinnis, "A Rehearsal to Bioregionalism" in *Bioregionalism,* ed. M. V. McGinnis (London: Routledge, 1999), 8–9.
52. Dryzek, *Politics of the Earth,* 175–177.

53. J. Baird Callicott, "Science, Value, and Ethics: A Hierarchical Theory," in *Democracy and the Claims of Nature: Critical Perspectives for a New Century,* ed. Ben A. Minteer and Bob Pepperman Taylor (Lanham, Md.: Rowman & Littlefield, 2002), 102.

54. Holmes Rolston III, "Environmental Ethics: Values in and Duties to the Natural World," in *Ecology, Economics, Ethics: The Broken Circle,* ed. F. Herbert Bormann and Stephen R. Kellert (New Haven, Conn.: Yale University Press, 1991), 73–96.

55. Merchant, *Death of Nature*, xx.

56. John Opie, *Nature's Nation: An Environmental History of the United States* (Fort Worth, Texas: Harcourt Brace, 1998), 414–417.

57. Sylvia Noble Tesh, *Uncertain Hazards: Environmental Activists and Scientific Proof* (Ithaca, N.Y.: Cornell University Press, 2000), 40–61. Of course, historians would view as problematic Tesh's argument that environmentalism was created in the 1960s.

58. William Leiss, *Ecology versus Politics* (Toronto: University of Toronto Press, 1979), 190.

59. E. Donald Elliott, "Toward Ecological Law and Policy," in *Thinking Ecologically: The Next Generation of Environmental Policy,* ed. Marian R. Chertow and Daniel C. Esty (New Haven, Conn.: Yale University Press, 1997), 173–174.

60. Robyn Eckersley, "Politics," in *A Companion to Environmental Philosophy,* ed. Dale Jamieson (Malden, Mass.: Blackwell, 2001), 316–330.

61. Barry, *Rethinking Green Politics*, 251.

62. O'Neill, "Deliberative Democracy," 269.

63. Michael E. Soulé and Gary Lease, *Reinventing Nature? Responses to Postmodern Deconstruction* (Washington, D.C.: Island Press, 1995), xvi.

64. Soulé, "Social Siege," 148–149.

65. Worster, *Nature's Economy*, 388–433.

66. Stephen Bocking, "Stephen Forbes, Jacob Reighard and the Emergence of Aquatic Ecology in the Great Lakes Region," *Journal of the History of Biology* 23 (1990): 461–498; Ronald Tobey, *Saving the Prairies: The Life Cycle of the Founding School of American Plant Ecology, 1895–1955* (Berkeley: University of California Press, 1981).

67. Sharon E. Kingsland, "An Elusive Science: Ecological Enterprise in the Southwestern United States," in *Science and Nature: Essays in the History of the Environmental Sciences*, ed. Michael Shortland (Oxford: British Society for the History of Science, 1993), 151–179.

68. John Sheail, "Pollution and the Protection of Inland Fisheries in Inter-war Britain," in *Science and Nature: Essays in the History of the Environmental Sciences*, ed. Michael Shortland (Oxford: British Society for the History of Science, 1993), 41–56.

69. Weiner, *Models of Nature*.

70. See especially Paul Sears, *Deserts on the March* (Norman: University of Oklahoma Press, 1935).

71. Worster, *Nature's Economy*.

72. Stephen Bocking, *Ecologists and Environmental Politics: A History of Contemporary Ecology* (New Haven, Conn.: Yale University Press, 1997), 13–37.

73. Gregg Mitman, *The State of Nature: Ecology, Community, and American Social Thought, 1900–1950* (Chicago: University of Chicago Press, 1992).

74. Peder Anker, *Imperial Ecology: Environmental Order in the British Empire, 1895–1945* (Cambridge: Harvard University Press, 2001).

75. Eugene Cittadino, "The Failed Promise of Human Ecology," in *Science and Nature: Essays in the History of the Environmental Sciences*, ed. Michael Shortland (Oxford: British Society for the History of Science, 1993), 251–283.

76. Paolo Palladino, "On 'Environmentalism': The Origins of Debates over Policy for Pest-Control Research in America, 1960–1975," in *Science and Nature: Essays in the History of the Environmental Sciences*, ed. Michael Shortland (Oxford: British Society for the History of Science, 1993), 181–212.

77. Stephen Bocking, "Ecosystems, Ecologists and the Atom: Environmental Research at Oak Ridge National Laboratory," *Journal of the History of Biology* 28, no. 1 (1995): 1–47.

78. Wilson recalled how as a beginning biologist he "saw science, by which I meant (and in my heart I still mean) the study of ants, frogs, and snakes, as a wonderful way to stay outdoors." Edward O. Wilson, *Consilience: The Unity of Knowledge* (New York: Vintage, 1999), 3.

79. Takacs, *Idea of Biodiversity*; Ramachandra Guha, "The Authoritarian Biologist and the Arrogance of Anti-Humanism: Wildlife Conservation in the Third World," *The Ecologist* 27, no. 1 (1997): 14–20.

80. See, for example, S.T.A. Pickett and P. S. White, *The Ecology of Natural Disturbance and Patch Dynamics* (Orlando, Fla.: Academic Press, 1985).

81. Worster, *Nature's Economy*.

82. C. S. Holling, "The Resilience of Terrestrial Ecosystems: Local Surprise and Global Change," in *Sustainable Development of the Biosphere,* ed. W. C. Clark and R. E. Munn (Cambridge: Cambridge University Press, 1986), 292–320.

83. James Fairhead and Melissa Leach, "Webs of Power and the Construction of Environmental Policy Problems: Forest Loss in Guinea," in *Discourses of Development: Anthropological Perspectives,* ed. R. D. Grillo and R. L. Stirrat (Oxford: Berg, 1997), 35–57; Kristin Shrader-Frechette, "Ecology," in *A Companion to Environmental Philosophy,* ed. Dale Jamieson (Malden, Mass.: Blackwell, 2001), 309.

84. Daniel B. Botkin, *Discordant Harmonies: A New Ecology for the Twenty-First Century* (New York: Oxford University Press, 1990).

85. Kristin S. Shrader-Frechette and Earl D. McCoy, "Natural Landscapes, Natural Communities, and Natural Ecosystems," *Forest and Conservation History* 39 (1995): 138–142.

86. Callicott, "Scientific Substance of the Land Ethic," 214.

87. Donald Worster, "Nature and the Disorder of History," in Michael E. Soulé and Gary Lease, *Reinventing Nature? Responses to Postmodern Deconstruction* (Washington, D.C.: Island Press, 1995), 82.

88. Martin Mittelstaedt, "Clear-cuts Likened to Natural Fires: Ontario Ministry under Attack for Idea Termed Pseudoscientific and Ridiculous," *The Globe and Mail* (Toronto), 23 November 2001. Viewed online at http://www.globeandmail.ca.

89. Samuel Hays, "The Role of Urbanization in Environmental History," in *Explorations in Environmental History,* 69–100 (Pittsburgh: University of Pittsburgh Press, 1998), 86–89.

90. Willett Kempton, James S. Boster, and Jennifer A. Hartley, *Environmental Values in American Culture* (Cambridge, Mass.: MIT Press, 1995).

91. Dryzek, *Politics of the Earth*, 94; Mark Sagoff, *The Economy of the Earth: Philosophy, Law, and the Environment* (Cambridge: Cambridge University Press, 1988)

92. Dryzek, *Politics of the Earth*, 167.

93. Bob Pepperman Taylor, "Aldo Leopold's Civic Education," in *Democracy and the Claims of Nature: Critical Perspectives for a New Century,* ed. Ben A. Minteer and Bob Pepperman Taylor (Lanham, Md.: Rowman & Littlefield, 2002), 183.

94. Bryan G. Norton, "Democracy and Environmentalism: Foundations and Justifications in Environmental Policy," in *Democracy and the Claims of Nature: Critical Perspectives for a New Century,* ed. Ben A. Minteer and Bob Pepperman Taylor (Lanham, Md.: Rowman & Littlefield, 2002), 16.

95. Bob Pepperman Taylor and Ben A. Minteer, "Introduction," in *Democracy and the Claims of Nature: Critical Perspectives for a New Century,* ed. Ben A. Minteer and Bob Pepperman Taylor (Lanham, Md.: Rowman & Littlefield, 2002), 4.

96. Shrader-Frechette, "Ecology".

97. IJC, Great Lakes Research Advisory Board, *The Ecosystem Approach: Scope and Implications of an Ecosystem Approach to Transboundary Problems in the Great Lakes Basin* (Windsor, Ont.: IJC, 1978); Rawson Academy, *Towards an Ecosystem Charter for the Great Lakes–St. Lawrence* (Rawson Occasional Paper no. 1, 1989).

98. See, for example, J. R. Vallentyne and A. L. Hamilton, "Managing Human Uses and Abuses of Aquatic Resources in the Canadian Ecosystem," in *Canadian Aquatic Resources,* ed. M. C. Healey and R. R. Wallace, *Canadian Bulletin of Fisheries and Aquatic Sciences* 215 (1987): 513–533.

99. An early statement of these ideas is in James J. Kay, "A Nonequilibrium Thermodynamic Framework for Discussing Ecosystem Integrity," *Environmental Management* 15 (1991): 483–495.

100. R. A. Ryder and C. J. Edwards, eds., *A Conceptual Approach for the Application of Biological Indicators of Ecosystem Quality in the Great Lakes Basin,* Report to the Great Lakes Science Advisory Board of the International Joint Commission, 1985 (Windsor, Ont.: IJC, 1985)

101. T.F.H. Allen, B. L. Bandurski, and A. W. King, *The Ecosystem Approach: Theory and Ecosystem Integrity* (Washington, D.C.: IJC, 1993).

102. Shrader-Frechette, "Ecology," 306–307.

103. See, for example, F. Berkes and C. Folke, eds., *Linking Social and Ecological Systems: Management Practices and Social Mechanisms for Building Resilience* (Cambridge: Cambridge University Press, 1998); K. Kohm and J. Franklin, eds., *Creating a Forestry for the 21st Century: The Science of Ecosystem Management* (Washington, D.C.: Island Press, 1997).

104. David L. Hull, *Science as a Process: An Evolutionary Account of the Social and Conceptual Development of Science* (Chicago: University of Chicago Press, 1988).

105. Norton, "Democracy and Environmentalism," 29–30.

106. Barry, *Rethinking Green Politics,* 223.

107. Simon Schama, *Landscape and Memory* (Toronto: Random House, 1995); Peter Coates, *Nature: Western Attitudes since Ancient Times* (Berkeley: University of California Press, 1998).

CHAPTER 4   *Science and Natural Resources Management*

1. Kevin Cox, "Fishery Could End Cod Stocks, DFO Says," *The Globe and Mail* (Toronto), 23 November 2002. Viewed online at http://www.globeandmail.ca.

2. Daniel Pauly et al., "Towards Sustainability in World Fisheries." *Nature* 418 (2002): 689–695; quote from interview with Pauly, *Nature* 421 (2003): 23.

3. Donald Ludwig, Ray Hilborn, and Carl Walters, "Uncertainty, Resource Exploitation, and Conservation: Lessons from History," *Science* 260 (1993): 17, 36. One recent example has been Pacific Northwest salmon stocks; see Robert T. Lackey, "Salmon Policy: Science, Society, Restoration, and Reality," *Environmental Science and Policy* 2 (1999): 369–379.

4. Evelyn Pinkerton, "Local Fisheries Co-management: A Review of International Experiences and Their Implications for Salmon Management in British Columbia," *Canadian Journal of Fisheries and Aquatic Sciences* 51 (1994): 2363–2376; Lackey, "Salmon Policy."

5. Ludwig, Hilborn, and Walters, "Uncertainty"; Ehsan Masood, "Fisheries Science: All at Sea When It Comes to Politics?" *Nature* 386 (1997): 105–106.

6. C. S. Holling, Fikret Berkes, and Carl Folke, "Science, Sustainability and Resource Management," in *Linking Social and Ecological Systems: Management Practices and Social Mechanisms for Building Resilience,* ed. Fikret Berkes and Carl Folke (Cambridge: Cambridge University Press, 1998), 342–362; Ludwig, Hilborn, and Walters, "Uncertainty."

7. *www.ices.dk/marineworld/fishsyst.asp.*

8. Jeffrey A. Hutchings, Carl Walters, and Richard L. Beamish, "Is Scientific Inquiry Incompatible with Government Information Control?" *Canadian Journal of Fisheries and Aquatic Sciences* 54 (1997): 1198–1210.

9. Stephen Bocking, "Fishing the Inland Seas: Great Lakes Research, Fisheries Management and Environmental Policy in Ontario," *Environmental History* 2, no. 1 (1997): 52–73.

10. Farley Mowat, "Foreword," in Elizabeth May, *At the Cutting Edge: The Crisis in Canada's Forests.* Toronto: Key Porter Books, 1998; Mowat, "Foreword", xi.

11. Masood, "Fisheries Science," 105.

12. Ken Lertzman, Jeremy Rayner, and Jeremy Wilson, "Learning and Change in the British Columbia Forest Policy Sector: A Consideration of Sabatier's Advocacy Coalition Framework," *Canadian Journal of Political Science* 29, no. 1 (1996): 111–133.

13. Geoff Cushon, "The Art of Uncertainty: Science and the Management of Natural Resources," Sustainable Development Research Institute, University of British Columbia, Discussion Paper DP–92–04, August 1992.

14. James M. Acheson, James A. Wilson, and Robert S. Steneck, "Managing Chaotic Fisheries," in *Linking Social and Ecological Systems: Management Practices and Social Mechanisms for Building Resilience,* ed. Fikret Berkes and Carl Folke (Cambridge: Cambridge University Press, 1998), 390–413.

15. Garrett Hardin, "The Tragedy of the Commons," *Science* 162 (1968): 1243–1248.

16. Hutchings et al., "Scientific Inquiry."

17. Elinor Ostrom et al., eds., *The Drama of the Commons* (Washington, D.C.: National Academy Press, 2002), 3.

18. Ray Hilborn, "Living with Uncertainty in Resource Management," *North American Journal of Fisheries Management* 7 (1987): 1; see also Ray Hilborn, Ellen K. Pikitch, and Robert C. Francis, "Current Trends in Including Risk and Uncertainty in Stock Assessment and Harvest Decisions," *Canadian Journal of Fisheries and Aquatic Sciences* 50 (1993): 874–880.

19. Quoted in Terry Glavin, *Dead Reckoning: Confronting the Crisis in Pacific Fisheries* (Vancouver, B.C.: Douglas & McIntyre, 1996), 18.

20. May, *Cutting Edge*, 33.
21. Ibid., 34.
22. R.I.C.C. Francis and R. Shotton, "'Risk' in Fisheries Management: A Review," *Canadian Journal of Fisheries and Aquatic Sciences* 54 (1997): 1699–1715.
23. Alan C. Finlayson, *Fishing for Truth: A Sociological Analysis of Northern Cod Stock Assessments from 1977–1990* (St. John's, Nfld.: Institute of Social and Economic Research, 1994).
24. Evelyn Pinkerton, "Integrated Management of a Temperate Montane Forest Ecosystem through Holistic Forestry: A British Columbia Example," in *Linking Social and Ecological Systems: Management Practices and Social Mechanisms for Building Resilience,* ed. Fikret Berkes and Carl Folke (Cambridge: Cambridge University Press, 1998), 363–389.
25. Lackey, "Salmon Policy."
26. Carl Walters, "Challenges in Adaptive Management of Riparian and Coastal Ecosystems," *Conservation Ecology* 2, no. 1 (1997), www.consecol.org/vol1/iss2/art1.
27. C. S. Holling, "The Resilience of Terrestrial Ecosystems: Local Surprise and Global Change," in *Sustainable Development of the Biosphere,* ed. W. C. Clark and R. E. Munn (Cambridge: Cambridge University Press, 1986), 292–320.
28. Ludwig et al., "Uncertainty." In forestry, professional concern over this phenomenon is reflected in how the majority of Canadian foresters believe that allowable cuts are set too high (May, *Cutting Edge*, 37).
29. C. S. Holling and G. K. Meffe, "Command and Control and the Pathology of Natural Resource Management," *Conservation Biology* 10, no. 2 (1996): 328–337.
30. Fraser River Sockeye Public Review Board, *Fraser River Sockeye 1994: Problems & Discrepancies* (Ottawa: The Board, 1995).
31. Milton M. R. Freeman, "Graphs and Gaffs: A Cautionary Tale in the Common-Property Resources Debate," in *Common Property Resources: Ecology and Community-Based Sustainable Development,* ed. F. Berkes (London: Belhaven Press, 1989), 92–109.
32. Gifford Pinchot, *The Fight for Conservation* (New York: Doubleday, Page & Company, 1910).
33. Michael Howlett and Jeremy Rayner, "Do Ideas Matter? Policy Network Configurations and Resistance to Policy Change in the Canadian Forest Sector," *Canadian Public Administration* 38, no. 3 (1985): 382–410.
34. Hamish Kimmins, *Balancing Act: Environmental Issues in Forestry* (Vancouver: University of British Columbia Press, 1992), 3.
35. Samuel Hays, "Public Values and Management Response," in *Explorations in Environmental History* (Pittsburgh: University of Pittsburgh Press, 1998), 51.
36. Kimmins, *Balancing Act*, 31.
37. David Perry, "The Scientific Basis of Forestry," *Annual Review of Ecological Systems* 29 (1998): 435–466.
38. Hays, "Public Values," 52–53.
39. Glavin, *Dead Reckoning*, 36.
40. Joanna M. Beyers and L. Anders Sandberg, "Canadian Federal Forest Policy: Present Initiatives and Historical Constraints," in *Sustainability the Challenge: People, Power and the Environment,* ed. L. Anders Sandberg and Sverker Sorlin (Montreal: Black Rose, 1998), 103.
41. Paul Starr, John H. Annala, and Ray Hilborn, "Contested Stock Assessment: Two

Case Studies," *Canadian Journal of Fisheries and Aquatic Sciences* 55 (1998): 529–537.

42. Thomas A. Hanley, "Interaction of Wildlife Research and Forest Management: The Need for Maturation of Science and Policy," *Forestry Chronicle* 70, no. 5 (1994): 527–532.

43. R. Michael M'Gonigle, "The Political Ecology of Biodiversity: A View from the Western Woods," in *Biodiversity in Canada: Ecology, Ideas and Action,* ed. S. Bocking (Peterborough: Broadview Press, 2000), 391–414.

44. Robert T. Lackey, "Pacific Salmon, Ecological Health, and Public Policy," *Ecosystem Health* 2, no. 1 (1996): 61–68.

45. Howlett and Rayner, "Do Ideas Matter?"

46. Jeremy Wilson, "Forest Conservation in British Columbia, 1935–85: Reflections on a Barren Political Debate," *BC Studies* no. 76 (1987/88): 3–32.

47. For reports of the Clayoquot Sound Scientific Panel, see: www.cortex.org/clay.htm.

48. Alfonso Peter Castro and Erik Nielsen, "Indigenous People and Co-Management: Implications for Conflict Management," *Environmental Science & Policy* 4 (2001): 229–239.

49. Hanna J. Cortner, "Making Science Relevant to Environmental Policy," *Environmental Science & Policy* 3 (2000): 21–30.

50. Lackey, "Pacific Salmon."

51. Robert L. Stephenson and Daniel E. Lane, "Fisheries Management Science: A Plea for Conceptual Change," *Canadian Journal of Fisheries and Aquatic Sciences* 52 (1995): 2051–2056; see also Perry, "Scientific Basis of Forestry."

52. Hanley, "Interaction of Wildlife Research"; Royal Society of Canada, *Aquatic Science in Canada: A Case Study of Research in the Mackenzie Basin* (Ottawa: Royal Society, 1995); G. L. Baskerville, "Gaelic Poetry for Deaf Seagulls—Encore," *Forestry Chronicle* 70, no. 5 (1994): 562–564.

53. Ken Lertzman, Jeremy Rayner, and Jeremy Wilson, "Learning and Change in the British Columbia Forest Policy Sector: A Consideration of Sabatier's Advocacy Coalition Framework," *Canadian Journal of Political Science* 29, no. 1 (1996): 111–133.

54. Robert G. Healy and William Ascher, "Knowledge in the Policy Process: Incorporating New Environmental Information in Natural Resources Policy Making," *Policy Sciences* 28, no. 1 (1995): 1–19.

55. Stephenson and Lane, "Fisheries Management Science."

56. David Spurgeon, "Canada's Cod Leaves Science in Hot Water," *Nature* 386 (1997): 107.

57. Lydia K. Bergen and Mark H. Carr, "Establishing Marine Reserves: How Can Science Best Inform Policy?" *Environment* 45, no. 2 (2003): 8–19.

58. Carl J. Walters and C. S. Holling, "Large-Scale Management Experiments and Learning by Doing," *Ecology* 71, no. 6 (1990): 2060–2068.

59. Ray Hilborn, Ellen K. Pikitch, and Robert C. Francis, "Current Trends in Including Risk and Uncertainty in Stock Assessment and Harvest Decisions," *Canadian Journal of Fisheries and Aquatic Sciences* 50 (1993): 874–880. For a contrary view, see Andrew A. Rosenberg and Victor R. Restrepo, "Uncertainty and Risk Evaluation in Stock Assessment Advice for U.S. Marine Fisheries," *Canadian Journal of Fisheries and Aquatic Sciences* 51 (1994): 2715–2720.

60. Francis and Shotton, " 'Risk' in Fisheries Management."

61. Walters and Holling, "Large-Scale Management Experiments."
62. Rosenberg and Restrepo, "Uncertainty and Risk Evaluation."
63. C. S. Holling, , ed., *Adaptive Environmental Assessment and Management* (New York: Wiley, 1978); Walters and Holling, "Large-Scale Management Experiments."
64. BC Ministry of Forests 2001. www.for.gov.bc.ca/hfp/amhome/Amdefs.htm.
65. Kai N. Lee, *Compass and Gyroscope: Integrating Science and Politics for the Environment* (Washington, D.C.: Island Press, 1993); Walters, "Challenges in Adaptive Management."
66. Walters et al., "Rivers Inlet Sockeye Salmon."
67. Walters and Holling, "Large-Scale Management Experiments"; Walters, "Challenges in Adaptive Management."
68. Thomas R. Stanley, "Ecosystem Management and the Arrogance of Humanism," *Conservation Biology* 9, no. 2 (1995): 255–262; Brent S. Steel and Edward Weber, "Ecosystem Management, Decentralization and Public Opinion," *Global Environmental Change* 11 (2001): 119–131.
69. Quoted in Reed S. Noss and J. Michael Scott, "Ecosystem Protection and Restoration: The Core of Ecosystem Management," in *Ecosystem Management: Applications for Sustainable Forest and Wildlife Resources,* ed. Mark S. Boyce and Alan Haney (New Haven, Conn.: Yale University Press, 1997), 239.
70. Robert T. Lackey, "Seven Pillars of Ecosystem Management," *Landscape and Urban Planning* 40, no. 1/3 (1997): 21–30
71. Aldo Leopold, *Sand County Almanac* (New York: Oxford University Press, 1949).
72. See George Van Dyne, ed., *The Ecosystem Concept in Natural Resource Management* (New York: Academic Press, 1969).
73. Alan Rike Drengson and Duncan MacDonald Taylor, *Ecoforestry: The Art and Science of Sustainable Forest Use* (Gabriola Island, B.C.: New Society Publishers, 1997); David G. Brand et al., "The Model Forest Concept: A Model for Future Forest Management?" *Environmental Reviews* 4 (1996): 65–90; Jerry F. Franklin, "Ecosystem Management: An Overview," in *Ecosystem Management: Applications for Sustainable Forest and Wildlife Resources,* ed. Mark S. Boyce and Alan Haney (New Haven, Conn.: Yale University Press, 1997), 21–53.
74. Samuel Hays, "A Challenge to the Profession of Forestry," in *Explorations in Environmental History* (Pittsburgh: University of Pittsburgh Press, 1998), 174, 179.
75. R. J. Beamish and D. R. Bouillon, "Pacific Salmon Production Trends in Relation to Climate," *Canadian Journal of Fisheries and Aquatic Science* 50 (1993): 1002–1016.
76. Mark S. Boyce and Alan Haney, eds. *Ecosystem Management: Applications for Sustainable Forest and Wildlife Resources* (New Haven, Conn.: Yale University Press, 1997); Scott A. Mullner, Wayne A. Hubert, and Thomas A. Wesche, "Evolving Paradigms for Landscape-Scale Renewable Resource Management in the United States," *Environmental Science and Policy* 4 (2001): 39–49.
77. Steel and Weber, "Ecosystem Management."
78. Harold L. Schramm and Wayne A. Hubert. "Ecosystem Management: Implications for Fisheries Management," *Fisheries* 21 (1996): 6–11.
79. John Gordon and Jane Coppock, "Ecosystem Management and Economic Development," in *Thinking Ecologically: The Next Generation of Environmental Policy,* ed. Marian R. Chertow and Daniel C. Esty (New Haven, Conn.: Yale University Press, 1997), 44.

80. Holling and Meffe, "Command and Control"; Steel and Weber, "Ecosystem Management"; Hanna J. Cortner and Margaret A. Moote, *The Politics of Ecosystem Management* (Washington, D.C.: Island Press, 1999); Norman L. Christensen, "Implementing Ecosystem Management: Where Do We Go From Here?" in *Ecosystem Management: Applications for Sustainable Forest and Wildlife Resources,* ed. Mark S. Boyce and Alan Haney (New Haven, Conn.: Yale University Press, 1997), 325–341.

81. Perry, "Scientific Basis of Forestry."

82. Beyers and Sandberg, "Canadian Federal Forest Policy."

83. Glavin, *Dead Reckoning*, 45.

84. Joel B. Hagen, *An Entangled Bank: The Origins of Ecosystem Ecology* (New Brunswick, N.J.: Rutgers University Press, 1992); Stephen Bocking, "Visions of Nature and Society: A History of the Ecosystem Concept," *Alternatives* 20, no. 3 (1994): 12–18.

85. Cortner, "Making Science Relevant"; Steel and Weber, "Ecosystem Management."

86. Ostrom et al., *Drama of the Commons.*

87. Dharam Ghai and Jessica M. Vivian, *Grassroots Environmental Action: People's Participation in Sustainable Development* (London: Routledge, 1995).

88. Richard Judd, *Common Lands, Common People: The Origins of Conservation in Northern New England* (Cambridge: Harvard University Press, 1997).

89. Peter N. Duinker, "Community Forests in Canada: An Overview," *Forestry Chronicle* 70, no. 6 (1994): 711–720; Evelyn Pinkerton, ed., *Co-operative Management of Local Fisheries: New Directions for Improved Management and Community Development* (Vancouver: University of British Columbia Press, 1989).

90. Oran R. Young, "Institutional Interplay: The Environmental Consequences of Cross-Scale Interactions," in *The Drama of the Commons,* ed. Elinor Ostrom et al. (Washington, D.C.: National Academy Press, 2002), 263–291; Castro and Nielsen, "Indigenous People and Co-Management."

91. Gisli Pálsson, "Learning by Fishing: Practical Engagement and Environmental Concerns," in *Linking Social and Ecological Systems: Management Practices and Social Mechanisms for Building Resilience,* ed. Fikret Berkes and Carl Folke (Cambridge: Cambridge University Press, 1998), 48–66.

92. Pinkerton, *Co-operative Management of Local Fisheries*, 22–23.

93. Fikret Berkes, "Indigenous Knowledge and Resource Management Systems in the Canadian Arctic," in *Linking Social and Ecological Systems: Management Practices and Social Mechanisms for Building Resilience,* ed. Fikret Berkes and Carl Folke (Cambridge: Cambridge University Press, 1998), 98–128.

94. C. S. Holling, Fikret Berkes, and Carl Folke, "Science, Sustainability and Resource Management," in *Linking Social and Ecological Systems: Management Practices and Social Mechanisms for Building Resilience,* ed. Fikret Berkes and Carl Folke (Cambridge: Cambridge University Press, 1998), 342–362.

95. James M. Acheson, James A. Wilson, and Robert S. Steneck, "Managing Chaotic Fisheries," in *Linking Social and Ecological Systems: Management Practices and Social Mechanisms for Building Resilience,* ed. Fikret Berkes and Carl Folke (Cambridge: Cambridge University Press, 1998), 390–413.

96. Steel and Weber, "Ecosystem Management"; Cortner and Moote, *Politics of Ecosystem Management.*

97. Young, "Institutional Interplay."

98. Gail Osherenko, "Can Comanagement Save Arctic Wildlife?" *Environment* 30, no. 6 (1988): 6–13, 29–34.
99. Pálsson, "Learning by Fishing."
100. Freeman, "Graphs and Gaffs."
101. Noss and Scott, "Ecosystem Protection and Restoration."
102. Herb Hammond, *Seeing the Forest among the Trees: The Case for Wholistic Forest Use* (Vancouver, B.C.: Polestar, 1991); Drengson and Taylor, *Ecoforestry*; Pinkerton, "Integrated Management."
103. Cushon, "Art of Uncertainty."

CHAPTER 5   *Science and the Global Environment*

1. According to David John Frank, the proliferation of international environmental treaties can be explained not only in functional terms—the increasing scale of environmental problems—but as a consequence of the influence since 1945 of the notion, rooted in science, of the earth as a global, interdependent ecosystem essential to life. David John Frank, "Science, Nature, and the Globalization of the Environment, 1870–1990," *Social Forces* 76, no. 2 (1997): 409–437.
2. Clark A. Miller, "Scientific Internationalism in American Foreign Policy: The Case of Meteorology, 1947–1958," in *Changing the Atmosphere: Expert Knowledge and Environmental Governance,* ed. Clark A. Miller and Paul N. Edwards (Cambridge: MIT Press, 2001), 167–217.
3. Stephen H. Schneider, *The Genesis Strategy: Climate and Global Survival* (New York: Delta, 1976).
4. On the history of climate as a scientific and political issue, see Matthew Paterson, *Global Warming and Global Politics* (London: Routledge, 1996), 16–48.
5. Paul N. Edwards, "Representing the Global Atmosphere: Computer Models, Data, and Knowledge about Climate Change," in *Changing the Atmosphere: Expert Knowledge and Environmental Governance,* ed. Clark A. Miller and Paul N. Edwards (Cambridge: MIT Press, 2001), 47; Social Learning Group, *Learning to Manage Global Environmental Risks*, volume 2: *A Functional Analysis of Social Responses to Climate Change, Ozone Depletion, and Acid Rain* (Cambridge: MIT Press, 2001), 2.33–34.
6. Social Learning Group, *Learning to Manage*, 2.8–9.
7. Clark A. Miller and Paul N. Edwards, "Introduction: The Globalization of Climate Science and Climate Politics," in *Changing the Atmosphere: Expert Knowledge and Environmental Governance,* ed. Clark A. Miller and Paul N. Edwards (Cambridge: MIT Press, 2001), 2.
8. Richard Wolfson and Stephen H. Schneider, "Understanding Climate Science," in *Climate Change Policy: A Survey,* ed. Stephen H. Schneider, Armin Rosencranz, and John O. Niles (Washington, D.C.: Island Press, 2002), 4–6, 13–17.
9. Ibid., 5.
10. Ibid., 23–30.
11. Aant Elzinga, "From Arrhenius to Megascience: Interplay between Science and Public Decisionmaking," *Ambio* 26, no. 1 (1997): 53; Edwards, "Representing the Global Atmosphere," 58.
12. Eleanor G. Turman, "Regional Impact Assessments: A Case Study of California,"

in *Climate Change Policy: A Survey,* ed. Stephen H. Schneider, Armin Rosencranz, and John O. Niles (Washington, D.C.: Island Press, 2002), 89–111.

13. Paul N. Edwards, "Global Comprehensive Models in Politics and Policymaking," *Climatic Change* 32 (1996): 149–161; Edwards, "Representing the Global Atmosphere," 51.

14. Social Learning Group, *Learning to Manage,* 2.23.

15. Edwards, "Representing the Global Atmosphere."

16. National Research Council, *Abrupt Climate Change: Inevitable Surprises* (Washington, D.C.: National Academy Press, 2002), 1. Available at *www.nap.edu.*

17. Stephen H. Schneider and Kristin Kuntz-Duriseti, "Uncertainty and Climate Change Policy," in *Climate Change Policy: A Survey,* ed. Stephen H. Schneider, Armin Rosencranz, and John O. Niles (Washington, D.C.: Island Press, 2002), 53–87.

18. Michael Glantz, *Societal Responses to Regional Climate Change: Forecasting by Analogy* (Boulder, Colo.: Westview Press, 1988).

19. Quoted in Wolfson and Schneider, "Understanding Climate Science," 46.

20. IPCC, *Introduction to the Intergovernmental Panel on Climate Change (IPCC),* at *www.ipcc.ch,* 6.

21. United States Climate Change Science Program and the Subcommittee on Global Change Research, *Our Changing Planet: The Fiscal Year 2003 U.S. Global Change Research Program and Climate Change Research Initiative* (November 2002), 20.

22. Ibid.

23. Paterson, *Global Warming,* 134–151.

24. See, for example, Eugene B. Skolnikoff, "The Role of Science in Policy: The Climate Change Debate in the United States," *Environment* 41, no. 5 (1999): 16–20, 42–45.

25. Clark A. Miller, "Challenges in the Application of Science to Global Affairs: Contingency, Trust, and Moral Order," in *Changing the Atmosphere: Expert Knowledge and Environmental Governance,* ed. Clark A. Miller and Paul N. Edwards (Cambridge: MIT Press, 2001), 249.

26. Miller and Edwards, "Globalization of Climate Science," 9.

27. Milind Kandlikar and Ambuj Sagar, "Climate Change Research and Analysis in India: An Integrated Assessment of a South–North Divide," *Global Environmental Change* 9 (1999): 123.

28. See Royal Society, *The Role of Land Carbon Sinks in Mitigating Global Climate Change* (July 2001), available at *www.royalsoc.ac.uk/policy*; David Suzuki Foundation, *Taking Credit: Canada and the Role of Sinks in International Climate Negotiations* (Vancouver, B.C.: David Suzuki Foundation, 2001); available at *www.davidsuzuki.org.*

29. Stewart Cohen et al., "Climate Change and Sustainable Development: Towards Dialogue," *Global Environmental Change* 8, no. 4 (1998): 341–371.

30. John O. Niles, "Tropical Forests and Climate Change," in *Climate Change Policy: A Survey,* ed. Stephen H. Schneider, Armin Rosencranz, and John O. Niles (Washington, D.C.: Island Press, 2002), 337–371.

31. Simon Shackley, "The Intergovernmental Panel on Climate Change: Consensual Knowledge and Global Politics," *Global Environmental Change* 7, no. 1 (1997): 77–79; Simon Shackley and Brian Wynne, "Integrating Knowledges for Climate Change: Pyramids, Nets, and Uncertainties," *Global Environmental Change* 5, no. 2 (1995):

113–126; Richard M. Moss, "The IPCC: Policy Relevant (Not Driven) Scientific Assessment," *Global Environmental Change* 5, no. 3 (1995): 171–174.

32. Shackley, "Consensual Knowledge."

33. Piers M. Blaikie, "Post-modernism and Global Environmental Change," *Global Environmental Change* 6, no. 2 (1996): 81–85; Shackley and Wynne, "Integrating Knowledges for Climate Change."

34. Cohen et al., "Climate Change and Sustainable Development"; Shackley, "Consensual Knowledge."

35. Cohen et al., "Climate Change and Sustainable Development."

36. Dale Jamieson, "Climate Change and Global Environmental Justice," in *Changing the Atmosphere: Expert Knowledge and Environmental Governance,* ed. Clark A. Miller and Paul N. Edwards (Cambridge: MIT Press, 2001), 287–307.

37. Paterson, *Global Warming,* 89; Kandlikar and Sagar, "South-North Divide," 131.

38. Anil Agarwal, "A Southern Perspective on Curbing Global Climate Change," in *Climate Change Policy: A Survey,* ed. Stephen H. Schneider, Armin Rosencranz, and John O. Niles (Washington, D.C.: Island Press, 2002), 375–391.

39. T. Hyder, "Climate Negotiations: The North/South Perspective," in *Confronting Climate Change: Risks, Implications, and Responses,* ed. I. Mintzer (New York: Cambridge University Press, 1992), 326.

40. Kandlikar and Sagar, "South-North Divide," 130.

41. Ibid.

42. Ecologic Institute for International and European Environmental Policy, *Participation of Non-Governmental Organizations in International Environmental Governance: Legal Basis and Practical Experience* (Berlin: Ecologic, June 2002); available at: *www.umweltbundesamt.de.*

43. Vandana Shiva, "'The Greening of the Global Reach." In *Global Ecology: A New Arena of Political Conflict,* ed. Wolfgang Sachs (London: Zed Books, 1993), 150.

44. Elzinga, "From Arrhenius to Megascience"; Shackley, "Consensual Knowledge"; Kandlikar and Sagar, "South-North Divide," 120, 133.

45. On the influence of the 1996 report see Paul N. Edwards and Stephen H. Schneider, "Self-Governance and Peer Review in Science-for-Policy: The Case of the IPCC Second Assessment Report," in *Changing the Atmosphere: Expert Knowledge and Environmental Governance,* ed. Clark A. Miller and Paul N. Edwards (Cambridge: MIT Press, 2001), 221–222.

46. It is worth noting that political effectiveness differs from ecological effectiveness. Research on flexibility mechanisms such as emissions trading and credits for carbon sinks may enhance the political effectiveness of climate science by reducing the costs of complying with the Kyoto Protocol. However, if these mechanisms serve as alternatives to meaningful reductions in greenhouse gas emissions, they will render action less ecologically effective.

47. One striking indication of the political salience of uncertainty in climate science was a May 11, 2001 letter from the White House to Dr. Bruce Alberts, president of the National Academy of Science, requesting the Academy's assistance in its review of U.S. policy on climate change. The White House had only two requests to make of the nation's premier science advisory body. The first was: "We seek the Academy's assistance in identifying the areas in the science of climate change where there are the greatest certainties and uncertainties." National Research Council, *Climate*

Change Science: An Analysis of Some Key Questions (Washington, D.C.: National Academy Press, 2001), appendix A; available at *www.nap.edu.*

48. Skolnikoff, "Role of Science in Policy."
49. Mike Hulme et al., "Climate Change Scenarios for Global Impacts Studies," *Global Environmental Change* 9 (1999): S3–S19.
50. Skolnikoff, "Role of Science in Policy"; Edwards, "Representing the Global Atmosphere."
51. Schneider and Kuntz-Duriseti, "Uncertainty," 62–70.
52. Riley E. Dunlap, "Lay Perceptions of Global Risk: Public Views of Global Warming in Cross-National Context," *International Sociology* 13, no. 4 (1998): 473–498.
53. Sheldon Rampton and John Stauber. *Trust Us, We're Experts! How Industry Manipulates Science and Gambles with Your Future* (New York: Tarcher/Putnam, 2001), 267–288.
54. Stephen D. Norton and Frederick Suppe, "Why Atmospheric Modeling Is Good Science," in *Changing the Atmosphere: Expert Knowledge and Environmental Governance,* ed. Clark A. Miller and Paul N. Edwards (Cambridge: MIT Press, 2001), 67; Edwards and Schneider, "Self-Governance and Peer Review."
55. Stephen Bocking, "Betting on the Future," *Alternatives Journal* 29, no. 1 (2003): 42–43.
56. Bjørn Lomborg, *The Skeptical Environmentalist: Measuring the Real State of the World* (Cambridge: Cambridge University Press, 2001), 258–324.
57. Armin Rosencranz, "U.S. Climate Change Policy," in *Climate Change Policy: A Survey,* ed. Stephen H. Schneider, Armin Rosencranz, and John O. Niles (Washington, D.C.: Island Press, 2002), 221–234.
58. Kai S. Anderson, "The Climate Policy Debate in the U.S. Congress," in *Climate Change Policy: A Survey,* ed. Stephen H. Schneider, Armin Rosencranz, and John O. Niles (Washington, D.C.: Island Press, 2002), 235–250.
59. Roger A. Pielke, Daniel Sarewitz, and Radford Byerly Jr., "Decision Making and the Future of Nature: Understanding and Using Predictions," in *Prediction: Science, Decision Making, and the Future of Nature,* ed. Daniel Sarewitz, Roger A. Pielke Jr., and Radford Byerly Jr. (Washington, D.C.: Island Press, 2000), 361–387.
60. Sonja Boehmer-Christiansen, "Scientific Consensus and Climate Change: The Codification of a Global Research Agenda," *Energy and Environment* 4, no. 4 (1993): 362–407.
61. Edwards, "Global Comprehensive Models."
62. Schneider and Kuntz-Duriseti, "Uncertainty," 66–68.
63. Karen T. Litfin, "Framing Science: Precautionary Discourse and the Ozone Treaties," *Millennium: Journal of International Studies* 24, no. 2 (1995): 251–277.
64. Edwards, "Global Comprehensive Models."
65. It can be argued that if comprehensive predictive models do not directly address any dimensions of policymaking, but have simply, at a cost of more than $1 billion per year, produced an epistemic community, then that is not good value (Edwards, "Global Comprehensive Models").
66. Willett Kempton, James S. Boster, and Jennifer A. Hartley, *Environmental Values in American Culture* (Cambridge, Mass.: MIT Press, 1995).
67. Social Learning Group, *Learning to Manage,* volume 1: *A Comparative History of Social Responses to Climate Change, Ozone Depletion, and Acid Rain* (Cambridge: MIT Press, 2001), 273.

68. Robert M. Margolis and Daniel M. Kammen. "Energy R&D and Innovation: Challenges and Opportunities," in *Climate Change Policy: A Survey,* ed. Stephen H. Schneider, Armin Rosencranz, and John O. Niles (Washington, D.C.: Island Press, 2002), 469–494.

69. Shardul Agrawala, Kenneth Broad, and David H. Guston, "Integrating Climate Forecasts and Societal Decision Making: Challenges to an Emergent Boundary Organization," *Science, Technology, & Human Values* 26, no. 4 (2001): 454–477.

70. Tanvi Nagpal, "Voices from the Developing World: Progress toward Sustainable Development," *Environment* 37, no. 8 (1995): 10–15, 30–35.

71. Lawrence H. Goulder and Brian M. Nadreau, "International Approaches to Reducing Greenhouse Gas Emissions," in *Climate Change Policy: A Survey,* ed. Stephen H. Schneider, Armin Rosencranz, and John O. Niles (Washington, D.C.: Island Press, 2002), 115.

72. Jonathan Baert Wiener, "Designing Global Climate Regulation," in *Climate Change Policy: A Survey,* ed. Stephen H. Schneider, Armin Rosencranz, and John O. Niles (Washington, D.C.: Island Press, 2002), 152.

73. Ibid., 152–153.

74. "Global Warming Information Page," *www.globalwarming.org/polup/pol7–30.htm.*

75. Daniel Sarewitz and Roger Pielke Jr., "Breaking the Global-Warming Gridlock," *Atlantic Monthly* 286, no. 1 (July 2000): 54–64.

76. Joel Tarr, *The Search for the Ultimate Sink: Urban Pollution in Historical Perspective* (Akron, Ohio: University of Akron Press, 1996).

77. Robert W. Kates and Thomas J. Wilbanks, "Making the Global Local: Responding to Climate Change Concerns from the Ground Up," *Environment* 45, no. 3 (2003): 12–23.

78. Clark A. Miller, "Challenges in the Application of Science to Global Affairs: Contingency, Trust, and Moral Order," in *Changing the Atmosphere: Expert Knowledge and Environmental Governance,* ed. Clark A. Miller and Paul N. Edwards (Cambridge: MIT Press, 2001), 271.

CHAPTER 6   *Science in a Risky World*

1. "China's Chernobyl?" *The Economist,* April 26, 2003, 9–10.

2. The phrase, "pursuit of safety" is from Aaron Wildavsky, *The Search for Safety* (New Brunswick, N.J.: Rutgers University Press, 1988).

3. Carlo C. Jaeger et al., *Risk, Uncertainty, and Rational Action* (London: Earthscan, 2001), 14.

4. Stephen Bocking, *Ecologists and Environmental Politics: A History of Contemporary Ecology* (New Haven, Conn.: Yale University Press, 1997), 197–198.

5. Stephen H. Linder, "The Social and Political (Re)Construction of Risk," in *Flashpoints in Environmental Policymaking: Controversies in Achieving Sustainability,* ed. Sheldon Kamieniecki, George A. Gonzalez, and Robert O. Vos (Albany, N.Y.: SUNY Press, 1997), 63–82.

6. Insightful examinations of this phenomenon include Walter A. Rosenbaum, "Regulation at Risk: The Controversial Politics and Science of Comparative Risk Assessment," in *Flashpoints in Environmental Policymaking: Controversies in Achieving Sustainability,* ed. Sheldon Kamieniecki, George A. Gonzalez, and Robert O. Vos

(Albany, N.Y.: SUNY Press, 1997), 31–61; and Sheila Jasanoff, "The Songlines of Risk," *Environmental Values* 8 (1999): 135–152.

7. Rosenbaum, "Regulation at Risk."
8. Steven Gibb, "Science and Economics Prominent on EPA Agenda," *Issues in Science and Technology* 17, no. 3 (2001): 57–60.
9. Rosenbaum, "Regulation at Risk."
10. Clinton J. Andrews, *Humble Analysis: The Practice of Joint Fact-Finding* (Westport, Conn.: Praeger, 2002), 74–75.
11. See, for example, James K. Hammitt, "Data, Risk, and Science," in *Thinking Ecologically: The Next Generation of Environmental Policy,* ed. Marian R. Chertow and Daniel C. Esty (New Haven, Conn.: Yale University Press, 1997), 152–153; see also Frank Fischer, *Citizens, Experts, and the Environment: The Politics of Local Knowledge* (Durham, N.C.: Duke University Press, 2000), 263–264.
12. Jaeger et al., *Risk,* 89.
13. Quoted in Dan Fagin and Marianne Lavell, *Toxic Deception: How the Chemical Industry Manipulates Science, Bends the Law, and Endangers Your Health* (Secaucus, N.J.: Birch Lane Press, 1996), 68.
14. J. Van Oostdam, "Human Health Implications of Environmental Contaminants in Arctic Canada: A Review," *Science of the Total Environment* 230 (1999): 50.
15. Bocking, *Ecologists and Environmental Politics,* 8.
16. EPA, Science Advisory Board, "Reducing Risk: Setting Priorities and Strategies for Environmental Protection," SAB-EC 90–021, September 1990.
17. EPA, *Guidelines for Ecological Risk Assessment,* EPA/630/R–95/002F, April 1998; see also National Science and Technology Council, Committee on Environment and Natural Resources, *Ecological Risk Assessment in the Federal Government,* CENR/5–99/001, May 1999.
18. Robert T. Lackey, "Fisheries Management: Integrating Societal Preference, Decision Analysis, and Ecological Risk Assessment," *Environmental Science and Policy* 1 (1998): 329–335.
19. J. R. Ravetz, "Usable Knowledge, Usable Ignorance: Incomplete Science with Policy Implications," in *Sustainable Development of the Biosphere,* ed. W. C. Clark and R. E. Munn (Cambridge: Cambridge University Press, 1986), 415–432.
20. Lackey, "Fisheries Management."
21. This is, for example, the typology adopted by the Codex Alimentarius, the international system of standards and guidelines for food products. Often invoked in controversies over food additives, pesticide residues, and biotechnology, it emphasizes its status as a "science-based" approach to decision-making. See United Nations, Food and Agriculture Organization, "Definitions for the Purposes of the Codex Alimentarius," www.fao.org/DOCREP/005/Y2200E/y2200e07.htm.
22. National Research Council, *Risk Assessment in the Federal Government: Managing the Process* (Washington, D.C.: National Academy Press, 1983); Jasanoff, "Songlines of Risk," 146.
23. Jaeger et al., *Risk,* 135.
24. Ibid., 108.
25. Jasanoff, "Songlines of Risk."
26. William W. Lowrance, *Of Acceptable Risk: Science and the Determination of Safety* (Los Altos, Calif.: William Kaufmann, 1976).
27. Linder "(Re)Construction of Risk."

28. Joel Tickner and Carolyn Raffensperger, "The Politics of Precaution in the United States and the European Union," *Global Environmental Change* 11 (2001): 175–180.

29. Sheila Jasanoff, "Civilization and Madness: The Great BSE Scare of 1996," *Public Understanding of Science* 6 (1997): 221–232.

30. Mark R. MacDonald, "Socioeconomic versus Science-Based Regulation: Informal Influences on the Formal Regulation of rbST in Canada," in *Risky Business: Canada's Changing Science-Based Policy and Regulatory Regime,* ed. G. Bruce Doern and Ted Reed (Toronto: University of Toronto Press, 2000), 166–168.

31. Tickner and Raffensperger, "Politics of Precaution."

32. Rosenbaum, "Regulation at Risk."

33. Theo Colborn, Dianne Dumanoski, and John Peterson Myers, *Our Stolen Future* (New York: Plume, 1996, 1997).

34. Daniel Metlay, "From Tin Roof to Torn Wet Blanket: Predicting and Observing Groundwater Movement at a Proposed Nuclear Waste Site," in *Prediction: Science, Decision Making, and the Future of Nature,* ed. Daniel Sarewitz, Roger A. Pielke Jr., and Radford Byerly Jr. (Washington, D.C.: Island Press, 2000), 199–228.

35. Douglas Powell et al., "Gene Escape, or the Pall of Silence over Plant Biotechnology Risk," in Douglas Powell and William Leiss, *Mad Cows and Mother's Milk: The Perils of Poor Risk Communication* (Montreal: McGill-Queen's University Press, 1997), 153–181.

36. Rosenbaum, "Regulation at Risk."

37. Paul Slovic et al., "Intuitive Toxicology. II. Expert and Lay Judgements of Chemical Risks in Canada," *Risk Analysis* 15, no. 6 (1995): 661–675; see also Christina Chociolko, "The Experts Disagree: A Simple Matter of Facts Versus Values?" *Alternatives* 21, no. 3 (1995): 18–25.

38. Harry Otway and Detlof von Winterfeldt, "Expert Judgement in Risk Analysis and Management: Process, Context, and Pitfalls," *Risk Analysis* 12, no. 1 (1992): 83–93.

39. E. Ann Clark, "Regulation of GM Crops in Canada: Science-Based or . . . ?" Unpublished paper, 2003.

40. EU–U.S. Biotechnology Consultative Forum, *Final Report*, December 2000, http://europa.eu.int/comm/external_relations/us/biotech/biotech.htm, 5.

41. Sheila Jasanoff, *The Fifth Branch: Science Advisers as Policymakers* (Cambridge: Harvard University Press, 1990).

42. Fagin and Lavell, *Toxic Deception.*

43. Samuel Hays, "The Role of Values in Science and Policy: The Case of Lead," in *Explorations in Environmental History* (Pittsburgh: University of Pittsburgh Press, 1998), 291–311.

44. Rosenbaum, "Regulation at Risk".

45. Jaeger et al., *Risk,* 214.

46. Jasanoff, "Songlines of Risk"; Rosenbaum, "Regulation at Risk"; Gibb, "Science and Economics."

47. Fischer, *Citizens,* 127.

48. Peter Montague, "The Uses of Scientific Uncertainty," *Rachel's Environment & Health News,* 1 July 1999, *www.rachel.org/erf/bulletin/bulletin.cfm?Issue_ID=1508.*

49. Lackey, "Fisheries Management."

50. Rosenbaum, "Regulation at Risk."

51. Kristin Shrader-Frechette, "Science, Environmental Risk Assessment, and the Frame Problem," *BioScience* 44 (1994): 548–551.

52. Fischer, *Citizens*, 56.

53. Jasanoff, "Songlines of Risk."

54. John Ahearne, "Integrating Risk Analysis into Public Policymaking," *Environment* 35, no. 2 (1993): 16–20, 37–40.

55. Nuclear Regulatory Commission, *Reactor Safety Study—An Assessment of Accident Risk in U.S. Commercial Nuclear Power Plants*, WASH 1400, NUREG 75/014.1975.

56. Joe Bowersox, "The Legitimacy Crisis in Environmental Ethics and Politics," in *Democracy and the Claims of Nature: Critical Perspectives for a New Century*, ed. Ben A. Minteer and Bob Pepperman Taylor (Lanham, Md.: Rowman & Littlefield, 2002), 80–81.

57. Alan Irwin, Alison Dale, and Denis Smith, "Science and Hell's Kitchen: The Local Understanding of Hazard Issues," in *Misunderstanding Science? The Public Reconstruction of Science and Technology*, ed. Alan Irwin and Brian Wynne (Cambridge: Cambridge University Press, 1996), 47–64.

58. Rosenbaum, "Regulation at Risk."

59. Lackey, "Fisheries Management."

60. Rosenbaum, "Regulation at Risk," 35–37.

61. Ulrich Beck, *Risk Society: Towards a New Modernity* (London: Sage, 1992).

62. Ibid., 29.

63. On Beck, see Fischer, *Citizens*, 47–60; Brent K. Marshall, "Globalisation, Environmental Degradation and Ulrich Beck's Risk Society," *Environmental Values* 8 (1999): 253–275; Maurie J. Cohen, "Science and Society in Historical Perspective: Implications for Social Theories of Risk," *Environmental Values* 8 (1999): 153–176.

64. Fischer, *Citizens*, 60.

65. Paul Slovic, "Perception of Risk," *Science* 236 (1987): 280–285.

66. Cass R. Sunstein, *Risk and Reason: Safety, Law, and the Environment* (Cambridge: Cambridge University Press, 2002), 55.

67. Sheldon Rampton and John Stauber, *Trust Us, We're Experts! How Industry Manipulates Science and Gambles with Your Future* (New York: Tarcher/Putnam, 2001), 170, 182.

68. This distinction emerged in the early 1980s, most prominently in NRC, *Risk Assessment*.

69. Douglas Powell and William Leiss, *Mad Cows and Mother's Milk: The Perils of Poor Risk Communication* (Montreal: McGill-Queen's University Press, 1997), ix.

70. Sylvia Noble Tesh, *Uncertain Hazards: Environmental Activists and Scientific Proof* (Ithaca, N.Y.: Cornell University Press, 2000).

71. Fischer, *Citizens*, 132–138.

72. Jaeger et al., *Risk*, 84–85.

73. John Eyles et al., "The Social Construction of Risk in a Rural Community: Responses of Local Residents to the 1990 Hagersville (Ontario) Tire Fire," *Risk Analysis* 13, no. 3 (1993): 281–290; Chociolko, "The Experts Disagree"; Jaeger et al., *Risk*, 104–106.

74. Fischer, *Citizens*, 137–138.

75. Ibid., 122–123; Paul Slovic, "Perceived Risk, Trust, and Democracy," *Risk Analysis* 13, no. 6 (1993): 675–682.

76. Jaeger et al., *Risk*, 184–192.

77. EU–U.S. Biotechnology Consultative Forum, *Final Report*, 5.

78. L. Alvarez, "Europe Acts to Require Labeling of Genetically Altered Food," *New York Times*, 3 July 2003, A3.

79. Irwin et al., "Science and Hell's Kitchen."
80. Fischer, *Citizens*, 137.
81. Jonathon Porritt, *Playing Safe: Science and the Environment* (New York: Thames & Hudson, 2000), 39; Jane Gregory and Steve Miller, *Science in Public: Communication, Culture, and Credibility* (New York: Plenum, 1998), 159–160.
82. MacDonald, "Socioeconomic versus Science-Based Regulation," 172–173.
83. Jasanoff, "Civilization and Madness."
84. W. E. Harris, "Siting a Hazardous Waste Facility: A Success Story in Retrospect," *Risk Analysis* 13, no. 1 (1993): 3–4.
85. Fischer, *Citizens*, 130–131.
86. Jasanoff, "Civilization and Madness."
87. Presidential/Congressional Commission on Risk Assessment and Risk Management, *Framework for Environmental Health Risk Management*, Final Report, Vol. 1, 1997, 1.
88. NRC, *Risk Assessment*.
89. Fischer, *Citizens*, 64.
90. See, for example, Irwin et al., "Science and Hell's Kitchen."
91. Robert Gottlieb, *Forcing the Spring: The Transformation of the American Environmental Movement* (Washington, D.C.: Island Press, 1993), 304; William Leiss, "Between Expertise and Bureaucracy: Risk Management Trapped at the Science-Policy Interface," in *Risky Business: Canada's Changing Science-Based Policy and Regulatory Regime,* ed. G. Bruce Doern and Ted Reed (Toronto: University of Toronto Press, 2000), 58.
92. Gottlieb, *Forcing the Spring*, 170, 175.
93. Fischer, *Citizens*, 151–157.
94. Jessica Glicken, "Getting Stakeholder Participation 'Right': A Discussion of Participatory Processes and Possible Pitfalls," *Environmental Science and Policy* 3 (2000): 305–310.

CHAPTER 7   *Credible and Effective Science*

1. National Council for Science and the Environment, *Recommendations for Improving the Scientific Basis for Environmental Decisionmaking: A Report from the First National Conference on Science, Policy, and the Environment, December 7–8, 2000* (National Academy of Sciences, Washington, D.C.).
2. Daryl Chubin and Edward Hackett, *Peerless Science: Peer Review and U.S. Science Policy* (Albany: State University of New York Press, 1990); Ann Weller, *Editorial Peer Review: Its Strengths and Weaknesses* (Medford, Mass.: Information Today, 2001).
3. Sheila Jasanoff, *The Fifth Branch: Science Advisers as Policymakers* (Cambridge: Harvard University Press, 1990), v.
4. Deborah M. Brosnan, "Can Peer Review Help Resolve Natural Resource Conflicts?" *Issues in Science and Technology* 16, no. 3 (2000): 32–36.
5. Paul N. Edwards and Stephen H. Schneider, "Self-Governance and Peer Review in Science-for-Policy: The Case of the IPCC Second Assessment Report," in *Changing the Atmosphere: Expert Knowledge and Environmental Governance,* ed. Clark A. Miller and Paul N. Edwards (Cambridge: MIT Press, 2001), 219–246.
6. Brosnan, "Can Peer Review Help."

7. Jasanoff, *Fifth Branch.*
8. Jeremy Cherfas, "Greenpeace and Science: Oil and Water?" *Science* 247 (1990): 1288–1290.
9. Edwards and Schneider, "Self-Governance and Peer Review," 230–231.
10. Justin E. Bekelman, Yan Li, and Cary P. Gross, "Scope and Impact of Financial Conflicts of Interest in Biomedical Research: A Systematic Review," *Journal of the American Medical Association* 289, no. 4 (2003): 454–465.
11. Edwards and Schneider, "Self-Governance and Peer Review," 231.
12. Jasanoff, *Fifth Branch,* 61–83; see also Brosnan, "Can Peer Review Help."
13. Brosnan, "Can Peer Review Help."
14. Frank Fischer, *Citizens, Experts, and the Environment: The Politics of Local Knowledge* (Durham, N.C.: Duke University Press, 2000), 106.
15. Edwards and Schneider, "Self-Governance and Peer Review," 231–245.
16. Brosnan, "Can Peer Review Help."
17. Leslie R. Alm, *Crossing Borders, Crossing Boundaries: The Role of Scientists in the U.S. Acid Rain Debate* (Westport, Conn.: Praeger, 2000).
18. William Leiss, "Between Expertise and Bureaucracy: Risk Management Trapped at the Science-Policy Interface," in *Risky Business: Canada's Changing Science-Based Policy and Regulatory Regime,* ed. G. Bruce Doern and Ted Reed (Toronto: University of Toronto Press, 2000), 65.
19. Dan Fagin and Marianne Lavell, *Toxic Deception: How the Chemical Industry Manipulates Science, Bends the Law, and Endangers Your Health* (Secaucus, N.J.: Birch Lane Press, 1996); Sheldon Rampton and John Stauber, *Trust Us, We're Experts! How Industry Manipulates Science and Gambles with Your Future* (New York: Tarcher/Putnam, 2001).
20. Stephen Bocking, "Genetic Illusions," *Alternatives Journal* 28, no. 4 (2002): 11–12. This phenomenon was also demonstrated in reporting on the work of the authoritative-sounding European Working Group on Environmental Tobacco Smoke and Lung Cancer. Coverage of the group's conclusion that passive smoking posed little risk to health failed to note that it had been funded by the tobacco industry. George Davey Smith and Andrew N. Phillips, "Passive Smoking and Health: Should We Believe Philip Morris's 'Experts'?" *British Medical Journal* 313 (1996): 929–933.
21. Wallace Immen, "Fragile Moraine Poorly Managed: Scientists," *The Globe and Mail* (Toronto), 2 February 2000. Viewed online at http://www.globeandmail.ca.
22. Leiss, "Between Expertise and Bureaucracy"; G. Bruce Doern and Ted Reed, "Conclusions: New Institutions and Prospects for Change," in *Risky Business: Canada's Changing Science-Based Policy and Regulatory Regime,* ed. G. Bruce Doern and Ted Reed (Toronto: University of Toronto Press, 2000), 370–371.
23. Jeffrey A. Hutchings, Carl Walters, and Richard L. Beamish, "Is Scientific Inquiry Incompatible with Government Information Control?" *Canadian Journal of Fisheries and Aquatic Sciences* 54 (1997): 1198–1210.
24. See: www.efsa.eu.int.
25. Jasanoff, *Fifth Branch,* 209–216; Terry J. Keating, "Lessons from the Recent History of the Health Effects Institute," *Science, Technology & Human Values* 26, no. 4 (2001): 409–430.
26. Samuel Hays, "The Future of Environmental Regulation," in *Explorations in Environmental History,* 101–128 (Pittsburgh: University of Pittsburgh Press, 1998), 120.

27. Stephen Bocking, "Bottom Line Hooks Salmon Science," *Alternatives Journal* 29, no. 2 (2003): 39–40.
28. Fischer, *Citizens*, 194.
29. Ibid., 143–218.
30. Ibid., 205.
31. See N. Katherine Hayles, "Searching for Common Ground," in *Reinventing Nature? Responses to Postmodern Deconstruction,* ed. Michael E. Soulé and Gary Lease (Washington, D.C.: Island Press, 1995), 59.
32. Brian Wynne, "Misunderstood Misunderstandings: Social Identities and Public Uptake of Science," in *Misunderstanding Science? The Public Reconstruction of Science and Technology,* ed. A. Irwin and B. Wynne (Cambridge: Cambridge University Press, 1996), 19–46.
33. On boundary organizations see David H. Guston, *Between Politics and Science: Assuring the Integrity and Productivity of Research* (Cambridge: Cambridge University Press, 2000); and Guston, ed., "Special Issue: Boundary Organizations in Environmental Policy and Science," *Science, Technology, & Human Values* 26, no. 4 (2001): 399–500.
34. Paul N. Edwards, "Representing the Global Atmosphere: Computer Models, Data, and Knowledge about Climate Change," in *Changing the Atmosphere: Expert Knowledge and Environmental Governance,* ed. Clark A. Miller and Paul N. Edwards (Cambridge: MIT Press, 2001), 33–35.
35. Social Learning Group, *Learning to Manage*, vol. 2: *A Functional Analysis of Social Responses to Climate Change, Ozone Depletion, and Acid Rain* (Cambridge: MIT Press, 2001), 74.
36. Jonathan Baert Wiener, "Designing Global Climate Regulation," in *Climate Change Policy: A Survey,* ed. Stephen H. Schneider, Armin Rosencranz, and John O. Niles (Washington, D.C.: Island Press, 2002), 161–162.
37. Aaron Wildavsky, *But Is It True? A Citizen's Guide to Environmental Health and Safety Issues* (Cambridge: Harvard University Press, 1995), 201–222.
38. Andrew C. Revkin, "F.D.A. Considers New Tests for Environmental Effects," *New York Times*, 14 March 2002, A20.
39. Social Learning Group, *Learning to Manage*, 2.31–48.
40. Jasanoff, *Fifth Branch*.
41. Daniel Pauly et al., "Towards Sustainability in World Fisheries," *Nature* 418 (2002): 689–695; Oran R. Young, "Taking Stock: Management Pitfalls in Fisheries Science," *Environment* 45, no. 3 (2003): 24–33.
42. Stephen Bocking, *Ecologists and Environmental Politics: A History of Contemporary Ecology* (New Haven, Conn.: Yale University Press, 1997), 101–104.
43. Peter M. Haas, *Saving the Mediterranean: The Politics of International Environmental Cooperation* (New York: Columbia University Press, 1990).
44. Don Munton, "Fumes, Forests, and Further Studies: Environmental Science and Policy Inaction in Ontario," *Journal of Canadian Studies* 37, no. 2 (2002): 130–163.
45. Stephen Bocking, "Ecosystems, Ecologists and the Atom: Environmental Research at Oak Ridge National Laboratory," *Journal of the History of Biology* 28, no. 1 (1995): 1–47.
46. Social Learning Group, *Learning to Manage*, 2.15.

47. Social Learning Group, *Learning to Manage*, vol. 1: *A Comparative History of Social Responses to Climate Change, Ozone Depletion, and Acid Rain* (Cambridge: MIT Press, 2001).

48. John Dryzek, *The Politics of the Earth: Environmental Discourses* (Oxford: Oxford University Press, 1997), 38–40.

49. John A. Hannigan, *Environmental Sociology: A Social Constructionist Perspective* (London: Routledge, 1995), 53–56.

50. M. C. Healey and T. M. Hennessey, "The Utilization of Scientific Information in the Management of Estuarine Ecosystems," *Ocean and Coastal Management* 23 (1994): 167–191.

51. Katherine Harrison and George Hoberg, "Setting the Environmental Agendas in Canada and the United States: The Cases of Dioxin and Radon," *Canadian Journal of Political Science* 24 (1991): 25; see also Hannigan, *Environmental Sociology*, 54–56; John Barry, *Rethinking Green Politics: Nature, Virtue and Progress* (London: Sage Publications, 1999), 30.

52. Wildavsky, *But Is It True?*

53. Hannigan, *Environmental Sociology*, 45.

54. Alan Irwin, Alison Dale, and Denis Smith, "Science and Hell's Kitchen: The Local Understanding of Hazard Issues," in *Misunderstanding Science? The Public Reconstruction of Science and Technology*, ed. Alan Irwin and Brian Wynne (Cambridge: Cambridge University Press, 1996), 47–64; Jane Gregory and Steve Miller, *Science in Public: Communication, Culture, and Credibility* (New York: Plenum, 1998), 98–99.

55. Royal Society of Canada, *Aquatic Science in Canada: A Case Study of Research in the Mackenzie Basin* (Ottawa: Royal Society, 1995), 60.

56. Social Learning Group, *Learning to Manage*, 2.75.

57. Michael E. Kraft, "Clean Air and the Adirondacks: Science, Politics, and Policy Choice," *Environmental Science and Policy* 1 (1998): 167–173.

58. Social Learning Group, *Learning to Manage*, 1.276–277.

59. Social Learning Group, *Learning to Manage*, 2.18.

60. Susan E. Cozzens and Edward J. Woodhouse, "Science, Government, and the Politics of Knowledge," in *Handbook of Science and Technology Studies,* ed. Sheila Jasanoff, Gerald E. Markle, James C. Petersen, and Trevor Pinch (Thousand Oaks, Calif.: Sage Publications, 1995), 533–553.

61. Social Learning Group, *Learning to Manage*, 2.189.

62. Andrew Webster, *Science, Technology and Society: New Directions* (New Brunswick, N.J.: Rutgers University Press, 1991), 93.

63. Karen T. Litfin, "Framing Science: Precautionary Discourse and the Ozone Treaties," *Millennium: Journal of International Studies* 24, no. 2 (1995): 251–277.

64. Penelope Canan and Nancy Reichman, *Ozone Connections: Expert Networks in Global Environmental Governance* (Sheffield: Greenleaf Publishing, 2001).

65. Kal Raustiala, "Nonstate Actors in the Global Climate Regime," in *International Relations and Global Climate Change,* ed. Urs Luterbacher and Detlef F. Sprinz (Cambridge: MIT Press, 2001), 95–117.

66. Jasanoff, *Fifth Branch*, 243.

67. Peter Cullen, "The Turbulent Boundary between Water Science and Water Management," *Freshwater Biology* 24 (1990): 201–209.

68. Sheila Jasanoff, "The Problem of Rationality in American Health and Safety Regulation," in *Expert Evidence: Interpreting Science in the Law,* ed. R. Smith and B. Wynne (New York: Routledge, 1989), 151–183.

69. Jonathon Porritt, *Playing Safe: Science and the Environment* (New York: Thames & Hudson, 2000), 85.

70. Ken Lertzman, Jeremy Rayner, and Jeremy Wilson, "Learning and Change in the British Columbia Forest Policy Sector: A Consideration of Sabatier's Advocacy Coalition Framework," *Canadian Journal of Political Science* 29, no. 1 (1996): 111–133.

71. Todd Wilkinson, *Science under Siege: The Politician's War on Nature and Truth* (Boulder, Colo.: Johnson Books, 1998).

72. Hessing and Howlett, *Canadian Natural Resource and Environmental Policy,* 153.

73. Melody Hessing and Michael Howlett, *Canadian Natural Resource and Environmental Policy: Political Economy and Public Policy* (Vancouver: University of British Columbia Press, 1997), 221–222.

74. Doern and Reed, "Conclusions," 374.

75. Jasanoff, *Fifth Branch,* 214–216; Keating, "Lessons from the Recent History."

76. Jasanoff, *Fifth Branch,* 49–60.

77. Samuel Hays, "Clean Air: From the 1970 Act to the 1977 Amendments," in *Explorations in Environmental History* (Pittsburgh: University of Pittsburgh Press, 1998), 228–230.

78. Social Learning Group, *Learning to Manage,* 1.327–329; 2.96–98, 109.

79. Poul Harremoës et al., *The Precautionary Principle in the 20th Century: Late Lessons from Early Warnings* (London: Earthscan, 2002).

80. William Leiss, *Governing Food: Science, Safety and Trade: Rapporteur's Report* (Canada–UK Colloquium, November 2–5, 2000), http://qsilver.queensu.ca/sps/WorkingPapers/files/CanUK2000.pdf 7.

81. Joel Tickner and Carolyn Raffensperger, "The Politics of Precaution in the United States and the European Union," *Global Environmental Change* 11 (2001): 175–180.

82. Porritt, *Playing Safe,* 42.

83. Harremoës et al., *Precautionary Principle,* 4–6.

84. Tickner and Raffensperger, "Politics of Precaution."

85. Ibid.

86. Wildavsky, *But Is It True?*

87. Rampton and Stauber, *Trust Us,* 127.

88. Henry I. Miller and Gregory Conko, "The Science of Biotechnology Meets the Politics of Global Regulation," *Issues in Science and Technology* 17, no. 1 (2000): 47–54.

89. Harremoës et al., *Precautionary Principle,* 207–208.

90. Stephen R. Dovers and John W. Handmer, "Ignorance, the Precautionary Principle, and Sustainability," *Ambio* 24, no. 2 (1995): 92–97.

91. Jasanoff, *Fifth Branch*; Liora Salter, *Mandated Science: Science and Scientists in the Making of Standards* (Dordrecht: Kluwer, 1988).

92. Richard Levins, "The Strategy of Model Building in Population Biology," *American Scientist* 54 (1966): 421–431.

93. Brian Wynne and Sue Mayer, "How Science Fails the Environment," *New Scientist,* 5 June 1993, 33–35.

94. Jane Lubchenco, "Entering the Century of the Environment: A New Social Contract for Science," *Science* 279 (1998): 491–497.

95. James Brown, *Who Rules in Science? An Opinionated Guide to the Wars* (Cambridge: Harvard University Press, 2001), 91.

96. On long-term research at Hubbard Brook see Bocking, *Ecologists and Environmental Politics*, 116–147; for the NSF LTER program see: U.S. Long Term Ecological Research Network, *www.lternet.edu/*; on endocrine disruptors see Theo Colborn, Dianne Dumanoski, and John Peterson Myers, *Our Stolen Future* (New York: Plume, 1996); on air pollution see Hays, "Clean Air," 238–241.

97. Social Learning Group, *Learning to Manage*, 1.243–244.

98. Michael E. Kowalok, "Research Lessons from Acid Rain, Ozone Depletion, and Global Warming," *Environment* 35, no. 6 (1993): 12–20, 35–38.

99. Brown, *Who Rules*, 88–91; see also Philip Kitcher, *Science, Truth, and Democracy* (New York: Oxford University Press, 2001), 111–116.

100. Social Learning Group, *Learning to Manage*, 2.108.

101. Douglas Powell and William Leiss, *Mad Cows and Mother's Milk: The Perils of Poor Risk Communication* (Montreal: McGill-Queen's University Press, 1997), 42–74.

102. Eyal Press and Jennifer Washburn, "The Kept University," *Atlantic Monthly*, March 2000, 39–54.

CHAPTER 8   *Democratic Environmental Science*

1. Carson, Rachel, *Silent Spring* (New York: Houghton-Mifflin, 1962), 64.

2. Ibid., 127.

3. Ibid., x.

4. Bryan G. Norton, "Sustainability: Descriptive or Performative?" in *The Moral Austerity of Environmental Decision Making: Sustainability, Democracy, and Normative Argument in Policy and Law,* ed. John Martin Gillroy and Joe Bowersox (Durham, N.C.: Duke University Press, 2002), 60–61.

5. Frank Fischer, *Citizens, Experts, and the Environment: The Politics of Local Knowledge* (Durham, N.C.: Duke University Press, 2000), 111–112.

6. William M. Lafferty and James Meadowcroft, eds., *Democracy and the Environment: Problems and Prospects* (Cheltenham: Edward Elgar, 1996).

7. John Dryzek, "Strategies of Ecological Democratization," in *Democracy and the Environment: Problems and Prospects,* ed. William M. Lafferty and James Meadowcroft (Cheltenham: Edward Elgar, 1996), 113.

8. Social Learning Group, *Learning to Manage Global Environmental Risks*, vol. 1: *A Comparative History of Social Responses to Climate Change, Ozone Depletion, and Acid Rain* (Cambridge: MIT Press, 2001), 349–354.

9. Robert Paehlke, "Environmental Challenges to Democratic Practice," in *Democracy and the Environment: Problems and Prospects,* ed. William M. Lafferty and James Meadowcroft (Cheltenham: Edward Elgar, 1996), 18–38.

10. Thomas Princen, "Distancing: Consumption and the Severing of Feedback," in *Confronting Consumption,* ed. Thomas Princen, Michael Maniates, and Ken Conca (Cambridge: MIT Press, 2002), 103–131.

11. Stephen Bocking, "Arctic Contaminants and Country Foods: Scientific and Indigenous Perspectives on Environmental Risks," *Environmental Practice* 3, no. 2 (2001): 103–112.

12. Social Learning Group, *Learning to Manage*, 1.8.

13. Melody Hessing and Michael Howlett, *Canadian Natural Resource and Environmental Policy: Political Economy and Public Policy* (Vancouver: University of British Columbia Press, 1997), 125–134.

14. Hanna J. Cortner, "Making Science Relevant to Environmental Policy," *Environmental Science & Policy* 3 (2000): 21–30.

15. Fischer, *Citizens*, 129.

16. Thomas C. Beierle and Jerry Cayford, *Democracy in Practice: Public Participation in Environmental Decisions* (Washington, D.C.: Resources for the Future, 2002), 75.

17. William B. Shutkin, *The Land that Could Be: Environmentalism and Democracy in the Twenty-First Century* (London: MIT Press, 2001).

18. Dryzek, "Strategies of Ecological Democratization," 109.

19. Jane Jacobs, *The Death and Life of Great American Cities* (New York: Vintage, 1961).

20. Martin Jänicke and Helmut Weidner, eds., *Successful Environmental Policy: A Critical Evaluation of 24 Cases* (Berlin: Sigma, 1995).

21. Bryan G. Norton, "Democracy and Environmentalism: Foundations and Justifications in Environmental Policy," in *Democracy and the Claims of Nature: Critical Perspectives for a New Century,* ed. Ben A. Minteer and Bob Pepperman Taylor (Lanham, Md.: Rowman & Littlefield, 2002), 23–24.

22. John Dryzek, *The Politics of the Earth: Environmental Discourses* (Oxford: Oxford University Press, 1997), 84–101; Bruce A. Williams and Albert R. Matheny, *Democracy, Dialogue, and Environmental Disputes: The Contested Languages of Social Regulation* (New Haven, Conn.: Yale University Press, 1995).

23. Fischer, *Citizens*, 148.

24. Fischer, *Citizens*, 233.

25. Aaron Wildavsky, *But Is It True? A Citizen's Guide to Environmental Health and Safety Issues* (Cambridge: Harvard University Press, 1995).

26. Brian Wynne, "Public Understanding of Science," in *Handbook of Science and Technology Studies,* ed. Sheila Jasanoff, Gerald E. Markle, James C. Petersen, and Trevor Pinch (Thousand Oaks, Calif.: Sage Publications, 1995), 363.

27. Amy Gutmann, "Democracy," in *A Companion to Contemporary Political Philosophy,* ed. Robert E. Goodin and Philip Pettit (Oxford: Blackwell, 1993), 411–421; Mark Sagoff, *The Economy of the Earth: Philosophy, Law, and the Environment* (Cambridge: Cambridge University Press, 1988).

28. Fischer, *Citizens*, 35.

29. Daniel Press, *Democratic Dilemmas in the Age of Ecology: Trees and Toxics in the American West* (Durham, N.C.: Duke University Press, 1994), 63–64.

30. Hessing and Howlett, *Canadian Natural Resource and Environmental Policy*, 278.

31. Ecologic, *Participation of Non-Governmental Organizations in International Environmental Governance: Legal Basis and Practical Experience* (Berlin: Ecologic, June 2002), 218.

32. Jänicke and Weidner, eds., *Successful Environmental Policy*.

33. Daniel J. Fiorino, "Environmental Policy and the Participation Gap," in *Democracy and the Environment: Problems and Prospects,* ed. William M. Lafferty and James Meadowcroft (Cheltenham: Edward Elgar, 1996), 200–201; Dryzek, "Strategies of Ecological Democratization."

34. Stephen Turner, "What is the Problem with Experts?" *Social Studies of Science* 31, no. 1 (2001): 123–149.

35. Quoted in Ben A. Minteer, "Deweyan Democracy and Environmental Ethics," in *Democracy and the Claims of Nature: Critical Perspectives for a New Century,* ed. Ben A. Minteer and Bob Pepperman Taylor (Lanham, Md.: Rowman & Littlefield, 2002), 40.

36. Clark A. Miller, "Challenges in the Application of Science to Global Affairs: Contingency, Trust, and Moral Order," in *Changing the Atmosphere: Expert Knowledge and Environmental Governance,* ed. Clark A. Miller and Paul N. Edwards (Cambridge: MIT Press, 2001), 265–268.

37. Brian Wynne, "Misunderstood Misunderstandings: Social Identities and Public Uptake of Science," in *Misunderstanding Science? The Public Reconstruction of Science and Technology,* ed. A. Irwin and B. Wynne (Cambridge: Cambridge University Press, 1996), 41.

38. Alan Irwin and Brian Wynne, eds., *Misunderstanding Science? The Public Reconstruction of Science and Technology* (Cambridge: Cambridge University Press, 1996), 215.

39. Chunglin Kwa, "The Rise and Fall of Weather Modification: Changes in American Attitudes toward Technology, Nature, and Society," in *Changing the Atmosphere: Expert Knowledge and Environmental Governance,* ed. Clark A. Miller and Paul N. Edwards (Cambridge: MIT Press, 2001), 135–165.

40. Turner, "Problem with Experts."

41. Jonathon Porritt, *Playing Safe: Science and the Environment* (New York: Thames & Hudson, 2000), 109.

42. Wildavsky, *But Is It True?*

43. Gregory and Miller, *Science in Public,* 89.

44. Wynne, "Public Understanding of Science," 366.

45. John A. Hannigan, *Environmental Sociology: A Social Constructionist Perspective* (London: Routledge, 1995), 104–106.

46. Wynne, "Misunderstood Misunderstandings," 26.

47. Hessing and Howlett, *Canadian Natural Resource and Environmental Policy,* 129, 208.

48. Sheldon Rampton and John Stauber, *Trust Us, We're Experts! How Industry Manipulates Science and Gambles with Your Future* (New York: Tarcher/Putnam, 2001), 215.

49. Stephen Turner, *Liberal Democracy 3.0* (London: Sage Publications, 2003), 6–7.

50. Dan Fagin and Marianne Lavell, *Toxic Deception: How the Chemical Industry Manipulates Science, Bends the Law, and Endangers Your Health* (Secaucus, N.J.: Birch Lane Press, 1996), 52.

51. Stephen Bocking, "Genetic Illusions," *Alternatives Journal* 28, no. 4 (2002): 11–12.

52. Rampton and Stauber, *Trust Us,* 178–179.

53. Robert Paehlke, "Cycles of Closure in Environmental Politics and Policy," in *Democracy and the Claims of Nature: Critical Perspectives for a New Century,* ed. Ben A. Minteer and Bob Pepperman Taylor (Lanham, Md.: Rowman & Littlefield, 2002), 293.

54. Riley E. Dunlap, "Lay Perceptions of Global Risk: Public Views of Global Warming in Cross-National Context," *International Sociology* 13, no. 4 (1998): 473–498.

55. Robert G. Healy and William Ascher, "Knowledge in the Policy Process: Incorporating New Environmental Information in Natural Resources Policy Making," *Policy Sciences* 28, no. 1 (1995): 1–19.

56. Timothy Luke, "Eco-Managerialism: Environmental Studies as a Power/Knowledge Formation," in *Living with Nature: Environmental Politics as Cultural Discourse,* ed. Frank Fischer and Maarten A. Hajer (Oxford: Oxford University Press, 1999), 105.

57. Turner, "Problem with Experts."

58. Ibid.

59. Dunlap, "Lay Perceptions of Global Risk."

60. Fischer, *Citizens*, 113.

61. Robert Gottlieb, *Forcing the Spring: The Transformation of the American Environmental Movement* (Washington, D.C.: Island Press, 1993), 117–204.

62. Quoted in David Harvey, "The Environment of Justice," in *Living with Nature: Environmental Politics as Cultural Discourse,* ed. Frank Fischer and Maarten A. Hajer (Oxford: Oxford University Press, 1999), 158.

63. Bruce Rich, *Mortgaging the Earth: The World Bank, Environmental Impoverishment, and the Crisis of Development* (Boston: Beacon Press, 1994); Catherine Caulfield, *Masters of Illusion: The World Bank and the Poverty of Nations* (New York: Henry Holt, 1996); Dana Clark, Jonathan Fox, and Kay Treakle, eds., *Demanding Accountability: Civil-Society Claims and the World Bank Inspection Panel* (Lanham, Md.: Rowman & Littlefield, 2003).

64. James Brown, *Who Rules in Science? An Opinionated Guide to the Wars* (Cambridge: Harvard University Press, 2001), 180–184.

65. E. Ann Clark, "Regulation of GM Crops in Canada: Science-Based or . . . ?" (unpublished paper, 2003).

66. Fischer, *Citizens*, 148–151.

67. Ecologic, *Participation of Non-Governmental Organizations*, 40–42.

68. Leslie R. Alm, *Crossing Borders, Crossing Boundaries: The Role of Scientists in the U.S. Acid Rain Debate* (Westport, Conn.: Praeger, 2000), 48–52.

69. Simone Chambers, "Deliberative Democratic Theory," *Annual Review of Political Science* 6 (2003): 307–326.

70. Samuel Hays, "Foreword to Frederick Frankena, *Strategies of Expertise in Technical Controversies*," in *Explorations in Environmental History* (Pittsburgh: University of Pittsburgh Press, 1998), 193–195.

71. Bruce V. Lewenstein, "Science and the Media," in *Handbook of Science and Technology Studies,* ed. Sheila Jasanoff, Gerald E. Markle, James C. Petersen, and Trevor Pinch (Thousand Oaks, Calif.: Sage Publications, 1995), 343–360; Susan E. Cozzens and Edward J. Woodhouse, "Science, Government, and the Politics of Knowledge," in *Handbook of Science and Technology Studies,* ed. Sheila Jasanoff, Gerald E. Markle, James C. Petersen and Trevor Pinch (Thousand Oaks, Calif.: Sage Publications, 1995), 533–553.

72. Quoted in Fischer, *Citizens*, 29.

73. See *www.epa.gov/airnow*.

74. Turner, *Liberal Democracy 3.0*, 19.

75. Jessica Glicken, "Getting Stakeholder Participation 'Right': A Discussion of Participatory Processes and Possible Pitfalls," *Environmental Science and Policy* 3 (2000): 305–310.

76. Christina Chociolko, "The Experts Disagree: A Simple Matter of Facts Versus Values?" *Alternatives* 21, no. 3 (1995): 18–25.

77. Steven Yearley, "Nature's Advocates: Putting Science to Work in Environmental Or-

ganizations," in *Misunderstanding Science? The Public Reconstruction of Science and Technology,* ed. Alan Irwin and Brian Wynne (Cambridge: Cambridge University Press, 1996), 181.

78. Cozzens and Woodhouse, "Science, Government, and the Politics of Knowledge," 544–548.
79. Fischer, *Citizens*, 37–40.
80. Wildavsky, *But Is It Safe?*
81. Clark, "Regulation of GM Crops."
82. Charles Herrick and Dale Jamieson, "The Social Construction of Acid Rain: Some Implications for Science/Policy Assessment," *Global Environmental Change* 5, no. 2 (1995): 105–112.
83. Jeremy Cherfas, "Greenpeace and Science: Oil and Water?" *Science* 247 (1990): 1288–1290.
84. Cozzens and Woodhouse, "Science, Government, and the Politics of Knowledge," 540; Social Learning Group, *Learning to Manage Global Environmental Risks*, volume 2: *A Functional Analysis of Social Responses to Climate Change, Ozone Depletion, and Acid Rain* (Cambridge: MIT Press, 2001), 20–21.
85. Hanna J. Cortner, "Making Science Relevant to Environmental Policy," *Environmental Science & Policy* 3 (2000): 21–30.
86. Steven Yearley, "The Environmental Challenge to Science Studies," in *Handbook of Science and Technology Studies,* ed. Sheila Jasanoff, Gerald E. Markle, James C. Petersen, and Trevor Pinch (Thousand Oaks, Calif.: Sage Publications, 1995), 476.
87. Fischer, *Citizens*, 172–176.
88. Ibid.
89. M. P. Robinson and M. M. Ross, "Traditional Land Use and Occupancy Studies and Their Impact on Forest Planning and Management in Alberta," *Forestry Chronicle* 73, no. 5 (1997): 596–605.
90. Sheila Jasanoff, "NGOs and the Environment: From Knowledge to Action," *Third World Quarterly* 18, no. 3 (1997): 579–594.
91. Fischer, *Citizens*, 129.
92. Bruce A. Williams and Albert R. Matheny, *Democracy, Dialogue, and Environmental Disputes: The Contested Languages of Social Regulation* (New Haven, Conn.: Yale University Press, 1995), 177–180.
93. Ibid.
94. Chambers, "Deliberative Democratic Theory."
95. Shutkin, *Land that Could Be*; see also Scott Campbell, "Green Cities, Growing Cities, Just Cities? Urban Planning and the Contradictions of Sustainable Development," *Journal of the American Planning Association* 62, no. 3 (1996): 304–305; Fischer, *Citizens*, 226–227; Robert Costanza, "Ecological Economics: Reintegrating the Study of Humans and Nature," *Ecological Applications* 6, no. 4 (1996): 978–990.
96. Chambers, "Deliberative Democratic Theory," 310.
97. Fischer, *Citizens*, 224–229.
98. David H. Guston, "Evaluating the First U.S. Consensus Conference: The Impact of the Citizens' Panel on Telecommunications and the Future of Democracy," *Science, Technology, & Human Values* 24, no. 4 (1999): 451–482.
99. Alan Irwin, "Business as Usual? Re-assessing Scientific Institutions and Global Environmental Challenges," *Global Environmental Change* 8, no. 3 (1998): 279–283.

100. Costanza, "Ecological Economics."
101. Philip Kitcher, *Science, Truth, and Democracy* (New York: Oxford University Press, 2001).
102. Williams and Matheny, *Democracy, Dialogue, and Environmental Disputes*, 57.
103. National Research Council, *Our Common Journey: A Transition toward Sustainability. Report of the Board on Sustainable Development* (Washington, D.C.: National Academy Press, 1999), 5.
104. John B. Robinson, "Risks, Predictions and other Optical Illusions: Rethinking the Use of Science in Social Decision-Making," *Policy Sciences* 25 (1992): 237–254.
105. Stewart Cohen et al., "Climate Change and Sustainable Development: Towards Dialogue," *Global Environmental Change* 8, no. 4 (1998): 341–371.
106. John B. Robinson, *Life in 2030: Exploring a Sustainable Future for Canada* (Vancouver: University of British Columbia Press, 1995).
107. Fischer, *Citizens*, 247–248; Brian Martin and Evelleen Richards, "Scientific Knowledge, Controversy, and Public Decision Making," in *Handbook of Science and Technology Studies,* ed. Sheila Jasanoff, Gerald E. Markle, James C. Petersen, and Trevor Pinch (Thousand Oaks, Calif.: Sage Publications, 1995), 506–526.
108. Alan Irwin, Alison Dale, and Denis Smith, "Science and Hell's Kitchen: The Local Understanding of Hazard Issues," in *Misunderstanding Science? The Public Reconstruction of Science and Technology*, ed. Alan Irwin and Brian Wynne (Cambridge: Cambridge University Press, 1996), 52–57.

CHAPTER 9   *Achieving Effective and Democratic Science*

1. Mike Fortun and Herbert J. Bernstein, *Muddling Through: Pursuing Science and Truths in the 21st Century* (Washington, D.C.: Counterpoint, 1998); Clinton J. Andrews, *Humble Analysis: The Practice of Joint Fact-Finding* (Westport, Conn.: Praeger, 2002).
2. William C. Clark and Giandomenico Majone, "The Critical Appraisal of Scientific Inquiries with Policy Implications," *Science, Technology, & Human Values* 10, no. 3 (1985): 6–19.
3. Between 1985 and the late 1990s Clark and Majone's scheme apparently did not attract much interest from scholars. The only study in which it was applied, to my knowledge, was my own analysis of aquatic science in northern Canada, conducted during 1993–94; see Royal Society of Canada, *Aquatic Science in Canada: A Case Study of Research in the Mackenzie Basin* (Ottawa: Royal Society, 1995).
4. Robin O'Malley, Kent Cavender-Bares, and William C. Clark, "Providing 'Better' Data: Not as Simple as It Might Seem," *Environment* 45, no. 4 (2003): 8–18; David W. Cash et al., "Knowledge Systems for Sustainable Development," *Proceedings of the National Academy of Sciences* 100, no. 14 (2003): 8086–8091.

References

Acheson, James M., James A. Wilson, and Robert S. Steneck. "Managing Chaotic Fisheries." In *Linking Social and Ecological Systems: Management Practices and Social Mechanisms for Building Resilience,* ed. Fikret Berkes and Carl Folke, 390–413. Cambridge: Cambridge University Press, 1998.

Agarwal, Anil. "A Southern Perspective on Curbing Global Climate Change." In *Climate Change Policy: A Survey,* ed. Stephen H. Schneider, Armin Rosencranz, and John O. Niles, 375–391. Washington, D.C.: Island Press, 2002.

Agrawala, Shardul, Kenneth Broad, and David H. Guston. "Integrating Climate Forecasts and Societal Decision Making: Challenges to an Emergent Boundary Organization." *Science, Technology, & Human Values* 26, no. 4 (2001): 454–477.

Ahearne, John. "Integrating Risk Analysis into Public Policymaking." *Environment* 35, no. 2 (1993): 16–20, 37–40.

Alexander, Donald. "Bioregionalism: Science or Sensibility." *Environmental Ethics* 12, no. 2 (1990): 161–171.

Allen, T.F.H., B. L. Bandurski, and A. W. King. *The Ecosystem Approach: Theory and Ecosystem Integrity.* Washington, D.C.: IJC, 1993.

Alm, Leslie R. *Crossing Borders, Crossing Boundaries: The Role of Scientists in the U.S. Acid Rain Debate.* Westport, Conn.: Praeger, 2000.

Alvarez, L. "Europe Acts to Require Labeling of Genetically Altered Food." *New York Times,* 3 July 2003, A3.

Anderson, Kai S. "The Climate Policy Debate in the U.S. Congress." In *Climate Change Policy: A Survey,* ed. Stephen H. Schneider, Armin Rosencranz, and John O. Niles, 235–250. Washington, D.C.: Island Press, 2002.

Andrews, Clinton J. *Humble Analysis: The Practice of Joint Fact-Finding.* Westport, Conn.: Praeger, 2002.

Anker, Peder. *Imperial Ecology: Environmental Order in the British Empire, 1895–1945.* Cambridge: Harvard University Press, 2001.

Apffel-Marglin, Frédérique. "Introduction: Rationality and the World." In *Decolonizing Knowledge: From Development to Dialogue,* ed. Frédérique Apffel-Marglin and Stephen A. Marglin, 1–39. New York: Oxford University Press, 1996.

Balogh, Brian. *Chain Reaction: Expert Debate and Public Participation in American Commercial Nuclear Power, 1945–1975.* Cambridge: Cambridge University Press, 1991.

Barry, John. *Rethinking Green Politics: Nature, Virtue and Progress*. London: Sage Publications, 1999.

Baskerville, G. L. "Gaelic Poetry for Deaf Seagulls—Encore." *Forestry Chronicle* 70, no. 5 (1994): 562–564.

Baumgartner, Frank R., and Bryan D. Jones. "Agenda Dynamics and Policy Subsystems." *Journal of Politics* 53 (1991): 1044–1074.

Beamish, R. J., and D. R. Bouillon. "Pacific Salmon Production Trends in Relation to Climate." *Canadian Journal of Fisheries and Aquatic Science* 50 (1993): 1002–1016.

Beck, Ulrich. *Risk Society: Towards a New Modernity*. London: Sage, 1992.

Beierle, Thomas C., and Jerry Cayford. *Democracy in Practice: Public Participation in Environmental Decisions*. Washington, D.C.: Resources for the Future, 2002.

Bekelman, Justin E., Yan Li, and Cary P. Gross. "Scope and Impact of Financial Conflicts of Interest in Biomedical Research: A Systematic Review." *Journal of the American Medical Association* 289, no. 4 (2003): 454–465.

Bergen, Lydia K., and Mark H. Carr. "Establishing Marine Reserves: How Can Science Best Inform Policy?" *Environment* 45, no. 2 (2003): 8–19.

Berkes, Fikret. "Indigenous Knowledge and Resource Management Systems in the Canadian Arctic." In *Linking Social and Ecological Systems: Management Practices and Social Mechanisms for Building Resilience,* ed. F. Berkes and C. Folke, 98–128. Cambridge: Cambridge University Press, 1998.

———. *Sacred Ecology: Traditional Ecological Knowledge and Resource Management*. Philadelphia: Taylor & Francis, 1999.

Berkes, F., and C. Folke, eds. *Linking Social and Ecological Systems: Management Practices and Social Mechanisms for Building Resilience*. Cambridge: Cambridge University Press, 1998.

Beyers, Joanna M., and L. Anders Sandberg. "Canadian Federal Forest Policy: Present Initiatives and Historical Constraints." In *Sustainability the Challenge: People, Power and the Environment,* ed. L. Anders Sandberg and Sverker Sorlin, 99–107. Montreal: Black Rose, 1998.

Blaikie, Piers M. "Post-modernism and Global Environmental Change." *Global Environmental Change* 6, no. 2 (1996): 81–85.

Bocking, Stephen. "Stephen Forbes, Jacob Reighard and the Emergence of Aquatic Ecology in the Great Lakes Region." *Journal of the History of Biology* 23 (1990): 461–498.

———. "Visions of Nature and Society: A History of the Ecosystem Concept." *Alternatives* 20, no. 3 (1994): 12–18.

———. "Ecosystems, Ecologists and the Atom: Environmental Research at Oak Ridge National Laboratory." *Journal of the History of Biology* 28, no. 1 (1995): 1–47.

———. "Fishing the Inland Seas: Great Lakes Research, Fisheries Management and Environmental Policy in Ontario." *Environmental History* 2, no. 1 (1997): 52–73.

———. *Ecologists and Environmental Politics: A History of Contemporary Ecology*. New Haven, Conn.: Yale University Press, 1997.

———. "Arctic Contaminants and Country Foods: Scientific and Indigenous Perspectives on Environmental Risks." *Environmental Practice* 3, no. 2 (2001): 103–112.

———. "Genetic Illusions." *Alternatives Journal* 28, no. 4 (2002): 11–12.

———. "Betting on the Future." *Alternatives Journal* 29, no. 1 (2003): 42–43.

———. "Bottom Line Hooks Salmon Science." *Alternatives Journal* 29, no. 2 (2003): 39–40.

Boehmer-Christiansen, Sonja. "Scientific Consensus and Climate Change: The Codification of a Global Research Agenda." *Energy and Environment* 4, no. 4 (1993): 362–407.

Botkin, Daniel B. *Discordant Harmonies: A New Ecology for the Twenty-First Century.* New York: Oxford University Press, 1990.

Bowersox, Joe. "The Legitimacy Crisis in Environmental Ethics and Politics." In *Democracy and the Claims of Nature: Critical Perspectives for a New Century,* ed. Ben A. Minteer and Bob Pepperman Taylor, 71–90. Lanham, Md.: Rowman & Littlefield, 2002.

Boyce, Mark S., and Alan Haney, eds. *Ecosystem Management: Applications for Sustainable Forest and Wildlife Resources.* New Haven, Conn.: Yale University Press, 1997.

Brand, David G., O. Thomas Bouman, Luc Bouthiller, Winifred Kessler, and Louis Lapierre. "The Model Forest Concept: A Model for Future Forest Management?" *Environmental Reviews* 4 (1996): 65–90.

Brody, Jane. "Even Low Lead Levels Pose Perils for Children." *New York Times*, 5 August 2003, F7.

Brosnan, Deborah M. "Can Peer Review Help Resolve Natural Resource Conflicts?" *Issues in Science and Technology* 16, no. 3 (2000): 32–36.

Brown, James. "Privatizing the University—The New Tragedy of the Commons." *Science* 290 (2000): 1701–1702.

———. *Who Rules in Science? An Opinionated Guide to the Wars.* Cambridge: Harvard University Press, 2001.

Burns, Ric, and James Sanders. *New York: An Illustrated History.* New York: Alfred A. Knopf, 1999.

Callicott, J. Baird. "The Scientific Substance of the Land Ethic." In *Aldo Leopold: The Man and His Legacy,* ed. Thomas Tanner, 87–104. Ankeny, Iowa: Soil Conservation Society of America, 1987.

———. "The Land Ethic." In *A Companion to Environmental Philosophy,* ed. Dale Jamieson. Malden, Mass.: Blackwell, 2001.

———. "Science, Value, and Ethics: A Hierarchical Theory." In *Democracy and the Claims of Nature: Critical Perspectives for a New Century,* ed. Ben A. Minteer and Bob Pepperman Taylor, 91–114. Lanham, Md.: Rowman & Littlefield, 2002.

Campbell, Scott. "Green Cities, Growing Cities, Just Cities? Urban Planning and the Contradictions of Sustainable Development." *Journal of the American Planning Association* 62, no. 3 (1996): 296–312.

Canan, Penelope, and Nancy Reichman. *Ozone Connections: Expert Networks in Global Environmental Governance.* Sheffield: Greenleaf Publishing, 2001.

Carson, Rachel. *Silent Spring.* New York: Houghton-Mifflin, 1962.

Cash, David W., William C. Clark, Frank Alcock, Nancy M. Dickson, Noelle Eckley, David H. Guston, Jill Jäger, and Ronald B. Mitchell. "Knowledge Systems for Sustainable Development." *Proceedings of the National Academy of Sciences* 100, no. 14 (2003): 8086–8091.

Castro, Alfonso Peter, and Erik Nielsen. "Indigenous People and Co-Management: Implications for Conflict Management." *Environmental Science & Policy* 4 (2001): 229–239.

Caulfield, Catherine. *Masters of Illusion: The World Bank and the Poverty of Nations.* New York: Henry Holt, 1996.

Chambers, Simone. "Deliberative Democratic Theory." *Annual Review of Political Science* 6 (2003): 307–326.

Cherfas, Jeremy. "Greenpeace and Science: Oil and Water?" *Science* 247 (1990): 1288–1290.

Chociolko, Christina. "The Experts Disagree: A Simple Matter of Facts Versus Values?" *Alternatives* 21, no. 3 (1995): 18–25.

Christensen, Norman L. "Implementing Ecosystem Management: Where Do We Go From Here?" In *Ecosystem Management: Applications for Sustainable Forest and Wildlife Resources,* ed. Mark S. Boyce and Alan Haney, 325–341. New Haven, Conn.: Yale University Press, 1997.

Chubin, Daryl, and Edward Hackett. *Peerless Science: Peer Review and U.S. Science Policy.* Albany: State University of New York Press, 1990.

Cittadino, Eugene. "The Failed Promise of Human Ecology." In *Science and Nature: Essays in the History of the Environmental Sciences*, ed. Michael Shortland, 251–283. Oxford: British Society for the History of Science, 1993.

Clark, Dana, Jonathan Fox, and Kay Treakle, eds. *Demanding Accountability: Civil-Society Claims and the World Bank Inspection Panel.* Lanham, Md.: Rowman & Littlefield, 2003.

Clark, E. Ann. "Regulation of GM Crops in Canada: Science-Based or . . . ?" Unpublished paper, 2003.

Clark, William C., and Giandomenico Majone. "The Critical Appraisal of Scientific Inquiries with Policy Implications." *Science, Technology, & Human Values* 10, no. 3 (1985): 6–19.

Coates, Peter. *Nature: Western Attitudes since Ancient Times.* Berkeley: University of California Press, 1998.

Cohen, Maurie J. "Science and Society in Historical Perspective: Implications for Social Theories of Risk." *Environmental Values* 8 (1999): 153–176.

Cohen, Stewart, David Demeritt, John Robinson, and Dale Rothman. "Climate Change and Sustainable Development: Towards Dialogue." *Global Environmental Change* 8, no. 4 (1998): 341–371.

Colborn, Theo, Dianne Dumanoski, and John Peterson Myers. *Our Stolen Future.* New York: Plume, 1996.

Commoner, Barry. *The Closing Circle: Nature, Man, and Technology.* New York: Alfred A. Knopf, 1971.

Cortner, Hanna J. "Making Science Relevant to Environmental Policy." *Environmental Science & Policy* 3 (2000): 21–30.

Cortner, Hanna J., and Margaret A. Moote. *The Politics of Ecosystem Management.* Washington, D.C.: Island Press, 1999.

Costanza, Robert. "Ecological Economics: Reintegrating the Study of Humans and Nature." *Ecological Applications* 6, no. 4 (1996): 978–990.

Coutinho, Marilia. "Ecological Metaphors and Environmental Rhetoric: An Analysis of The Ecologist and Our Common Future." *Environment and History* 3 (1997): 177–195.

Cox, Kevin. "Fishery Could End Cod Stocks, DFO Says." *The Globe and Mail* (Toronto), 23 November 2002.

Cozzens, Susan E., and Thomas F. Gieryn. "Introduction: Putting Science Back in Society." In *Theories of Science in Society,* ed. Susan E. Cozzens and Thomas F. Gieryn, 1–14. Bloomington: Indiana University Press, 1990.

Cozzens, Susan E., and Edward J. Woodhouse. "Science, Government, and the Politics of Knowledge." In *Handbook of Science and Technology Studies,* ed. Sheila Jasanoff, Gerald E. Markle, James C. Petersen and Trevor Pinch, 533–553. Thousand Oaks, Calif.: Sage Publications, 1995.

Crowcroft, Peter. *Elton's Ecologists: A History of the Bureau of Animal Population.* Chicago: University of Chicago Press, 1991.

Cullen, Peter. "The Turbulent Boundary between Water Science and Water Management." *Freshwater Biology* 24 (1990): 201–209.

Cushon, Geoff. "The Art of Uncertainty: Science and the Management of Natural Resources." Sustainable Development Research Institute, University of British Columbia, Discussion Paper DP–92–04, August 1992.

Daily, Gretchen C., ed. *Nature's Services.* Washington, D.C.: Island Press, 1997.

David Suzuki Foundation. *Taking Credit: Canada and the Role of Sinks in International Climate Negotiations.* Vancouver, B.C.: David Suzuki Foundation, 2001. Available at *www.davidsuzuki.org.*

Dewey, John. *The Public and Its Problems.* New York: Swallow, 1927.

Doern, G. Bruce, and Ted Reed. "Conclusions: New Institutions and Prospects for Change." In *Risky Business: Canada's Changing Science-Based Policy and Regulatory Regime,* ed. G. Bruce Doern and Ted Reed, 363–385. Toronto: University of Toronto Press, 2000.

Dovers, Stephen R., and John W. Handmer. "Ignorance, the Precautionary Principle, and Sustainability." *Ambio* 24, no. 2 (1995): 92–97.

Drengson, Alan Rike, and Duncan MacDonald Taylor. *Ecoforestry: The Art and Science of Sustainable Forest Use.* Gabriola Island, B.C.: New Society Publishers, 1997.

Dryzek, John. "Strategies of Ecological Democratization." In *Democracy and the Environment: Problems and Prospects,* ed. William M. Lafferty and James Meadowcroft, 108–124. Cheltenham: Edward Elgar, 1996.

———. *The Politics of the Earth: Environmental Discourses.* Oxford: Oxford University Press, 1997.

Duinker, Peter N. "Community Forests in Canada: An Overview." *Forestry Chronicle* 70, no. 6 (1994): 711–720.

Dunlap, Riley E. "Lay Perceptions of Global Risk: Public Views of Global Warming in Cross-National Context." *International Sociology* 13, no. 4 (1998): 473–498.

Dunlap, Thomas. *Saving America's Wildlife: Ecology and the American Mind, 1850–1990.* Princeton, N.J.: Princeton University Press, 1988.

Eckersley, Robyn. "Politics." In *A Companion to Environmental Philosophy,* ed. Dale Jamieson, 316–330. Malden, Mass.: Blackwell, 2001.

Ecologic—Institute for International and European Environmental Policy. *Participation of Non-Governmental Organizations in International Environmental Governance: Legal Basis and Practical Experience.* Berlin: Ecologic, June 2002. Available at: *www.umweltbundesamt.de.*

Economist, The. "China's Chernobyl?" 26 April 2003, 9–10.

Edwards, Paul N. "Global Comprehensive Models in Politics and Policymaking." *Climatic Change* 32 (1996): 149–161.

———. "Representing the Global Atmosphere: Computer Models, Data, and Knowledge about Climate Change." In *Changing the Atmosphere: Expert Knowledge and Environmental Governance,* ed. Clark A. Miller and Paul N. Edwards, 31–65. Cambridge: MIT Press, 2001.

Edwards, Paul N., and Stephen H. Schneider. "Self-Governance and Peer Review in Science-for-Policy: The Case of the IPCC Second Assessment Report." In *Changing the Atmosphere: Expert Knowledge and Environmental Governance,* ed. Clark A. Miller and Paul N. Edwards, 219–246. Cambridge: MIT Press, 2001.

Elliott, E. Donald. "Toward Ecological Law and Policy." In *Thinking Ecologically: The Next Generation of Environmental Policy,* ed. Marian R. Chertow and Daniel C. Esty, 170–186. New Haven, Conn.: Yale University Press, 1997.

Elliott, Lorraine. *The Global Politics of the Environment.* New York: New York University Press, 1998.

Elzinga, Aant. "From Arrhenius to Megascience: Interplay between Science and Public Decisionmaking." *Ambio* 26, no. 1 (1997): 72–80.

Environmental Protection Agency, Science Advisory Board. "Reducing Risk: Setting Priorities and Strategies for Environmental Protection." SAB-EC 90–021, September 1990.

Environmental Protection Agency. *Guidelines for Ecological Risk Assessment.* EPA/630/R–95/002F, April 1998.

European Commission. *Science and Society Action Plan.* Luxembourg: Office for Official Publications of the European Communities, 2002.

EU–U.S. Biotechnology Consultative Forum. *Final Report.* December 2000. http://europa.eu.int/comm/external_relations/us/biotech/biotech.htm.

Eyles, John, et al. "The Social Construction of Risk in a Rural Community: Responses of Local Residents to the 1990 Hagersville (Ontario) Tire Fire." *Risk Analysis* 13, no. 3 (1993): 281–290.

Ezrahi, Yaron. *The Descent of Icarus: Science and the Transformation of Contemporary Democracy.* Cambridge: Harvard University Press, 1990.

Fagin, Dan, and Marianne Lavell. *Toxic Deception: How the Chemical Industry Manipulates Science, Bends the Law, and Endangers Your Health.* Secaucus, N.J.: Birch Lane Press, 1996.

Fairhead, James, and Melissa Leach. "Webs of Power and the Construction of Environmental Policy Problems: Forest Loss in Guinea." In *Discourses of Development: Anthropological Perspectives,* ed. R. D. Grillo and R. L. Stirrat, 35–57. Oxford: Berg, 1997.

Finlayson, Alan C. *Fishing for Truth: A Sociological Analysis of Northern Cod Stock Assessments from 1977–1990.* St. John's, Nfld.: Institute of Social and Economic Research, 1994.

Fiorino, Daniel J. "Environmental Policy and the Participation Gap." In *Democracy and the Environment: Problems and Prospects,* ed. William M. Lafferty and James Meadowcroft, 194–212. Cheltenham: Edward Elgar, 1996.

Fischer, Frank. *Citizens, Experts, and the Environment: The Politics of Local Knowledge.* Durham, N.C.: Duke University Press, 2000.

Fleming, D. "Roots of the New Conservation Movement." *Perspectives in American History* 6 (1972): 7–94.

Fortun, Mike, and Herbert J. Bernstein. *Muddling Through: Pursuing Science and Truths in the 21st Century.* Washington, D.C.: Counterpoint, 1998.

Foucault, Michel. *Power/Knowledge: Selected Interviews & Other Writings, 1972–1977.* New York: Pantheon Books, 1980.

Francis, R.I.C.C., and R. Shotton. "'Risk' in Fisheries Management: A Review." *Canadian Journal of Fisheries and Aquatic Sciences* 54 (1997): 1699–1715.

Frank, David John. "Science, Nature, and the Globalization of the Environment, 1870–1990." *Social Forces* 76, no. 2 (1997): 409–437.

Franklin, Jerry F. "Ecosystem Management: An Overview." In *Ecosystem Management: Applications for Sustainable Forest and Wildlife Resources,* ed. Mark S. Boyce and Alan Haney, 21–53. New Haven, Conn.: Yale University Press, 1997.

Fraser River Sockeye Public Review Board. *Fraser River Sockeye 1994: Problems & Discrepancies.* Ottawa: The Board, 1995.

Freeman, Milton M. R. "Graphs and Gaffs: A Cautionary Tale in the Common-Property Resources Debate." In *Common Property Resources: Ecology and Community-Based Sustainable Development,* ed. F. Berkes, 92–109. London: Belhaven Press, 1989.

Ghai, Dharam, and Jessica M. Vivian. *Grassroots Environmental Action: People's Participation in Sustainable Development.* London: Routledge, 1995.

Gibb, Steven. "Science and Economics Prominent on EPA Agenda." *Issues in Science and Technology* 17, no. 3 (2001): 57–60.

Gieryn, Thomas F. *Cultural Boundaries of Science: Credibility on the Line.* Chicago: University of Chicago Press, 1999.

Glacken, Clarence J. *Traces on the Rhodian Shore: Nature and Culture in Western Thought from Ancient Times to the End of the Eighteenth Century.* Berkeley: University of California Press, 1967.

Glantz, Michael. *Societal Responses to Regional Climate Change: Forecasting by Analogy.* Boulder, Colo.: Westview Press, 1988.

Glavin, Terry. *Dead Reckoning: Confronting the Crisis in Pacific Fisheries.* Vancouver, B.C.: Douglas & McIntyre, 1996.

Glicken, Jessica. "Getting Stakeholder Participation 'Right': A Discussion of Participatory Processes and Possible Pitfalls." *Environmental Science and Policy* 3 (2000): 305–310.

Gordon, John, and Jane Coppock. "Ecosystem Management and Economic Development." In *Thinking Ecologically: The Next Generation of Environmental Policy,* ed. Marian R. Chertow and Daniel C. Esty, 37–48. New Haven, Conn.: Yale University Press, 1997.

Gottlieb, Robert. *Forcing the Spring: The Transformation of the American Environmental Movement.* Washington, D.C.: Island Press, 1993.

Goubert, Jean-Pierre. *The Conquest of Water: The Advent of Health in the Industrial Age,* trans. Andrew Wilson. Cambridge: Polity Press, 1986.

Goulder, Lawrence H., and Brian M. Nadreau. "International Approaches to Reducing Greenhouse Gas Emissions." In *Climate Change Policy: A Survey,* ed. Stephen H. Schneider, Armin Rosencranz, and John O. Niles, 115–149. Washington, D.C.: Island Press, 2002.

Graber, David. "Resolute Biocentrism: The Dilemma of Wilderness in National Parks." In *Reinventing Nature? Responses to Postmodern Deconstruction,* ed. Michael E. Soulé and Gary Lease. Washington, D.C.: Island Press, 1995.

Greenwood, Ted. *Knowledge and Discretion in Government Regulation.* New York: Praeger, 1984.

Gregory, Jane, and Steve Miller. *Science in Public: Communication, Culture, and Credibility.* New York: Plenum, 1998.

Grove, Richard H. *Green Imperialism: Colonial Expansion, Tropical Island Edens and the Origins of Environmentalism, 1600–1860.* Cambridge: Cambridge University Press, 1995.

Guha, Ramachandra. "The Authoritarian Biologist and the Arrogance of Anti-Humanism: Wildlife Conservation in the Third World." *The Ecologist* 27, no. 1 (1997): 14–20.

Guston, David H. "Evaluating the First U.S. Consensus Conference: The Impact of the Citizens' Panel on Telecommunications and the Future of Democracy." *Science, Technology, & Human Values* 24, no. 4 (1999): 451–482.

———. *Between Politics and Science: Assuring the Integrity and Productivity of Research.* Cambridge: Cambridge University Press, 2000.

Guston, David H., ed. "Special Issue: Boundary Organizations in Environmental Policy and Science." *Science, Technology, & Human Values* 26, no. 4 (2001): 399–500.

Guthman, Julie. "Representing Crisis: The Theory of Himalayan Environmental Degradation and the Project of Development in Post-Rana Nepal." *Development and Change* 28 (1997): 45–69.

Gutmann, Amy. "Democracy." In *A Companion to Contemporary Political Philosophy,* ed. Robert E. Goodin and Philip Pettit, 411–421. Oxford: Blackwell, 1993.

Haas, Peter M. *Saving the Mediterranean: The Politics of International Environmental Cooperation.* New York: Columbia University Press, 1990.

Hagen, Joel B. *An Entangled Bank: The Origins of Ecosystem Ecology.* New Brunswick, N.J.: Rutgers University Press, 1992.

Halberstam, David. *The Best and the Brightest.* 1972. New York: Ballantine Books, 1993.

Hamlin, Christopher. *A Science of Impurity: Water Analysis in Nineteenth Century Britain.* Berkeley: University of California Press, 1990.

Hammitt, James K. "Data, Risk, and Science." In *Thinking Ecologically: The Next Generation of Environmental Policy,* ed. Marian R. Chertow and Daniel C. Esty, 150–169. New Haven, Conn.: Yale University Press, 1997.

Hammond, Herb. *Seeing the Forest among the Trees: The Case for Wholistic Forest Use.* Vancouver, B.C.: Polestar, 1991.

Hanley, Thomas A. "Interaction of Wildlife Research and Forest Management: The Need for Maturation of Science and Policy." *Forestry Chronicle* 70, no. 5 (1994): 527–532.

Hannigan, John A. *Environmental Sociology: A Social Constructionist Perspective.* London: Routledge, 1995.

Hardin, Garrett. "The Tragedy of the Commons." *Science* 162 (1968): 1243–1248.

Harremoës, Poul, David Gee, Malcolm MacGarvin, Andy Stirling, Jane Keys, Brian Wynne, and Sofia Guedes Vaz. *The Precautionary Principle in the 20th Century: Late Lessons from Early Warnings.* London: Earthscan, 2002.

Harris, W. E. "Siting a Hazardous Waste Facility: A Success Story in Retrospect." *Risk Analysis* 13, no. 1 (1993): 3–4.

Harrison, Katherine, and George Hoberg. "Setting the Environmental Agendas in Canada and the United States: The Cases of Dioxin and Radon." *Canadian Journal of Political Science* 24 (1991): 3–27.

Harvey, David. "The Environment of Justice." In *Living with Nature: Environmental Politics as Cultural Discourse,* ed. Frank Fischer and Maarten A. Hajer, 153–185. Oxford: Oxford University Press, 1999.

———. *The Condition of Postmodernity.* Cambridge: Blackwell, 1989.

Hayles, N. Katherine. "Searching for Common Ground." In *Reinventing Nature? Responses to Postmodern Deconstruction,* ed. Michael E. Soulé and Gary Lease, 47–63. Washington, D.C.: Island Press, 1995.

Hays, Samuel P. *Conservation and the Gospel of Efficiency: The Progressive Conservation Movement 1890–1920.* Cambridge: Harvard University Press, 1959.

———. "A Challenge to the Profession of Forestry." In *Explorations in Environmental History,* 172–184. Pittsburgh: University of Pittsburgh Press, 1998.

———. "Clean Air: From the 1970 Act to the 1977 Amendments." In *Explorations in Environmental History,* 221–279. Pittsburgh: University of Pittsburgh Press, 1998.

———. "Foreword to Frederick Frankena, *Strategies of Expertise in Technical Controversies.*" In *Explorations in Environmental History,* 185–197. Pittsburgh: University of Pittsburgh Press, 1998.

———. "Public Values and Management Response." In *Explorations in Environmental History,* 41–68. Pittsburgh: University of Pittsburgh Press, 1998.

———. "The Future of Environmental Regulation." In *Explorations in Environmental History,* 101–128. Pittsburgh: University of Pittsburgh Press, 1998.

———. "The Role of Urbanization in Environmental History." In *Explorations in Environmental History,* 69–100. Pittsburgh: University of Pittsburgh Press, 1998.

———. "The Role of Values in Science and Policy: The Case of Lead." In *Explorations in Environmental History,* 291–311. Pittsburgh: University of Pittsburgh Press, 1998.

———. "Value Premises for Planning and Public Policy: The Historical Context." In *Explorations in Environmental History,* 24–40. Pittsburgh: University of Pittsburgh Press, 1998.

Healey, M. C., and T. M. Hennessey. "The Utilization of Scientific Information in the Management of Estuarine Ecosystems." *Ocean and Coastal Management* 23 (1994): 167–191.

Healy, Robert G., and William Ascher. "Knowledge in the Policy Process: Incorporating New Environmental Information in Natural Resources Policy Making." *Policy Sciences* 28, no. 1 (1995): 1–19.

Heclo, Hugh. "The Sixties' False Dawn: Awakenings, Movements, and Postmodern Policymaking." *Journal of Policy History* 8, no. 1 (1996): 34–63.

Heinz, H. John III Center for Science, Economics and the Environment. *The State of the Nation's Ecosystems: Measuring the Lands, Waters, and Living Resources of the United States.* Cambridge: Cambridge University Press, 2002.

Herrick, Charles, and Dale Jamieson. "The Social Construction of Acid Rain: Some Implications for Science/Policy Assessment." *Global Environmental Change* 5, no. 2 (1995): 105–112.

Hessing, Melody, and Michael Howlett. *Canadian Natural Resource and Environmental Policy: Political Economy and Public Policy.* Vancouver: University of British Columbia Press, 1997.

Hilborn, Ray. "Living with Uncertainty in Resource Management." *North American Journal of Fisheries Management* 7 (1987): 1–5.

Hilborn, Ray, Ellen K. Pikitch, and Robert C. Francis. "Current Trends in Including Risk and Uncertainty in Stock Assessment and Harvest Decisions." *Canadian Journal of Fisheries and Aquatic Sciences* 50 (1993): 874–880.

Holling, C. S. "The Resilience of Terrestrial Ecosystems: Local Surprise and Global Change." In *Sustainable Development of the Biosphere,* ed. W. C. Clark and R. E. Munn, 292–320. Cambridge: Cambridge University Press, 1986.

Holling, C. S., ed. *Adaptive Environmental Assessment and Management.* New York: Wiley, 1978.

Holling, C. S., Fikret Berkes, and Carl Folke. "Science, Sustainability and Resource

Management." In *Linking Social and Ecological Systems: Management Practices and Social Mechanisms for Building Resilience,* ed. Fikret Berkes and Carl Folke, 342–362. Cambridge: Cambridge University Press, 1998.

Holling, C. S., and G. K. Meffe. "Command and Control and the Pathology of Natural Resource Management." *Conservation Biology* 10, no. 2 (1996): 328–337.

Howlett, Michael, and Jeremy Rayner. "Do Ideas Matter? Policy Network Configurations and Resistance to Policy Change in the Canadian Forest Sector." *Canadian Public Administration* 38, no. 3 (1985): 382–410.

Hull, David L. *Science as a Process: An Evolutionary Account of the Social and Conceptual Development of Science.* Chicago: University of Chicago Press, 1988.

Hulme, Mike, et al. "Climate Change Scenarios for Global Impacts Studies." *Global Environmental Change* 9 (1999): S3–S19.

Hutchings, Jeffrey A., Carl Walters, and Richard L. Beamish. "Is Scientific Inquiry Incompatible with Government Information Control?" *Canadian Journal of Fisheries and Aquatic Sciences* 54 (1997): 1198–1210.

Hyder, T. "Climate Negotiations: The North/South Perspective." In *Confronting Climate Change: Risks, Implications, and Responses,* ed. I. Mintzer. New York: Cambridge University Press, 1992.

ICES. *www.ices.dk/marineworld/fishsyst.asp*.

IJC. Great Lakes Research Advisory Board. *The Ecosystem Approach: Scope and Implications of an Ecosystem Approach to Transboundary Problems in the Great Lakes Basin.* Windsor, Ont.: IJC, 1978.

Immen, Wallace. "Fragile Moraine Poorly Managed: Scientists." *The Globe and Mail* (Toronto), 2 February 2000.

IPCC. *Introduction to the Intergovernmental Panel on Climate Change (IPCC).* At *www.ipcc.ch*, p. 6.

Irwin, Alan. *Citizen Science: A Study of People, Expertise and Sustainable Development.* London: Routledge, 1995.

———. "Business as Usual? Re-assessing Scientific Institutions and Global Environmental Challenges." *Global Environmental Change* 8, no. 3 (1998): 279–283.

Irwin, Alan, Alison Dale, and Denis Smith. "Science and Hell's Kitchen: The Local Understanding of Hazard Issues." In *Misunderstanding Science? The Public Reconstruction of Science and Technology,* ed. Alan Irwin and Brian Wynne, 47–64. Cambridge: Cambridge University Press, 1996.

Irwin, Alan, and Brian Wynne. "Introduction." In *Misunderstanding Science? The Public Reconstruction of Science and Technology,* ed. Alan Irwin and Brian Wynne, 1–17. Cambridge: Cambridge University Press, 1996.

Jacobs, Jane. *The Death and Life of Great American Cities.* New York: Vintage, 1961.

Jaeger, Carlo C., Ortwin Renn, Eugene A. Rosa, and Thomas Webler. *Risk, Uncertainty, and Rational Action.* London: Earthscan, 2001.

Jamieson, Dale. "Climate Change and Global Environmental Justice." In *Changing the Atmosphere: Expert Knowledge and Environmental Governance,* ed. Clark A. Miller and Paul N. Edwards, 287–307. Cambridge: MIT Press, 2001.

Jänicke, Martin, and Helmut Weidner, eds. *Successful Environmental Policy: A Critical Evaluation of 24 Cases.* Berlin: Sigma, 1995.

Jasanoff, Sheila. "The Problem of Rationality in American Health and Safety Regulation." In *Expert Evidence: Interpreting Science in the Law,* ed. R. Smith and B. Wynne, 151–183. New York: Routledge, 1989.

————. *The Fifth Branch: Science Advisers as Policymakers*. Cambridge: Harvard University Press, 1990.

————. "NGOs and the Environment: From Knowledge to Action." *Third World Quarterly* 18, no. 3 (1997): 579–594.

————. "Civilization and Madness: The Great BSE Scare of 1996." *Public Understanding of Science* 6 (1997): 221–232.

————. "The Songlines of Risk." *Environmental Values* 8 (1999): 135–152.

————. "Image and Imagination: The Formation of Global Environmental Consciousness." In *Changing the Atmosphere: Expert Knowledge and Environmental Governance*, ed. Clark A. Miller and Paul N. Edwards, 309–337. Cambridge: MIT Press, 2001.

Johnson, Kirk. "With Uncertainty Filling the Air, 9/11 Health Risks Are Debated." *New York Times*, 8 February 2002, A1.

————. "For a Changing City, New Pieces to a Lead-Poison Puzzle." *New York Times*, 30 September 2003, B1.

————. "Looking Outside for Lead Danger." *New York Times*, 2 November 2003, 31.

Johnson, Kirk, and Andrew Revkin. "Contaminants Below Levels for Long-Term Concerns." *New York Times*, 11 October 2001.

Judd, Richard. *Common Lands, Common People: The Origins of Conservation in Northern New England*. Cambridge: Harvard University Press, 1997.

Kaiser, Jocelyn. "Ecologists on a Mission to Save the World." *Science* 287, no. 5456 (2000): 1188–1192.

Kandlikar, Milind, and Ambuj Sagar. "Climate Change Research and Analysis in India: An Integrated Assessment of a South–North Divide." *Global Environmental Change* 9 (1999): 119–138.

Kates, Robert W., and Thomas J. Wilbanks. "Making the Global Local: Responding to Climate Change Concerns from the Ground Up." *Environment* 45, no. 3 (2003): 12–23.

Kay, James J. "A Nonequilibrium Thermodynamic Framework for Discussing Ecosystem Integrity." *Environmental Management* 15 (1991): 483–495.

Keating, Terry J. "Lessons from the Recent History of the Health Effects Institute." *Science, Technology & Human Values* 26, no. 4 (2001): 409–430.

Keller, Evelyn Fox. *Reflections on Gender and Science*. New Haven, Conn.: Yale University Press, 1985.

Kellert, Stephen R., and E. O. Wilson, eds. *The Biophilia Hypothesis*. Washington, D.C.: Island Press, 1993.

Kempton, Willett, James S. Boster, and Jennifer A. Hartley. *Environmental Values in American Culture*. Cambridge, Mass.: MIT Press, 1995.

Kimmins, Hamish. *Balancing Act: Environmental Issues in Forestry*. Vancouver: University of British Columbia Press, 1992.

Kingsland, Sharon E. "An Elusive Science: Ecological Enterprise in the Southwestern United States." In *Science and Nature: Essays in the History of the Environmental Sciences*, ed. Michael Shortland, 151–179. Oxford: British Society for the History of Science, 1993.

Kitcher, Philip. *Science, Truth, and Democracy*. New York: Oxford University Press, 2001.

Klesius, Michael. "The State of the Planet." *National Geographic*, September 2002, 102–115.

Knight, Richard L., and Suzanne Riedel, eds. *Aldo Leopold and the Ecological Conscience*. Oxford: Oxford University Press, 2002.

Kohm, K., and J. Franklin, eds. *Creating a Forestry for the 21st Century: The Science of Ecosystem Management*. Washington, D.C.: Island Press, 1997.

Kowalok, Michael E. "Research Lessons from Acid Rain, Ozone Depletion, and Global Warming." *Environment* 35, no. 6 (1993): 12–20, 35–38.

Kraft, Michael E. "Clean Air and the Adirondacks: Science, Politics, and Policy Choice." *Environmental Science and Policy* 1 (1998): 167–173.

Kwa, Chunglin. "The Rise and Fall of Weather Modification: Changes in American Attitudes toward Technology, Nature, and Society." In *Changing the Atmosphere: Expert Knowledge and Environmental Governance,* ed. Clark A. Miller and Paul N. Edwards, 135–165. Cambridge: MIT Press, 2001.

Lackey, Robert T. "Pacific Salmon, Ecological Health, and Public Policy." *Ecosystem Health* 2, no. 1 (1996): 61–68.

———. "Seven Pillars of Ecosystem Management." *Landscape and Urban Planning 40, nos. 1/3* (1997): 21–30.

———. "Fisheries Management: Integrating Societal Preference, Decision Analysis, and Ecological Risk Assessment." *Environmental Science and Policy* 1 (1998): 329–335.

———. "Salmon Policy: Science, Society, Restoration, and Reality." *Environmental Science and Policy* 2 (1999): 369–379.

Lafferty, William M., and James Meadowcroft, eds. *Democracy and the Environment: Problems and Prospects*. Cheltenham: Edward Elgar, 1996.

Latour, Bruno. *Pandora's Hope: Essays on the Reality of Science Studies*. Cambridge: Harvard University Press, 1999.

Lease, Gary. "Introduction: Nature under Fire." In *Reinventing Nature? Responses to Postmodern Deconstruction,* ed. Michael E. Soulé and Gary Lease, 3–15. Washington, D.C.: Island Press, 1995.

Lee, Kai N. *Compass and Gyroscope: Integrating Science and Politics for the Environment*. Washington, D.C.: Island Press, 1993.

Leiss, William. *Ecology versus Politics*. Toronto: University of Toronto Press, 1979.

———. *The Domination of Nature*. 1972. Montreal: McGill-Queen's University Press, 1994.

———. "Between Expertise and Bureaucracy: Risk Management Trapped at the Science-Policy Interface." In *Risky Business: Canada's Changing Science-Based Policy and Regulatory Regime,* ed. G. Bruce Doern and Ted Reed, 49–74. Toronto: University of Toronto Press, 2000.

———. *Governing Food: Science, Safety and Trade: Rapporteur's Report*. Canada–UK Colloquium, November 2–5, 2000. http://qsilver.queensu.ca/sps/WorkingPapers/files/CanUK2000.pdf

Leopold, Aldo. *Sand County Almanac*. New York: Oxford University Press, 1949.

Lertzman, Ken, Jeremy Rayner, and Jeremy Wilson. "Learning and Change in the British Columbia Forest Policy Sector: A Consideration of Sabatier's Advocacy Coalition Framework." *Canadian Journal of Political Science* 29, no. 1 (1996): 111–133.

Levins, Richard. "The Strategy of Model Building in Population Biology." *American Scientist* 54 (1966): 421–431.

Lewenstein, Bruce V. "Science and the Media." In *Handbook of Science and Technology Studies,* ed. Sheila Jasanoff, Gerald E. Markle, James C. Petersen, and Trevor Pinch, 343–360. Thousand Oaks, Calif.: Sage Publications, 1995.

Lexchin, Joel, Lisa Bero, Benjamin Djulbegovic, and Otavio Clark. "Pharmaceutical Industry Sponsorship and Research Outcome and Quality: Systematic Review." *British Medical Journal*, 31 May, no. 326 (2003): 1167–1170.

Linder, Stephen H. "The Social and Political (Re)Construction of Risk." In *Flashpoints in Environmental Policymaking: Controversies in Achieving Sustainability,* ed. Sheldon Kamieniecki, George A. Gonzalez, and Robert O. Vos, 63–82. Albany, N.Y.: SUNY Press, 1997.

Litfin, Karen T. *Ozone Discourses: Science and Politics in Global Environmental Cooperation.* New York: Columbia University Press, 1994.

———. "Framing Science: Precautionary Discourse and the Ozone Treaties." *Millennium: Journal of International Studies* 24, no. 2 (1995): 251–277.

Lomborg, Bjørn. *The Skeptical Environmentalist: Measuring the Real State of the World.* Cambridge: Cambridge University Press, 2001.

Lovelock, J. E. *Gaia: A New Look at Life on Earth.* Oxford: Oxford University Press, 1979.

Lowrance, William W. *Of Acceptable Risk: Science and the Determination of Safety.* Los Altos, Calif.: William Kaufmann, 1976.

Lubchenco, Jane. "Entering the Century of the Environment: A New Social Contract for Science." *Science* 279 (1998): 491–497.

Ludwig, Donald, Ray Hilborn, and Carl Walters. "Uncertainty, Resource Exploitation, and Conservation: Lessons from History." *Science* 260 (1993): 17, 36.

Luke, Timothy. "Eco-Managerialism: Environmental Studies as a Power/Knowledge Formation." In *Living with Nature: Environmental Politics as Cultural Discourse,* ed. Frank Fischer and Maarten A. Hajer, 103–120. Oxford: Oxford University Press, 1999.

MacDonald, Mark R. "Socioeconomic versus Science-Based Regulation: Informal Influences on the Formal Regulation of rbST in Canada." In *Risky Business: Canada's Changing Science-Based Policy and Regulatory Regime,* ed. G. Bruce Doern and Ted Reed, 156–181. Toronto: University of Toronto Press, 2000.

Margolis, Robert M., and Daniel M. Kammen. "Energy R&D and Innovation: Challenges and Opportunities." In *Climate Change Policy: A Survey,* ed. Stephen H. Schneider, Armin Rosencranz, and John O. Niles, 469–494. Washington, D.C.: Island Press, 2002.

Marsh, George Perkins. *Man and Nature: Or, Physical Geography as Modified by Human Action,* ed. David Lowenthal. Cambridge, Mass.: Belknap Press, 1965.

Marshall, Brent K. "Globalisation, Environmental Degradation and Ulrich Beck's Risk Society." *Environmental Values* 8 (1999): 253–275.

Martin, Brian, and Evelleen Richards. "Scientific Knowledge, Controversy, and Public Decision Making." In *Handbook of Science and Technology Studies,* ed. Sheila Jasanoff, Gerald E. Markle, James C. Petersen, and Trevor Pinch, 506–526. Thousand Oaks, Calif.: Sage Publications, 1995.

Masood, Ehsan. "Fisheries Science: All at Sea When It Comes to Politics?" *Nature* 386 (1997): 105–106.

Mathews, Freya. "Deep Ecology." In *A Companion to Environmental Philosophy,* ed. Dale Jamieson, 218–232. Malden, Mass.: Blackwell, 2001.

May, Elizabeth. *At the Cutting Edge: The Crisis in Canada's Forests.* Toronto: Key Porter Books, 1998.

McCormick, John. *Reclaiming Paradise: The Global Environmental Movement.* Bloomington: Indiana University Press, 1989.

McEvoy, Arthur. *The Fisherman's Problem: Ecology and Law in the California Fisheries, 1850–1980*. Cambridge: Cambridge University Press, 1986.

McGinnis, Michael Vincent. "A Rehearsal to Bioregionalism." In *Bioregionalism*, ed. M. V. McGinnis, 1–9. London: Routledge, 1999.

Merchant, Carolyn. *The Death of Nature: Women, Ecology, and the Scientific Revolution*. New York: HarperCollins, 1980.

————. *Radical Ecology: The Search for a Livable World*. New York: Routledge, 1992.

Metlay, Daniel. "From Tin Roof to Torn Wet Blanket: Predicting and Observing Groundwater Movement at a Proposed Nuclear Waste Site." In *Prediction: Science, Decision Making, and the Future of Nature*, ed. Daniel Sarewitz, Roger A. Pielke Jr., and Radford Byerly Jr., 199–228. Washington, D.C.: Island Press, 2000.

M'Gonigle, R. Michael. "The Political Ecology of Biodiversity: A View from the Western Woods." In *Biodiversity in Canada: Ecology, Ideas and Action*, ed. S. Bocking, 391–414. Peterborough: Broadview Press, 2000.

Miller, Clark A. "Challenges in the Application of Science to Global Affairs: Contingency, Trust, and Moral Order." In *Changing the Atmosphere: Expert Knowledge and Environmental Governance*, ed. Clark A. Miller and Paul N. Edwards, 247–285. Cambridge: MIT Press, 2001.

————. "Scientific Internationalism in American Foreign Policy: The Case of Meteorology, 1947–1958." In *Changing the Atmosphere: Expert Knowledge and Environmental Governance*, ed. Clark A. Miller and Paul N. Edwards, 167–217. Cambridge: MIT Press, 2001.

Miller, Clark A., and Paul N. Edwards. "Introduction: The Globalization of Climate Science and Climate Politics." In *Changing the Atmosphere: Expert Knowledge and Environmental Governance*, ed. Clark A. Miller and Paul N. Edwards, 1–30. Cambridge: MIT Press, 2001.

Miller, Henry I., and Gregory Conko. "The Science of Biotechnology Meets the Politics of Global Regulation." *Issues in Science and Technology* 17, no. 1 (2000): 47–54.

Minteer, Ben A. "Deweyan Democracy and Environmental Ethics." In *Democracy and the Claims of Nature: Critical Perspectives for a New Century*, ed. Ben A. Minteer and Bob Pepperman Taylor, 33–48. Lanham, Md.: Rowman & Littlefield, 2002.

Mitman, Gregg. *The State of Nature: Ecology, Community, and American Social Thought, 1900–1950*. Chicago: University of Chicago Press, 1992.

Mittelstaedt, Martin. "Clear-cuts Likened to Natural Fires: Ontario Ministry under Attack for Idea Termed Pseudoscientific and Ridiculous." *The Globe and Mail* (Toronto), 23 November 2001.

Montague, Peter. "The Uses of Scientific Uncertainty." *Rachel's Environment & Health News*, 1 July 1999, www.rachel.org/erf/bulletin/bulletin.cfm?Issue_ID=1508.

Moss, Richard M. "The IPCC: Policy Relevant (Not Driven) Scientific Assessment." *Global Environmental Change* 5, no. 3 (1995): 171–174.

Mowat, Farley. "Foreword." In Elizabeth May, *At the Cutting Edge: The Crisis in Canada's Forests*. Toronto: Key Porter Books, 1998.

Moynihan, Ray. "Who Pays for the Pizza? Redefining the Relationships between Doctors and Drug Companies. 1. Entanglement." *British Medical Journal* 326 (May 31, 2003):1189–1192.

Mullner, Scott A., Wayne A. Hubert, and Thomas A. Wesche. "Evolving Paradigms for Landscape-Scale Renewable Resource Management in the United States." *Environmental Science and Policy* 4 (2001): 39–49.

Munton, Don. "Fumes, Forests, and Further Studies: Environmental Science and Policy Inaction in Ontario." *Journal of Canadian Studies* 37, no. 2 (2002): 130–163.

Nagpal, Tanvi. "Voices from the Developing World: Progress toward Sustainable Development." *Environment* 37, no. 8 (1995): 10–15, 30–35.

Nash, Roderick Frazier. *The Rights of Nature: A History of Environmental Ethics*. Madison: University of Wisconsin Press, 1989.

National Council for Science and the Environment. *Recommendations for Improving the Scientific Basis for Environmental Decisionmaking: A Report from the First National Conference on Science, Policy, and the Environment, December 7–8, 2000*. National Academy of Sciences, Washington, D.C. Available online: *www.NCSEonline.org/ 2000conference*

National Research Council. *Risk Assessment in the Federal Government: Managing the Process*. Washington, D.C.: National Academy Press, 1983.

————. *Our Common Journey: A Transition toward Sustainability. Report of the Board on Sustainable Development*. Washington, D.C.: National Academy Press, 1999. Available at: *http://books.nap.edu/catalog/9690.html*

————. *The Science of Regional and Global Change: Putting Knowledge to Work*, Washington, D.C.: National Academy Press, 2000. Available at: *www.nap.edu/books/ 0309073278/html/R1.html*.

————. *Climate Change Science: An Analysis of Some Key Questions*. Washington, D.C.: National Academy Press, 2001. Available at *www.nap.edu*.

————. *Abrupt Climate Change: Inevitable Surprises*. Washington, D.C.: National Academy Press, 2002. Available at *www.nap.edu*

National Science and Technology Council, Committee on Environment and Natural Resources. *Ecological Risk Assessment in the Federal Government*. CENR/5–99/001, May 1999.

Nature. "Is the University-Industrial Complex out of Control?" *Nature* 409, no. 6817 (11 January 2001): 119.

Nelkin, Dorothy. "Science, Technology, and Political Conflict: Analyzing the Issues." In *Controversy: The Politics of Technical Decisions*, ed. D. Nelkin, 3d ed., ix–xxv. Newbury Park, Calif.: Sage, 1992.

————. "Science Controversies: The Dynamics of Public Disputes in the United States." In *Handbook of Science and Technology Studies,* ed. Sheila Jasanoff, Gerald E. Markle, James C. Petersen, and Trevor Pinch, 444–456. Thousand Oaks, Calif.: Sage Publications, 1995.

New York City Department of Health and Mental Hygiene. *Lead Poisoning Prevention Program, Annual Report 2001*. New York, December 2002.

Newbold, Heather, ed. *Life Stories: World-Renowned Scientists Reflect on Their Lives and the Future of Life on Earth*. Berkeley: University of California Press, 2000.

Niles, John O. "Tropical Forests and Climate Change." In *Climate Change Policy: A Survey,* ed. Stephen H. Schneider, Armin Rosencranz, and John O. Niles, 337–371. Washington, D.C.: Island Press, 2002.

Norton, Bryan G. "Democracy and Environmentalism: Foundations and Justifications in Environmental Policy." In *Democracy and the Claims of Nature: Critical Perspectives for a New Century,* ed. Ben A. Minteer and Bob Pepperman Taylor, 11–32. Lanham, Md.: Rowman & Littlefield, 2002.

————. "Sustainability: Descriptive or Performative?" In *The Moral Austerity of Environmental Decision Making: Sustainability, Democracy, and Normative Argument in Policy and Law,* ed. John Martin Gillroy and Joe Bowersox, 51–62. Durham, N.C.: Duke University Press, 2002

Norton, Stephen D., and Frederick Suppe. "Why Atmospheric Modeling Is Good Science." In *Changing the Atmosphere: Expert Knowledge and Environmental Governance,* ed. Clark A. Miller and Paul N. Edwards, 67–105. Cambridge: MIT Press, 2001.

Noss, Reed F., and J. Michael Scott. "Ecosystem Protection and Restoration: The Core of Ecosystem Management." In *Ecosystem Management: Applications for Sustainable Forest and Wildlife Resources,* ed. Mark S. Boyce and Alan Haney, 239–264. New Haven, Conn.: Yale University Press, 1997.

Novick, Peter. *That Noble Dream: The "Objectivity Question" and the American Historical Profession.* Cambridge: Cambridge University Press, 1988.

Nuclear Regulatory Commission. *Reactor Safety Study—An Assessment of Accident Risk in U.S. Commercial Nuclear Power Plants.* WASH 1400. NUREG 75/014.1975.

Odum, Eugene. "The Strategy of Ecosystem Development." *Science* 164 (1969): 262–270.

O'Malley, Robin, Kent Cavender-Bares, and William C. Clark. "Providing 'Better' Data: Not as Simple as It Might Seem." *Environment* 45, no. 4 (2003): 8–18.

O'Neill, John. "Deliberative Democracy and Environmental Policy." In *Democracy and the Claims of Nature: Critical Perspectives for a New Century,* ed. Ben A. Minteer and Bob Pepperman Taylor, 257–275. Lanham, Md.: Rowman & Littlefield, 2002.

Ong, Elisa, and Stanton Glantz. "Constructing 'Sound Science' and 'Good Epidemiology': Tobacco, Lawyers, and Public Relations Firms." *American Journal of Public Health* 91, no. 11 (2001): 1749–1757.

Opie, John. *Nature's Nation: An Environmental History of the United States.* Fort Worth, Texas: Harcourt Brace, 1998.

Osherenko, Gail. "Can Comanagement Save Arctic Wildlife?" *Environment* 30, no. 6 (1988): 6–13, 29–34.

Ostrom, Elinor, et al., eds. *The Drama of the Commons.* Washington, D.C.: National Academy Press, 2002.

Otway, Harry, and Detlof von Winterfeldt. "Expert Judgement in Risk Analysis and Management: Process, Context, and Pitfalls." *Risk Analysis* 12, no. 1 (1992): 83–93.

Paehlke, Robert. "Environmental Challenges to Democratic Practice." In *Democracy and the Environment: Problems and Prospects,* ed. William M. Lafferty and James Meadowcroft, 18–38. Cheltenham: Edward Elgar, 1996.

———. "Cycles of Closure in Environmental Politics and Policy." In *Democracy and the Claims of Nature: Critical Perspectives for a New Century,* ed. Ben A. Minteer and Bob Pepperman Taylor, 279–299. Lanham, Md.: Rowman & Littlefield, 2002.

Palladino, Paolo. "On 'Environmentalism': The Origins of Debates over Policy for Pest-Control Research in America, 1960–1975." In *Science and Nature: Essays in the History of the Environmental Sciences,* ed. Michael Shortland, 181–212. Oxford: British Society for the History of Science, 1993.

Pálsson, Gisli. "Learning by Fishing: Practical Engagement and Environmental Concerns." In *Linking Social and Ecological Systems: Management Practices and Social Mechanisms for Building Resilience,* ed. Fikret Berkes and Carl Folke, 48–66. Cambridge: Cambridge University Press, 1998.

Paterson, Matthew. *Global Warming and Global Politics.* London: Routledge, 1996.

Pauly, Daniel, Villy Christensen, Sylvie Guénette, Tony J. Pitcher, U. Rashid Sumaila,

Carl J. Walters, R. Watson, and Dirk Zeller. "Towards Sustainability in World Fisheries." *Nature* 418 (2002): 689–695.

Percival, Robert V. "Global Environmental Accountability: The Missing Link in the Pursuit of Sustainable Development?" In *The Moral Austerity of Environmental Decision Making: Sustainability, Democracy, and Normative Argument in Policy and Law,* ed. John Martin Gillroy and Joe Bowersox, 194–206. Durham, N.C.: Duke University Press, 2002.

Perry, David. "The Scientific Basis of Forestry." *Annual Review of Ecology and Systematics* 29 (1998): 435–466.

Pickett, S.T.A., and P. S. White. *The Ecology of Natural Disturbance and Patch Dynamics.* Orlando, Fla.: Academic Press, 1985.

Pielke, Roger A., Daniel Sarewitz, and Radford Byerly Jr. "Decision Making and the Future of Nature: Understanding and Using Predictions." In *Prediction: Science, Decision Making, and the Future of Nature,* ed. Daniel Sarewitz, Roger A. Pielke Jr., and Radford Byerly Jr., 361–387. Washington, D.C.: Island Press, 2000.

Pinchot, Gifford. *The Fight for Conservation.* New York: Doubleday, Page & Company, 1910.

Pinkerton, Evelyn. "Local Fisheries Co-management: A Review of International Experiences and Their Implications for Salmon Management in British Columbia." *Canadian Journal of Fisheries and Aquatic Sciences* 51 (1994): 2363–2376.

———. "Integrated Management of a Temperate Montane Forest Ecosystem through Wholistic Forestry: A British Columbia Example." In *Linking Social and Ecological Systems: Management Practices and Social Mechanisms for Building Resilience,* ed. Fikret Berkes and Carl Folke, 363–389. Cambridge: Cambridge University Press, 1998.

Pinkerton, Evelyn, ed. *Co-operative Management of Local Fisheries: New Directions for Improved Management and Community Development.* Vancouver: University of British Columbia Press, 1989.

Platt, Rutherford H., Paul K. Barten, and Max J. Pfeffer. "A Full Clean Glass? Managing New York City's Watersheds." *Environment* 42, no. 5 (2000): 8–20.

Porritt, Jonathon. *Playing Safe: Science and the Environment.* New York: Thames & Hudson, 2000.

Porter, Theodore M. *Trust in Numbers: The Pursuit of Objectivity in Science and Public Life.* Princeton, N.J.: Princeton University Press, 1995.

Pound, R., R. Wilson, and N. Ramsey. "Memorial Minute—Kenneth Tompkins Bainbridge." *Harvard University Gazette,* 7 May 1998, *www.news.harvard.edu/gazette/1998/05.07/MemorialMinute-.html*

Powell, Douglas, and William Leiss. *Mad Cows and Mother's Milk: The Perils of Poor Risk Communication.* Montreal: McGill-Queen's University Press, 1997.

Powell, Douglas, and William Leiss, with Angela Griffiths and Katherine Barrett. "Gene Escape, or the Pall of Silence over Plant Biotechnology Risk." In Douglas Powell and William Leiss, *Mad Cows and Mother's Milk: The Perils of Poor Risk Communication,* 153–181. Montreal: McGill-Queen's University Press, 1997.

Presidential/Congressional Commission on Risk Assessment and Risk Management. *Framework for Environmental Health Risk Management.* Final Report, Vol. 1, 1997. Available at http://www.riskworld.com/Nreports/1996/risk_rpt/Rr6me001.htm.

Press, Daniel. *Democratic Dilemmas in the Age of Ecology: Trees and Toxics in the American West.* Durham, N.C.: Duke University Press, 1994.

Press, Eyal, and Jennifer Washburn. "The Kept University." *Atlantic Monthly*, March 2000, 39–54.

Princen, Thomas. "Distancing: Consumption and the Severing of Feedback." In *Confronting Consumption,* ed. Thomas Princen, Michael Maniates, and Ken Conca, 103–131. Cambridge: MIT Press, 2002.

Pyne, Stephen J. *World Fire: The Culture of Fire on Earth*. Seattle: University of Washington Press, 1995.

Rampton, Sheldon, and John Stauber. *Trust Us, We're Experts! How Industry Manipulates Science and Gambles with Your Future*. New York: Tarcher/Putnam, 2001.

Raustiala, Kal. "Nonstate Actors in the Global Climate Regime." In *International Relations and Global Climate Change,* ed. Urs Luterbacher and Detlef F. Sprinz, 95–117. Cambridge: MIT Press, 2001.

Ravetz, J. R. "Usable Knowledge, Usable Ignorance: Incomplete Science with Policy Implications." In *Sustainable Development of the Biosphere,* ed. W. C. Clark and R. E. Munn, 415–432. Cambridge: Cambridge University Press, 1986.

———. "Uncertainty, Ignorance and Policy." In *Science for Public Policy,* ed. H. Brooks and C. Cooper, 77–93. Oxford: Pergamon Press, 1987.

Rawson Academy of Aquatic Science. *Towards an Ecosystem Charter for the Great Lakes–St. Lawrence*. Rawson Occasional Paper no. 1, 1989.

Revkin, Andrew C. "F.D.A. Considers New Tests for Environmental Effects." *New York Times*, 14 March 2002, A20.

———. "Exxon-Led Group Is Giving a Climate Grant to Stanford." *New York Times*, 21 November 2003, A26.

Rich, Bruce. *Mortgaging the Earth: The World Bank, Environmental Impoverishment, and the Crisis of Development*. Boston: Beacon Press, 1994.

Richardson, Mary, Joan Sherman, and Michael Gismondi. *Winning Back the Words: Confronting Experts in an Environmental Public Hearing*. Toronto: Garamond Press, 1993.

Robinson, John B. "Risks, Predictions and other Optical Illusions: Rethinking the Use of Science in Social Decision-Making." *Policy Sciences* 25 (1992): 237–254.

———. *Life in 2030: Exploring a Sustainable Future for Canada*. Vancouver: University of British Columbia Press, 1995.

Robinson, M. P., and M. M. Ross. "Traditional Land Use and Occupancy Studies and Their Impact on Forest Planning and Management in Alberta." *Forestry Chronicle* 73, no. 5 (1997): 596–605.

Rolston, Holmes III. "Environmental Ethics: Values in and Duties to the Natural World." In *Ecology, Economics, Ethics: The Broken Circle,* ed. F. Herbert Bormann and Stephen R. Kellert, 73–96. New Haven, Conn.: Yale University Press, 1991.

Rosenbaum, Walter A. "Regulation at Risk: The Controversial Politics and Science of Comparative Risk Assessment." In *Flashpoints in Environmental Policymaking: Controversies in Achieving Sustainability,* ed. Sheldon Kamieniecki, George A. Gonzalez, and Robert O. Vos, 31–61. Albany, N.Y.: SUNY Press, 1997.

Rosenberg, Andrew A., and Victor R. Restrepo. "Uncertainty and Risk Evaluation in Stock Assessment Advice for U.S. Marine Fisheries." *Canadian Journal of Fisheries and Aquatic Sciences* 51 (1994): 2715–2720.

Rosencranz, Armin. "U.S. Climate Change Policy." In *Climate Change Policy: A Survey,* ed. Stephen H. Schneider, Armin Rosencranz, and John O. Niles, 221–234. Washington, D.C.: Island Press, 2002.

Royal Society of Canada. *Aquatic Science in Canada: A Case Study of Research in the Mackenzie Basin*. Ottawa: Royal Society, 1995.

Royal Society. *The Role of Land Carbon Sinks in Mitigating Global Climate Change*. July 2001. Available at *www.royalsoc.ac.uk/policy*.

Russell, Edmund. *War and Nature: Fighting Humans and Insects with Chemicals from World War I to Silent Spring*. Cambridge: Cambridge University Press, 2001.

Ryder, R. A., and C. J. Edwards, eds.. *A Conceptual Approach for the Application of Biological Indicators of Ecosystem Quality in the Great Lakes Basin*. Report to the Great Lakes Science Advisory Board of the International Joint Commission, 1985. Windsor, Ont.: IJC, 1985.

Sachs, Wolfgang. "Sustainable Development and the Crisis of Nature: On the Political Anatomy of an Oxymoron." In *Living with Nature: Environmental Politics as Cultural Discourse,* ed. Frank Fischer and Maarten A. Hajer, 23–41. Oxford: Oxford University Press, 1999.

Sagoff, Mark. *The Economy of the Earth: Philosophy, Law, and the Environment*. Cambridge: Cambridge University Press, 1988.

———. "On the Value of Natural Ecosystems: The Catskills Parable." *Politics and the Life Sciences* 21, no. 1 (2002): 16–21.

Salter, Liora. *Mandated Science: Science and Scientists in the Making of Standards*. Dordrecht: Kluwer, 1988.

Sarewitz, Daniel, and Roger Pielke Jr. "Breaking the Global-Warming Gridlock." *Atlantic Monthly* 286, no. 1 (July 2000): 54–64.

Schama, Simon. *Landscape and Memory*. Toronto: Random House, 1995.

Schneider, Stephen H. *The Genesis Strategy: Climate and Global Survival*. New York: Delta, 1976.

Schneider, Stephen, and Penelope Boston, eds. *Scientists on Gaia*. Cambridge: MIT Press, 1993.

Schneider, Stephen H., and Kristin Kuntz-Duriseti. "Uncertainty and Climate Change Policy." In *Climate Change Policy: A Survey,* ed. Stephen H. Schneider, Armin Rosencranz, and John O. Niles, 53–87. Washington, D.C.: Island Press, 2002.

Schramm, Harold L., and Wayne A. Hubert. "Ecosystem Management: Implications for Fisheries Management." *Fisheries* 21 (1996): 6–11.

Sears, Paul. *Deserts on the March*. Norman: University of Oklahoma Press, 1935.

Sellars, Richard West. *Preserving Nature in the National Parks: A History*. New Haven, Conn.: Yale University Press, 1997.

Sellers, Christopher C. *Hazards of the Job: From Industrial Disease to Environmental Health Science*. Chapel Hill: University of North Carolina Press, 1997.

Sessions, George. "Ecocentrism, Wilderness, and Global Ecosystem Protection." In *Deep Ecology for the Twenty-First Century,* ed. George Sessions, 356–375. Boston: Shambhala, 1995.

Sessions, George, ed. *Deep Ecology for the Twenty-First Century*. Boston: Shambhala, 1995.

Shackley, Simon. "The Intergovernmental Panel on Climate Change: Consensual Knowledge and Global Politics." *Global Environmental Change* 7, no. 1 (1997): 77–79.

Shackley, Simon, and Tora Skodvin. "IPCC Gazing and the Interpretative Social Sciences: A Comment on Sonja Boehmer-Christiansen's: 'Global Climate Protection Policy: The Limits of Scientific Advice.'" *Global Environmental Change* 5, no. 3 (1995): 175–180.

Shackley, Simon, and Brian Wynne. "Integrating Knowledges for Climate Change: Pyramids, Nets, and Uncertainties." *Global Environmental Change* 5, no. 2 (1995): 113–126.

Sheail, John. "Pollution and the Protection of Inland Fisheries in Inter-war Britain." In *Science and Nature: Essays in the History of the Environmental Sciences*, ed. Michael Shortland, 41–56. Oxford: British Society for the History of Science, 1993.

Shepard, Paul, and Daniel McKinley, eds. *The Subversive Science: Essays toward an Ecology of Man*. Boston: Houghton Mifflin, 1969.

Shiva, Vandana. *The Violence of the Green Revolution: Third World Agriculture, Ecology and Politics*. Penang: Third World Network, 1991.

———. "The Greening of the Global Reach." In *Global Ecology: A New Arena of Political Conflict,* ed. Wolfgang Sachs, 149–156. London: Zed Books, 1993.

———. "Western Science and Its Destruction of Local Science." In *The Post-Development Reader,* ed. Majid Rahnema and Victoria Bawtree, 161–167. London: Zed Books, 1997.

Shrader-Frechette, Kristin. "Science, Environmental Risk Assessment, and the Frame Problem." *BioScience* 44 (1994): 548–551.

———. "Ecology." In *A Companion to Environmental Philosophy,* ed. Dale Jamieson, 304–315. Malden, Mass.: Blackwell, 2001.

Shrader-Frechette, Kristin S., and Earl D. McCoy. "Natural Landscapes, Natural Communities, and Natural Ecosystems." *Forest and Conservation History* 39 (1995): 138–142.

Shutkin, William B. *The Land that Could Be: Environmentalism and Democracy in the Twenty-First Century*. London: MIT Press, 2001.

Sillitoe, Paul. "The Development of Indigenous Knowledge: A New Applied Anthropology." *Current Anthropology* 39, no. 2 (1998): 223–252.

Skolnikoff, Eugene B. "The Role of Science in Policy: The Climate Change Debate in the United States." *Environment* 41, no. 5 (1999): 16–20, 42–45.

Slovic, Paul. "Perception of Risk." *Science* 236 (1987): 280–285.

———. "Perceived Risk, Trust, and Democracy." *Risk Analysis* 13, no. 6 (1993): 675–682.

Slovic, Paul, et al. "Intuitive Toxicology. II. Expert and Lay Judgements of Chemical Risks in Canada." *Risk Analysis* 15, no. 6 (1995): 661–675.

Smith, George Davey, and Andrew N. Phillips. "Passive Smoking and Health: Should We Believe Philip Morris's 'Experts'?" *British Medical Journal* 313 (1996): 929–933.

Smith, Michael. *Pacific Visions: California Scientists and the Environment 1850–1915*. New Haven, Conn.: Yale University Press, 1987.

Social Learning Group. *Learning to Manage Global Environmental Risks*. Volume 1: *A Comparative History of Social Responses to Climate Change, Ozone Depletion, and Acid Rain*. Volume 2: *A Functional Analysis of Social Responses to Climate Change, Ozone Depletion, and Acid Rain*. Cambridge: MIT Press, 2001.

Soulé, Michael E. "The Social Siege of Nature." In Michael E. Soulé and Gary Lease, *Reinventing Nature? Responses to Postmodern Deconstruction,* 137–170. Washington, D.C.: Island Press, 1995.

Soulé, Michael E., and Gary Lease. *Reinventing Nature? Responses to Postmodern Deconstruction*. Washington, D.C.: Island Press, 1995.

Spurgeon, David. "Canada's Cod Leaves Science in Hot Water." *Nature* 386 (1997): 107.

Stanley, Thomas R. "Ecosystem Management and the Arrogance of Humanism." *Conservation Biology* 9, no. 2 (1995): 255–262.

Starr, Paul, John H. Annala, and Ray Hilborn. "Contested Stock Assessment: Two Case Studies." *Canadian Journal of Fisheries and Aquatic Sciences* 55 (1998): 529–537.

Steel, Brent S., and Edward Weber. "Ecosystem Management, Decentralization and Public Opinion." *Global Environmental Change* 11 (2001): 119–131.

Stephenson, Robert L., and Daniel E. Lane. "Fisheries Management Science: A Plea for Conceptual Change." *Canadian Journal of Fisheries and Aquatic Sciences* 52 (1995): 2051–2056.

Stine, Jeffrey R. *A History of Science Policy in the United States, 1940–1985.* Washington, D.C.: Government Printing Office, 1986.

Sunstein, Cass R. *Risk and Reason: Safety, Law, and the Environment.* Cambridge: Cambridge University Press, 2002.

Takacs, David. *The Idea of Biodiversity: Philosophies of Paradise.* Baltimore, Md.: Johns Hopkins University Press, 1996.

Tarr, Joel. *The Search for the Ultimate Sink: Urban Pollution in Historical Perspective.* Akron, Ohio: University of Akron Press, 1996.

Taylor, Bob Pepperman. "Aldo Leopold's Civic Education." In *Democracy and the Claims of Nature: Critical Perspectives for a New Century,* ed. Ben A. Minteer and Bob Pepperman Taylor, 173–187. Lanham, Md.: Rowman & Littlefield, 2002.

Taylor, Bob Pepperman, and Ben A. Minteer. "Introduction." In *Democracy and the Claims of Nature: Critical Perspectives for a New Century,* ed. Ben A. Minteer and Bob Pepperman Taylor, 1–7. Lanham, Md.: Rowman & Littlefield, 2002.

Tesh, Sylvia Noble. *Uncertain Hazards: Environmental Activists and Scientific Proof.* Ithaca, N.Y.: Cornell University Press, 2000.

Thompson, Michael. "Policy-Making in the Face of Uncertainty: The Himalayas as Unknowns." In *Water and the Quest for Sustainable Development in the Ganges Valley,* ed. G. P. Chapman and M. Thompson, 25–38. London: Mansell, 1995.

Tickner, Joel, and Carolyn Raffensperger. "The Politics of Precaution in the United States and the European Union." *Global Environmental Change* 11 (2001): 175–180.

Tobey, Ronald. *Saving the Prairies: The Life Cycle of the Founding School of American Plant Ecology, 1895–1955.* Berkeley: University of California Press, 1981.

Turman, Eleanor G. "Regional Impact Assessments: A Case Study of California." In *Climate Change Policy: A Survey,* ed. Stephen H. Schneider, Armin Rosencranz, and John O. Niles, 89–111. Washington, D.C.: Island Press, 2002.

Turner, Stephen. "What is the Problem with Experts?" *Social Studies of Science* 31, no. 1 (2001): 123–149.

———. *Liberal Democracy 3.0.* London: Sage Publications, 2003.

United Nations, Food and Agriculture Organization. "Definitions for the Purposes of the Codex Alimentarius." www.fao.org/DOCREP/005/Y2200E/y2200e07.htm.

United States Climate Change Science Program and the Subcommittee on Global Change Research. *Our Changing Planet: The Fiscal Year 2003 U.S. Global Change Research Program and Climate Change Research Initiative.* November 2002.

Vallentyne, J. R., and A. L. Hamilton. "Managing Human Uses and Abuses of Aquatic Resources in the Canadian Ecosystem." In *Canadian Aquatic Resources,* ed. M. C. Healey and R. R. Wallace. *Canadian Bulletin of Fisheries and Aquatic Sciences* 215 (1987): 513–533.

Van Dyne, George, ed. *The Ecosystem Concept in Natural Resource Management*. New York: Academic Press, 1969.

Van Oostdam, J., et al. "Human Health Implications of Environmental Contaminants in Arctic Canada: A Review." *Science of the Total Environment* 230 (1999): 1–82.

Walters, Carl. "Challenges in Adaptive Management of Riparian and Coastal Ecosystems." *Conservation Ecology* 2, no. 1 (1997). www.consecol.org/vol1/iss2/art1.

Walters, Carl, R. D. Goruk, and Donald Radford. "Rivers Inlet Sockeye Salmon: An Experiment in Adaptive Management." *North American Journal of Fisheries Management* 13 (1993): 253–262.

Walters, Carl J., and C. S. Holling. "Large-Scale Management Experiments and Learning by Doing." *Ecology* 71, no. 6 (1990): 2060–2068.

Watson-Verran, Helen, and David Turnball. "Science and Other Indigenous Knowledge Systems." In *Handbook of Science and Technology Studies,* ed. Sheila Jasanoff, Gerald E. Markle, James C. Petersen and Trevor Pinch, 115–139. Thousand Oaks, Calif.: Sage Publications, 1995.

Weber, Max. "Bureaucracy." In *From Max Weber: Essays in Sociology,* ed. H. Gerth and C. Wright Mills, 196–244. New York: Oxford University Press, 1946.

Webster, Andrew. *Science, Technology and Society: New Directions*. New Brunswick, N.J.: Rutgers University Press, 1991.

Weiner, Douglas R. *Models of Nature: Ecology, Conservation, and Cultural Revolution in Soviet Russia*. Bloomington: Indiana University Press, 1988.

Weller, Ann. *Editorial Peer Review: Its Strengths and Weaknesses*. Medford, Mass.: Information Today, 2001.

Wiener, Jonathan Baert. "Designing Global Climate Regulation." In *Climate Change Policy: A Survey,* ed. Stephen H. Schneider, Armin Rosencranz, and John O. Niles, 151–187. Washington, D.C.: Island Press, 2002.

Wildavsky, Aaron. *The Search for Safety*. New Brunswick, N.J.: Rutgers University Press, 1988.

———. *But Is It True? A Citizen's Guide to Environmental Health and Safety Issues*. Cambridge: Harvard University Press, 1995.

Wilkinson, Todd. *Science under Siege: The Politician's War on Nature and Truth*. Boulder, Colo.: Johnson Books, 1998.

Williams, Bruce A., and Albert R. Matheny. *Democracy, Dialogue, and Environmental Disputes: The Contested Languages of Social Regulation*. New Haven, Conn.: Yale University Press, 1995.

Wilson, Edward O. *The Diversity of Life*. Cambridge: Harvard University Press, 1992.

———. *Consilience: The Unity of Knowledge*. New York: Vintage, 1999.

———. *The Future of Life*. New York: Vintage Books, 2003.

Wilson, Jeremy. "Forest Conservation in British Columbia, 1935–85: Reflections on a Barren Political Debate." *BC Studies* no. 76 (1987/88): 3–32.

Wolfson, Richard, and Stephen H. Schneider. "Understanding Climate Science." In *Climate Change Policy: A Survey,* ed. Stephen H. Schneider, Armin Rosencranz, and John O. Niles, 3–51. Washington, D.C.: Island Press, 2002.

Worster, Donald. *Rivers of Empire: Water, Aridity, and the Growth of the American West*. New York: Oxford University Press, 1985.

———. *Nature's Economy: A History of Ecological Ideas*. Cambridge: Cambridge University Press, 1994.

———. "Nature and the Disorder of History." In *Reinventing Nature? Responses to*

Postmodern Deconstruction, ed. Michael E. Soulé and Gary Lease, 65–85. Washington, D.C.: Island Press, 1995.

Wynne, Brian. "Establishing the Rules of Laws: Constructing Expert Authority." In *Expert Evidence: Interpreting Science in the Law*, ed. Roger Smith and Brian Wynne, 23–55. London: Routledge, 1989.

———. "Public Understanding of Science." In *Handbook of Science and Technology Studies,* ed. Sheila Jasanoff, Gerald E. Markle, James C. Petersen, and Trevor Pinch, 361–388. Thousand Oaks, Calif.: Sage Publications, 1995.

———. "Misunderstood Misunderstandings: Social Identities and Public Uptake of Science." In *Misunderstanding Science? The Public Reconstruction of Science and Technology,* ed. A. Irwin and B. Wynne, 19–46. Cambridge: Cambridge University Press, 1996.

Wynne, Brian, and Sue Mayer. "How Science Fails the Environment." *New Scientist,* 5 June 1993, 33–35.

Yearley, Steven. "The Environmental Challenge to Science Studies." In *Handbook of Science and Technology Studies,* ed. Sheila Jasanoff, Gerald E. Markle, James C. Petersen, and Trevor Pinch, 457–479. Thousand Oaks, Calif.: Sage Publications, 1995.

———. "Nature's Advocates: Putting Science to Work in Environmental Organizations." In *Misunderstanding Science? The Public Reconstruction of Science and Technology,* ed. Alan Irwin and Brian Wynne, 172–190. Cambridge: Cambridge University Press, 1996.

Young, Oran R. "Institutional Interplay: The Environmental Consequences of Cross-Scale Interactions." In *The Drama of the Commons,* ed. Elinor Ostrom et al., 263–291. Washington, D.C.: National Academy Press, 2002.

———. *The Institutional Dimensions of Environmental Change: Fit, Interplay, and Scale.* Cambridge: MIT Press, 2002.

———. "Taking Stock: Management Pitfalls in Fisheries Science." *Environment* 45, no. 3 (2003): 24–33.

INDEX

acid rain, 102; controversy over, 169, 214–215; and scientific uncertainty, 29

acid rain research, 195; influence of, 177, 181; and scientific disciplines, 196

adaptive management, 93–95, 96, 104, 188

Adirondacks, 181

administrative agencies: capacity to learn, 186–187, 188–190; and democracy, 148, 211–212; and knowledge brokers, 186; and natural resources, 80, 90, 94–95, 102–104; and peer review, 166–167; and scientific expertise, 21–23, 24, 33, 34, 39, 80, 84, 171, 178, 189, 192

administrative rationalism, 21–22, 143, 186, 208; opposition to, 22–23, 40

adversarial science. *See* science, in legal contexts

advocacy coalitions, 179, 187

Agarwal, Anil, 121–122

agriculture, 40–41, 51. *See also* biotechnology

Agriculture, Department of (U. S.), 21

air pollution, 4, 138, 195. *See also* acid rain; climate change; ozone layer

Alar controversy, 176

Alaska, 168

Alberta, 31, 158, 219

Alberta-Pacific Corporation, 219–220

Alberts, Bruce, 248n47

Allee, Warder Clyde, 65

American Crop Protection Association, 35

Andrews, Clinton, 227

animals, attitudes towards, 53–54

animal trials, in risk assessment, 140

aquaculture, research on, 172, 210

Arctic institute of North America, 219

arctic: and climate change, 114–115, 130–131; and contaminants, 106, 201

Arrhenius, Svante, 108

asbestos, 8; and deception, 34, 153

Association for Small Island States, 214

Atomic Energy Commission (U. S.), 23; and ecological research, 18, 66, 179

authority of science, 4, 10, 11, 16–44, 80, 178; challenges to, 10, 25–38, 63, 146–147

backcasting, 224

Bacon, Francis, 49, 208

Bahro, Rudolf, 200

Bainbridge, Kenneth, 25

Bangladesh, 110

Barber, Benjamin, 215–216

Barber, Richard, 229n1

Barlow, Maude, 156

Barnes, Barry, 4

Barry, John, 62

basic research: and applied science, 175; role of, 176, 194–195, 217

Beck, Ulrich, 41, 148, 150–151

Beierle, Thomas, 202

Berejikian, Jeffrey, 181

Berkes, Fikret, 101

Bernstein, Herbert, 227

Bessey, Charles, 64

ABOUT THE AUTHOR

Stephen Bocking is professor in the Environmental and Resource Studies Program at Trent University. He is the author of *Ecologists and Environmental Politics: A History of Contemporary Ecology* (1997) and editor of *Biodiversity in Canada: Ecology, Ideas, and Actions* (2000).